Where Is My Doorway To Possibilities?

By Nilofer Safdar

Copyright Notice

TABLE OF CONTENTS

❖

INTRODUCTION

❖

This book is not perfect. In fact this is a most imperfect book. You will find weird and wacky language in here. You will find spelling mistakes, grammatical mistakes, all kinds of mistakes. But that is not what this book is about. It is not a language book. Although it is a language book. It talks about the language of energy, it talks about the language of possibility. And if you let it, it will change you. It will change you in ways you cannot even fathom. It will change you in ways you have never even considered. And it will immerse you in this wonderful magical mystical world of possibilities. IF YOU ALLOW IT.........WILL YOU?

This book is dedicated to this amazing man Gary Douglas, who has created this wonderful body of work called Access Consciousness, which is changing thousands of lives all over the world. This book is also dedicated to Dr Dain Heer, the co founder of Access, who is willing to see a different possibility and be a different possibility.

This book is dedicated to the thousands of men and women all over the world who are creating their own realities and making choices that are changing the whole world. And last but not the least, this book is dedicated to you, the seeker. This book is dedicated to your courage and your perseverance and your tenacity in searching for possibilities even when you are surrounded by limitations. Thank you for being you. And thank you for being a part of this journey with me.

I have been doing telesummits since 2011. In fact I have done 7 since then. Out of the 7, 5 have been all Access Consciousness Telesummits. I actually discovered Access Consciousness in the first telesummit I did and fell in love with it. I fell in love with the ease and simplicity of the tools and the speed at which change can occur.

I love these all Access Consciousness telesummits. I get to experience all the tools of Access in action in different areas like money, business, sex, relationships, body, creation etc. In fact I jokingly like to tell people that it's like getting my own personal session from so many different facilitators.

This book is a compilation of the interview series called, "Where Is My Doorway To Possibilities" which ran from January to March 2015.

Throughout the book you will find the Access Consciousness Clearing Statement. For those of you who have never heard the Access clearing statement, that's that crazy phrase - *Right and Wrong, Good and Bad, POD and POC, All 9, Shorts, Boys and Beyonds*™.

In this book there is copyrighted content belonging to Access Consciousness® and a list of these is at the back.

I wonder what else is possible now that hasn't been available before?

Nilofer Safdar

Certified Facilitator Access Consciousness, CFMW

Host Illusion To Illumination Summit

AMAZING BONUSES

Scan this code to get for the free book updates, interviews, transcripts, bonuses and great free training!

Please send your purchase receipt to www.whereismydoorwaytopossi-bilities.com to get these phenomenal bonuses-

1. Audio Clearings From Each Chapter

2. 10 Tools To Embracing All Of You by Rachel Silber

3. RISE of the Super Heroes (mp3 audio) by Rhonda Burns

4. Other fantastic mystery bonuses

Visit www.whereismydoorwaytopossibilities.com for more…….

CHAPTER ONE

❖

THE TROUBLEMAKERS

Nilofer: I started playing around with this telesummit in September and it was in November that I was in the Mumbai Level 2 and 3 that I actually got the energy of what the tele-summit would like to be. Dr Dain Heer was sharing this story about how his horse threw him into a tree and it opened up a doorway to a totally different reality for him. And when he said that, I said, "Oh, that's the energy it is." So I'm curious. When I invited each one of you and you saw what the theme of the summit was, what did it open up for you?

Rebecca: Well for me the doorway to possibilities has been something that I've been asking, have been tripping down, have been rolling myself through head-first, whether the door was open or not. I was really excited to be invited to this summit and It goes from now until the end of March. That's 3 months of opening doors to possibilities! I really wonder where we are all going to end up 3 months from now just by choosing to be on the summit or choosing just to even listen to one of interviews. That's where I see we can go and that drew me when I first saw the pictures on the title.

Katherine: When we are looking at making decisions, we usually look at one doorway. And there are infinite doorways available to us and the joy of choosing a doorway that's light or choosing a possibility that's light and then not knowing what's on the other side of that. Not knowing what it creates but still being willing to open the door. So I'm excited about that window of "Ok, I'm looking at 5 doors in my life. How many doors are actually available if we get out of conclusion that we have to choose the right doorway?

Nilofer: I'm curious, how do you perceive the energy since the New Year?

Rebecca: Amazing. Even on New Year's day the change was palpable immediately. I was talking to Simone Milasas and we were working on the El Lugar project and everything was exploding and firing out and one thing after the other. It was like "This is day 1 of 2015! Holy moly, I've done more in this one day in a week or a month on this project that we've been like waiting for and waiting for, like come on, can we do this? And it's like "Oh, we can do it now." It's like "Ok, I'm on board." Like where the hell do we get to go? That's been what it's like for me. It's phenomenal.

Nilofer: Wouldn't you say that the energy is so palpable and so fast that even your ability to create crap is exponentialized?

Simone Padur: I'd totally vouch for that too.

Katherine: Well, it is this idea of speed that it's just not one door you are looking to open in these multitude of possibilities. It's like opening 5 doors at once or 20 doors at once or even a 100 doors at once. Yes, that's speed to crap or possibility and we get to choose.

Rachel Silber: Sometimes it may not be doors, sometimes it may just be other possibilities or other things that just end up showing up.

George: Yes, if we are focusing on creating crap and we've created too much, now the speed is really forcing us to engage into our lives and become super-present with everything that's going on because we go unconscious and we can create that unconscious crap pretty damn quick.

Pratima Nagaraj: I also perceive that our level of awareness has expanded so much, it's exponential since the new year started. I guess for me, I have been buying into all of the stuff I have been aware as mine and it feels like the crap has increased so much more but that's no longer mine because it's just a level of awareness.

Nilofer: Julia, I remember you asking a question on one of the tele-calls to Gary and he responded by saying something "a few seconds of unconsciousness will create some trillion years of crap."

Julia: Oh yes! I remember that. I think I was drunk in New York and it created a lot of crap. What I'm really excited about with this telesummit is that those 10 seconds of unconsciousness are going to create a future of unconsciousness and the 10 seconds of consciousness are the 10 seconds of actually looking at your life, saying this is my life, this is what I'm choosing right now and then looking to the future and saying "this is the future that I'm going to have" and making the choices today to create that future, that for me is where the doorways to possibilities lie, it's right now.

We have this tendency to create for right now, to do everything now and if we actually create today for the future, we can create now and for the future and so when I think about this telesummit, I think we have this time together and all of these amazing conversations and if we all go at it from the perspective of "what's the future I'd like to have?" not just this scrambling of "oh, I'm so wrong. How do I stop being so wrong?" If we look at it from "Ok, so maybe everything isn't going to change in this 10 seconds or maybe it will" but if we look at the future and choose and ask and look at this telesummit based on where we want to be in a year or 2 years or whatever, I think that's what's going to create the ripples and the waves that's going to allow this summit to change the world.

Rachel: That's a great point, Julia. I find that some of the classes that I'd taken 2 or 3 years ago are sending ripples out to everything. I mean, everything in my life is changing and shifting based on classes that I'm still just processing, not necessarily listening to again, but the effect of the clearings and everything is changing things just now. And you are right, that getting out of the wrongness of us, we've been doing that for how many trillions of years? Isn't it time to say "Ok, I'm still here. There's got to be something good here, right?" So what can I create?

What can I do today to change the world?

Julia: I have to comment on your tagline "Fa-SILLY-tating", that's hysterical. (laughs) It's so you! I love you.

Katherine: Well, Julia, I love what you said because it's like when we are in the present moment that 10 seconds of consciousness which also creates for the future or a future or futures, we are also eliminating and eradicating the past. So we are getting out of the story that we are stuck, or life is hard or it has to be difficult and we are actually creating possibilities through the eradication of history or past or stuckness. Well, I think it's brilliant.

Simone Padur: I don't know if any of you have noticed this for yourself, but what I've noticed particularly with this new year, is that reference points which I've had from the past, have just been bubbling up and it's so different than it's ever been before. Has anybody else noticed that?

Nilofer: Oh my god, yes, me for sure.

(Everybody laughs)

Rebecca: It's just you.

Nilofer: And what you brought up about reference points, I wonder if that is really your reference points or are you just aware of so many people. I was with people on the new year and people were creating a whole lot of crap and I was just "oh my god, oh my god, oh my god", I would just bring myself back to this moment of "Oh, this is not mine. This is not mine. This is not mine." (laughs) So the tool 'Who does that belong to?'

Rebecca: Yes

Katherine: Is this mine?

Rebecca: No! (laughs) I mean I did a 3 day 'Who does this belong to?' challenge just before the holidays. I thought "You know what, now is the time more than ever and I knew I wasn't going to do it by myself so

I invited the world to come with me too, to inspire me along. You know there's a difference, but you don't know what has changed until much later. I was out on New Year's eve. It was just past midnight and I was in a club and there was strip lighting everywhere and the whole world was tripping out around me but I was fully present and I know that that person is drunk off their ass and this person has been doing drugs and this person wants to go out and have a night and pass out in some stranger's bed and I was able to be aware of all of that but without the judgment and still have a great time in the middle of it and to be able to pick and choose the people that could be the contribution and the gift to me having a phenomenal night without having to buy or heal or get caught up in everyone else's crazy. And it was the first time that I really experienced it to that level. The gift that these tools are, I am just in awe of them, just the simplest tools …

Julia: What is the "Who does it belong to?" challenge for some of those out there who might not know.

Rebecca: "Who does this belong to?" challenge has probably been a difficult challenge for me. You are going to become really, really familiar with this question "Who does this belong to?" The whole idea of this is that 99% of all of your thoughts, feelings and emotions and a lot of your physical sensations aren't actually yours. And you are aware of everything that is going on around you.

So by asking "who does this belong to?" for 3 days straight for every single thought, feeling, emotion – "Oh, I feel like a coffee. Who does that belong to?" "I feel really tired today. Who does that belong to?" "Oh, I wonder if I should create this business? Who does that belong to?" Everything that is going on up here and in your body, asking that question for it and if it's not yours, returning it to sender. So Day 1, you are pretty good. Day 2, you probably forgot. Day 3, you have got damn sick of this question, and then Day 4, you are like "Oh, it's over. And I knew that none of this was mine!" (laughs) That's the "Who does this belong to?" challenge.

Question: I just wanted to say thank you for Access. It has changed my life. I love it. What process or question can I use to 1) Stop the tailgating in traffic?

Katherine: What if it's not about dealing with the traffic so much as not making yourself crazy while you are in traffic. And what are the possibilities that you could create while you feel "that you don't have a choice" or that you are at the effect of being behind, I think I actually did a video on this where I invited people to see what they could create when they are in traffic and they may not actually be able to do anything about it and what could they create for the future, through thoughts, through possibilities instead of being disgruntled that they are in traffic. How could you use "being stuck" to your advantage?

Nilofer: That's a good question.

Rachel: So what are the most fun things that you've done, Katherine, in the car? (laughs)

Katherine: What are the most fun things? When I am in the car, I actually love pulling money to me. So when I'm driving forward or even if I'm stuck, I envision all the amount of money that's coming into my life. I also envision the classes I'm creating. I envision people's lives that are changing. I love playing with the molecules when I'm driving because I feel like even if I'm stuck in traffic, I'm creating my future.

Nilofer: Oh wow.

Rebecca: Yes, don't do that.

Katherine: It doesn't work at all. (laughs)

Rachel: I actually play with the traffic itself and just move anything that's stuck anywhere, almost like undoing knots in a way and just this weird kind of symphony fun thing. I'm waving my hands and people turn around and stare, as they are driving past me and I just have fun. One hand on the wheel, one hand waving, and I have fun with that. I love the money creation idea and then I do all sorts of clearings like songs, which is fun too.

Rebecca: Rachel, I love that. I do that too. I'm always going out and realising "Oh, why are these people on the road?" and I'm like "Oh, it's 5 o'clock traffic. It's full of stupids here and there." And I'm like "Oh I don't want this" and then I just go like (makes separating hand gesture) and the cars turn and they turn and they move and they clear the jam and the other thing that I do when traffic is back to back to back, is that I generally call my assistant or I call someone that I'm creating with. Like "I'm in traffic, lets create." Because they know that if I'm not doing anything while I'm in a slow line –I do not do slow. Ever. Ever. So I just call someone, because then I can create something and keep my mind off creating crap. And yes, you can use questions at the same time. This works for me.

Simone: What I like to do especially when I see somebody get frustrated and traffic is doing weird things, I actually make the demand that when I see something is going to happen, I'm like "No, no, lets not do that." I'll just actually say "be aware" and all of a sudden it's almost like that person snaps into their body and is like "Oh, I was almost going to hit that tree" and they do something different, so I use that a lot. (laughs)

Nilofer: The second part of the question is – "My neighbour plays the piano all day long. I love the piano but I would just like to have peace and quiet when I come home, so how do I change it?"

Rhonda: Awesome. I walk around singing this little song in my head "what else is possible? What can I do to change this?"

Rebecca: I think I have some choreography to go with it, like swing. Now I wish I wasn't on my throne.

Rachel: Take up drums and see what they feel about that.

Nilofer: I love that!

Rebecca: Or even just - How obnoxious could you be?

Pratima: How much fun could you have with it? I have my neighbours doing renovation work with drilling and hacking which was really bothering me, so I asked the entities to actually contribute and help me and they had to literally stop the work for a few days because they were missing something and they just couldn't go ahead and I had my peace and quiet. (laughs)

Katherine: You could also plant in your neighbour's head that they are really hungry or that they need to go run an errand or they need to do something to get them off of playing the piano. So it's like "I think I'm hungry. Oh, I think I better make dinner. Oh, I think I might need to go run an errand" What could you create?

Rebecca: "I'm not going to do that." Just leave. Just go.

Simone: Why can't you just request?

Rebecca: Or just request. You can text them requests. "Hey, can you play this song?" and then 2 minutes later "Wait, wait, I've changed my mind. I really want this song."

Pratima: I had posted this question on Facebook asking people for fun ideas and the most hilarious idea I got was "Go knock on the neighbour's door and tell them 'Hey, I'm doing witchcraft and running some spells, so if your noise is disturbing my spells and something happens, please don't blame me for it. You continue." So that was the most fun part.

Rachel: Or you could involve the entities when you make a request. Like "I have this entity friend here who would like you to play this" and then when they play it, come up with a different one. "You know there is a whole coven of them here. They are just hanging out. I don't know."

Nilofer: Oh God, this is so funny. Part 3 of the question – "So what am I doing to attract so much drama and negativity from people at work. All of these issues I believe are happening because of something in me and I don't know how to change these issues."

Rachel: As long as you believe that they are issues, they will still be issues. What if you didn't have a point of view about them?

Rebecca: Enough said.

Rachel: What else could be possible? I know, because I got that big-time. Here I am, living in Guatemala, facilitating mostly in English, some in Spanglish as well, and I just kept repeating this point of view of "I don't know how to facilitate in Spanish. I don't know how to facilitate in Spanish." And someone called me on it, like "Well, you won't get any further in Spanish if you have this point of view about it." I'm like "Oh my goodness, that really is a point of view. I didn't even recognize it." So what if they didn't have a point of view that it's a problem?

Rebecca: Yes, you nailed it, Rachel.

Nilofer: Let's talk about people around you being negative?

Katherine: There is this idea that a point of view creates our reality. So if you have this point of view that there are disgruntled/negative people around you, you are going to create that. If you have the point of view that your life is magical, you'll create that. If you have the point of view that your co-workers are fun, you will create that. And so my question to you is– like Rachel was saying – what points of view do you have that are actually creating your life as true for you and what points of view would you like to have about creating your future? What points of view about creating a different possibility could you have?

Nilofer: The other thing is you could use all their negativity to your advantage. How can I use all of this to my advantage? I love that one.

Julia – How many thoughts can you plant in their head using Katherine's idea from before? There are so many goodies to put in there.

Nilofer: Who does not have negative people around them? I mean, the world is full of people who have a lot of interesting stuff going on.

Rebecca: You can plant in their head "Oh, I am such a bad friend. I'm being so mopey and horrible around Rebecca. I should be nice to her. I should buy her lunch." What do you want to happen today? Oh, who do I want to go to lunch with? Or "Oh, maybe that person could deliver flowers to me." What would be fun to creating your work day? And the funny thing is the more that you become happier around these people, that they are not choosing happiness, that the more they will judge you, so then the more money you make, so the more fun you'll have, so the more they'll judge you, so the more fun you'll get. Did everyone get that?

I love what's being talked about with all of this because I think another piece to look at here is if we are being triggered by trauma and drama or if we are being triggered by negative people and we are using that as a way to slow us down or distract us, I think maybe a good question that people can start asking is *"What do I love about being inside of the trauma and drama? What do I love about being a part of the negative patterns that keeps me from having more of me, or keeps me from being more productive or keeps me from creating more?"* You wouldn't choose it unless on some level, you are enjoying something about it. "What do I love about this? What do I hate about this? What do I love about this? What do I hate about this?" Maybe start moving some energy from there.

Simone: I would also start like playing with them like "How can I screw with these people today that would be fun for me right away?"

Rebecca: Simone, you are a horrible person.

Rebecca: She likes it. She's laughing.

Nilofer: And the other thing I love playing with this is I go "How can I contribute to the choices they are making?" and if they are being really trauma and drama, so I just contribute more to that so at some point it gets so much for them, they get like "Oh, I don't know what to do? This is too much for me. I have to change something here!!!"

Rebecca: Nilofer, I think you got all the trouble-makers on this hangout, every single one!

Nilofer: I'm the biggest one.

Pratima: And like Gary says, or you could just go and tell them that "hey, if I were you with so much trauma and drama, I would kill myself."

Rachel: "I don't know what you are still doing alive on the planet."

Rebecca: I love it.

POSSIBILITIES WITH YOUR PARTNER

Nilofer: Ok, more questions folks. – "So what clearing can be said when you are on one level of consciousness and your partner or spouse is not in the same space?"

Julia: Leave them! Bye bye.

Rebecca: See you later alligator!

Rachel: Go on away for a while.

Katherine: I like playing with this one because there are days when your partner is having a bad day, if you let that bad day affect you, you change your reality. I like playing with – "What can I do to be the joy of me?" I'm not coming up with the right question but I've noticed that if I don't dumb myself down to fit into their reality, I actually can be aware of their bad day or aware of their different level of consciousness and still have fun with it. And at some point, like George says, you may need to make a different choice and find a different partner but if it's just a day or a week or a month or a moment, well, "How can I choose the joy of me?" regardless of what they are choosing.

And most of us, when somebody is having a bad day, we want to go into their Universe to fix it, and when we go into their Universe, we stop being ourselves. We stop accessing our awareness. We stop accessing our joy. One of the tools I love is "Stop it! Walk away. Stop it!" I'm going for a walk. I'm going for a run. I'm going to a party. I'm going to go find a neighbor to play with. How could you literally walk away?

There are a lot of questions you can ask but I think the biggest thing is not going into their Universe to try and fix where they are in the moment because they'll just have to resist you even more which will piss you off even more and the next thing you know, a month later, you are still in their Universe, pissed off and you stop choosing the joy and magic of you.

Rachel: Yeah. That part that you were saying Katherine, that allowance, letting them have that space of sitting in their poopy diaper and being there if that's what's working for them, being in allowance of that is one of the greatest, most caring gifts that we could really be for them that they can just be as pissed off as they require to be at that moment and they can indulge whatever that energy is and we honor that. We can, like you said, walk away for however long we need to, for a walk, for you know, a run, a Starbucks, calling a friend, whatever.

Reading a book even, not being stuck in the world but still not going into their space and trying to fix them, just letting them be whatever they require until they choose something that's a little bit different.

Rachel: Or, like George was saying, ditch them.

Katherine: What stupidity am I using to create the partner I am choosing? (laughs) And then POD POC it. Either the partner will change their behavior or you'll get a new partner.

Rachel: I've run stupidity clearings on relationships before. (laughs)

Rebecca: That's a great idea. And the other part of this is the judgment of levels of consciousness. Like "Oh my partner is less conscious than I am". Well the thing is, people choose to be more conscious in some areas or not in some – how can you actually rate if someone is being more or less conscious? That's just going into the judgment and the conclusion and computation and how can you have your doorway of possibilities if you are doing that? So **unless** you finally stop going into "oh, my partner is being less conscious than I am", well, where are you choosing to be less conscious right now, because you kept going into conclusion right there. So I wonder if you got out of the consciousness scale – his consciousness – my consciousness is bigger than your consciousness, where could you actually get to go? And especially in relationships, there can be a doorway to possibility greater than anything you've ever imagined because really if you are choosing consciousness in your relationship and maybe if you were choosing that, you won't require them to be your definition of consciousness.

Simone: Also allowing them to have a different point of view, just because they have a different point of view than you doesn't mean that there is this level of consciousness, it's just that they have a different point of view. Even though you might not agree with it, I found that just being willing to look at that, even with friendships, and just being like "Actually we never agree on this subject, so why don't we just talk about something else?"

Rebecca: Yes, subject closed.

Nilofer: I'd like to talk about resonance when it comes to personal relationships. Really early on when I started my personal transformation journey, I was so attached to the relationships and the friendships that I had. When I really started to change and shift, I would notice that they would try to judge me or try to bring me down because really, they didn't want to lose me and I had to start creating a whole new paradigm with relationships because I love moving fast and there's just a lot of those circles that weren't able to keep up with me, so I just began looking at everything as resonance.

"Ok, am I resonating in a different place than they are?" and if I just allowed that am I ok with me flying even if they decided to come with me or not? And so just coming from that place for me has made it a lot easier to deal with relationships than just being in allowance of the resonance and the frequencies of it all.

Julia: I had a really sobering experience last night along these lines. My sister wrote a book. Kind of an autobiography about her life and I'm reading this book the first time and I was just gobsmacked because she does a bit of Access and stuff, but the level of intelligence that she has, that she let out or let people know, I was like "Woah! How could I have let somebody who is so intelligent, how could I have treated them as though they didn't know something or as though they were less than me or less conscious? I'm reading this book and it's this story of our lives growing up and it was so sobering to see how I had treated her as somebody that was less. I think that the way out of that is to just be with that person, just to be present with them and to say "Hey, I chose this person to be in my life" and sometimes, it is bye-bye time but a lot of time we assume that people aren't as conscious as us, or we assume that people are so frustrating. Because, it's sort of an Access thing, "Oh, stupid people!" But if we actually are willing not to put our blinders on and be, "What is actually going on here?" and "Is there something that I'm not willing to see? That I've just assumed that because I do Access I know everything." That level of vulnerability, that actual willingness to be wrong, really be wrong and to re-evaluate all the structure that you have built your life on, I think that's what can make a relationship work too.

Nilofer: Yes, that's so amazing, Julia, because I have been present to that also. I just became aware of how much I used to think my husband does not have allowance for me, and I just became aware of how much allowance I don't have for him. And the day I realized that, it just has changed so much for us, because now I look at a situation and I just go "Am I being in allowance here?" and that just changes everything.

Pratima: For me, it was also what Rebecca said, not judging your partner's choices as right or wrong because there is no right or wrong choice. There is just making the choice in those 10 seconds and it's just looking at "Ok, so they are choosing it." And you just choose what works for you without giving up 'you' using a process as well, and acknowledging that they are not giving up being them with the choices they are making. So what if you could honor that?

Judgment

Question: "Thank you for offering this phenomenal experience. Much gratitude to all of you. My question is related to the 'no judgment' aspect of Access. If Access is about no judgment, when you label or define something as crap, aren't you in judgment simply based on labeling it as crap?"

Julia: (laughs) Unless it is awareness.

Katherine: Well, isn't poo poo? You know like sometimes crap is just crap. And it's not necessarily a judgment, it's an awareness.

Rachel: Whoever has to change the poopy diaper knows.

Katherine: What's interesting is that a lot of times the judgments that stick us the most are the ones that appear to be kind. Like "She's so pretty", "he's so handsome", "he's so nice", "she's so kind". Those actually can be more of a judgment than "that's a poopy diaper", "That's frigging crap." Because sometimes crap is crap and it literally depends on your point of view or where you are functioning. So labeling something as "negative" isn't always a judgment. 99% of the time what I look at when somebody is talking is – "Is there a charge in their Universe when they are talking about something?" and if there is a charge, there is usually a judgment attached to it. But if the energy is really clean or if there is space where they are talking, even if they are talking about a crappy situation and there's no charge – like George was saying, there's no trigger, it's just space so the judgment isn't actually there anymore. So that's my point of view.

George: It's a tail-on to that, in the question there's a pre-supposition that judgment is a bad thing and part of what I love about Access is that judgment isn't wrong either. We don't make judgment wrong and it's great to become aware of judgment because then we can step into awareness that we are judging and then discharge whatever the pattern is from there.

Overwhelm

Question: "What can I do or ask to handle overwhelm, that is, too many possibilities, too much to do and no focus?"

Rebecca: What a horrible life you have! (laughs) You have too many things to create, too many possibilities, too much to do, like, oh my gosh, your life must suck!

Simone: This is just funny... sorry.

Simone: I was looking into this today and I was going into overwhelm and then I remembered this tool that I love to use and it is "What requires my attention?" So I start with it at the beginning of the day and be "Ok, what requires my attention today?" or "What requires my attention now?" or "Do I do this now or later?" and all of a sudden things became really clear and it just becomes easy.

Nilofer: Simone, have you noticed with that question that a whole lot of things that were on your "to-do" list just seem to fall away?

Simone: It's amazing!

Rebecca: I was talking to Blossom Benedict about this. She's like "How many things are you doing? What's on your plate?" And I said, "Maybe 5 or 6" and she said, "Is that enough?" and it was like "No". And for me, I need somewhere between 12 to 20 things to do pretty much all the time. I put on Facebook the other day like "Oh, I have 50 tabs open on my computer. I'm using at least 18 of them at the same time. Do you do this? What's going on?" Telling people that they weren't wrong for filling up their entire computer screen. Just because all the things they are doing, because that's actually the way that they function, it's a genius way of being! And I was wondering what if you didn't have to focus and what if you didn't have to remember? What if you were just this crazy Tasmanian devil that's just possibly doing all the things all at once all the time and you never stopped and you never gave in and always kept going and you always kept creating? What would be your reality?

Rebecca: Right! And you can never get bored that way. Thank god! Oh my gosh, if I got bored, the world would end.

Katherine: Well along the lines of what Simone said, I ask "What is contribution today?" And I am shocked that the amount of people that come into my life that will go to the DMV for me or wash my car for me or do my grocery shopping. My "to-do" list gets done by other people for me because I am willing to receive contribution. I laughed the other day because all of the daily tasks that people do, I have people that are willing to do them for me and I didn't necessarily seek hiring them, they just started coming into my life. What are you refusing to receive contribution for and from? And what if your "to-do" list could be the Universe helping create magic for you? So that's a fun one.

Body

Question: "Any advice on being able to hear the body when recovering from addiction and chemical dependency? And there is a sense of no longer being able to trust the answers the body is offering up."

Julia: Have you tried getting any body processes run? The first thing I would go with is body processes. Access Consciousness body processes acknowledge the body in a way that nothing that I've ever known has. There is a specific body process called the Trifold Sequencing Systems For Drug Induced Scenarios And Perfectionism. That's a really amazing process. So this might be a big contribution to this person to get this process run.

It's run on the sensory cortex of your brain and the way that the process runs is when you are high or you have an addiction to alcohol or drugs, everything that occurs in your life when you are on alcohol or the drugs, the reason that you are using the addiction is to be unconscious or to not really look at what's going on in your life. So what happens is when we are high or we are stoned, we are drunk, all of those awarenesses from when we have made ourselves that unconscious gets stored in the sensory cortex of the brain, so this body process, The Trifle Sequencing System, actually clears out the sensory cortex of the brain and offers a sense of relief that I can not describe. And it works through all lifetimes. So it's this lifetime, past lifetimes, any lifetime you were a man, a woman, maybe you were Al Capone, whatever it was, that body process will clear that.

So the Access body processes are a huge, huge part of actually having an awareness of what your body is telling you because if you have had the addiction, there's likely going to be a place where the communication with your body just isn't happening. You have done so much to try to be unconscious and to try not to listen, because the awarenesses that you have had may have been kind of painful. And there is no wrongness in that.

If you hadn't had that addiction, where would you be? Maybe you would have committed suicide by now or been down a life path – maybe you wouldn't be at this place where you actually have a conscious choice. So the addiction is not a wrongness. It actually could have been a huge gift at that time. So if you get out of judgment of that addiction, that's a huge step. And then another step that I would say is is looking into this body process if you haven't already done it, it's a huge, huge gift. If there's **any** body facilitators in your area, I would definitely recommend getting hold of them. And it's just an honoring of the body and it is clearing out all of these places where you are stuck and don't have an awareness of what your body is actually saying to you.

Nilofer: And the other thing is the book, 'Right Recovery For You' by Marilyn Bradford. It's brilliant. I interviewed her in the last summit I did and she said, "The first thing you go to is 'What's right about this addiction I am not getting?'" Just what you were talking about Julia. So if you were to just keep repeating that 'What's right about this addiction I am not getting, you get out of the wrongness of you.

Katherine: And one thing that you can ask, because I heard the person asking how can they hear their body more, there are so many things – running the body process, absolutely, reading Marilyn's book, absolutely, whether you are dealing with addiction or anything, not willing to be aware of, "What am I aware of that I'm not willing to be aware of," and if you ask that question a lot, every day, something's bound to open up.

When I'm in body pain or dealing with stuff, I'm always "Body, what are you aware of that I don't want to hear?" One of the things that you can also ask is "What am I not willing to hear?" Most of us are unwilling to hear how aware we are, how amazing we are, how brilliant we are. And I think Julia mentioned it, most people who turn to drugs or alcohol are so flipping aware of everyone's thoughts around them that they think by doing the drugs or alcohol, it will actually shut down the awareness. What the problem is, is it turns up the volume. So then they have even more crazy thoughts in their head. So asking "What are you aware of?" and just return to sender, could also be a huge contribution. If you begin to acknowledge it's not a wrongness and that it was just a choice, your body will forgive you and want to create a different possibility with you immediately. What questions could you ask that would be an honoring of your body?

Rebecca: That's so brilliant, Katherine. And what just popped up in my head from you talking about that was your body is there all the time. Your body doesn't leave. It's there when you get up in the morning, it stays when you do stupid shit, it's there when you do great stuff. So is it that you are not trusting your body or that you are not trusting you? And would you be willing to receive the kindness that your body has for you? It's there all the time and virtually has your back. So I wonder if you started to trust you, maybe you'll get what awareness your body is asking for to show up.

Simone: I also wonder if you've touched on how often people who have addictions, they are so aware that they are trying to block out some of all of the stuff that they are hearing. So I wonder also if they could say something like "Ok, truth, my body, what would you like to do? Truth, my body, what would you like to do?" Because often they are so aware of other people's bodies and what they require and so to really go "Ok, what is it that we require?"

Nilofer: Wow that's so great Simone.

Rebecca: That's a brilliant question.

Nilofer: Oh my god, "my body" (laughs)

Rebecca: You mean, you could take care of you? What the hell! (laughs)

Katherine: Nilofer, I just want to say thank you for putting this to-gether, for putting all of us together and foreseeing a possibility that no one else may have seen. When we follow our knowing and we literally open a door to a possibility that no one else on the planet can see, we invite everyone into something new and amazing and so thank you for being the gift and invitation to all of us, to everyone who will listen to the summit, because truly, like what Rebecca said in the beginning of this hangout, I wonder what we'll create. Because the seeds that we are planting today in the present moment, they are not only creating a different future, they are eradicating a past so that we can have even more possibilities. So thank you for your genius, thank you for your magic and it's so brilliant. I'm honored to be a part of it.

Nilofer: When I actually started doing my tele-summits, my point of view was "I get to talk to all these brilliant people one-on-one. I'm going to get a private session from each one of them!"

I've seen people who are there on the summit who come in as a total newbie and then I see their conversation after a year and they are a totally different person. And I go "Oh my god! That's what this is creating!" It's not about me, that's a very small point of view I have, it's just not about me, it's about what we are creating in the Universe and I just feel so grateful for that and I'm so grateful for all of you for being a part of it. Thank you so much.

Pratima: Being a part of the summit along with so many amazing facilitators is like a huge contribution to me too. Just exploring what I'm going to talk, just listening to other facilitators speaking.

Rachel: It invites every single one of us to step into – literally, not just us participating in the tele-summit, but every single person who is listening now and in the future to creating an entirely new way of being in the world, an entire new way of seeing the world and an entire new world. And hats off, really, it's amazing.

Simone: Thanks for bringing the trouble-makers together, Nilofer.

Nilofer: Yeah, how much trouble can we all get into collectively? Oh my god. Thank you so much. Thank you so much everyone for being on this hangout together.

Rebecca: I just want to invite people, this book is packed. There's brilliance in this, so I would really invite you to use this as an opportunity to choose and to follow your knowing and to take care of you like "Ok, what would my life be like in 5 years if I choose to read this now and in the future?" And don't feel like you have to do what everyone else is doing. Don't do what everyone else does. And really how much fun can we have? How much can we change the whole fucking world?

Pratima: And also we've just stepped into a brand new year and for me, the theme of the year is about creating possibility. So what if this summit could contribute to everybody in creating infinite possibilities? That's an awesome way to begin a new year to me.

Rebecca: Oh yes.

Simone: And this stuff is so much fun, for me and for probably all of us right here right now, it's play, it's things like magic that you can just throw around and chuck around and just play with it.

Nilofer: You know what actually happens with me is when I'm doing these interviews, a few minutes into the interview, I just become aware of this sense of peace and joy and happiness in my Universe and I'm like grinning. "Oh, I'm happy. I'm happy."

AMAZING BONUSES

Would you like to have the clearing loops from all the clearings in this book? Visit www.whereismydoorwaytopossibilities.com

---

ALL OUR CONTRIBUTORS

Aditi Iyer

Bhagyalakshmi Murali

Cara Wright

Christine McIver

Gary Douglas

Delany Delaney &
Glen Sheppard

Stephanie Richardson

Heather Karian Nichols

Julia Sotas

Kalpana Raghuraman

Katherine McIntosh

Louise Derksen

Melanie Clampit

Nirmala Raju

Pratima Nagaraj

Rachel Silber

Rebecca Hulse

Rhonda Burns

Ritu Motial

Simone Padur

Nilofer Safdar

CHAPTER TWO

WHAT IF YOU'RE ALREADY ON YOUR WAY TO BECOMING LIMITLESS?

By Rebecca Hulse

International #1 Best-Selling Author,

Access Consciousness® Certified Facilitator,

Speaker & Writer

Have you been searching for ways to eliminate problems or change parts of your life? What about ways to improve it, and the search for more… ? What if you were already far more limitless than you thought?

What could you create?

When Nilofer invited me to be a part of this book, I wondered what contribution this chapter could be. From the magic we've created together at the Illusion to Illumination Summit, I had a taste of the possibilities; however I didn't realize the depth of tools and conversation we had until I read the transcript that was the start point for this chapter. From reading through it and adding on, I realized we're far closer to being limitless than we ever thought possible. How does it get any better than that? Does that make your world light up (perhaps with a little bit of excitement, fear and knowing)?

Is now the time to be limitless? Is this something you've been asking for?

If so I invite you to read on…

Choosing To Shake Out Of It! Changing Your Reality From Train Wreck To Infinite Being

Have you ever woken up feeling like you got hit with a train in your sleep? And wondered what the hell you were doing all night to create this? I've definitely had more than a few of those. Some of those states that lasted all day, or and some that were a repeat pattern daily.

One morning, I got smart and demanded a different possibility. It was one of those train wreck mornings where I did not want to get out of bed, that morning I thought, "Oh this bed is so nice. I just got hit by a train and I am never like this. I deserve to mope a bit." (Normally I think, "Yes! I'm going to do this! I'm going to create this! Ok, let's go!) Who the hell am I being? "I deserve to mope a bit?" What kind of infinite being's reality is that?

The moment I shook myself out of this it and chose to get up and get going, things started to happen like magic. I had coffee in my hands. Simple thoughts like "I never had any breakfast. I really want some breakfast…" created people that lived in our house walking up and asking, "Do you want my breakfast? It's nice. I just don't want to eat it." There's this energy here that is available for everyone to choose whether you believe it or not.

You just have to be conscious of what you're creating.

Acknowledgment doesn't mean that you are stuck up. Acknowledgement means that you are willing to have more of what you'd like to create. That's why I'm on Facebook all the time. It's the easiest way for me to acknowledge everything around.

We can choose to facilitate limitation, or we can choose to create possibility. If you have to facilitate limitations on the way to creating the possibility that you've perceived, that's the place where these the amazing tools of the clearing statement comes in. Otherwise, are we using limitations as an excuse to stop ourselves from having possibility?

I have seen people who come to classes and they just want to talk about their limitations. What if we were to bypass the limitations? What if we were to start creating from possibilities? After some time, you don't have time for limitations anymore. "I have too much going on, and I can't do limitations" can become your reality. Then we would get so busy world-dominating, reality-shaking and creating a new possibilities. Who has time for limitations? Who has time to get upset or to worry about what someone said when they were having a horrible day and accidentally blurted something out of their mouth that wasn't even to do with you anyway?

So I wonder, is it as simple as choosing possibility instead of limitation? Could it be that easy? How easy do you actually want it to be? Really? If it was easy, how much more would you create? Do you really believe you're the type to sit back and only create just enough? Literally, we don't want to be aware we are that potent, and we could create this kind of change.

I totally get it. I did not want to be aware I was that potent either. When I first started using the tools of Access Consciousness® and going to classes, I was in an advanced class with Gary Douglas (founder) and Dr. Dain Heer (co-founder). It was lots of fun, I was laughing and I maybe asked 1 or 2 questions. They weren't massive questions, but I came back to a class 3 or 4 months later and they still knew who I was. I thought to myself, "Wait, me being happy and being me created so much change that so many people remember who I was and that I made a difference to them? Something's a little bit different." I wonder how often we all are being the change and don't realize it or don't value it? If we didn't discount it, could the difference we naturally be go much further? What am I going to create especially in the next year that is inspiring everyone to be like this?

What could we create if we were willing to be that big or to be that phenomenal? What could we create if we were willing to be us, and acknowledge we are the change? It is the reality change, and It is the world change, that will create this. If you are too busy looking and facilitating the limitations so you can get over your blocks, so you can get possibilities, to feel good about yourself to consider changing the world - the doorway doesn't open. If you are too busy looking at your limitations so you can get over your blocks, see possibilities, and feel good about yourself--the doorway to world-changing possibilities doesn't open.

If you choose the reality-shaking or the world-changing from the start, the Universe says: "Yes girl, I've got your back," and then those limitations can simply disappear.

I remember Dr. Dain Heer (co-founder of Access Consciousness®) say in a class, "Just by being you, just by being present, you change everything. You are such a huge contribution." When I walked away from that class and I asked myself, "What contribution am I being that I'm not acknowledging?" that started to shift and change things for me. I started being present to the contribution I was being, and I started to acknowledge that contribution.

Have you ever been present to the contribution that you are being? Look at you being you; look at the energy of this…

*Everywhere that you think "Oh my god, I don't even want to look at that!" will you destroy and un-create that? Right and wrong, good and bad, POD and POC, all nine, Shorts, boys and beyonds**

So now, take this energy of you being you, what does the world look like in 5 years if you be you? Now let's go even further. What does the Universe look like in 200 years if you be you? Look at everything that exists: what does would consciousness look like or be like in a thousand years if you be you? What would consciousness be like if you choose chose this?

I wonder what new possibilities would show up for the planet?

Creating Massive Change By Being You

So how do you choose you being you?

Is being you what you've been looking for? Perhaps the first step is acknowledging that being you is really what you're looking for. Once you have that the acknowledgement that you know what you're choosing, and what you're looking for, you then know what does and doesn't match the energy. Whenever I sense that, *(can you say more about what 'that' is? The energetic match?)* it gives me the fire, the desire, and the capacity I didn't even know was possible to filter it *(also more about what 'it' is?)* into the everyday life. A lot of the time when I'm being, I don't think at all, especially when I'm working or creating.

If you are being you and demanding whatever it takes for creations that you are looking for to show up, how much more do people respond to you? How much does that command people to be present in your present? I know people get frustrated and caught up in, "Oh this isn't happening. All these people aren't doing anything!" By You commanding their presence and by being that presence yourself makes them snap out of it.

One of the first questions from Access Consciousness® that caught my attention was, "What would my life be like in 5 years if I chose this?" I've been running that one for about a year and a half now and I'm looking at how my life has shown up and from as a result of *(?)* choosing from that question. If this is year one from of using that question, I wonder what year 5 will be like? Five years is way too far out in the future, but if *this* is what it has created right away, that's a phenomenal possibility.

Choosing the Doorway to Infinite Possibilities

To me, the doorway to possibilities is about the space where you are willing to receive the invitation to one. The Universe is constantly offering us the stuff that we are or are not willing to receive and access. The doorway to possibilities is the space where you are willing to receive the invitation of possibilities that you've always been getting but have never been willing to receive.

Possibility is undefined. Possibility is the space in which anything is possible Anything can be created, anything can exist, and there is no limitation. That's why we say infinite possibilities because there really is an infinite amount. The whole reason why it's almost not worth describing is that because the definition is a limitation alone. So with possibilities, what are you really aware of when it comes to possibilities? Is it something that you can use to your advantage? Is it something you have or haven't been choosing? An invitation? I would invite everyone to look at what is possibility to you.

The other question that I've been asking recently is "What choice or what possibilities do I have available that nobody else does?" There's only one Nilofer, there's only one Dr. Dain Heer, there's only Gary Douglas, there's only one me and there's only one you. Why the hell would I try to be anyone else except me?

What would the world be like if there was no you? That doesn't light me up at all.

Using The Infinite Colors of Infinite Intensity And Infinite Possibilities To Overcome Your Perceived Limitations

Are limitations what you use to define the problem that you'd like to have? A limitation can be anything, and it depends on the person, really. What are you making your limitations? Everything that you have decided your limitations are, will you destroy and uncreate them all? Right and wrong, good and bad, POD and POC, all nine, shorts, boys and beyonds. *

What if we chose to not define our problems? Would you have any problems? Damn! Then it's just an interesting possibility. That thing of just being happy for no reason could actually be a reality. It's not like that manic kind of happiness where you are giggling, but it's more like that energy of joy and a sense of peace.

What's funny about true joy and ease is that a lot of time it has been damn uncomfortable, horribly uncomfortable: *I'm being vulnerable here, it hasn't all been easy.* How often have we truly ever allowed ourselves ease and joy? Anytime recently in the last four trillion years?

What has been really amazing is I'm now willing to receive the unexpected. The number of unexpected things that are showing up in my Universe has been just amazing. Now, when something which is unexpected shows up, I think, "Oh, that's unexpected. Hmm, but that's so much fun. I'll just play with it."

What if life was here to surprise and delight you? This is something that we can all have and be. It's delicate, not balanced, but a composition of where, as an infinite being, you are not just being infinite, you are using all your capacities too. You are willing to have them, you are willing to receive them and that means that other people will find you really intense.

It's almost like when you have earphones in your ears and someone speaks to you and you are going "YES!" You're just speaking normally and everyone else is like "you're shouting". Please, the intensity is too much!

Isn't that the place where we actually dumb ourselves down because people aren't willing to receive us? What if it wasn't the people that receive you, what if it was the Universe that was going to receive you? If you think about it, a person choosing to be finite, or the Universe: what which one is really going to receive you more? The Universe has been receiving you since you've existed!

What we choose is to expect this person that is just trying to get along and doesn't know that there's possibilities out there to receive the brilliance of us, when there's something that's an entire Universe that has been begging to receive us for all eternity. It's like when a woman chooses a guy that really doesn't actually like her. All the while, there this other guy has been like taking care of her and honoring her his entire life. It's that kind of insanity that goes on with us.

The Universe is begging to receive us. If we were to function from that, everything would change!

Trusting Your Own Potency And Awareness

For what reason would you let someone else's awareness or conclusion overpower your own? Everything that brought up or let down, will you destroy and un-create all that? Right and wrong, good and bad, POD and POC, all nine, shorts, boys and beyonds*

So my question is for what reason would you let someone else's awareness or conclusion overpower your awareness? Do you believe you're still stuck in that blame and shame thing - blaming yourself for everything? **Is there a different possibility available?**

If so, what possibility would you be interested in creating beyond blaming yourself?

If you choose to continue blaming yourself, will that reality ever get created? What would you really like to choose? Everything that doesn't allow that, will you destroy and un-create it? Right and wrong, good and bad, POD and POC, all nine, shorts, boys and beyonds*

This is the kind of thing, where we could also use a 1-2-3**. 1-2-3 is this massive, energetic, super-power explosion that every single infinite being has the capacity to do. And it's as simple as gathering the awareness of the energy that we could create, and letting it out in a big explosion on 3. It's fun!

So this particular one will be to creating that future where we all empower each other.

Everything that we can now contribute as infinite beings and the Universe can contribute to creating that as the reality, we now just flick that energy at anywhere that you would like on 3.

Grab that energy you're aware of, even just reading the pages. Become aware of the possibility that you would also like to add to this, and everyone who ever reads this. Now on 3 we are going to flick all that energy out to the Universe to create it. 1-2-3. And that is a 1-2-3.

How does it get any better than that?

I wonder, what else do you know about infinite possibilities that nobody else knows? What does everyone know about possibilities that they have been denying or refusing that it is now the time for? Everything that that brought up; and everywhere you swore you would never look at possibilities like that again; and everywhere that you've got a pattern or implant that says that this was a horrible thing; and every time you look this big or got this much or were this intense that you destroyed everything, would you be willing to destroy and un-create that and actually see the truth of what's possible? Right and wrong, good and bad, POD and POC, all nine, Shorts, boys and beyonds*

Refusing to Accept "The Wrongness of Us"

Every time that I let go of what should be and shouldn't be, my life creates itself on its own and it's way beyond what I could have imagined possible. The other thing I want to talk about is the wrongness of us and going into the judgment of us. What if we didn't go there?

I have had 17 years of dance training, which is 17 years of looking in the mirror and making myself wrong, and picking up the judgments of everyone else and choosing to believe they're ~~mine~~ yours because ~~I~~ you don't like that those are someone else's judgments. *When we do this, ~~we~~ You* put them in ~~your~~ *our bodies* and go on judging that people aren't really being that mean to themselves. Isn't this insane?

You were born judgment-free. You were born without the wrongness of you!

This is the same thing as what we looked at about as being you. Can you truly be you without judging you? Like while you are judging you?

Or does that very choice alone stop you from being you?

Do you have anyone in your life that is always unapologetically them, no matter what? What does that create in their *life* lives? And what does it do for you – having them in your life? Do you not also wonder if that could also be you and something that you too could create? The world would change.

One of the questions that Gary Douglas, founder of Access Consciousness® gave me in a class was "What would it take for you to out-create yourself one thousand fold today?" I have been in that question and then sometimes, I'll ask just for fun: "What would it take for me to out-create Gary and Dain today?"

The temple of consciousness will get you and pick you up in a chariot and make your life amazing.

This is one of the things that I've had constant conversations with Gary about - the piece of choice being a manipulation. I've said over and over again "but it's not *just* choice!" If Gary, someone else, or I say "choice" about something, you do not have to run a body process a million times. You don't have to get your bars run every week for a year to have this finally change. You don't have to run a clearing statement for 30 days, 30 times like a day for this to change. It's literally right here waiting for you. And it's not a wrongness if you don't want it or require it, it's just there as an offer or invitation that you either get to choose or not choose. It makes things simple, it makes things easy. To me, that's really what choice is. Would you like to be you? You don't have to! I'm willing to be the invitation for it if you would like it, but at the same time, there's nothing wrong with you if you don't.

Recognizing That You Are A Different Person Everyday:

A Different Possibility Is Always Available

Have you ever wondered how you choose? A lot of people don't know how to choose. I'll let you in on a secret - I don't know how to choose either! For some reason I just do it, it's a weird capacity everyone has the ability to have that remains a total mystery. Do you know how to make your heart beat? I don't! I don't know how to choose either, what I do know is that my heart beats and I choose. :)

The reason I say that is because I'm a different person every day. Are you the same person you were a year ago? Or what even about six months ago?

Forget it, even one day ago! Just one day ago.

The secret to choice is you don't need to know how to do it. Do you know how to breathe or is it something you innately do? What if choice is actually as natural to you as breathing? Does that feel light to you? Would you be willing to play with it? Have fun even?

Just choose anything! There's no right or wrong in that. When you choose it, it gives you an awareness of "Oh, this is working for me; this isn't working for me. Ok, I'm going to play with this some more. I'm not going to play with this anymore." And that's that.

And if you come across a moment when you are really struggling with "I don't know how to choose", this is what I do: I ask, "How do I choose today?" or "What would choosing to me look like today?" Or I'll go outside and say "Ok, nature, ok Universe, ok anyone, like I'm being real dumb today. What is choice? Show me choice." Anything that I'm not currently getting, I'll generally go outside (and even to my cat, because I don't know how, but my cat's always choosing consciousness), and I'll be like "Show me consciousness." Or "Show me choice." Or "Show me possibility." The thing is, if you ask, they will receive. They will come to you. Ask and you shall receive actually does work!

The other question that I ask when I'm not getting something is: "What would it take for me to get what choice is?" You don't actually have to know the answer to anything anymore. What if you just needed to be smart enough to ask a question? I'll hear someone say something and I'll sit there like a dog watching television and I'm going "I'm not getting this" and then the next moment I ask, "what would it take for me to get it?" It can be as simple as that.

I've often found that when I sit there like a dog watching television and I don't get something, it's because that's not my issue at all. So I look there and *I realize:* I'm like "oh I don't get this," but then it's not my stuff, that's why I don't get it. This is also something that I talk about with my mum. When she gets so lost she says, "I didn't get this. How did this take so long and reach so much?" All it takes is for me to ask here: "Well, when did you finish it or change it?" and then she goes *says* "Oh, five seconds before you started talking about it." What if you were that fast too?

Bypassing Judgment To Make More Money

Have you ever had a conversation about how we personally could be that world *would* change, and being willing to choose it even if we're scared shitless about doing it? I would like to bring together a group of people that would like to change the world. Those who have an ability or see a possibility that has not yet shown up or they are not yet choosing it, with being that world change, with changing other people's reality.

Isn't that we always wanted to be anyway? How much of a contribution is just being us? Have you ever considered it's the change that walks through the world effortlessly? And then when we create something, it has the impact of an explosion – only of change rather than destruction. This is the kind of thing that sounds irresistible to me. Does it light you up?

What's funny to me about this, is when you are willing to be and choose to be that much of a contribution, the rest of your life becomes easy. Things flow into your life at a rapid rate like caring friends, adventures, and experiences, and money money money!

I personally love talking about money; investing in beautiful antique jewelry is one of my favorite things. A $50 note that's purple and it's *is* just so beautiful, coincidentally so is a Euro $500 note! Has anyone has looked at money and thought it was beautiful? A lot of people talk don't talk about money as if it is beautiful, but it is something that I see as quite beautiful.

Money is especially *beautiful* when you talk about *the* possibilities of money. If there is something that has been sticking you, especially if you've been struggling to get the money so you can do the things you want to do to change the world, what if you didn't have to wait? What if you went ahead anyway? If money was no issue, what would you choose?

What if you never went into the wrongness of "oh my god, I don't have any money. What's going on?" anymore? How much would the flood-gates of wealth could open for you? Using the Access Consciousness® tool *Interesting Point of View* is one of my best money tools.

If my money goes on a flatline or drops below what I've thought is an "okay level" repeating to myself "Interesting point of view I have this point of view about money" really changes my perspective. It takes money panic of "Oh my god it's Christmas and my money is going down the drain faster than draino!" to "Oh, my money just took a hike. I wonder what this is? I wonder what's going on here?"

It turns the panic and contraction around really quickly because it's alleviating the polarity. What if money was not a limitation and what if just because those numbers didn't match up, that didn't mean that you weren't going to create it anyway?

What if having no money is not a limitation?

At the start of 2014, I didn't have a job, I barely had an Access Bars business and I'd just come back from a dancing contract on cruise ships where I'd shopped my way through the Caribbean. I had a con-siderable family wealth that I was living off, but nothing sustainable or a creation of my own. By the end of the year, I had travelled to Costa Rica twice, did a tour around the United States, gone to two advanced

Access Consciousness® 7 days and a bunch of other classes in between all on my own income and creation.

I started the year with no money that I had personally earned, and ended it with phenomenal amounts. This has been my awareness, "If you didn't have to use money to create, maybe you would use you."

Where To From Here?

For me writing chapters in books and sharing these wonderful tools is a gift come true. These tools have personally affected my life so deeply and I'm still in awe that I was smart enough to use them!

My greatest tip with the energy transformation tools of Access Consciousness® is to treat them like a shed full of tools – they are always there if you desire them, but they only work if you use them.

A rusty set of shears doesn't cut so well as a well oiled and loved pair, and a messy toolshed where you can't tell what's what will never inspire you to choose and use them. Some tools won't resonate with you as well as others – that doesn't mean you have to use them.

Simply take what lights you up and pings you and leave the rest at the store. You can always come back later for more – and there is always more.

Thank you for reading this chapter and more importantly for choosing you and choosing to be here on this beautiful planet. Truly if the Universe and consciousness didn't want you here, you wouldn't still be alive (has it tried to drop a crane on your head yet? :) Enjoy the wonderful adventure and I hope to meet you in person someday soon.

The Access Bars

The Access Bars are 32 points on the head that when gently touched, effortlessly and easily release anything that doesn't allow you to receive.

The Access Bars have assisted tens of thousands of people worldwide to change many aspects of their body and their life including sleep, health and weight, money, sex and relationships, anxiety, stress, disabilities and so much more.

Bars Demonstration Video. Download Version + Printable Chart - http://bit.ly/2aBuxUb

Global Access Bars Class With Gary - http://bit.ly/2aGD3er

Global Bars with Dr Dain Heer Single - http://bit.ly/2aBdtbs

Global Bars with Dr Dain Heer – 2 Attendees - http://bit.ly/2aHCEPd

❖

CHOICE, CHANGE & PLAY: KEYS TO DISCOVERING AND STEPPING THROUGH YOUR DOORWAY TO INFINITE POSSIBILITY

by Melanie Clampit

Empowerment Coach, Access Consciousness™
Certified Facilitator, Author, Leader &
Conscious Revolutionary

Choice ~ Change ~ Play

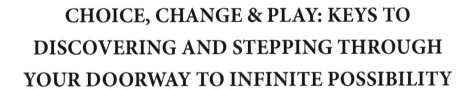: So I was just tapping into the energy of the call and I was looking at the topic that you have chosen and for all our listeners, I love what you have said, "Choice, Change and Play".

Wow! So can you talk about all three different elements in that.

M: Absolutely. I know for me these are 3 elements haven't always been the easiest areas. For me, and for many people, choice, change and play are places where many of us get stuck – stuck on what to choose, trying to make the right choice, and trying not to make the wrong choice.

I spent years thinking I needed to make the correct and right choice to get me where I'd like to go. It didn't work so well. Transition, fear of change, and being uncomfortable in the un- known and unfamiliar can be challenging.

Play is about wondering and being in the question. It's also about curiosity. With both choice and change I'm looking at how I can take the energy of play, curiosity, and wonder, and bring that into choice. Bringing these elements into creating ease with change. Because change isn't always comfortable. But what if we have choice about how we engage with the changes?

What If Nothing Ever Shows Up Like You Think It Will?

N: So you have written in your description, 'Tips and tools for how to choose when nothing looks like you imagined', can you say more about that?

M: That's right. Have you ever had a really specific way you thought something had to show up and all of a sudden everything is totally different than you thought it would be?

N: Oh that never happens to me!

M: No. Never!

Well, one of the things I've noticed with using Access ConsciousnessTM tools, and something I've heard, the co-founders, Gary Douglas and Dr. Dain Heer saying so often, is that nothing ever shows up like you think it will. I admit when I first heard this I thought to myself, "I have no idea what they are talk- ing about actually."

What I've noticed over the last 3 1/2 years is that truly nothing has shown up like I ever imagined it would, and the choices that I have in front of me are also not choices that I had ever imagined for myself.

In addition, often when we are looking to create a different future, there isn't a defined picture about what it is that we would like to create or how we could go about creating it, there just an energy, an awareness.

The undefined space of awareness, energy, and possibilities was a pretty tricky area for me, and it actually often stopped me from choosing, because I was always looking for something familiar, known, and to have it figured out before choosing. I was always looking for some kind of solidity to go towards.

What I'm noticing is when I become aware of an energy that I'd like to create in my future, I don't have any solid place to create from – there are none of the road signs I expected.

So, I wanted to offer some of the Access Consciousness tools for how to navigate when what is before you is undefined and has no form or solidity?

When you don't have words or definition how do you create your future and what do you base your choices on if you don't have something solid to move towards?

N: Oh totally. Totally.

M: Before this interview, I was looking at the different gifts in the product package that I put together and one of the pieces in there is a guided audio of a creation exercise, some people in Access call it the 'Energy Ball' exercise.

In that exercise, I'm inviting the listener to get the energy of what they would like as their future, just the energy of it, and then play with it on an energetic level. Because, what if living in a world of possibilities, what if being a doorway to possibilities is something that is probably going to go beyond anything that may be recognizable to you?

You may actually have to become someone who is so different from who you are right now, you may not even recognize you. Right?

N: Wow. You know, this is something I heard Shannon O'Hara speak about during her class yesterday. She said, "You know, when things are really uncomfortable for me, I make a demand for myself. I make a demand that I will be or do whatever it takes to have more, to have more ease, and to create more in that space." And I said wow. How often do we go to that space and we make it a wrongness?

M: Absolutely. I noticed that so often when I was actually becoming the difference that I was asking for, when I was actually quite different from who I usually was, I would judge it as wrong. So I was actually moving in the direction that would create what I was asking for but would stop it by going into wrongness.

What I didn't know is that I would be uncomfortable sometimes, very uncomfortable, and that I would actually have to be different.

Are You Willing To Be So Different You May Not Recognize Your Life?

It was like I had a point of view that everything around me would shift and warp and change, but I wouldn't. Over the last year and a half I chosen to put myself into constant change, kind of a crash course in using the tools with change. Pretty strategic, actually. I basically demanded that I be or do whatever it would take for me to have greater ease with change, jumped in and worked that muscle.

It was only recently I realized how different my life is and how much more ease with change I have. One of the things that I had to choose for myself, like Shannon was saying, was to demand of myself to be or do whatever it took to create ease with change, discomfort, and difference.

I realized that to create a living dream, an ideal job, a great relationship, the money, and what I know is possible it is actually going to require me to be different?

And what if different isn't wrong? What if different was just different? And what if you could kind of loosen the hold you have on who you think you are and who you think you are not, so that you may actually become everything that's possible for you to be?

What if we do actually live in a Universe of ask and you shall receive? What if this is really true?

What if you can begin to ask:

What can I be or do different today to have greater ease with the changing unrecognizable me right away?

M: When we actually make that choice, when we choose it, we may not have any idea how it is going to occur. I haven't known how anything was going to occur in my life. The only thing I know is that I chose and allowed the change. I consciously continued to choose over and over again and I got more playful with it.

The play, the wonder and the curiosity are part of what helps have more ease with the unrecognizable you, unrecognizable relationships and unrecognizable life. Many of us are asking for a totally different life and living, a totally different reality.

I was asking for my life to be different, my money flows to be different, all my relationships to be different, I was basically asking for an entirely different life. But the piece I wasn't really getting here was that I wasn't yet willing to be as different as it was going to take to have it and allow myself to receive all of it.

One of the keys to changing this was a growing willingness to be unrecognizable to myself, to let my life be different, and to not make any of it wrong.

Judgment Is Not Part Of The Equation

N: It's amazing. Wow! Unrecognizable to me. Wow. I mean, for me it's almost like unrecognizable – Am I willing to be unrecognizable to others? Am I willing to receive judgments from others, for being unrecognizable? But really, I mean, it is about being unrecognizable to me. Right?

M: I think so. If you are willing to be unrecognizable to you, are you actually willing to have more allowance for other people? It's a strange kind of thing. When I am willing to be unrecognizable to me, I am willing to let other people be whoever they were too.

N: Even if they judge, you have more allowance for that.

M: In order to become unrecognizable to you, or quite different than what you're used to, you cannot judge you. In order to allow that level of change, judgment cannot be part of that equation.

N: Wow. The energy that we all are perceiving at this moment is really that energy of no judgment that you be for yourself. Wow.

M: So truly, what would it take for you to not judge you? One of the reasons that I held on to judgment of myself for such a long time was that I thought it was sort of a checking system where I could make sure I was going in the right direction. To ensure that I would constantly be choosing more, choosing correctly, and choosing something greater. It was as if I couldn't have consciousness if I didn't judge me, which was one of the greatest lies that I've ever bought.

I'm discovering it's the opposite. If you choose not to judge you, you can receive everything. You can receive all of you. You also trust you when you're not judging you. When you trust you, you can make choices based on the awareness of what your choice will create not on the judgments of right and wrong, good or bad.

A Magnanimous Universe

Gary and Dain just did a 3 day tele-series, called "Living in a World of Possibilities" and on the last call they introduced something called the "magnanimous Universe". Magnanimous is greatly generous; a generosity of spirit, a kindness.

What if that is actually who you are?

What if we are the energy of the magnanimous Universe?

Can you perceive that energy? Is there any judgment in there?

It is as if judgment can't do anything, has no effect whatsoever, in the energy of magnanimous Universe.

N: I was in the shower and looking at generosity of spirit, and guess what I put on in my iPod?

M: What?

N: *What energy, space and consciousness can me and my body be, to be the generosity of spirit we truly be for all eternity?*

M: (laughs) Don't you love consciousness. That is awareness!

N: And now you are talking about it. Wow.

M: What's interesting about change is this – we have so many fixed points of view about what it takes to change something, what change is, what change isn't, what can be changed what cannot, right?

We've been talking for a while, so let's take a moment to check something out here.

What If Change Is Different Than You Think?

Ask for the energy of who you were, your life, the possibilities available to you 20 minutes ago when we started this chapter. Don't think too much about it, just ask to become aware of the energy before we started, just get a sense.

And now look at who you are right now and also look and perceive the energy of who you'll be in 5 years, 10 years, 50 years as a result of just these 20 minutes and now, what will the world be like in 50 years as a result of what we just changed in this conversation?

So are there more possibilities or less?

N: Definitely more. And thank you. Thank you for that. I never looked at change like that.

M: What if every time you choose what's light or true for you, every time you choose based on your awareness, you change something?

What if every single time you stopped and didn't buy someone's thought, feeling, or emotion as yours and returned it to sender, you changed something?

What if the change are you creating is not only for you, but for all of us? What if every choice counts, every choice creates? (laughs) How does it get better than that?

What If Everything Is Just An Interesting Point Of View?

Caller: "So what would it take to have more allowance for me while becoming different? I hear a lot of "Who do you think you are?" and "Never change.""

M: Are you willing to give yourself permission to be you regardless of what anyone else thinks? Choosing allowance with you is an amazing tool for working with this.

Allowance is where everything is just an interesting point of view. If you say to yourself, "Interesting point of view, they have that point of view or Interesting point of view that I have that point of view", over and over and over again it will begin to change this.

This is a powerful Access Consciousness tool that can create greater allowance of you being different and greater allowance of others who struggle with your changes. This is a fantastic tool for anyone who would like to stop judging themselves and have ease with other people's judgments.

I Choose Not To Judge Me Today

N: Yes, it's almost like you catch yourself. 'Oh, I'm judging myself. Never mind, I won't do it now.'

M: Yes. One of the things that I played with was just that exact thing. Every time I noticed myself judging, I would stop. I would acknowledge it was a choice and I would say "I choose not to judge me for this." And then a bit later I would perceive myself start judging and again say, "I choose not to judge me for this." I would even tell myself, "I can judge myself tomorrow if I would really like to. I can judge me for this later but I'm not choosing that right now." And it worked for me brilliantly. You know what is funny, I never remember to judge myself later.

N: (laughs) You know, this weekend I had one of my friends over and we were doing clearing for each other and stuff like that and she had some body stuff going on and at the end of the conversation, for the first time in my life, I actually perceived the energy of total non- judgment for my body. It was just the energy of wow.

M: That's beautiful.

N: My body is phenomenal the way it is. I am phenomenal the way I am. That was just such a beautiful energy.

M: And what would it take for even more of that?

N: What would it take for me to have that a godzillion times?

Outgrowing The Other Flowers In The Garden

M: There is one more thing that I would like to add for the person who wrote in. It has helped me so much to realize that I don't have to wait for anyone else to be different before I can choose to be different and that not everyone is going to like who I am or the change.

When you are part of a system, like in relationships or with family members, people become dependent. They have all these connection and reference points to you. And often that's how they stabilize their own identity and reality. So when you are someone who is that divergent, who is willing to outgrow everyone in the garden, you sort of threaten the ecosystem that they have created and are relying on not to change.

There are many different Access tools you can use to create more ease with this, but in the end it really comes down to choice. What would it take to be light with it? What would it take to be playful about it?

What if when people judged you, you don't have to judge them back or defend your choices?

What if you could actually continue to care for the people in your life that are struggling with the changes that you are making?

What if it's actually ok? What if that's not wrong either? I hear many people talk about this. So often we want people to behave a certain way for us, to accept, celebrate, and give us permission to be who we are. But why aren't we giving them permission to be them when they are upset with our changes? It goes both ways.

All Energy Can Be Generative, Even Judgment

N: The other thing is that it's all just energy. So what would it take for us to be willing to just take that energy, to receive that energy, to receive the contribution from that energy with no point of view?

M: Exactly. That's exactly where that tool, 'Interesting point of view, they have that point of view,' comes in. Because when we don't have a point of view attached there is no charge, nothing that sticks us, it is just an energy and we can receive it and it can even be generative, which is such a different way of looking at this. I know it blew my mind.

Again, some of this stuff kind of makes sense. You get a sense of "yes, yes this is true". Although it doesn't always make cognitive sense, does it?

Also, I invite you not to believe anything that I tell you. Don't believe anything anyone tells you. Try it out and see what works for you.

N: So talk more about change.

Is This The Change I've Been Asking For?

M: Do we have a caller with a question about change?

Caller: "Change is happening for the efforts I take and make, but I can't see and experience it. Hence, I go to try new things and end upon the hamster-wheel of 'this isn't working for me'. I don't have joy in the experience and I'm always impatient. What stupidity am I using here to do this reversal of energy rather than going with the flow?"

M: That's a great question. So let me see if I have this clearly. You're asking for change but then not noticing, enjoying or acknowledging the change?

N: Yes

M: That's kind of a push-pull energy isn't it?

One of the things that I've noticed with change that has been really helpful for me is that I don't actually always know that it is happening or I just start to feeling kind of weird and uncomfortable.

So for example, you might notice that my voice is a little scratchy. I've lost my voice for the last few days and had some fever as my body is going through a lot of change. Now for a lot of people, they look at these symptoms and they go, "Oh my, I'm sick. Oh my gosh, I'm ill."

Instead I asked, "*Is this the change I've been asking for*?" There was a sense of lightness, remember what is light is true for you.

Then I asked, "Body, are you sick?" It was heavy, remember heavy means it's a lie and not true for you.

So what if it is actually true that it is change even if it looks nothing like it? *The truth will always feel lighter and a lie will feel heavy.*

What if the lightness and the expansiveness of what's true was more valuable to you than having the cognitive solidification you think is going to prove to you that change is happening?

With many things in my life, if it starts to feel weird and kind of funky, that's one of the first questions I ask myself, **"Is this the change I've been asking for?"**

When something falls through that I thought was happening, there are a couple of questions I start with. **"What's right about this that I'm not getting?"** and "Is this the change that I've been asking for?" Within a few weeks at least, there is new information that comes up and I go "Oh my goodness, that totally makes sense why this happened, this happened, this happened." Although I couldn't see it at the time.

Living With Joy In The Present And Creating For Tomorrow

I get so many of you would like more yesterday – more, faster, better. What if you were totally present in your life today? What if you were enjoying the movement of your body, the nature around you, the space around you, the people around you?

What if you could actually be here and be living present enough to make the choices today that will create the future you desire tomorrow?

What if you can enjoy everything as it changes? What if you don't have to reject anything in order to choose different? What if you can still play with a sense of joy in living and create? Sometimes we take change and we put it outside of living.

What would it take to have greater ease and joy in the life that I'm living?

N: Like change becomes almost like not a part of your living but something different?

M: Exactly. What if change is part of your living? What if you included it? For some people I've noticed there can be this intensity with things being different and things changing. There's kind of a force or a push that's in it. There's a judgment that things need to be different, things need to change, and a world of judgment of them if it does not show up right this red hot minute.

What if you can be the invitation of something new, the invitation of possibility and the invitation of change. You notice a different energy with that?

There's a receiving. So, what if you actually allowed yourself to receive the changes that you've been asking for? This kind of goes back to things looking different than you imagined.

Truth, how many times has the Universe delivered what you are asking for but because you have a fixed point of view about how it needs to show up and what it needs to look like you didn't recognize it and refused it? Everything that brings up or lets down will you destroy and un-create it?

Right and wrong, good and bad, POD and POC all nine, shorts, boys and beyonds.

Wonder And Play Increases Receiving

M: One of the times that I noticed receiving the most change with the most ease is when I'm having a good time. It's when I let go of my intense laser-focus on that life and the reality that I must have now! When I go, "I wonder what fun thing I can do today to enjoy this day to the fullest?" I'm having a fabulous time. I get out of the way so that I can actually receive everything I'm asking for, including the information and awareness of what I can choose today to create a different tomorrow.

What if you don't actually have to work really hard to have the changes you are asking for? What if bringing more wonder, play, and happiness into your life creates a kind of vacuum to receiving everything you're asking for?

Striving Versus Embracing

Caller: "What am I allowing to hold me back from reaching my full potential?"

M: *Everything that you've already decided that you aren't, that you actually already are, will you please destroy and un-create all that? Right and wrong, good and bad, POD and POC all nine, shorts, boys and beyonds.*

M: It's a funny idea to me, "full potential". What is "full potential" anyway? Do you notice any judgment in that? And I also wonder whose point of view that is? Is it actually your point of view? "that you are holding back from reaching your full potential."

N: It's almost like someone impelled them with it.

M: In my point of view this idea that there is a place of full potential we must attain is based totally on judgment. We're looking for the right, good, perfect and higher self that we could be, that we are striving to be, that we aren't. Basically what that is saying is, "You are not your full potential, you are lacking," which you aren't. It is all judgment.

What if you acknowledged and knew that you are an infinite being and that you are in a magnanimous Universe? What if acknowledging that will allow you to embrace and be everything you are?

Just notice what feels lighter.

Striving to reach your full potential? Or...

Embracing and allowing yourself to be more of what you already are?

In my point of view one thing that draws people so strongly to motivation and striving for your highest potential is that these systems often give you logical concrete steps and you can start ticking things off your to-do list to self realization. This never worked for me, it only created more judgment because my life was not changing the way it should be, even though I was following checklist and rules.

What I'm inviting you to is something different, unfortunately or fortunately depending on your point of view. You don't get a checklist. You don't get the comfort of the familiar, not always, and you don't get a really defined place that you strive for and arrive at. Although I have found that it's usually better than what I could have asked for. For me it's the greatest adventure I can imagine.

Everywhere you bought that possibility and being an infinite being was a definable place you would reach, rather than receiving and acknowledging and being everything you already are, will you please destroy and un-create it all? Right and wrong, good and bad, POD and POC all nine, shorts, boys and beyonds.

M: I think so many of us have been raised in a reality where we've been impelled with this point of view that we must be in constant judgment of us, that we are lacking in some way and have a sense that at the center of us there's something innately wrong that we must vigilantly strive to change. This is not the invitation for more of that. This is an invitation to drop it, to let it go.

What if there is nothing wrong with you, and there never was?

Everywhere you've been implanted and explanted to believe any of that, to believe that judgment is real, to believe that you are wrong, to believe you have to strive and attain something that you aren't, will you please revoke, recant, rescind, renounce, denounce, reclaim, destroy and un-create it all?

Right and wrong, good and bad, POD and POC all nine, shorts, boys and beyonds.

Simply The Gift Of You

Caller: "I was wondering how do I make the choice? I know the tools of Access, and even though it seems simple, it is quite an 'Aha' moment for me to say, "I choose" at the start of the sentence, like: "I choose not to judge myself." It is so simple and I'm weird. It's more of a comment. (laughs) Awesome!"

M: (laughs) You know what? It is simple. It is weird. It is different and it works. We are not and living is not as complicated as we try to make it.

What if you allowed yourself to be the simplicity that you truly be?

Anywhere that you've ever judged you for being simple will you destroy and uncreate that? Right and wrong, good and bad, POD and POC all nine, shorts, boys and beyonds.

Everywhere you complicate your world, your life, your dreams, your brain, your everything by pulling in other people's confusion, complication, and complexity into your world to eliminate simplicity. Will you please destroy and un-create that?

Right and wrong, good and bad, POD and POC all nine, shorts, boys and beyonds.

M: In this is the gift of you, beneath the lies that we have bought. The lies we have been implanted and explanted to believe like simple is weird and different is wrong. Herein lies the treasure that you are seeking. These lies are covering up your power, your potency, your capacity for choice, for change and play, to be the joyful being that you are.

If you choose to totally clear the lies and never buy them as real again, what would happen in our world? What would happen to this reality? Would it all change?

So because we are looking a different point of view on what change is, let's just check in again one more time.

Choice And Change In The Space Of No Judgment

We came together in a space of no judgment. We are having a conversation. We are talking about possibilities. We are opening up to different points of view and we are allowing ourselves to receive even more of the energy, space and consciousness that is us.

As a result of us being us here together, right now, yes, even if you're reading this chapter, I'd like you to perceive what the world will be like in 50 years as a result of this interaction. Now I'd like for you to perceive what the world will be like in 50 years if we had not come together and had this conversation right now.

N: One is defined and one is totally undefinable – totally unrecognizable.

M: Now look at your own life, in your own living. If you hadn't gotten on this call, picked up this book or had this conversation today, what would your life have been like in 10 years? And POD and POC all that. As a result of this conversation, what is it that you created in your life, living and reality in 10 years?

For me, it almost brings me to tears. Well, it does. To perceive the change we can create together when we are all being us and we are in the question, and all of you choosing to be here. Your choices create change and new awareness for you and your choice is also creating a different reality for all of us. It has changed the fabric of this reality and it changed the future.

Everywhere that you have been judging that you are not changing, that you are not contributing to the world in the most dynamic way you would like to be, I invite you to perceive what we created here together. And further I invite you to begin acknowledging what you have created and what you've changed in the past that you had no idea you were changing and contributing. Anything that doesn't allow that will you destroy and uncreate it? Right and wrong, good and bad, POD and POC all nine, shorts, boys and beyond.

You Can't Help Changing The Fabric Of Reality Because You Are The Fabric

What if choice and change is different than you thought it was? What if it is more dynamic that you thought? And what if you are already the gift and the change that this world has been asking for?

I am so grateful for each one of you, for your contribution, for everything that you are and that you are choosing right now. For everything you have ever chosen and everything you will choose.

You can't help changing the fabric of reality because you are the fabric, and as you change, so it changes.

EMBRACE ALL OF YOU

Get the phenomenal bonus from Rachel Silber - 10 Tools To Embracing All Of You (Audio + Poster).
Visit www.whereismydoorwaytopossibilities.com

CHAPTER FOUR

THE BEGINNING OF INFINITE POSSIBILITIES

By Gary Douglas

Founder, Access Consciousness®

Facilitator, Leader & Innovator

Author & Speaker on Consciousness

Global Bars Day

Nilofer: "Thank you so much. Thank you so much for being on the call with us. How did we get to be so lucky to have you with us?"

Gary: "That's because you are smart!"

Nilofer: "Gary, thank you so much for being you and for the tools of Access. In the three years that I've been using these tools, my whole life has undergone a total transformation and the Global Bars Day yesterday (6th Jan 2015) was absolutely phenomenal."

Gary: "It was amazing! People from around the world were running Bars; the laughter that was coming out of them and the happiness was just amazing. It was great."

Nilofer: "Yes, it was so amazing. Wow ! I was just seeing all the places like Japan, Hong Kong and of course here in the Middle East. To see the Bars spreading all over the world, wow, that's so amazing, Gary."

Gary: "Yes, that's so great. It was more than double (the number of people) that we had last year and more than double the number of different places, which was really cool."

Nilofer: "Wow ! Wow! This is just the beginning of the year. So I wonder what else is possible for the rest of the year now?"

Gary: "Exactly! That's the reason we are talking about possibilities, isn't it?"

The Beginning Of Infinite Possibilities

Nilofer: "Yes. So Gary, The Beginning of Infinite Possibilities, what do you know about that that none of us know?"

Gary: "Well, you know, the thing that's interesting to me is, to have possibilities; you have to start from a question and not a conclusion and you have to make choices, which open the door to greater possibilities. So you want the questions first, then you want the choices that come from having the question and then you want the infinite possibilities from there. So you have to look at it from 'O.K, so what question do I need to BE, what question do I need to ask?' What I see most people doing is, I see them asking the question with the idea that 'what I want is this, so if I ask this question then that should give me this', which is a conclusion that they are trying to use to create a question so they can choose; which makes absolutely no sense.

It makes no sense because it's really not a question, it's really a conclusion that they are using as if that's the sum total of what they need to do and when you come from conclusion to create possibility, no possibility can actually exist. All you can do is, create less."

Nilofer: "What I've seen is, the energy is so different from the end of the year to the beginning of the year and everything seems to be actualizing so fast, so if you go to conclusion, that's what you are actualizing now."

Gary: "That's correct. If you start from conclusion, all you can do is create a conclusion to function from and when you create a conclusion, you are coming from judgment or decision or computation or conclusion, any of those are all judgmental realities. If you live from a judgment, the reality of judgment, all you can do is create something that creates more judgment. You don't have real choice."

What Is Real CHOICE?

Gary: "Real choice is the awareness that everything is available to us if we are willing to actually receive it.

So, one of the things we talked about recently was the time when we were in Costa Rica. We were right next to a volcano, an active volcano. There was smoke coming out of the rim of the volcano and that kind of stuff. On the sides of the volcano, there were horses and cows grazing. Everybody asked, 'Aren't you afraid that the volcano is going to go off?' I said, 'No. As long as the cows and the horses are still grazing there, it's not going to go off.' The one thing about animals is that they live in the present, never the past. They don't trust that yesterday's reality will be today's reality. They have a different reality about how everything is. It's all about being aware of what choices you have.

So, if the volcano were to be going off, the horses and the cows would have started to go away, they would be running away. That's because they are always aware of what's happening. They sense everything through the Earth and everything else and they don't cut off any of their awareness. They highlight their awareness in order to create. So they create from now and they create future. So they are always looking to 'I've got to eat well now so I don't have to starve in the future.' Or 'I have to eat well now so I have plenty in my gut for the future.' They have these different points of view in life than we do. We could learn a lot from the animals, I think, because if we would really look at these things and go, **'What is it that I want to create here?'** and look at it from that point of view. We've got to learn to function from these questions-

'What is this? What do I do with it? Can I change it? If so, how do I change it?'

If you function from those elements of life, everything becomes easier, and becomes greater, but we tend to avoid having that kind of greatness under some weird guise that that's smarter or greater or better, which is not really true. We need to be more perceptive, more aware of things at all times – like the horse makes the choice to eat on the side of a volcano, he's willing to know if it is going to go off so he goes away from it. We would eat on the side of a volcano and die there.

That's what happened when – what's that famous Italian volcano that went off three hundred years ago? Pompei! They heard the volcano erupting. The horses were trying to get away but they kept on eating and having a good time. They didn't try to get away, until it was too late and most people function from that. They just go 'Oh well, it'll be fine. It was fine yesterday so it'll be fine in the future.' Whereas horses do not have that – animals do not have that point of view. What was fine yesterday may turn out badly tomorrow so they want to be aware of it. They don't want to function from a fixed point of view ever. So it's a possibility for them."

Nilofer: "So we also have these awarenesses, but it's just that we turn them off don't we?

Gary: "Yes."

Nilofer: "It's like our body is always giving us that awareness, when you feel that weirdness in your body, when you wake up, or something like that and instead of going to question, we just go into conclusion. 'Oh, I have this pain, or this thing, or how do I fix this?' Instead of asking what it is?"

Gary: "Exactly. You've got to be willing to see that there's a greater possibility in life. What most of us try to do instead is get it right. You spend the majority of life trying to do the right thing, get the right thing, function the right way, be the right way, whatever that is. The more you try to function from the right or the wrong point of view, the less of you and the less possibilities you actually have available. It's kind of sad."

Nilofer: "We are also trying to make the right choices and we do not choose."

Gary: "Yes."

What Is Truly Possible

Nilofer: "What is giving up your ideals and seeing what is truly possible?"

Gary: "The ideal is what we think everything should turn out like. If you think the ideal scene is to meet the love of your life, get married and live happily ever after, is that realistic? Is that an awareness or is that a conclusion?"

Nilofer: "A total conclusion."

Gary: "Yes. It's a total conclusion. So, a question should be 'Is this somebody I'm really going to want to stay with for a long time?' I personally think that they should make it very hard to get married and easy to get divorced, because then people would have to really work to get married to somebody they want to be with and then if they get divorced, 'O.K. goodbye, see you later,' and it would be over with but they don't do it that way. They make it hard to get divorced and easy to get married. Kind of crazy I think."

Nilofer: "Gary, I wonder what will happen if you became the Prime Minister of a country. I wonder what would change."

Gary:" Well, the number one thing that would change is I would make all laws obsolete after a year. So in order to keep the world – you know, the country, functioning, we would have to spend all our time doing laws, reiterating laws to make sure that we had somebody to take care of the criminals, somebody to take care of everything and we wouldn't have time to do silly stuff. We'd actually have to be aware of what we were choosing at every moment. Does that sound like fun?"

Nilofer: "It sounds like total fun. Which country are you running for president, Gary?

Gary:" I don't think I will, thank you very much. I have actually no interest."

Motivation

Caller: "I have a question. Lately, I've been feeling like I have no motivation at all and that I'm not committed to my life and not willing to be committed and I have no clue what to create. There's a lot of no motivation and depression, so what can I do about it?"

Gary: "Wow, welcome to humanoid reality. O.K. Number 1, there's nothing wrong with you. Number 2, motivation is as though there's an outside choice, that's necessary. In reality, what you've got to do is, you've got to do 10 second increments of choice. You go, 'I've got 10 seconds to live the rest of my life. What do I choose?' If you started living from what you were going to choose instead of what you thought you had to do, would your life be different?"

"Yes. So the difficulty is most of us think we've got to have motivation. No, you just have to have choice."

Caller: "So how do I get clear on making a choice?"

Gary: "Well, you ask a question. **'What would I like to do? What would be fun for me to do? In this 10 seconds, what would be fun for me to do?'** You've got to learn to live more as you did as a child. You know with kids, they are only good for 10 seconds sometimes for pretty much anything. My grandson picked up a shaver that Dain had left around. He picked it up and goes, 'what's this?' I said, 'Well, that's Dain's shaver. You need to give that to Dain.' So he said, 'O K. So why did you bring it here? ' Dain's not here at the moment, so I'll take care of it' I replied. He said, 'I'll take it to Dain but Dain's not home.' So he threw it on the floor. You know, if you would allow yourself to have that kind of quixotic point of view, where you are just willing to do whatever works at the moment and you would do that for 3 days, you'd get clear about what you really want to create in life.

When you go to create something, you ask 'If I choose this, what would my life be like in 5 years? If I don't choose this, what will my life be like in 5 years?'. You've never been asked to choose, pretty much your whole life you've been told you have to make the right decision, the right choice. So all you've learnt is to judge yourself non-stop, which doesn't actually give you any clarity or any capacity to create, does it? No. So you've got to look at **'What do I really want to create here and how can I create it? How can I have everything I really want? What do I really want?'** I need to know what it is that I really want, but in order to know what I really want, I have to choose and that's what we are talking about in this whole thing here. 'What do I have to choose?' Well, it's not what you have to choose, it's what would I like to choose?"

Stagnant Energy

Caller: "Can you say something about stagnant energy? Like there is stagnancy in creation."

Gary: "O K, let me ask you something. Can energy ever be stagnant? Really?"

Caller: "No."

Gary: "No, it's not like water, where it can be contained. Energy can never be contained. So it is not possible for energy to be stagnant, but it is possible for you to stop *you* from creating. It takes a hell of a lot of energy and if you could put that energy against stopping you from creating, what would happen if you used that energy to create with?"

Caller: "Do you have anything else on stopping me?"

Gary: "Yes. *You.* So you might run '

What do I hate about being successful? Everything that comes up, times a godzillion, right and wrong, good and bad, POD and POC all nine, shorts, boys and beyonds.'

Keep running that until you get over the idea that you have a hate of being successful and you might actually have a choice to be successful. Right now, you are trying to hate success and stay away from success instead of choosing."

Caller: "True."

Gary: "You know, if you chose success you'd be asking, *"What can I do to be successful at this no matter what?"*

The Magnanimous Universe

Gary: "The Universe has no judgment. It is magnanimous. You know, it's like the birds that get up in the morning and sing for us. They don't go 'I'm having a bad day, so I won't sing for you.' Or 'I actually can't believe you are such a mean person.' They don't do that. They get up; they sing their hearts out every day. The fruit trees don't go, 'You didn't water me correctly, so I'm not going to give you any fruit.'

They push through; they collect whatever they can from every place and deliver whatever fruit they can. When you get that the world – the Universe is a magnanimous place, that has no charge in it and if you really will start to function from no judgment, you too can be magnanimous. Most of us have learnt this sort of weird exchange thing. We have this thing where everything is an exchange and people function from 'If I do this for this person, then they are going to do this for me.' 'I never do that. I do whatever I'm going to do, with no idea of whether I'm going to get anything in return or not; because the gifting is the return for me and in the Universe, that's how the Universe works. It gifts to you with no expectation in return and in so doing, it receives the gift of being itself, and that's the one thing that most of us are not willing to have."

Nilofer: "Wow. So how do you *be* that Gary?"

Gary: "By choice. By always doing what works for you regardless of what anybody else thinks. You know people have said to me, 'you can't just give that person that kind of money!' I go, 'why not? They deserve it.' 'O.K. Why not?' 'Well, because it's wrong.' 'Why?' 'That's because it's not what you should do.' 'Why?' 'That's not normal here. People don't pay that kind of money.' 'O.K. but I want to pay that kind of money.' 'Well, you can't do that because you are going to spoil them and they are not going to be able to do it for anybody else.' So that's their choice."

Nilofer: "When kids are small, they have that. I mean, I've seen my sons and they have that generosity of spirit with things and it's just amazing to watch them. Sometimes it brings up this thing, 'Oh my god, they are doing too much. They are giving too much!' It is that magnanimity that you are talking about, isn't it?"

Gary: "Yes. Little kids may not want to share their toys, but they will share who they are with another kid instantaneously. I mean, my grandson Zander, goes to Chuck E Cheese, a place I would never go to in a million years. You know, I went there when my kids were young and I would never want to go again, and anyways, he goes to Chuck E Cheese and says, 'Oh, I met a friend there.' I go, 'Oh you did?' He goes, 'yes'. 'O.K. So what's your friend's name?' He tells me their name and I said, 'How did you meet this person?' 'I saw them and I knew they were my friends. 'I mean, you walk in some place and you look around for who you can discard, not who you can connect to.

Kids have this generosity of spirit. They want to know who else they can have in their lives. They have a willingness to give of themselves and to receive another without any judgment and they learn later on not to do that. 'You have to be more discriminating. You are choosing the wrong kind of friends.' Well, the thing is they don't have a point of view about wrong or right kind of friends. They have a point of view about who they can connect to in some way that works for them. We learn as we get older not to be that. 'Why do we teach our kids that?'

'That's protecting them.' So have we protected ourselves out of having?

Everything we've done to protect ourselves out of having, can we destroy and uncreate all that? Right and wrong, good and bad, POD and POC all nine, shorts, boys and beyonds.

So you've got to get what it is you want to create, what it is you want your life to look like, for your life to be like. What is it that's important to you?"

Nilofer: "That's also putting you in the computation of your life."

Gary: "Yes. Exactly. That's saying, you know, *'how about being magnanimous with you?' What a strange concept to be magnanimous with self.*"

Colors of Infinite Possibilities

Nilofer: "Gary, can you talk about the Colors of Infinite Possibilities?"

Gary: "Well, one of the things we found is that people go to judgment. The one thing you can't judge is colors. Well, you can, but it's a lot harder. '

What is the infinite possibility of the infinite colors of infinite possibilities that I'm not choosing? What could I choose?' Destroy and uncreate all that. Right and wrong, good and bad, POD and POC all nine, shorts, boys and beyond.

The colors of possibility have been dulled down to a few. 'I only like colors like this. I only can choose these things.' How many places have you lived your life that it's, 'I can only have this choice. I can't have anything or everything. I can only have these choices.' It's like – what colors do you wear? You know, one of the things I love about going to India is people wear some many different colors, it's amazing! In the United States people don't do that. They wear black all the frigging time."

Nilofer: "Yes. That's what I noticed, in the United States people wear these neutral colors and the only place they will have color is on their nails or on their lips. It's so funny to me."

Gary: "Yes. So their feet and their lips will be colorful but that's about it. Sometimes they'll have a scarf that's colorful but they even like subdued colors on their scarves and their clothes. Everything's beige and everything's grey and everything's like black, and that's the only colors they use because they've created out of having the infinite colors of all possibility, they choose colors that are neutral enough to make them fit into other people's reality.

That's the reason we are looking for the infinite colors of infinite possibility because that alone creates a place where you begin to see that there's so much more available that we don't ever choose. That we were taught as kids that you only have this choice or this choice. 'You can have chocolate, strawberry or vanilla.' 'Yes, but what about Rocky Road and what about Mint Chocolate Chip?' It's like, 'no, you can't have those.' 'Why? Why can't I have those?' 'That's not available.' 'Why isn't it available?'

We spend our lives choosing based on availability, based on other people's points of view. What if everything were available to us at all times and all we had to do was choose it? Well, that's infinite possibilities, and that's the beginning of learning how to choose from possibilities.

'What's really possible here that I've never considered?' is a great question to ask yourself. Do it on a daily basis. Do it when you wake up in the morning. 'What's really possible here that I've never chosen?' 'What's really possible here that I've never chosen?' 'What's really possible here that I've never chosen? 'If you start to look at what's actually possible you haven't chosen, you begin to realize, 'wait a minute, I have not given myself the infinite choice of infinite possibility. I have given myself a very limited menu of possibility.' Limited menu of possibility isn't that much fun, folks!"

Nilofer: " It's boring."

Gary: "It's boring! You know, it'll be like going to eat at McDonalds every frigging day."

Nilofer: "Oh, horrible!"

Gary: "You might be able to eat at McDonalds once every twenty seven years, but every day? No, not fun but I see people all the time who are trying to live their lives from living from a choice that's based on a particular kind of choice based on 'well, these are what my choices are.'

What if there was an infinite array of choice available? **What could you choose that you are currently not choosing?** You've got to be willing to look at that and choose from that and see the possibilities of that. Instead of trying to create from the limited reality and from the point of view that limited reality is the only thing that makes any sense. What if it was never about anything making sense? **What if it was about everything becoming a possibility?"**

Nilofer: "Wow. It's like going to a buffet, which has like 800 dishes on it. Then you can choose 'No, no, no, no, no, that!' "

Gary: "Yes, and what if you recognize – it's like, I personally hate Smorgasbord. I prefer going to restaurants that have a small elite menu where all the food is great, instead of a large amount to eat in order to make sure that you can stuff your gullet and look like a stupid turkey."

Frantic Energy, Trauma And Drama, Boredom

Caller: "I seem to be just like jumping from what calls my attention, like it's always like an emergency, just like frantic energy, like whatever calls my attention, I just seem to go from place to place. I'm kind of tired and…"

Gary: "Is that what you've defined as motivation? Or is that what you've defined as how you live a life?"

Caller: "I almost, feel like – if I could just plan ahead, – but when I plan ahead something always – it's another emergency that calls for my attention."

Gary: "O.K, so the horses on the side of the volcano…do they plan ahead?"

Caller: "No, they don't."

Gary: "No, they just live in each and every moment and then as something changes, they change and that's actually innately correct behavior for all of us. Do you allow yourself to change in the moment of an emergency? Or have you considered the possibility that maybe you could have an emergency that's beyond what anybody else can do?

'What else is possible that I've never considered?' "Emergencies happen in my life but I usually handle them in like 5-10 minutes."

Caller: "How do I prevent myself from getting frantic?"

Gary: "Well, you could acknowledge the fact that you love trauma and drama."

Caller: "Oh Gary ! I hate that."

Gary: "No, you don't because you keep choosing it."

Caller: "I know!"

Gary: "You keep choosing it. You must love it."

Caller: "I know."

Gary: "What do I love about the trauma and drama of my life?"

Caller: "Oh and then when I want to have downtime, I'm just – I'm so tired, my husband says,' why aren't you doing the housework?' and he's like…"

Gary: "Well, you can't deal with it till it's an emergency."

Caller: "Oh!! O.K."

Gary: "Otherwise you won't have any drama. I mean, how do you do without drama?! I was talking to my daughter the other day about my grandson being rather dramatic. He was talking about how 'that cookie is very dramatic.' You know, it's like now everything is dramatic because he heard the word 'dramatic.' It's like kids create from whatever they hear in your life. You know, what are you creating from the not – that you don't really have to? What if you had something greater that you haven't considered? You know, you might be careful because you might find out that you can actually handle everything with such ease that the only reason you are not handling it is to make sure that you have trauma and drama in your life."

Caller: "O.K"

Gary: "If you laughed, it must be true, sorry!"

Caller: "It must be true, I know! Crap. O.K. So then I'm just kind of like stuck. I don't know how to get out of this. I mean, how do I do it calm, cool and collected rather than creating drama?"

Gary: Ask "What do I love about trauma and drama?"

Also "What do I love about being a drama queen?" Keep doing it until you find 'oh my god, I'm such a drama queen. Holy shit!"

Caller: "If I go to the other extreme, I'm totally bored with my life. When I have ease, I'm like totally bored. So…"

Gary: "I know! That's the reason you keep creating the emergencies so you can have the trauma and drama because you think you are bored if you are not in trauma and drama.

As humanoids you need to actually function slightly different. One of the things you have to do is you have to function from the idea of 'O.K. So what 10 things could I do right now that would make my life fun?' That's because when you have more to do, you have more fun. If you don't have enough to do - I keep telling people, you are not really OCD, you are OCC. You are an obsessive compulsive creator and then if you don't spend all that time creating, you go to OCCC, which is obsessive compulsive creator of crap.

So apparently, you are doing the crap version and you might want to ask *"What can I create today that I've never even considered?"* If you have enough going on in your life, if you have 5-10 things going on in your life at all times, you wouldn't have time for trauma and drama. You'd have too much to do and too much that would be fun for you. There's another thing –if you decide to redecorate your house, so that you have painting and stuff to do, have you ever noticed that no trauma and drama occurs while you're doing that?"

Caller: "Yes. Why is that?"

Gary: "That's because you've got enough to do on your plate that you can't bother with the trauma and drama.

'I have to get this done.' So you go for it and you do it and you know, it's just that you get that that's the way to function for you and then it's not a wrongness or rightness or anything else, it's just a way that you function, then you won't get into the rightness or wrongness and you won't think that there's something bad happening because the reality is, nothing bad is happening. It's just that you are making it bad so you can have some fun."

'So what can I do that would be fun for me today?' instead of 'what can I do to create the drama and the trauma that will make my life exciting to the brain?'"

Caller: "Alright. So I've been asking the wrong questions."

Gary: "Yes, you've been asking the wrong question. Sorry."

Relationship

Caller: "I'm destroying and uncreating my relationship every day but it still seems like I'll create a relationship and then it'll get crappy."

Gary: "Are you asking - *What contribution is this person to my life?*"

Caller: "Maybe. Well, I am in appreciation. They are definitely a contribution but I think they are second guessing me as a contribution to them, or maybe that's a projection, but, I guess it's like…"

Gary: "I think that is a projection.

Well, let me ask you a question, Truth, are you trying to get into a relationship or get out of it before you get into it? What made you smile?"

Caller: "Well, I'm trying to get out of it before I get hurt, I don't know."

Gary: "You're trying to get out of it before you get into it. Your justification is 'I don't want to be hurt.' Actually it's a definition. Big deal!

Just know that you have different choices and as long as you have different choices, different possibilities can show up.

'What can I do or choose that will create something greater in my life? Well, yes. What would it be like if I choose this? What would this not be like?' You know, 'what will my life be like in five years if I choose this? What will my life be like in 5 years if I don't choose this?' So you become very clear in a short period of time. 'Oh, if I choose this it's going to turn out great.' Instead it may not turn out good at all though. We don't know until we get there."

Caller: "Yes. It just feels like it's kind of in this in-between phase. Am I in? Am I out? Am I out? Am I in? Are we…? It kind of feels like a limbo thing. I don't know. Uncomfortable…"

Gary: "The limbo, is it dancing? You might want to learn how to do that."

Caller: "Oh thanks. I have your book, I'll read it again. Divorceless Relationships."

Gary: "Oh good. Keep reading it and eventually, it'll sink in and then you'll start to create more and have more. Worry not, it will work."

Creation from Dynamism

Caller: "I've been more aware lately of an intense energy present when I choose from the question of 'what will be created in 5 years?' Amazing fun things are showing up. I perceive the energy of the Universe saying, 'keep going. I have your back.' The energy is so intense, I start to giggle, vibrate and scream with joy. What else can I create with this energy that I have not been willing to be aware of?"

Gary: "Well, I'm sorry that your life is that way. It's so much more fun to have trauma and drama. Oh yes. Well, what you've got to ask is 'what else is possible that I've never considered?' When you ask the question 'what else is possible that I've never considered?' it opens the door to you beginning to see the things you haven't chosen or that you haven't been aware of. It's like you probably have way more available – you know, it's like when you gain that awareness and start having fun, you start to gain more things, more rapidly than any other time and that is the point at which everything starts to create in a much more dynamic way. Creation through dynamism is much more fun than creation from patheto-ism."

Communication

Caller: "Gary, I love the way you communicate. It works. How can I communicate in a way that is effective and creates greater possibilities for those I speak to?"

Gary: "Always speak what people can hear, never what you want them to know and you ask a question 'what can this person hear?' not what do I want them to hear, or what do I want them to know.

I don't have the point of view that I want somebody to know anything. I have the point of view there's a possibility they can give me something if I can speak what they can hear. What that requires of you is, 'what can I speak so that they can hear?', then what happens is you begin to see where people's limitations get created based on their point of view or based on their choices or based on something else? Based on their choices. So then you begin to look at 'what choice do I have that they don't have? So you then can speak to a choice that they will not allow themselves to have in a way in which they can hear it so they don't make themselves wrong or go into judgment of themselves.

You know, most of the communication that goes on this planet is designed to put the person you are communicating with in judgment of themselves. Yes, just watch the way people talk to you and how often you come away from it feeling like you somehow need to judge yourself, like there's something terribly wrong with you. What if that's not necessary?"

Nilofer: "When you are actually functioning from that question of 'what can they hear?' you actually give them the energy of possibility, isn't it?"

Gary: "Well, it's like the thing is, you don't put out the energy of what possibility can occur. So it's like if you talk to somebody in such a way that they go into judgment of themselves, instead of talking about what they can hear, then they will usually go into judgment. The moment they go into judgment, they stop having a different possibility. They cut off all possibility in favor of that."

Quantum Entanglements

Nilofer:" How do the quantum entanglements come into play with the infinite possibilities ?"

Gary: "Well, the thing is that infinite possibilities are based on the quantum entanglements. If everything around you really wants to contribute to you, and it does, because the magnanimous Universe is wanting to give you everything you ask for; but the problem is most of you are not willing to ask for anything. What you tend to do is ask for something as small as possible rather than great enough to be everything you would like it to be. The quantum entanglements support whatever you ask for.

That's where you need to start with a question and then go to choice. If you start with a question, the Universe will give you multiple choices for multiple possibilities. The moment you make a choice, multiple possibilities start to show up. When those moments of multiple possibilities show up that is the place where you ask yourself ' what would I like to choose now?', which means you've gone back to question. but that place where you go back to question is the place in which you also open the door to greater possibilities and greater choices. Do you want to always be opening the door to greater choice and greater possibility? As long as you are opening that, you are expanding your life and you are expanding everybody's life around you."

Functioning Different In This Reality

Nilofer:" What allows you to function so differently in this reality?"

Gary: "That's because I spent a year going 'interesting point of view. I have this point of view' for every point of view I had, most of which turned out not to be mine and I began to realize that 'wow, I'm way more aware than I want to know I'm aware' because if I actually had to admit how aware I was, then I wouldn't have any of the problems I'm currently trying to create.

You know, it's like if you have awareness, nothing is a problem. Everything is 'O.K. What other choice do I have here?' It becomes a question of what other choice is available. If you go 'I have no choice' (and you've all heard people say that 'I had no choice. I had to do this'). Well, there's no such thing as 'I have no choice.' You still have infinite choice, no matter what choice is available.

How do you want to deal with it? Do you want infinite choice? Or do you want to pretend you don't have choice? Why would it be necessary to think you have no choice? If you think you have no choice then you can justify anything that is less than what is possible as true and real, when it's actually not.

Then, when you ask these questions some door opens where people are able to hear better than ever before and what they are able to hear, and what I'm able to say isn't much different and that's the gift of this last year and all the things we've done. We did a tele-call about possibility, **Living in Infinite Possibility.**

If you live from that point of view of, 'what is actually possible that I've never considered?' you start functioning from that, you start to look at everything that might occur or could occur, you don't have to live from what you think should not occur or should be or has to be, or ought to be. You get a choice. Once you get a choice, everything is much better."

Home of Infinite Possibilities Class - http://bit.ly/2dgocv3

Gary: "What is home to you? Home is where your heart is. Home is where you feel most comfortable. Home is where everybody judges you. What is home for you? So in Home of Infinite Possibilities, one of the things I want people to get to is a place where they recognize that home is wherever they are. Wherever you can be and if you can be wherever you are, then possibilities open up. You've got to be willing to be in a different way. It's the imperative of recognizing the value of being that most people do not have.

Right now this reality is dedicated to doing rather than being, isn't it? You always know what you are going to do. You sometimes know what you want to do but mostly you try not to do what you can do in the hopes that a different possibility is possible. What would occur if you didn't have that point of view? What would occur if you created some-thing greater by every choice you make?

What's most important from my perspective is, you have to get that choice is one of the greatest gifts that we've got as beings. You know, for years, metaphysical people said, oh, you know it's like a free will Uni-verse'. If it's a free-will Universe then why do you keep saying you have no choice? How can it be a free-will Universe and you have no choice at the same time? What has to be different? What is different? What needs to be different?

Well, that's a place where choice comes in. You have to get that choice is the free-will that you were given but we try to function from no choice or lack of choice or limited choice as though that's real choice and it's not. So what can be created that we've not considered? What is possible you haven't considered? What we haven't considered is that choice is the source of all creation.

We keep looking for something else to create for us, or something outside of us to create. You know, whether it is motivation - 'I need to be motivated', well that's something outside of us pushing us to do something. When the reality is, the only thing that'll ever push you to create anything is *you*. You have to be the source for pushing your creation into existence, not somebody else."

Nilofer: "That's not really a push also, isn't it? If you are being the source of your own creation, you don't have to push anything."

Gary: "You don't push anything because push is not about how you create; choice is about how you create."

Nilofer: " Gary, especially in the last few months, I've been aware of this energy of just joy and peace and happiness. So is that when you are being you, when you are just being?"

Gary: "Yes, when you are being, that's what you have because literally one thing that is actually true is, you as a being have infinite choice and with infinite choice comes infinite possibility and with infinite possibility comes the gift of being. When you are willing to be everything you are, everything becomes possible. Nothing is a limitation but what you create it from.

How's that for fun?

So, giving up your ideals and seeing what is truly possible. Your choice changes reality and the infinite colors of infinite possibility."

Gary's Package: http://connect.tpniengage.com/go/128291

Call number 1 from the 'Need and Tug' series

Gary: "Oh good, that's a great call. It would give you some clarity about how you start to create in life."

Nilofer: "So I remember I got you to sign my book 'The Place' and you wrote in it 'Need and tug' and then a month later, there was this tele-call series that came up 'Need and Tug', so it's like,' Yay! Wow!' So can you talk about what is 'need and tug'? What is the difference between need and neediness?"

Gary: "The problem is that people have the idea that if they need something, it's because they can't have it and they value what they need; they don't value what they have. So for me, I look at something and I go "ok, this is what I'd like to have" but if you go "I'm going to have that" that's where you create the need for a possibility and the tug is the energy, which you use to pull it into existence. So if you function from real need and tug, it's about pulling into existence that which you desire, that which you would like to create, that which you would like to have and it explains that you choose a sense and emotion for you to begin to get there."

Call number 1 from the 'Lies of Money'

Gary: "That's a good one because it starts to bring in place all the places where you say money is created from what it isn't. For years people said "oh money is just energy". Is it really energy or is it something else? It's not energy. It the awareness that you have greater – you have more choices when you have money than when you don't have money and the recognition of why you would want to have money. Not that you have to have money but if you know that you are going to have more choice when you have money than you do when you don't have money, which one would you choose? No money or money?"

Nilofer: "Definitely money."

Gary: "Yes, it's like, 'I really want more choices and more possibility', but that's my point of view. Choices and possibility make sense to me, they don't to others. I always think that you would not have choice for what reason? Why would you not always look to what's possible rather than what you think it ought to be or has to be? Create a different reality; create a different possibility. What's most important to you?"

Nilofer: "You just fried us again, Gary."

Gary: "I know. It's one of my best talents. What can I tell you?"

Call number 1 from the 'Purpose of life' series

Gary: "The whole idea for the 'Purpose of life' was to get you out of the idea that you had to have a fixed point of view that there is a better purpose, you know. It's like whatever your purpose is and whatever you really want to create in your life is really what you should create. I know when I was doing metaphysical stuff, I would say, 'Well, my purpose is to have this' and they would go 'well, that's not a big enough purpose'. 'What do you mean it's not a big enough purpose?' I would reply. 'Well, it's not big enough. Mine is big and mine is, you know, mine is to bring more spirituality in this world.' I go, 'but...but spirituality already exists in the world. Wouldn't it be to wake people up to what they could choose spiritually?' 'No, you are wrong.' I got judged for everything. Every time I came to any kind of awareness of what I would like to create, they told me I was wrong. So I gave up my purposes in life instead of choosing my purposes. So part of that call was designed to get to the point where you bring back your capacity to create based on what you'd really like to choose and how it's not wrong and the purpose of life might be to have fun.If the purpose of life is to have fun... are you having any?"

<u>**Get Gary's Package Here**</u> - http://connect.tpniengage.com/go/128291

Different Possibility, Different Reality

Nilofer: "Gary, so what else do you want to tell us that we are not willing to know?"

Gary: "Well, most of you are firmly impressed with how pathetic you are. So what does it take to make yourself that pathetic? Does it take a lot of energy, a lot of time? Does it take none? Does it take some? What does it take? What if, instead of using that energy that you use to make you pathetic, you made you dynamic, great and amazing? Would that be different? Would that be possible? Would that be more viable to you than what you've been choosing?

The thing is that if you personally can look at your life and say "well, I fucked that up" that means you have a lot of power because it takes a lot to mess up any part of your life. So what would it be like if looking at how you messed it up like "ok, I've got enough power to mess that up. *What if I use that power in a different direction and created something? What could I create if I did that?" - different possibility, different reality.* So there you go, and then what part of possibility can you create and can you choose then? What aren't you choosing? Choose to create a life based on possibility. You would choose a life based on question and choice and in so doing, you'll create possibilities other people can't have, will not have and will never choose.

Will that set you apart? In a sense, yes, but aren't you kind of apart already? Can you never acknowledge how different you are and how you are not like others? I don't think any of you have ever really been like others but you try to make yourself like others.

How much energy does it take to disavow you and disempower you in order to be like other people? You know, you probably had a family who wants you to be – they want you to be the way they want you to be. How many of you have spent a lot of time to create that? If you never created that again, what else would be possible? Everything that is, times a godzillion, will you destroy and uncreate all that? Right and wrong, good and bad, POD and POC, all nine, shorts, boys and beyonds."

CHAPTER FIVE

MAGIC OF THE UNIVERSE

By Aditi Iyer

Certified Facilitator - Access Consciousness

Certified Facilitator - Talk to the Entities

'High Functioning Autistic Alien'

Allround Joyful Person

N: What do you know about the magic of the Universe that nobody else knows?

A: The magic of the Universe – it's you. You know, the strangest thing, when you asked me to be on the summit, I felt kind of "Me? Really? Why?" and I remember writing to you that I don't have a clue what to do. And you were "whatever you want!" I just wrote "Magic of the Universe." And I had no clue where this was going. I had no sense of it. And I just had these four words "Magic of the Universe". And ever since you invited me and I said yes, it's just been about having to show up as me. I'm discovering all of these things about me and acknowledging them. And today, I acknowledge it. I am magic. Magic isn't some big fireworks in the sky. It's the small moments that you acknowledge you and when you acknowledge the joy that you be. That is truly the magic.

N: You said that "magic is when you be you" and it's when you stepped into being you.

A: Yes

N: So how did that show up for you?

A: That showed up with me having to do a lot of work, like really really destroying and un-creating a lot of points of view that I had of myself and a lot of judgments that I bought over the years. And it's very easy to buy into that. I mean I see myself as a satellite dish of the Universe, picking up everybody's judgment. And when you get to the point where you realise that none of those judgments are about you and they are not of you, it's just a whole lot simpler. And I know that I perceive more thoughts than I can count and it's all at the same time. And it's really looking at it – when you have that sense of "oh my god, I can perceive every single person's thoughts and everybody connected to that person. And everybody beyond that person and everybody they have been in all the lifetimes".

You have to go to "Ok, what part of this is relevant to me?" And what that does is - it clears up the space for you to recognise what it is to be you and who you be. And for me, I just say it, when I ask that question and I have too many thoughts and I'm thinking way too much and I'm going like "Really? This? That?" and I'm going "Oh my god, there's another thought there. Oh my god, there's another thought there. Who does this belong to? Who does it belong to? Who does it belong to?"

So "Who does it belong to?" doesn't work for me sometimes. And in those moments I ask "ok, what part of this is relevant to me?" and then *whoosh!* And everything just fades away. And all I'm left with is me.

And in that moment when I ask myself "Ok, so what would be fun for me to create today?" I notice that I love to laugh and I love laughing everyday. Whenever I ask the question, "What would be fun for me to create today?" I just laugh.

What Question Can You Be

What is the question that you could ask that would give you that space? Everything that doesn't allow you to perceive, know, be and receive that, will you destroy and un-create it all? Right and wrong, good and bad, POD and POC, all nine, shorts, boys and beyond.

N: I love that thing that you spoke about – "everyone else's thoughts and everyone else connected to them and connected to them and connected to them" and I guess, most of us, we go to this place of "who does this belong to? So this is all the people I know!" but it's actually what you spoke about and it's so many layers of that, which really creates that *ooh* in our Universe.

A: Yeah and that *ooh* is never yours. That's the best part of it. Like even that is not yours. Oh my god, do I have anything? No!

N: What's really funny is, it was New Year's Ev. I was at a get-together and I was high. I was high without having a single drop of alcohol. And somebody is like telling me "you are high" and I didn't get it at that moment. But later when I was in bed and I was lying down, I asked "oh, how many people are around me who are high?" And I'm just acting out who they all are being. That tool "who does this belong to?" and "what part of this is relevant for me?" I think with "who does this belong to?", each one of us has our own spin-off of that which really works for us.

A: So what question would give you that space that you've not been willing to receive?

Because the question is around you. You just have to ask for it. The Universe is right there in your face sometimes, knocking on your head or prodding you in the back, asking, just saying "Ok, just see, I'm here. I'm here to give you everything." You just have to be willing to receive.

Joy And Magic

A: So, take a deep breath in. And as you breath out, lower all the barriers that you are perceiving around you. These may not even be your barriers. You perceive them. So just lower them. You can return as many as you want to people, to whomever it belongs to. And keep lowering them. Now notice all of the energy, that twinkles around you, that sparkles. It may sound like bells, it may feel like a tickle, and no-tice how the molecules of your body vibrate. And all of the barriers that you may notice going up again, lower them down. Return them to sender if you'd like. And notice how you expand. And allow this energy to caress you, to kiss you, to sparkle around you. What would it take for you to receive this more and more? What would that create for you, for you body, for the planet?

What energy, space and consciousness would you and your body have to be to receive that? And everything that doesn't allow that, destroy and un-create it all.

Right and wrong, good and bad, POD and POC, all nine, shorts, boys and beyonds.

Do you notice the joy around you? Do you notice how every molecule is just so happy to have you? Notice how there's no judgment, there's no thought. When you choose magic and joy, when you choose to be the space and receive from the Universe, there is no right and wrong, because when there is magic and there's joy, no judgment can exist.

Whenever you get into that space when you have so many thoughts, what if you just chose this? And what would that create? And everything that doesn't allow you to perceive, know, be and receive that, destroy and un -create it all. Right and wrong, good and bad, POD and POC, all nine, shorts, boys and beyonds.

Caller: Yes, that was really wonderful and it has opened up. When you started, you said the magic of the Universe is you. You said it is to acknowledge the joy.

Is it again related with what Gary talks about – the 10 second incre-ment and being in that point of awareness all the time?

A: Absolutely. Absolutely. It's a choice. Every 10 seconds is a choice to be joy for me. What do I choose to be right now? Ok, I'm done with that. I'll just be really depressed. Try that for 10 seconds. I dare you. It's not that easy!

It is when you have choice and when you are willing to receive that choice and you have no barriers to it, you will find yourself looking for the joy and the joy will be right in front of you. It's not that the depression is not, it's not that the sad and pathetic is not, but you will choose what is expansive to you. You are an infinite being. You have infinite choice.

So in these 10 seconds would you choose something that expands or something that contracts? And that's still a choice.

If you do something that gives you joy – like I love cone ice creams. I love sitting and eating them like a child. It's not that I don't perceive the judgments around me, it's that I don't care, because I'm choosing for me.

And there are days when I'll just say "Ma, I'm just going to be depressed" and she's like "ok." My mother's pretty cool that way. And I can't do it for longer than that. The moment that she says "ok", it's like there's nothing for me to be depressed about anymore. But that's a choice. And 10 seconds later, there's nothing. I choose something different.

Because actually if you look at it, and if you consider it and you realise and you notice that judgment doesn't seem to exist whenever you are being the joy, whenever you are choosing to be the magic. You will notice how much energy other people use to be depressed, to be sad and to be all "poor, pathetic me" and victims. And if you start noticing that whenever you are around those people and you choose joy, they can't be like that anymore. They can't even stand to be around you.

The best thing was the moment I chose joy a few times, I noticed that there was nobody around me and that's when I realised how many people just love choosing being sad and pathetic. It's a choice. Magic is a choice.

Caller: I've had this pain – I know it's an intensity in my neck. I watched a video of Dain's talking about detoxing from this reality and I'm wondering if it is from detoxing from this reality?

A: So are you detoxing from this reality? Or you are noticing other people, other energy?

How many people are invested in you not leaving this reality, Not having your own reality?

Everything that is and all of the oaths, vows, swearings, fealties, comealties, commitments, contracts that you have with any and all of them, through all time space dimensions and realities, will you now destroy and un-create all that? Right and wrong, good and bad, POD and POC, all nine, shorts, boys and beyonds.

Caller: Yes. I have one person in my life who if I hurt myself, they are very happy. It's very obvious that they are very happy.

A: Oh really?

Caller: Yes. They are very happy if I get hurt at all. If I fall, man, they are just "did you fall!", like they are just so excited that I've hurt myself. (laughs) It's like…

A: So how much energy are you using to hold yourself back that your body is like "oh, crap"?

Caller: I'm using a lot of energy. I'm starting to free it up, but yes, I'm using a lot of energy.

A: *Everything that is, and all of the barriers that you've created in your body, so that you never have to choose that, will you destroy and un -create it all? Right and wrong, good and bad, POD and POC, all nine, shorts, boys and beyonds.*

What secret agendas do you have with judgment that keeps you from being the magic and joy you truly be? And everything that is, will you destroy and un-create it all? Right and wrong, good and bad, POD and POC, all nine, shorts, boys and beyonds.

A: *What energy, space and consciousness can you and your body be to be the source point for the creation of intensely infinite joy and magic that you truly be? Everything that doesn't allow that, will you destroy and un -create it all? Right and wrong, good and bad, POD and POC, all nine, shorts, boys and beyonds.*

A: Do you notice that the planet is asking you to be you? Do you notice that the planet is begging for people to choose joy?

N: Yes

A: What capacities do you have with joy? I've always noticed that when I'm happy, I'm really happy and I'm being joy, I will get everything I ask for - like today, I was going to a friend's house and I was on my two-wheeler, and I got from my house to her house, which is about 10 kilometers, without putting a foot down. I never had to put a foot down. I always go through green lights. The road always clears. And this is one of the most busiest areas, the old part of town, and I got through without ever putting my foot down in 15 minutes, which in many cases, especially here in Chennai, it's not heard of. That's the joy you be. You always create for yourself. You have capacity. And when you are being that joy and when you are willing to have that space and choose that space and choose that magic, the entire planet is waiting to gift to you. I noticed that I was tapping into the nine trannies for that.

The Nine Trannies

A: Ok, I can't remember exactly what the nine trannies are, to be very honest. (laughs) I refer to them as the "super-powers" - the superpowers that I know are possible. When I was a child growing up, Superman, and Batman and all of that was more possible to me. You ask me about, Superman and what Superman did and Star Trek, that was more real to me.

There's one tranny called translocation that is my capacity. I will move through space. My body moves through space. And I always create that for myself. I've always been told I walk way too fast. Last year when I was in Venice, every few seconds I had to stop and look back to see where my friends were, because I was walking so fast. And it's a potency. These capacities are potencies. We buy so much from this reality about how we should move that we haven't actually accessed what is possible with our bodies. Now that's magic as well.

N: We all are just basking in the energy, Aditi. (laughs)

A: I know, am I making sense here? Like am I suddenly...?

N: (laughs) No, it's just the energy. Just we are so enjoying being in the energy. Yes it's awesome.

A: If you wake up in the morning and go "*What would be outrageously happy to do today that would change this reality right away?*" *What would we create? Everything that doesn't allow that, will you destroy and un-create it all? Right and wrong, good and bad, POD and POC, all nine, shorts, boys and beyonds.*

Did everybody's body just relax?

N: (laughs) Yes, we just all became outrageously happy. I'm just like so happy.

A: And the best part is when you include your body in all of this, I've noticed that if somebody switches on music in my house, I will dance. It does not look very pleasant and I really don't care. (laughs) Your body enjoys that energy as well. That's the joy your body feels when you step up to and acknowledge your capacity.

I've always noticed that when I have a pain in my body and it's like "Ok, what am I aware of here?" and it's like "Ok, it's time for me to step up." My body is giving me awareness about it constantly. I have a capacity here. Ok, cool. How could I use that now to my advantage? And you'll always find that your body will contribute to the joy and your body will match that energy and will want more of it.

What energy, space and consciousness can you and your body be to be the source point of creation of intensely infinite joy and magic that dom-inates and out-creates all other energies on, through and for the planet with total ease? And everything that doesn't allow that, will you destroy and un-create it all? Right and wrong, good and bad, POD and POC, all nine, shorts, boys and beyonds.

It's where you are gifting to the planet, when you are being joy and your body is also being that. You are gifting to the planet. The planet is joy. How much of what we see in the newspapers would exist if we just chose joy? How much of that would even be relevant?

You've got to get that when you choose magic and joy you are choosing beyond this reality, beyond what you've been told this reality is, or what is possible with this reality. There's something beyond that.

Sense the fog in this reality for a moment? Notice how contractive and disgusting it gets?

Now, as an infinite being, can you perceive just beyond that? Notice how expansive it is? Notice how the molecules shift and change so easily? Notice what is available to you now. Notice what is possible now. Does anything they say in the news make sense when you perceive that energy?

N: No, it doesn't.

A: Exactly. Because that energy is the joy this Universe is, the magic that it is and that it offers you. And like the lady was asking, whenever you feel that pain - are you avoiding joy and magic? Is it pressing up against you so intensely, waiting for you to choose, waiting for you to claim, own and acknowledge this as your reality? And if you would acknowledge that and be that, what else is possible that we haven't even considered?

This planet is gifting to you. This Universe is gifting to you, because you are a gift. Why don't you acknowledge that gift that you be? You are gifting to the planet and to the Universe and that is gifting to you again and that expands and expands and expands and expands so much so that none of the wars and none of the stupidity on this planet, the insanity on this planet could exist. What is your gift to the planet and to the Universe is the joy and the magic that you be?

What if you could walk into a room, walk into your prime minister's office or the parliament and be the energy that completely changes it? How potent would that be? How much of the crap that people create would exist? And yes, it wouldn't be fun, because you know, there's not enough trauma and drama. But how much fun would that be? Notice the molecules dancing with you. Notice the joy. Notice the ease in your body when you do that. How much are you abusing you and your body by not acknowledging that? You be that magic.

What have you made so vital, valuable and real about creating the reference points to this reality that keeps you from ever claiming, owning and acknowledging and choosing magic as a possibility? And everything that is times a godzillion, will you destroy and un-create it all? Right and wrong, good and bad, POD and POC, all nine, shorts, boys and beyonds.

N: When you perceive the energy of the doorway to possibilities, what is that for you?

A: Choice. It's just choice. I would choose infinite possibility any day over sad and pathetic. I did sad and pathetic for years. I did believe that I have to be in this reality, I have to go according to what they say in this reality. But that never worked for me.

I went from spending 6 months locked up in my room and never leaving the house to not being able to sit at home, to going abroad and travelling and travelling alone. And for me, that was the biggest change and the thing that changed that for me was the bars. I never let go of the knowing that something greater was possible, but for me the reality at that time was "I couldn't have it." And there was this moment when I just said "ah, screw it. Either something changes or I'm done" – I'm not going to kill myself. I tried that once, it did not work. It's the most painful experience of my life. I just said, "ok, I'm never going to choose anything beyond this. I'm never going to have a good time. I'm never going to leave the house. Whatever that is. However that shows up." Three weeks later, somebody had run my bars for me and I asked them again, "will you run my bars?" and I did it again and I did it again for 5 days.

And I was like "ok, I want to learn the bars." And I went to a bars facilitator here in Chennai, Sudha Murari, and she taught me the bars and she said, "Oh, this is fun. You know after this you have Foundation, Level 1 and you have this, you have that. It's so much fun." And I was like "Oh, I want all of that. I want all of that." From that I went to a Right Voice for You breakthrough, and I enjoyed myself. I thoroughly enjoyed myself.

And it was Vanitha Subramaniam's class. She told me she was doing a Foundation & Level 1 and I'm like "I'm there!" I didn't know what made me say that or where I was going to get the money from. I didn't really care. It wasn't like I had an income. I just chose it. I just knew that I had to do that. And it's opened me up to being able to be this, in this moment. Just that space and that joy that I always knew was possible, I just never knew that I could be that.

Choice is the doorway to possibility, and choosing to be whatever you are and all that you are and all that you be. And believe me, there's a joy in life. Or actually, don't believe me.

N: (laughs) So, yeah, I actually want to point something out. So when you were talking about choice and you said that thing of 'I just chose it. I just said "ok, I'm going for foundation level 1 and I don't care. I mean I'm just going. I chose it. I didn't have the money, I didn't have anything but I chose it." And it's like I could just perceive people's thoughts that how did you choose it? How did you create the money? How did you blah blah blah… But that's the thing you know, if you can just perceive the energy she was being when she made that choice, that's what it is.

A: Yes, it's like nobody's judgment about how did I get the money – none of that could hold me back because that wasn't real to me at all. That choice was more real to me than anything else that I could see.

Even the fear - I hadn't flown in 12 years when I first flew to Mumbai. I was staying in a hotel all by myself and I'd never done that in my life. I didn't know a single soul in Mumbai at that time.

I was crying when the flight took off that day. I still remember that. I was crying and I noticed that my body was just like "such joy!" Such joy. "Yeay! We are finally doing this. You're getting out of this shit." It was that! The moment you choose everything – and being that magic, I know that that was the magic that the Universe just gifted me. I just chose it. And everything showed up. And notice the space that you can choose from. It is always available to you. Ask for it to expand, to substantiate in and as your reality. Everything that doesn't allow that, destroy and un-create it all. Right and wrong, good and bad, POD and POC, all nine, shorts, boys and beyonds.

I'm not saying that going into judgment is not easy. Is it going to be easy right away? It's a choice you make. And the more you make that choice, the less hard and the less solid it can be. Today I wake up with joy because I choose that.

Question: (laughs) "Hi, thank you so much. I'm crying as I listen to you. How do I come out and be me when it has not ever been safe to be me?" and the other thing is "My body is trembling listening to you, what you are saying about not ever leaving the house again is how I feel right now. I've never felt comfortable in this reality. Inside it hurts. I feel trapped. Please help."

A: So, first of all, wherever you are, if you never had the bars run, please have it run. Your body is enjoying this energy. The molecules of your body are dancing. When you are crying – and I have done this many times so I can honestly say – your body is bringing down the walls and all of that solidity that it has bought as real but never known to be true. Your body is just breaking it down and all the molecules around you are dancing.

This is the first time somebody is speaking or somebody is talking to the energy around you. If you are on this call and if you have chosen to listen to this, it's because everything has led you to this moment. Receive it. And if you can get your bars run, please get it run and ask your body everyday "Do you want to get your bars run? Do you want to get your bars run? Do you want to get your bars run?" And I'm sure there's somebody around you who will be willing to run your bars for you. If you need to pay them ask them "ok, how much do I need to pay? Can we exchange something for it?" There's always a way. It's not like I had an income. I borrowed from my mother and I went. And my mother has never asked for it back because she's like "Are you kidding me? Look at everything that's changed." And it is the same for her also by the way. I just want to say this, I go for all the Access classes all around the world and I go through the entire classes and she's at home totally enjoying the energy. She never has to step her foot out and she's happy. She's living a retired life now and is like "Yeah, yeah, go for all the classes. Do all the work. I'll enjoy it." (laughs) So she has never asked for it back.

And the thing about not leaving the house is – ok, so what are you aware of? And what part of that is relevant to you? Notice how that just clears the energy? That's your question. What part of this is relevant to me? And notice how it clears up even more. And everything that is, will you destroy and un-create it all? Right and wrong, good and bad, POD and POC, all nine, shorts, boys and beyonds.

Crying is a good thing. Crying is actually a very happy thing for your body so allow that.

Magic

N: What else do you know about magic that nobody else knows?

A: It's a choice. That's the one thing I really do know about it. And it's a choice I make every day. Actually, it's a choice I make every moment and even when it's most uncomfortable for me, I will make it, because that is more real to me than what this reality says. It is not about pulling a rabbit out of a hat, it's about walking into a room and having nobody frown or cry. And not because I'm dancing around doing anything, but because I'm there. I have a garden in my house now and I have this amazing lady who comes and cleans my house. She doesn't clean my house so much as looks after my garden now, because I really don't care. I'll do the dishes, let her just come and look after the garden because my garden grows so beautifully when she is around. And I noticed all of the little fairies and sprites. I've noticed leprechauns in my garden. And it's such a joy for me. And it's the Earth gifting to me. That's a magic too: the elements and the energies of the Earth are just gifting all the time. And I know that it's a choice. I know that it's a choice every single day.

What Does Relevant Mean?

A: Does it have anything to do with you? Whatever you are sensing, whatever you are feeling. I don't like the word 'feeling' about it, but I'll go with that right now. *So whatever you are aware of, does it have anything to do with you? Does it have anything to do with your reality? How many people around you are depressed? How many people around you are sad all the time? And who are you trying to take it out of? Wow. And everything that is, will you destroy and un-create it all? Right and wrong, good and bad, POD and POC, all nine, shorts, boys and beyonds.*

How much energy are they using to do the depressed, the sad, and pathetic and poor me? Is that your reality? Can they be depressed and can they be invested in that if you are choosing joy all the time?

A: What else about magic? What do you know about magic that you've never been willing to acknowledge?

N: (laughs) I don't know anything.

A: No, Nilofer doesn't know anything about magic. Like Nilofer and magic are like no, it cannot exist on the same page. Otherwise she'd have like millions of people signing up to her – like millions and millions. Like the entire planet would have been signed up on this summit. Because she has no clue about magic. It's an alien concept to her. And joy? Are you kidding me? She can't do joy. Have you seen her face?

She cries all the time. Have you listened to her? This is her crying. It just looks like it's smiling, but it's not.

N: What do you know about magic that you are not willing to know? – I like that. It's really, really amazing with all these calls, there's not so much talking as is you stepping into into the energies you know.

It's the energy. The call starts and it's just the energy. Everyone is actually choosing that. Choosing that joy, that peace, that magic and there's not really much to talk about actually. (laughs)

A: This is all about the energy. And that's the beauty and magic of it.

Listen to all the sounds near my house now. They are blowing the conch and they are ringing the bell. See, magic!

N: You speak about 'That is what the Earth requires of you', talk more about that.

A: Gary said this a lot and hearing him say it was the first time that I acknowledged that I was aware of it as well. Which is, that the Earth is dying. We have been taking and taking and taking from the Earth, but we never really gifted anything to the Earth. And we think gifting to the Earth is going organic or being vegan and clean living and all of that. What if there's more than that? What's the choice beyond that?

The Earth is energy. What energy does it require of you? And what energy does it require you to receive and acknowledge? I'm always amazed at my garden. Everyday, there is some new color of flower or something like that, and it's not a very big garden but every molecule of it is just so beautiful. And I live near the beach and I live near this area that is really wooded, which is very rare in a city like Chennai and every morning I can hear birds. And this place has been calling to me for many years and I lived here for 5 years, then I had to shift out and then I shifted in again. And I've noticed how the energy of this area has changed. And I noticed that every single molecule in this area is just waiting for somebody to acknowledge it. And I acknowledge the energy of this area everyday. I do 1-2-3s and 1-2-3-4s and yes, that definitely is a contribution. The real contribution that I've noticed is just saying "Hi" to the Earth, "hi" to the Universe. And it's so beautiful. There's so much beauty around us that we don't even notice. Just saying "hi" to it, there's so much more beauty that reveals itself to you every single day, every single moment.

N: You know, when you said "Just say "hi" to the planet, say "hi" to the Universe", the whole energy just opened up even more.

So it can't be that easy, right? We really have to do a lot of hard work. Go 1-2-3... (laughs)

A: Yes, and then you have to go and meet the shaman, he is called White Princess. He lives in particular areas in US. And you can't find him – he keeps shifting around. He keeps shifting around. And you have to be very very astute. You have to do years and years and years of meditation before you can get there.

N: (laughs) Oh my god, that's so awesome! Thank you so much, Aditi. You are such a contribution in this call. It was like having a shower of energy. Thank you so much.

RISE OF THE SUPER HEROES

A Gift from Rhonda Burns for a 110+ minute call out of an 8-week series -

Call # 2 of 8 - RISE of the Super Heroes

Activating and amplifying the authentic gifts within you.

Get it at www.whereismydoorwaytopossibilities.com

CHAPTER SIX

BEYOND THE CREATIVITY TRAP –
UNCOVERING EVERYDAY GENIUS IN ALL
AREAS OF LIFE

By Stephanie Richardson

Facilitator, Access Consciousness®
Artist & Photographer Author & Speaker

What Would You Like To Create In Your Life

What is it that you would like to create in your life that you have yet to create? For years in my own life I found it difficult to get out of the ruts I had created for myself. I judged everything that I created. I compared my talent, and creative abilities, and my success against the people who were the top in the fields I wanted to succeed in and judged myself for not succeeding faster. I was spinning my wheels and I was miserable.

Judging ourselves is one of the first places that we get hung up. Comparing ourselves against other people and looking at where they seem to have gifts that we don't or success that we don't shuts down the access that we have to all the gifts we have available. It sends a beacon out to the world that what we value, more than anything else, is comparison, judgment, and struggle.

If we want to have something different than we have had so far, we have to do something different. But when we get into the cycle of comparison and judgment, it can be really hard to see beyond the limitations that have become so palpably real. We literally begin to use our creative capacities to create the limitations before us. Those limitations can seem so real that choice can seem as if they are an unreachable mythical beast.

What would happen if every time we looked at what somebody else was creating and used it to judge ourselves, or began to have judgment creep in, we stopped? What if every time we heard ourselves say, "I can't" or "I'm not as good as..." or "I'm not as creative as..." we just changed the conversation without judging ourselves? We can begin this really simply by saying to ourselves, "Oh, look at that. I just compared myself to that person. I just judged myself. Everything that that is, I destroy and uncreate it all."

It turns out, we don't have to take our judgments about ourselves very seriously! When we catch ourselves we can just say, "I just judged myself. Am I willing to change that? Am I willing to have something different" and then ask a new question like, "What would I like to create here?"

What if, instead of comparing, we allowed other's creations to inspire us to create more? What if we could look and ask, "Are those gifts, talents and abilities that I have?... Yes?... No?" If it's yes, "What can I choose today, that will begin to create this in my life right away?" You may actually have to learn a new skill, you may not, but the question opens the door for the information, the energy, and the people to begin to show up. I prefer to use the word "begin" In the question as it alleviates the element of time as the important factor. If I don't have it 100% tomorrow, there is nothing wrong... I can just ask, "Is it beginning?" If the answer is, "yes", you can ask a new question, "So, I know it's begun, now, what can I add today that will begin to create more of this in my life right away?" Curiosity and the willingness to play, along with gratitude, for even tiniest of things, actually begins to allow for more to show up.

Stumbling Blocks

When it comes to starting, two of the biggest stumbling blocks seem to be a lack of inspiration or a feeling overwhelm. Some people feel like they require inspiration to begin, and some people feel overwhelmed when they begin. Sometimes people experience a lack of inspiration at the same time they feel overwhelmed! When any of that shows up I first ask, "Who does that belong to? Is any of that mine?" We tend to be highly aware of everyone around us, could it be that we are picking up other people's boredom, other people's stress, or other people's lack of inspiration? Would you like to hold onto that for them? Probably not. Asking, "Who does that belong to?" allows you to let go of the thoughts and the feelings and the emotions that you have picked up from others along the way.

If you are having trouble starting or catch yourself saying things like, "One day.... When my kids are grown up, or when I make more money or when I lose ten pounds..." You can ask, "Is this something that I would actually like to choose?" Sometimes we haven't taken action because it isn't something we actually want to do or be. We may have bought into someone else's dreams of what a great life would entail. It may not actually be relevant for you.

If it is actually an activity or a target that you would like to pursue, you can start asking, "What can I choose today that will begin to create a future that I'd truly like to have right away?" And then, just start. What do I mean by start? Get the energy of what you would like to create and begin. It doesn't matter what you begin to do, you literally just start creating. If you want become a great artist, expand your business globally, or become an author, just begin! The biggest key is not to judge anything that you create. Just create and create and create and you can then choose what to put out in the world later.

There's this moment in either artwork or life or anything, where you may look at what you've created and think, "Oh, this is really good..." That moment, for me, can be a moment where doubt kicks in. The destructive voice of judgment, pipes up and says, "What if it only gets worse from here?"

Is, "What if it only gets worse from here?" actually a question? Or is it an expectation of failure?

Does it expand what's possible? Or does it ask for things to get worse?

When you find yourself slipping out of the present moment or slipping into judgment or thinking up worst case scenarios, how do you get out of it? Ask a different question. "What else is possible, that I haven't considered?" is a question you can ask that will get you moving back in the direction of creation.

Lets look at that in practice. Imagine you're working on a project. You think to yourself, "This is looking so good, I don't want to ruin it!" does that feel contracted? Or does that feel expanded? That tends to feel pretty contracted! If you ask a question in that same moment, "What else is possible that I haven't even considered?" Does that change the feeling of contraction at all? Does it begin to give you a place to begin creating again?

Any time you feel yourself holding on to any feelings or thoughts, whether the feeling is, "This is awesome!!" or the feeling is, "This is awful!" you can ask the question, "What else is possible?"

When something becomes precious to you, it's as if that is the best thing that you can have. It's where you've already decided that nothing else is possible, that was as far as you could go, that that was all you could create. And does that feel light? Or does that feel heavy? If it's heavy, it's a lie, and if it's light, it's actually true for you.

"You can always ask, "Is something else possible that I haven't considered?" If you get a sense of lightness when you ask, it's light for you, begin to ask, "What would it take for that to show up?"

Staying in question, following the energy, asking what else is possible, and being bluntly honest with yourself allow you to easily move beyond road blocks and discouragement. When you begin to think that nothing else is possible, be bluntly honest with yourself and then ask yourself, "Can I ask a question here? Universe, I'm not seeing where the possibility is here. Can you show me? What's possible here that I have not considered? And anywhere I'm unwilling to be that, to perceive that, to know that, to receive that, I destroy and un-create it all."

Bluntly Honest With Yourself

Just asking very simple questions, and really getting honest about what is true for you, is radically different for most people. One of my biggest awakenings was when I asked myself if I was truly willing to be happy. I thought I was a happy person by nature. So I was shocked when the answer at that time was, "No!

Weirdly, just by being totally honest, it changed immediately. What if the things that you've been hiding from you, as if they would trap you forever, are actually things that would set you free if you were willing to look at them with no point of view?

Anytime that you come to something that feels like a dead end, would you be willing to be bluntly honest? – Am I willing to have more possibilities here? Am I willing to have more money here? Am I willing to be creative here? Am I willing to have other people judge me? Am I willing to step into the greatness that's possible? And anytime that answer is, "No." What if that was ok?

Only by answering what's actually true for you in this moment, can you have a different choice, or a different awareness. Until then, you keep it all locked up. It's a big secret you are keeping from you. We lock all these things into our bodies, we lock all these things into our lives.

They are not really true for us, but when we hide them, we hold onto them. We make a choice. Our choice then becomes a decision. That decision becomes determining factor for the possibilities that we have available.

For instance, I had decided at some point that happiness was exhausting. And when I locked that into my life, could have anything else? Not really. "Happiness is exhausting" became one of the underlying rules to live by which is why, when I asked if I was willing to be happy, the answer was "No." But the moment I asked, "What's actually true here? Oh, I decided that happiness is exhausting," it no longer had to be true.

Creation

Why am I talking about this when the topic is creativity? All of these are things we use not to create our lives. Often, what comes up for people around creativity is less about creating and more about the things that are in the way. Time, money, energy, the things people think are their resources.

We could just choose to create, no matter what! But as long as you believe that the limitations of time, money, and energy are more real than your ability to create, then can you create? Not very dynamically.

So what do we do about those limitations when they seem so real? Let's look at time. You can begin by asking, "What would I actually like to create here? Would I like to create this limitation of time as real? Or could I actually choose to write (or draw, or go on a walk) for five minutes right now?" Next time you catch yourself catching up on social media, for instance, could I be using this moment to create what I've been saying I desire to create? Next time you hit the snooze button in the morning, "Would I like to sleep now? Would I like to take a moment for me?"

There are lots of those moments in a day, waiting in line at the grocery store, stopped at a traffic light, on the phone with your mom... Can you use any of those moments?

You can even begin to shift the way you spend time with friends. Would it be fun for any of your friends to have a writing night, or a crafting night, or a cooking night?

When it comes to money, a lot of people limit what they can create by thinking that they have to have certain supplies or certain equipment to begin. Can you begin with what you already have? If you want to be a photographer and you have a smart phone, can you begin with that? If you want to do art, do you need to begin with oil paint? Or can you begin with a pen and some copy paper? What have you decided are your requirements for starting? Would you be willing to destroy and uncreate everything that does not allow you to begin creating now?

If you are using money as a reason not to create, you have to make sure that you don't have enough money to afford what you have decided you can't afford to do. Do you think that may limit how much money you can have? Does that work for the rest of your life? If you don't have the money to do photography, will you have enough money to go on that vacation to Bali? Would you like to make a different choice now?

Each and every time we buy one of these limitations as real, we are saying that we have no other choice, that we are at the effect of all of the circumstances that surround us. Does that empower you to make a choice that would actually work for you? Does that acknowledge the gifts and the talents and abilities that you have that are waiting to be expressed in the world? Would you like to have more choice now?

Any time that stuckness or those lies are coming up, would you be willing to have a different reality? You can ask, "What can I choose here that if I chose it, would contribute to the future that I'd truly like to have? What can I choose here that if I chose it, would contribute to a greater future than I've ever imagined possible?" and, "What can I add today that will begin to bring that to fruition right away?" Is there a lightness, is there a space there? What if that lightness is you?"

Clearing The Original Issues Of Abuse

This (class) will start to unlock those insane places in people where they have received abuse. What would it take for you to be free, joyful and expansive with yourself and your body?

If you have suffered abuse of any kind and can not seem to totally heal you or your body, or get over behavior issues, then this 2.5 hour MP3 is for you! Just play this MP3 anywhere you can hear it and watch the change begin. It is that easy. This original abuse class developed by Gary Douglas has a profound healing and clearing effect on people including kids, adults and even animals! This audio is especially recommended if you are looking to release the places where abuse has been locked into your body. Try it out, you will not be disappointed.

Orig Abuse CD - http://bit.ly/2aBqlnz

The Original Clearing the Issues of Abuse
mp3- http://bit.ly/2b9Obq

CHAPTER SEVEN

❖

ROMANCE WITH MONEY

By Nirmala Raju (Nimi)

Entrepreneur, Spiritual Medium,

Healer & Facilitator of Consciousness

How My Romance Started

Nilofer: So, so, tell me what got you started on this whole thing about romance with money and creating this whole audio about the lottery and so on?

Nirmala: I posted some questions on Facebook about money and it created a lot of energy and at the same time I was also doing some audio loops for my newsletter subscribers. The more interactions I had the more I recognized that I was receiving loads of contribution from people – kindness, money and many other. Sensing this energy of receiving, I started buying lottery tickets once a week and I was winning continuously. I realized then that I have a capacity to tap into the awareness of winning money and in general for receiving. I started asking more and more questions and this energy showed up. It was like playing with the energy of money and having fun with it.

Nilofer: So basically what you are saying is you didn't make money significant?

Nirmala: Absolutely. Even when I bought lottery, I didn't make it so significant. I didn't have any expectations, I just bought it. I also remembered and acknowledged that whenever I played Bingo with my friends, I won. I have won full house - thrice consecutively . Actually, most of the time, I used to borrow from friends for Bingo, win money and give them back their money and take mine with me. How does it get any better than this?

I started acknowledging my capacity to create and generate money without having to have any investment.. Of course, you create from nothing because being the source of creation, you can be/do anything.

Are You Willing To Be The Gift You Are To The Universe

Nilofer: So what questions were you asking?

Nirmala: More like, "*what contribution can I be?*" and "*what gift can I be for me and the Universe?*" These questions brought up more questions for creating money. People used to comment on my Facebook, "your questions are really simple and they are not lengthy clearings, but they bring up judgment and the energy that's limiting us." In one of the calls, Gary talked about being a contribution to the world. In my point of view, when you are willing to be a contribution to the world and the Universe, the expansion we choose is much more. So, are you willing to be the contribution to the world? Not just for you. This changed a lot for me. *What contribution can I be? What gift can I be for the world? What can I change in the Universe today? What can I be or do different today that will change the financial reality on this planet?*

What If Money Can Be Fun

In general, most people go into tightness and lack thinking about money.. Regardless of whether you have money or not, there's always a sense of heaviness, a sense of tightness there - because if you have money, it's about possessing money, keeping money, growing money, investing money etc. If you don't have money, it's seeking money, getting money, receiving money, making money, creating money. So what if money can be just fun? Just like the excitement of being in romance.

So if all of us can have the energy of romance with money, what will it change for the planet? How would the financial reality be on the planet if all of us can function from that energy? When you have that kind of tightness or heaviness for money, would it come to you?

Nilofer: No

Nirmala: If someone else projects that kind of energy at you, would you go to them?

Nilofer: No, No

Nirmala: You wouldn't. When somebody has that energy of romance for you, would you love to go to them? Absolutely. If all of us have that, how would it be? Would we still have lack and poverty on the planet?

Would An Infinite Being Have Lack

What's stopping people from having fun with money? Most of the time it is self-judgment. 'I am this, I am that, I can be this, I can never be that etc.' So would an infinite being have any hesitation to be anything?

Nilofer: No

Nirmala: Are you willing to attract people? Are you willing to be so seductive that people can just show up and give you money? And these are the kind of questions I started posting on Facebook and started doing audio loops for creating more money winning lottery etc. One thing I keep seeing in people is, lack of self-worth. If you don't see yourself as a gift, would you be willing to create a life that will be a gift to you? Not really. Why would you have low self-worth? Because you are just buying into other people's sense of you or themselves. See, we – everyone of us is so unique that for all eternity in the entire Universe, we have only just one of us. There is nobody to compare; Nobody to compete with. Nobody can take our place. If we are not here, then there is going to be a void in the Universe. If only we get that, then we start creating the life we desire.

Caller: You are talking about romancing money, which sounds like a great idea but when one doesn't have romance or money in one's life, how does one embody those frequencies or those vibrations?

Nirmala: Ok, what does romance mean to you?

Caller: Romance means being cherished and adored for who I am someone paying me attention and being with me and wanting to be with me.

Nirmala: Ok. So, are you being that energy to you?

Caller: I have my phases. I leave myself, I come back. So…

Nirmala: Ok, why are you unable to be present for you all the time with that kind of romantic energy? So what judgments do you have about you?

Caller: I don't know. I would like to be more present for myself. I would like to be my beloved and my lover, but I know that I do keep leaving myself from time to time.

Nirmala: *Ok, if you knew why you are doing that, what would it be? So everything that doesn't allow you to know, be, perceive and receive that energy, will you now destroy and un-create all of it? Right and wrong, good and bad, POD and POC, all nine, shorts, boys and beyond.*

 Most of the time, it is the willingness to be. Willingness doesn't equal to choosing. For eg, Are you willing to get off the chair? Do you have any charge about it? No. You are willing to get up from the chair. But do you have to? Are you choosing to? You don't have to, but anytime you like to, you can get up because you have that choice.

Caller: Yes

Nirmala: *What are you not willing to be for you? If you are not willing to be something for you, that is where you are creating a no-choice Universe. So what are you not willing to be for you? Are you willing to be your lover?*

Everywhere you decided and concluded that you don't know, will you destroy and un-create all of it? Right and wrong, good and bad, POD and POC, all nine, shorts, boys and beyonds.

And one thing I keep noticing is, you keep saying "I don't know". Ok? Would you like to clear that?

Caller: Yes

Nirmala: Would an infinite being not know anything?

Caller: No, they would know everything.

Nirmala: Ok, can you say "I don't know" three times please?

Caller: I don't know. I don't know. I don't know.

Nirmala: All the SHICUUUU (Secret, Hidden, Invisible, Covert, Unseen, Unsaid, Unacknowledged and Undisclosed implants or explants that control us) implants creating this and all the quantum particulates and mobius strips that are holding all this in place, will you now destroy and un-create all of it? Right and wrong, good and bad, POD and POC, all nine, shorts, boys and beyonds.

So keep asking this question, **"What am I not willing to be for myself?"** and keep clearing.

Are You Willing To Seduce

Nirmala: There's another thing I keep seeing, Nilofer - The unwillingness. What is seduction? Basically, you are willing to be everything that people are looking for in you. Seduction doesn't have to be stripping. You are just willing to be everything for them. When I started Access, I was interviewed by a TV station here in London. I have been doing healing and mediumship work for a long time. So, in the interview, I was talking about Access Consciousness and I mentioned about the mediumship work and the interviewer got really interested in mediumship and asked more questions. The callers were also so hung up on mediumship. In the whole interview, Access got diluted. Lot of people called me after the interview and I was repeatedly trying to empower them with Access tools, but people were just looking to get answers through my mediumship work. So, I couldn't convert 95% of the calls into business. I asked Gary about it. And he asked me, "They were all looking for answers and they wanted you to be their guru. Were you willing to be their guru?" I wasn't.

He said, "Ok, people can go to any medium and people can come to you. Who would facilitate them into more consciousness? You or any other medium?" I said, "yes me, because my intention is to give them empowerment rather than answers." He said," Are you willing to trick them into consciousness just by your willingness to be their guru?" I realized that I don't have to be their guru to trick them into conscious-ness. I just got to be willing to be so. That's what it is all about.

Even six months back in Copenhagen, when Gary mentioned about seducing people into the class, my body literally shrunk and I asked Gary to help changing that. Gary did some clearing and said, "Some doors are open and the rest is your choice." Then you see, in a few months I have come up with a class called "Seducing money". There is a lot of clarity on this subject. Do you have to choose seduction? Not necessary. Just the willingness. Just like getting up from a chair. It's as simple as that. When you have the willingness, you have the choice. When you don't have the willingness, you spend so much energy in defending that.

Using The Limitations To Your Advantage

Question: "So I have been playing some clearings about money Gary suggested in some call. Also have done the money workbook like 20 times. Recorded money workbook questions as a night loop. Have been asking questions but somehow things are moving too slow for me to say "Oh this has changed like Nilofer said in her money work-book calls about experiences of others." It has been more than a year I have been using tools, clearings, questions. What's happening here? At times, I sense that tools don't work for me. At times they work magically. Any suggestions?

Nirmala: Ok, cool. So if you are on the call, can you just get the energy of this limitation? Where is it in your body? Got it? Does it have a boundary? Most of the time it does. Yeah? If there is a boundary, there is space around it. Can you sense the space? Does the space have boundary?

Nilofer: No

Nirmala: Not really. If the answer is yes, go beyond that boundary. Beyond that boundary you have space, because without space there is no boundary. Just go beyond it, beyond it. And who is this space? You are that space. So does that mean this limitation is within you? Who is holding this?

Nilofer: No, if I am the space then the limitation can't be in me.

Nirmala: Yes. So who is holding this limitation? If you are the space around this limiting energy, who is holding this? You are much bigger than that. Are you willing to be that?

Nilofer: Yes

Nirmala: Now being that space, can you ask this energy – this energy of limitation – to make money for you?

Nilofer: (laughs) I love that!

Nirmala: This is energy. This is just energy. Are you willing to release it so that it can go out and bring people to pay you money? Or you know, money in any other form? This is pure energy and it is up to you how you like to use this. Try this. Every time you go into this contraction of not having enough, that creates a kind of energy. How about using that energy to your advantage? Instead of assigning values and meaning to the energy, just use it. So everything that doesn't allow you to know, be, perceive and receive that, will you now destroy and un-create all of that please? Right and wrong, good and bad, POD and POC, all nine, shorts, boys and beyond… Cool!

Whenever such tightness comes up, this is what I do…

'I have some additional energy here. How can I use it to my advantage? How can I transmute this into joy? How can I release this and give it a job?' So what if not having money does not have much to do with doing, but just being?

Can You Be An Invitation To Money

Nilofer: Talk more about doing and being money.

Nirmala: Yeah. You know, the question you just read out, it was so heavy because the energy was all about doing. "I've done this. I've done that." Yes, there has been a lot of doing but from what space? If you are doing all this from the energy of desperation, then what are you creating? So, instead of seeking money, are you willing to be an invitation to money so that money can come to you? Are you willing to be attractive? How much charge do we have about being attractive? And how many DJCC's do we have about attracting? DJCC is definition, judgment, computation and conclusion. Are you willing to be paid for your beauty? How many of us went into contraction? When I asked that question, how many of you pictured selling the body? What if it's nothing to do with it? If we are unique and so beautiful, everyone of us has a key to consciousness, right? So are you willing to be paid for that? It's that willingness to receive. Are you willing to receive from everybody and everything? Just try this exercise. Get the energy of your beauty. Absolutely gorgeous. And people are queuing up to give you money. Ok? So how many people can you see? Anybody? Any volunteer?

Nilofer: I could volunteer. (laughs)

I can see like millions of people like that, but there's this voice which is going on in my head "but they are not!" (laughs)

Nirmala: Is it? So who does that voice belong to?

Nilofer: Not me, not people sure…

Nirmala: Would you like to return it and destroy and un-create every-where you've bought it as yours?

Nilofer: Yes, yes

Nirmala: Right and wrong, good and bad, POD and POC, all nine, shorts, boys and beyond… And can you also look at the people in the queue? What kind of people are there?

Nilofer: (laughs) You know what visual I'm getting? I'm getting a visual of the cavemen. (laughs)

Nirmala: Cool! How does it get any better than this? So does that mean you are only willing to receive from them? Or you are not willing to receive from them?

Nilofer: Yes, not willing to receive from them.

Nirmala: *Yes, so what judgments do you have about receiving money from certain kind of people? Everything that brings up, will you now destroy and un-create all of it? Right and wrong, good and bad, POD and POC, all nine, shorts, boys and beyond…*

Are you willing to receive from a homeless person?

Nilofer: No, I'll feel guilty about receiving from homeless person.

Nirmala: This exercise will give you insights into the points of view that are limiting you from receiving money. If you only see 5 people queuing up for you, you have decided and concluded that you can't receive from more than 5 people. If you only see women queuing up, you have decided that you can't receive from men. If you only see rich people, then you have decided that you can't receive from poor people.

What decisions and conclusions have you made about receiving money? Everything that brings up for everybody, can we all destroy and un-create all of it? Right and wrong, good and bad, POD and POC, all nine, shorts, boys and beyonds.

So, what else do you see?

Nilofer: I see flowers now.

Nirmala: Ok. So what else are you not willing to receive? How about receiving from every molecule of the Universe? Are you willing to copulate with every molecule of the Universe? Are you willing to receive from every molecule of the Universe without any defence, without any barrier? How would it be if you can be in communion with every molecule of the Universe? Why do we have to limit copulation to body parts? What if it doesn't have to be that way? If you can receive one cent from every molecule of your body, how much money will you be receiving?

Nilofer: A lot!

Nirmala: If you are willing to receive just one cent from every molecule of the Universe, how much money would you be receiving?

Nilofer: Oh my god, godzillion times! (laughs)

Nirmala: Just one cent! Are you willing to receive that?

Nilofer: Yes, absolutely

Nirmala: *Everything that doesn't allow us to receive that, be that energy, shall we now destroy and un-create all of that please? Right and wrong, good and bad, POD and POC, all nine, shorts, boys and beyonds.*

Your Judgment About Money

One of the questions I ask in the class is if money were a person, how would they be? Female, male? And how would they look? And where are they? (You know, in one of my classes somebody said "93 kilometers from me." Wow! So specific. 93 kilometers from me. (laughs)) And now, sense whether you would like to have romance with them? What judgments do you have about this person? And ask whether they will be willing to romance you. And then you will be able to see what judgments you have about you with respect to money.

Most of them are points of view we bought into. What if we can go into 'interesting point of view'?

Can You Get Out Of The Rabbit Hole, If You Are Not In It

Caller: I have actually gone into the shell and not willing to see what it is. I've tried my best. I always had everything and all of a sudden things are crumbling down, lot of drama, you know, lot of pain and lot going on that is distracting me and… what should I run to get out of this? Can you give me any process?

The thing is I have always had everything, so my life was always happy -go-lucky. But all of a sudden for the last 2 years, I've been – I've been running my processes, I've done up to level 1.

But still it's like I'm in this box trying to get out, cannot get out. Is there any process that I can run? It's not just money, everything.

Nirmala: Ok, are you really in that box?

Caller: Feels like it.

Nirmala: Gary asked us once in facilitators', "If you are not in the rabbit hole, can you get out of it?"

Caller: I don't know how to

Nirmala: (laughs) If you are not in the rabbit hole, can you get out of it?

Caller: Um, I feel like I'm in rabbit hole.

Nirmala: Ok, so is that really true? Who does that belong to?

Caller: No clue, honey. Nothing comes up. It's – That's another thing, you know, I just go blank.

Nirmala: Ok, so what are you not willing to see?

Caller: The truth?

Nirmala: What are you not willing to know?

Caller: Truth

Nirmala: Truth? Ok, what is that?

Caller: My capacity?

Nirmala: *Ok. So everywhere you are not willing to be all of you, will you now destroy and un-create all of it? Right and wrong, good and bad, POD and POC, all nine, shorts, boys and beyonds.*

So what would happen if you are being all of you? Who will die? Who will leave?

Caller: I think half of me will die.

Nirmala: Is this point of view from this lifetime?

Caller: No

Nirmala: *So everywhere you have stored all these memories in the cellular structure, your BHCEEMCs (When we talk about BHCEEMCs, we're talking to ALL your bodies, your subtle bodies as well as your physical body. When you talk about your body, you only mean the physical body. In Access we want to clear everything including the explants, so therefore we talk about BHCEEMCs, which includes all time, all space, all dimensions, all realities, simultaneously) through all dimensions and realities, will you now revoke, rescind, recant, renounce, denounce, destroy and un-create all of it? Right and wrong, good and bad, POD and POC, all nine, shorts, boys and beyonds.*

So what else would happen if you are all of you? So what happened in that particular lifetime when you were all of you? What did you destroy?

Caller: Everything and everyone.

Nirmala: *So, everywhere you are punishing yourself for that, will you now destroy and un-create all of it? Right and wrong, good and bad, POD and POC, all nine, shorts, boys and beyonds.*

And all the oaths, vows, commitments, comealties, fealties, swearings you have never to be all of you ever again, for all eternity, will you now revoke, rescind, recant, renounce, denounce, destroy and un-create all of it? Right and wrong, good and bad, POD and POC, all nine, shorts, boys and beyonds.

Where is the box now?

Caller: I can see it falling apart. It's like walls are breaking.

Nirmala: Ok, run this clearing for 30 days, 30 times a day if possible

Lies About You

Question: "So what would it take for me and my body to be willing to be so different than anybody else that I can just be me and receive money and judgment included with total, ease, joy and glory?"

Nirmala: *Cool, but what conclusions do you have about your body and you? How did you decide that you are not different? Just look at you. How can you be not different? You are not only different but so unique. So where have you decided that you are just somebody, you are just like everybody else? Where did you get that point of view from? What lies have you bought about yourself and your body? So what are you making real and true and solid about you and your body that really isn't? Would you be willing to destroy and un-create all of it? Right and wrong, good and bad, POD and POC, all nine, shorts, boys and beyonds.*

Can you ask yourself every day what gift am I being here? And the second part of the question, if I am right, it is about receiving judgment. When somebody judges you or throws their judgments at you, instead of resisting you can simply ask "How much money would I receive if I receive this judgment without any point of view?" It changes the energy.

Nilofer: I love it.

Nirmala: You would have read in Foundation Class that if you receive a judgment without a point of view, you get $5000. So every judgment thrown at us is an opportunity to make $5000. Why would you resist that? And another tool I use is this - when judgment comes my way, and if I am resisting, my body tenses up. Somewhere in the body, I sense this barrier and I start opening the doors in the barrier. It could be a small window. It could be a door. You keep opening and just withdraw all the energy you have invested in keeping this barrier. Just withdraw for 5 seconds and see whether the barrier can stand on its own. It can't. It will start crumbling and the tightness in your body will disappear. You will be able to receive judgment with total ease. If you really can't let that go, just try to open a little tiny hole in the barrier and see what difference that makes. Once you start allowing little bit of judgment then you'll be able to receive more and more. It's also, building the muscle for it. Does that help?

Nilofer: Yes. Awesome! I love it. Withdrawing energy from the barriers. That's amazing…

Winning The Lottery

Question: "Hi. Since I was young I knew I would win a lot of money playing the lottery. Then a couple of years ago my mom, best friend and I started to buy tickets together. We truly felt and believed we would win big. It hasn't happened yet. Do you have any awareness, and/or clearing for me to create a big win? Thank you."

Nirmala: Ok, so in my experience or point of view, not having any expectation helps a lot. So when you have expectation, what happens is every second you judge whether you are meeting your expectations, whether you are building the energy to meet the expectations. Then you are living in the judgment. Every judgment is a barrier to receive.

All the projections, rejections, expectations, separations you have on you with regards to winning the lottery, will you now revoke, recant, rescind, renounce, denounce, destroy and un-create all of it? Right and wrong, good and bad, POD and POC, all nine, shorts, boys and beyonds.

And not having any point of view about it helps a lot. As I said, I don't buy lottery very often. I haven't bought any lottery tickets for two months or so. I don't have a point of view about it. And what if you can receive money from other sources? When you invest so much energy on winning or receiving money from lottery, are you restricting yourself from receiving money from other sources. Are you just closing the paths? Or are you not willing to see other sources? And are you willing to be the source of creation rather than lottery being the source of creation?

What judgments do you have about winning lottery and you winning lottery and not winning lottery? If you go into the judgment that you are not winning lottery and you are a failure, is that a contribution to you? It's all about receiving, right? It doesn't have to be from lottery. When you are fixated on something, we are actually closing the doors for others. I give this example – from London to Dubai, I can take different routes. I can take a plane. I can take a ship. I can even swim. I can take a road trip. And mixture of all these. When I ask the Universe to give me money for a plane ticket to go to Dubai, am I restricting myself from receiving a free ride on a private jet? So what's your destination? Are you fixated on the vehicle rather than the destination?

Nilofer: Love it.

Nirmala: Yeah. So ask yourself what energy would you like to have? How that comes into your life is Universe's job.

Let Go Of All The Conclusions

Question: "I am excited about growing my Access bars business. Can you provide clearings to assist me in pricing and charging money for my bars sessions and expanding my financial income with joy and ease? I'd love to participate in more Access classes and what would it take to have fun actualizing money? Thank you."

Nirmala: *What have you made so vital, valuable and real about not having money that keeps you from having more money than god? Everything that is, will you now destroy and un-create all of it, please? Right and wrong, good and bad, POD and POC, all nine, shorts, boys and beyonds.*

Making something vital means you are willing to lose yourself and destroy yourself in order to possess something. So, we also make Access business so vital. Sometimes we go into the conclusion that we can only make money through Access classes. What if it's not true? **What if you can do anything that is fun for you and receive money? Are you willing to receive money just for having fun? Are you willing to be paid for laughing?**

Nilofer: (laughs) I love that!

Nirmala: Most of us go into the conclusion that it is not possible.

How about creating a new reality of getting paid for laughing. Everything that does not allow that, will you now destroy and un-create all of it, please? Right and wrong, good and bad, POD and POC, all nine, shorts, boys and beyonds.

And again, is there a conclusion when you say "I don't have money to do Access classes." What if Gary and Dain invite you to their classes? Instead of asking for money for Access classes, how about you just asking – "what would it take for me to be there (in the class) and have total fun?" Are you willing to receive that invitation?

Sexualness And Money

"What is your first memory of money?" Most of the time you create your reality from that point of view. And from whom did you learn about money? And from whom did you learn about romance? From whom did you learn about seduction? And whom are we mimicking in all this? Everything that brings up for everybody, shall we now destroy and un-create all of it please? Right and wrong, good and bad, POD and POC, all nine, shorts, boys and beyond…

"What sexualness are you refusing to be?" When I ask this question, most of us go into being sexual in our body or with our body.

Nilofer: Yes

Nirmala: Yes. How do we feel in the nature?

Nilofer: Oh we feel so expansive.

Nirmala: Absolutely. So, is that because the plants are are not covering themselves up? Not really. It's because they don't judge themselves. They don't judge you. It's that kind of nakedness. Being naked with your being, your true being without any pretension, without any mask is the true sexualness.- Not judging ourselves, not judging others. Have you hugged a tree Nilofer anytime?

Nilofer: Yes

Nirmala: The energy I receive from trees is amazing for me. I still haven't received such a hug from any body yet. That really shows what kind of barriers we put in between us. Nature doesn't have that. That's the energy of sexualness. Are we willing to be that? How many defence systems do we have to defend our labels? I am this. I am that. I am not this. I am not that. I can never be this. I won't be that. So is it all true for an infinite being?

Nilofer: No

Nirmala: What sexualness are you not willing to be? And if we can be that, how many people will queue up for us? If you can be that sexualness, in a crowd, it's like having a forest there. Try playing with that energy and see how that changes things around you. "What invitation are you being for money?" You can ask this question every day - What invitation can I be for money? So are you willing to be that energy everybody likes to go to? I've heard people saying that people suck energy from them. When you have that point of view, you avoid people around you. What contribution is that to you and your life? When people draw energy from you, they see you bigger than themselves. Why would you resist that? And for an infinite being, is there any lack of energy? Not really.

Are you willing to be the source of creation for you and everybody around you? Everything that doesn't allow that, will you now destroy and un-create all of it? Right and wrong, good and bad, POD and POC, all nine, shorts, boys and beyonds.

And another question is, **"What are you not willing to be for money?"** Basically money comes to happy people. Are you willing to be that energy?

Are you willing to be everything for money? So everything that doesn't allow us to be, know, perceive and receive all of that, shall we now destroy and un-create all of it please? Right and wrong, good and bad, POD and POC, all nine, shorts, boys and beyonds.

Willingness To Reject Money

Are you willing to let go of the significance of money? How many form, structure and significance we have about money? One question that came to me all of a sudden really struck me – "Are you willing to reject money?" How many of us are willing to reject money? 'Why would I ever reject money?' was the response I went into.

I could not even comprehend why anybody would reject money. Then I got the awareness that when you are not willing to reject money, you are making money so significant and it owns you. I'll give you an example where rejecting money would be an advantage to you. Well, let's say you are on a boat with a huge bundle of cash, in your boat. And your boat starts sinking. To get help it's going to take a few minutes and if you are willing to throw away your money, you could be afloat until then. If you are not willing to reject money, what will happen to you? Would you have the choice to throw it away? You don't have to choose to reject money, but you have to be willing to reject money. That's the essence.

Just Take a U-Turn

Caller: For many years I was very sick and I was constantly told "oh you just messed up. You'll never do anything again." But now I'm well again and I want to, but it seems like that is locked in my body and I can't. I'm only functioning from that and it's really affecting me being able to make any money to support myself and to make my life better, and I wondered if you could help me shift out of that block?

Nirmala: Ok, cool. So if we create so much mess in our life, what does that mean? It just means that we are so creative; we have so much creative energy. You are so potent and you have created so much mess. So that means abundant energy is available to you. It's with you

Caller: Yes

Nirmala: It's like you have a great car and you have the fuel to go extra mile and you have been going in the wrong direction.

Caller: Yes

Nirmala: Now you have to take a U-turn. That's all it is.

Caller: A U-turn! Oh wow.

Nirmala: Yes. That's all it is because you've got all the ingredients for creating. Your life is evidence of that. You've created so much. So much of what is not working for you, but still you have created that, right?

So that means, you can uncreate it.

Caller: That's where I get stuck. I'm scared of un-creating it. I'm scared of my potency because I've always been put down for it in a really big way.

Nirmala: Nice. Ok. So who is saying that? Who are you being when you say that?

Caller: All the people who put me down.

Nirmala: Ok, so would you like to live their life or would you like to live your life?

Caller: I would really like to live my life.

Nirmala: *Would you like to return all of that, all the projections, rejection, expectations, separations that are creating all this to all of them? And revoke, rescind, recant, renounce, denounce, destroy and un-create all of it, wherever you are buying into all these? Right and wrong, good and bad, POD and POC, all nine, shorts, boys and beyonds.*

Are you willing to be that energy of destruction?

Caller: Ah, could you explain more? That made me feel scared.

Nirmala: *If you have decided that there's so much limitation, you would like to destroy them, right? So to destroy them, you have to be the energy of destruction. Are you willing to be that? Everything that doesn't allow that, will you now destroy and un-create all of it? Right and wrong, good and bad, POD and POC, all nine, shorts, boys and beyonds.*

And also you mentioned something about your body. The limitations about your body, is that right?

Caller: Yes

Nirmala: So are you listening to your body?

Caller: I'm learning now to listen. Just in the last few months since I started with Access.

Nirmala: *Everywhere you are not in complete communion with your body, will you now destroy and un-create all of it? Right and wrong, good and bad, POD and POC, all nine, shorts, boys and beyonds.*

Are you punishing your body for some reason?

Caller: Yes

Nirmala: What would that be?

Caller: Well, I think I was punishing my body all my life because I was sexually abused when I was very young and I've learnt now that I don't need to do that, so I just started to learn to love my body, but it's a new experience because it's not familiar. I don't have any model for it.

Nirmala: Right. Ok. One thing I've noticed in people who are abused, is that they tend to prove that it is wrong by making their life difficult.

Caller: Oh wow. Wow, that's so true.

Nirmala: *If you demonstrate that how people can be messed up by abuse, then you think that abuse will stop in the world. So why does it have to be that? What if you can show them a different possibility through joy? Would you be willing to do that? Everything that doesn't allow that, will you now destroy and un-create all of it? Right and wrong, good and bad, POD and POC, all nine, shorts, boys and beyonds.*

And also ask this question to you, "**What are you trying to tell and demonstrate with your body?**"

Caller: Do you want me to answer right now?

Nirmala: You could but you don't have to. You can just bring up the energy and destroy and un-create all of it.

Caller: Yes

Nirmala: *Instead of demonstrating whatever it is you are trying to prove, what if you can choose something else now? Everything that doesn't allow that, will you now destroy and un-create all of it? Right and wrong, good and bad, POD and POC, all nine, shorts, boys and beyonds.*

How much of your potency are you using against you? Would you be willing to use it for you?

Caller: Yes

Nirmala: What would happen if you use it for you?

Caller: I wouldn't be creating all these limitations.

Nirmala: Yeah. So what if you can create something joyful instead of going into "I wouldn't be creating all these limitations"? How about choosing something expansive? Do you have a fun list?

Caller: (laughs) No, I don't have a fun list. I...

Nirmala: Would you be willing to make one for you?

Caller: Ok.

Right now it's like every part of my life is a challenge so I never get to the fun part. I don't allow myself to get to the fun part.

Nirmala: Yes. So when you are so focused on the challenges, you are investing all your potency in defending the challenges. How about shifting gears and looking at the fun part now?

Make a list of every fun thing that you would like to do or be or like to receive. Could be anything like - smiling at a stranger, cuddling a baby, receiving flowers, looking at flowers. Could be anything. Or even bungee jumping.

Caller: I just had... I do that a lot in my everyday life. I look for - I create a lot of fun moments for me and my son and also for other people, even for strangers, I do.

Nirmala: Do you do that for you?

Caller: Yes, I get a lot of joy out of it.

Nirmala: Fantastic. Are you willing to expand that?

Caller: Yes

Nirmala: If you already do 30 minutes of fun, go for 1 hour.

Caller: Yes

Nirmala: Doing fun things for you, not for anybody else. For you. For you.

Caller: I think I've been doing them for everybody else but I haven't thought about doing it for me. I get the joy from it, but I haven't thought about it being for me, because, you know, you don't do it for yourself. That's right. (laughs)

Nirmala: Start with you, and see how the world changes around you.

Caller: Wow, thank you. You really – I'm astonished at how you went to the heart of it and the energy of where I was immediately. I really love it.

Nirmala: Thank you for receiving. Receiving is a gift, you see.

Nilofer: Wow. It's been just so phenomenal, Nimi. You know, I'm getting comments on the webcast saying thank you, thank you, thank you! "A huge thank you. The most phenomenal one so far in the series. Nirmala is amazing. Thank you! What a phenomenal call." Wow, we have all kinds of fun stuff. Thank you.

Nirmala: Thank you very much for receiving.

Q&A

What can I be and what tools can I use to know I have and am money in totality? I have money, I'd just love to have more coming in continuously with ease. I appreciate very much everything that is showing up for me.

Be the questions you have just asked. You can also add, 'What energy space and consciousness can I and my body be that would allow me to create and generate money continuously with total ease?' Keep the desire going and have fun with creating and generating!

Would you speak and help us clear around the fear of success and fear of failure please?

What have you defined success or failure as? Whose standard are you validating? When there is nobody around you, what would be your success or failure? Are you trying to fit into the definitions of this reality? Is that why it is heavy for you?

Besides, fear is a distractor implant and clearing them would help. Most of the time fear of failure or success is related to safety or survival. How many life times you were tortured and killed for your success or failure that you decided you would never be that again for all eternity?

Everything that brings up will you destroy and uncreate all of it?

I keep regretting the past where I could have easily saved money and didn't, I feel angry with myself, what else is possible?

What would you be aware of if you are not judging yourself? What are you not willing to be aware of now? Is this anger yours in the first place? What conclusions are you going into about your capacity to create and generate money? What if the amount you could have saved would be just a pocket change if you only acknowledged your capacity?

What would it take to eliminate the lies of not enough?

What have you made so vital about holding on to this lie that keeps you from having infinite choices?

From whom did you buy this lie? Whose reality have you committed to validate? Everything that is will you destroy and uncreate all of it?

Gratitude is a great antidote to lack. Are you willing to do a gratitude list everyday and look at what you have in plenty in your life?

I am working with an MNC since 2 years. For the past few months i am wanting to generate multiple source of income & not just be restricted to one fixed job. What kind of questions should ask to create possibilities?

Just be the question. Be the energy of wonder and curiosity just like a child. What/who would like to contribute to your income today? What choices are available for you that you have not even considered yet?

If I should not have expectation, then should I even be setting targets about how much money I would like to have in my life?

You can have desires; you can have targets . Desire creates more. Target is movable. But if you are expecting a fixed outcome, you get into the judgment of your creation every second comparing it with the outcome you have in your mind. Judgment kills creation. Besides, if you are fixated on a particular outcome, would you even be able to see if something greater showed up?

How do I release a strong tightness in my chest and in my heart? I've trusted others instead of myself. How do I be me in the world?

Is it really true? Are you trying to define and understand who you are? Can an infinite being be put into boxes? Can't you be anything you wish to be? What can you be today that you have never considered before?

Would you be willing to let go of all the stories you are telling yourself and choose whoever you like to be in this 10 sec?

I'm aware that I slipped in smallness when I spoke up to someone and they didn't hear me. For me it created discomfort...........later, I did my best to let the other person that it didn't work for me. It created distance and anger from the other person, I was not blaming. How do I not go into the wrongness of me......and not keep hiding.

Are you resisting the judgments from the other person? What if you allow them to have their point of view and see them as just interesting?

What are you not willing to be here that if you are willing will create total ease in this situation?

How can I be more aware of when to buy and sell GOLD in terms of trading in KGs

Just ask the gold to tell you

I have always had this comfort with money... And always been sure that money will always be there.. being active doing things, creating things is what has helped create money... After Access, am actually in this space where i am concerned that I won't have enough money.. What is that... Is it my awareness about money.... Somehow the ease with money is going while it should be the other way around.... Clarity please.

Are you gaining more awareness about other people's financial realities around you? How can you use it to your advantage instead of against you?

How can I use and be the energy to receive the money that is owed to me?

Pull massive amount of energy from the person who owes you money and send back trickles of energy to them. See how that works for you. Have you also asked the money to return to you?

I would like for constant inflow of money to me... It comes stops, comes stops, comes stops... What is this about?

Good question. Aren't you looking for consistency or stability? How many stability points are you using that limits you from receiving money more than you can ever spend?

If you are given a choice to choose between one billion dollars once or five thousand dollars every month for rest of your life, which one would you choose? Both the choices are not wrong, but when you make one thing significant aren't you closing the door way to the other?

What would it take for you to have total ease with money regardless of the consistency in flow?

How can my body and I be a better 'Receiver' and 'BE' money with Ease joy and glory? How can I get past the fear of 'Not having enough' at any given moment- now or in the future?

What are you not willing to be/receive/know and perceive? Poc and Pod all that every day 30 times a day for 30 days. When you function as an infinite being nothing is impossible.

Would you be willing to speak about how people use the tools of Access to be unkind, I get that Access says just Be You......with no apology , is that permission to be mean, without taking any responsibility? I've witnessed people using the user whore (A user whore is one who will do something for money. If you are not willing to be a user whore, then you have to judge everything you do to determine whether you are not being that. You keep trying to prove you're not a whore by not taking money for things you do well) thing as a way to get whatever they want no matter what? That seems heavy to me , I do appreciate the tools of Ac-

cess. There's something in it though that seems to mixed up................I'm willing to do whatever it takes yet not willing to run someone over to get there................are we all in this together? What else is Possible? It seems some Access people don't give a **** and it's all about them...........I know you may say that's interesting point of view and could it possibly be true.

Access tools are very potent and of course people can choose how to use them. I have personally experienced this as well but I see that as my unwillingness to be unaware of what was coming. As infinite beings, don't we all choose what we create – whether to run people over or to be run over?

I choose to use the tools to create grand changes in my life and by doing so invite people to see different possibilities. What about you?

I would like to attend the facilitators training in Venice in March and I can't seem to create the money for it. I would have to create min. 5.000 Euro in order to attend and the idea of creating that much money in such short time is a beyond for me. And I keep putting this off because in the back of my mind there is this something telling me I can't do it. It feels like I am stuck, and where is the lie here? What else is possible here?

When you feel stuck, you require more information. Ask what information you would require and what/who can provide you that? Also destroy and uncreate all the conclusions you have about money. Who is bigger – you or 5000 EUR?

I have been living on rent for years. Buying my own house seemed long in the future always. Now that I know I can have anything I desire to buy a fun and elegant house. Please suggest clearings for night loop, questions to create, generate and have amazing house NOW. I have been asking this house to find me for long time and playing with questions too.

Ask the house that likes you to own it to reveal itself to you and ask your body to be a contribution. Have you asked where your body would like to live? Get the energy of the energy where your body likes to live in... pull massive amounts of energy from the Universe, send the trickle out to the entire Universe. Do this as often as you like and see what magic you can create.

FUN WITH VIDEOS WITH NILOFER

Recently Blossom Benedict posted a 30 Day Video Challenge. I created videos everyday as part of the challenge. It was totally fun. Simple tools of Access Consciousness and my insightful moments. I've posted them on my blog at www.nilofersafdar.com

---

CHAPTER EIGHT

ARE YOU USING THE MOLECULES OF YOUR BODY TO YOUR ADVANTAGE?

By Katherine McIntosh

Innovative Leader, Speaker

Facilitator on Business, Health,

Wealth, and living a vibrant lifestyle

CFMW

What Would It Be Like If You Created The Molecules Of Your Body As The Universe Of Infinite Possibilities

I left the conversation almost entirely as what it was because in the conversation there was so much magic. Do you ever have a conversation with a friend and know that the conversation just changed everything in your Universe? This conversation was one of those places.

What if your body held the key to opening a doorway to possibilities that you've never even considered? What if the molecules of your body were here to gift you a different way of being? This conversation for me was sharing my own personal journey of knowing that the molecules of our body are here to create magic. And it was to invite you into the places where you could create that in your body, life, and living. The molecules of the Universe are all around us and they are here to contribute to us and be the energy we desire to create and see on the planet. My hope is that this conversation gifts you a doorway into a new way of being with your body.

What if Judgment Wasn't Real? What Would You Create?

N: Wow. Wow. It's been an amazing series so far and every call is like wow! What else is possible? (laughs) So I wonder, I just wonder where we are going to go today?

K: (laughs) I wonder! I love that question.

I never know, but I'm always amazed where we go. So I wonder what we'll create today?

N: So where should we go Katherine, today? (laughs)

K: Yeah, I mean, I love the topic, right? We are inviting the molecules into this doorway of possibility and I was sharing with you before we started, like I had these 'aha's. I was at the hot springs just now, soaking my body in these hot springs and just looking at how we define our bodies, how we define who we are. And if we didn't define our molecules, or our bodies or our businesses or anything, what do the molecules of our body actually want to create?

And so, it's this idea that we can be whoever we want whenever we want and so can our bodies. And especially in this reality, we are told "this is your body, this is what you are doing with it. This is how you are going to either create it or not create it" and you have to fit it into this construct and I wonder, especially with these doorways to possibilities, how many of the molecules of our body are constantly seeking the possibility of something?

Most often, when we ignore how our bodies can contribute we are essentially saying: "sorry, I can't hear you. No, we have to go to the gym. This is how we are supposed to form the body." or "we need to go to this healer for the answer".

I really wonder with the molecules of our body, with our bodies being infinite, what's truly possible with the future when we are willing to open the infinite doorways to possibilities?

N: Wow. What's truly possible with the future? Wow. Wow.

K: Right?

N: You know, with 4 questions, you've fried us! (laughs) How does it get any better than that?

K: Exactly. Exactly. If we were willing to get out of form, structure, significance, definition, judgment, and conclusion, the molecules of our bodies want to live in joy, they want to be in space, they want to receive possibility.

What could we create if we invited ourselves on the journey that our body would like to take us on?

N: So I wonder what journey our body wants to take us on? Can you speak to that a little more and maybe share how it has shown up for you?

K: Yeah. I'll share how it showed up for me. I was born into an Irish Catholic family. I was definitely born into rules and regulations and the judgment of how you are supposed to function. If you go to church, you are a good girl. If you don't go to church, you are not a good girl. You have to go to penance and repent your sins and I didn't realize how much that one thing structured my reality through the window of judgment. I had to judge everything I did as good or bad. I had to judge everything I was as good or bad and right or wrong.

I was an athlete, I had really great communion with my body, I had really great agility and then when I turned 15, I started to enter into the age of really judging and criticizing my body, so I didn't see this beautiful, athletic, agile, capable body. I started to go to the place of judgment and say what was wrong with it instead of what was actually right with it.

And so I went on this 20 year long journey of trying to get my body to do what I thought it needed to do, to look the way I thought I wanted it to look, and when I got to the visual of what I thought I wanted my body to look like, I was dead inside.

I had no life left to give because my entire structure was created around judgment.

Am I eating enough? Am I eating too much? Am I exercising enough? Am I not exercising enough? What's right about me? What's wrong about me?

And so literally, I took up so much mental capacity in my life around my body, food, and my weight because I was structuring my life around judgment.

No Judgment Diet

And then I gave birth to a son and when he was 2 months old, I was doing my normal judging of my body. (laughs)

I was looking in the mirror and seeing all these things I didn't want to see. And then all of a sudden, I looked over at my son who was smiling and giggling and waving at me and I was like "wow! I just spent 6 minutes missing out on receiving his brilliance because I was too busy deciding, deciphering and judging what was wrong with me and my body."

N: Wow

K: And when that happened, it was like such an 'aha' in my whole being and I went "I'm stopping this right now". This pattern has to stop. I just missed out on 6 minutes of pure energy, joy, and gratitude from a being who had no judgment in his Universe.

And the light bulb that went off was like a voice of reason that said: "If I just missed out on that, where else am I missing out on receiving possibility because I'm too busy judging myself and my body?"

Everything I tried, whether it was a diet pill or an exercise regimen or the grapefruit diet, I still never had all of me with my body like I did before I was 15.

And so in that moment I said "this is stopping right now" and I went on pretty much what I call a year-long no-judgment diet. And so anytime I wanted to judge my body, judge the shape, judge the size, judge the food I was eating, judge the amount of exercise I was or was not doing, I literally would say "stop" and I'd walk away and I'd create what I call a generative thought.

So I'd create a thought that was like "oh, I love my body. Oh my god, my body is awesome. I wonder what space I could create today?" and what that did, Nilofer, is not only did it get me into a better space with my body where my body shows me the possibilities when I stop judging it, but I had all this space to create a six-figure business.

So I was nursing a baby and building a six-figure business (without knowing it) and a year later, I looked back and I went "oh my gosh!" I had so much space to create from because I wasn't taking up all this mental energy of my normal pattern of judging myself for food or my body.

Molecules Of Possibilities

K: Yeah. And so this idea of your molecules is that your molecules literally desire to gift you the space of you. However when we are in judgment, we can't receive the space of possibility. Judgment and awareness cannot exist at the same time.

So if everyone was to tap into the molecules of their body right now, into the molecules of the space around you, because the molecules of your body desire to interact with all the possibilities.

Right?

Or do they desire to criticize or conclude what you did or didn't do today?

It's like, no, your body is like "screw it!"

The molecules want to play in the space around us to help us create our future.

N: Wow

K: And so what I realized through my own journey of judgment, conclusion, enough/not enough, is that it was never enough.

I was never skinny enough. I was never pretty enough. I was never good enough in my body.

It's like that stopped me from creating my future. So when I started to communicate with the molecules to see what was possible, these doorways of my future opened in a way that I can't necessarily explain. I can only give you the energy transmission of all of it. When I changed this one thing, my whole visual way of seeing things changed.

And so our molecules in our bodies are so infinite, they are so willing to contribute to us every day and we are like "no, we can't hear you" because we are thinking about going to the gym or we are busy thinking about when our next meal is going to be or we are busy thinking about how much money isn't in our bank accounts. Right?

N: Wow

K: Yeah.

N: Wow. That is so amazing. So it was just like a choice on your part to say 'no', you know. "I'm not doing this anymore. I'm stopping this." And then going on a year long choice of saying "I'm not doing this anymore."

I Judge Myself Everyday

K: Yeah, and you know, people now ask me "Do you not judge yourself?" and I'm like "No! I judge myself every day. But every day I know that it is a choice." And the reality of it is, I'm not actually judging myself, I am picking up on all the judgments of this reality and thinking they are real.

I mean, how many people in this reality absolutely love their bodies? How many people in this reality don't judge how much or how little food they've eaten or need to eat?

Right?

So, because we are aware beings and 98% of our thoughts, feelings and emotions don't belong to us, we are picking up on other people's judgments thinking they are our judgments.

And so I probably have at least a 100 judgments that pass through my awareness every day and some of them I grab onto and I buy as real but I know now that none of them are actually mine. (laughs)

And so, it's this moment in time where I look at a fork in the road and I can either go left down the road of judgment or right down the road of possibilities.

And so it's not that the judgments don't occur for me, it's just that I know that they are not real anymore. And so I literally, I judge myself every day, or more appropriately, I am aware of all the judgments that are in the Universe around food, body, weight, and not enough. I sometimes still think they're mine. We're cute! (laughs) Right?

I know that I am no longer at the effect of them unless I choose to give them energy. It's what you said Nilofer, the key moment is that we think that to get judgment-free, we won't ever have anymore judgments, but that's not true.

If you are an aware being and you are aware of people all over the planet and you are aware of other countries and other cultures and your parents and your siblings and your children, you are going to pick up on their judgments and so judgments happen all day long.

It's just a matter of knowing you don't have to choose to buy them as real and then become at the effect of them, because when we choose judgment, we stop opening the doorway to possibilities. And we stop inviting our molecules to co-create a possibility or a future beyond what we can imagine.

N: Wow. You know, I love that, Katherine. You being so vulnerable to share that you do have the judgment because it is that. It is like most people buy into this "oh that means there is not going to be judgment anymore" but it is knowing that there is judgment and it's like every moment you are choosing a different possibility for yourself.

So, you know, how easy or how difficult was it when you actually started your year long no-judgment diet?

K: You know, when I started it, it was easy. I mean, roughly. It took me like 90 days to actually enter into the space of me. Right?

Because every day it was like "oh, I'm looking in the mirror. There's the judgment" or "I'm about to eat breakfast. There's the judgment." "Oh, I'm eating so much. There's the judgment." So it took me, like a habit, I had to re-form my way of being and in the beginning, the year was actually easy. It's funny now, you know, 2 years after my son was born – he's now almost 2 and 3 months, it's actually like I'm watching another layer of judgment rise to the surface and asking me and my molecules and my body, "what are you going to choose?

Here's another layer in which you could expand your life. Are you willing to actually go the distance to not buy that judgment as real?"

So in the last few months, I've had just interesting changes in my body as I become more aware and you know, moments of intensity and discomfort and judgment and it has actually become or has been a little more challenging in the last few months to continue to encourage myself to not buy the judgments as real.

But the truth is, I know it's not real and I'm just going through another level of change, so I wonder what this change will create? When we don't solidify anything as real, then we have a chance to change it.

N: I'm like listening to you and I'm going "I'm having that! I'm going on a year long no-judgment diet!" So what tools would you share with all of us who are wanting to step through that doorway of possibility of no judgment?

K: I think the biggest, the first thing is to choose it. The first thing is what you said – "I'm having that!" That's the first step, right? And then the second step is just to make the commitment so it's kind of like when Gary encourages us to ask the question "who does this belong to?" for 3 days straight.

There are moments when you totally remember to ask that question and then there are moments you forget, and then you just come back to it, right?

And so with this no judgment diet, it's to make the choice to say "no" and walk away from every judgment.

N: Oh wow.

K: Yeah, so it's making the choice and then it's just continuing to make the choice and not make yourself wrong when you forget. You just go back to it.

I have blonde hair, right? So I can always say "oh, I'm having a blonde moment. I forgot to do my no judgment diet today." And then I start again. Right?

So it's not that we ever get anything perfect, it's just that we continue to encourage the choice to be the dominant possibility.

N: Yeah, so it's like for me, you know, I am just aware in the day of the times when I'm so aware of the trauma and the drama and whatever, and then I'm also aware that I'm buying into it at some point and then I go "oh, so where is possibility here? Oh, it can't exist with all of this. Oh, never mind, you know, I'm not doing this anymore. I'm just choosing possibility."

Bodies

K: Right. And especially with the body, here's sort of what I've discovered for me, and I've discovered or helped a lot of intuitive people or people that are healers or people that are really aware. If you are somebody who has struggled with your body image, or struggled with the pain in your body or the disease in your body or struggled with your digestion, chances are that your body actually has a gift and capacity and brilliance with bodies that you have not yet acknowledged.

N: Wow

K: Yeah, and so for everyone who's listening, is it light for you that you have a gift and capacity with your body that you haven't yet acknowledged?

Ok, cool, so should we dive into the Access Consciousness clearing statement?

Everything that doesn't allow you to acknowledge the gift and capacities that you have with your body and other bodies, will you destroy and un-create it please? Right and wrong, good and bad, POC and POD, all nine, shorts, boys and beyonds.

Anything that doesn't allow you to dive into trusting that your molecules desire to contribute joy and possibility to you and your body, will you destroy and un-create that please? Right and wrong, good and bad, POC and POD, all nine, shorts, boys and beyonds.

What have you made so vital about using judgment as the source to creating your body? Everything that is times a godzillion, will you destroy and un-create it please? Right and wrong, good and bad, POC and POD, all nine, shorts, boys and beyonds.

You know, it's like we think that if we judge our bodies into "oh, you are not skinny enough, you are not pretty enough, you are not white enough, you are not dark enough, you are not tan enough, you have too many freckles, you know, you are wrinkling, you have too many grey hairs, we think that if we judge those pieces, that they'll change.

But the problem – and I think we know this from Access Consciousness – is that judgment actually solidifies it into place.

So if you judge that you are too fat or you're too skinny or that you are too old or you have too many wrinkles, you actually solidify that into your body as a reality rather than giving the molecules of your body a different possibility.

Judgment creates the solidity of it as if it's true.

And so for those of you on the call, think of someone in your life who does not look their age. They look younger than they actually are. Right?

Think of someone who maybe looks, you know, muscular-wise, they look 10 or 20 years younger.

Or think of somebody who doesn't have any issues with food, and tap into the space of who they are being with themselves and their body. There we go. Yeah, it's like when I ask that question, I see space.

N: You know what, Katherine, can I stop you for a minute here?

K: Yes please!

N: I actually cannot find anyone who is like that.

K: Really?

N: I mean, I look at the people who are skinny and when I tap into the space I'm like so aware of how they've created their body from a lot of judgment, like 2-3 people pop into my awareness who are like that. Wow.

K: Yeah

N: So this really is like, you know, how much people are creating their lives from judgment.

Ask Your Molecules To Show You The Space Of Possibility With Your Body

K: Yeah, and so with the topic of using the molecules to create a different possibility, everyone on the call you want to ask yourselves, ask your molecules to show you the space of possibility with your body it would like to create for you.

N: Oh

K: Right. The molecules are like "yes please! We've been waiting our entire lives to be able to contribute to you but you're busy judging, calculating, concluding."

It's just like when we ask the Universe to contribute to showing us a different possibility, we can do that with the molecules of our bodies. Our bodies desire to play with us. Right? And so, what would it be like if you created the molecules of your body as the Universe of infinite possibilities?

N: Wow.

K: Right. So I actually, Nilofer, do have a couple of people. Like I have a friend who is about to turn 50 and I'm 39 and he looks younger than I do by at least 5 years.

N: Wow

K: And I'm always like "wow, that's so amazing! I'll take more of that!" You know in my own journey, there's days when I look 25-30 and then there are days when I look older than I am. I mean it doesn't always happen that I look older (at least I hope not). When we are being space then people view us from space not conclusion. But when we are concluding about how we look, about our bodies, about what our bodies are capable of, then people pick up on those judgments and they see us through our own judgments.

N: Wow

K: Right. So everyone who's willing to see themselves through space, like if you were willing, Nilofer, to see your body through space, what would you see? Who would you be? How much more energy would you have? And would your future look different than it does now?

N: Wow. So I was facilitating someone a couple of weeks back on the body and we literally got to that space and that was I think the first time I really experienced that with my body and after 10 minutes, we were like done. We didn't have anything more to talk about because there was just possibility there.

K: Yeah, and I love that, Nilofer, because when there's possibility and there's space and there's silence and there's nothing to talk about, this reality goes into the judgment of 'something must be wrong'. (laughs)

N: Oh my god, no! She had come over and we were doing like a swap and we were facilitating each other and we were like after 10 minutes "oh wow!" and we were just happy to play with our bodies after that.

K: And that, Nilofer, is the difference that you be when you are willing to be space. And so, you know, people that do that, it's such a gift. Because every time we choose space. Every time we choose more. We invite our bodies, we invite our beings, we invite the molecules to continue to create a different possibility. But most people don't function from that reality, so that's the difference that you be.

N: Wow. You've just turned my whole reality upside down, Katherine! How does it get any better than that? (laughs)

K: (laughs) What else is possible?

N: What else is possible? And I'm just so aware of that space and of the space that I be and I'm like "I don't have any reference points anymore." How does it get any better than that?

K: Right, it's that!

N: How does it get any better than that?

Invite Your Body Into The New Space

K: Exactly. And when we don't have any reference points, my favorite tool I use when my reference points are gone is to ask the question: "What can I create from here?"

Here's a great tool, Nilofer – you want to invite your body into the new space. Right?

There are moments in my life and this isn't necessarily Access' point of view, this is my own journey through my own body from doing a lot of work with transforming my life. Sometimes with all the change, I forget to include my body in the journey. When that happens, I have to look back at my body and say "ok body, come on. You can come too!" Right?

And so if you are in this place where you've created a new space of possibility for yourself, invite the body along if it's not already with you. When we invite the body along, how much more can we actually create?

Because lucky for all of us listening on this call, we all have bodies. (laughs) Right?

We are really smart to have a body in this reality and so we are often creating all these possibilities in this Universe and sometimes, we are like "oh, wait. I feel strange. Or I feel weird. Or my body's hurting", you might want to ask "oh body, am I including you? Body, how can I contribute to you?

Would you like to come along too?"

Everything that doesn't allow you to invite your body into who you already are, into the space that you've been creating your whole life, will you destroy and un-create it please? Right and wrong, good and bad, POC and POD, all nine, shorts, boys and beyonds.

And I'm wondering Nilofer, if we could do 1-2-3 to invite our bodies to come along?

Yeah. Yeah, there we go. Will that work?

N: Oh my god, totally!

K: Cool

N: Wow

K: So everybody out there on the call if you could just expand out and if you are fast, you are going to go a hundred thousand miles out in every direction immediately. If you need a little more time, go ten miles out then a hundred miles, but yeah, you guys are fast. Ok, so 100,000 miles out in every direction and see if you want to go out a little bit more. There we go. Or a lot more. Right?

This is your journey, not mine. (laughs)

There you go. And then see all of the spaces that you've been creating your entire life and all of your lifetimes. There we go. And then we are going to go 1-2-3 to invite our bodies to come along and access all of that information, all of that space and all of those possibilities. Ok, ready? And so, with a 1-2-3, are you ready? 1-2-3!

And all we are doing is contributing energy to create a new possibility, right?

This is a possibility. Yeah, there we go! And if you are smiling, if your body just felt happier, if you just got happier, then that's all you need to know that it's working. (laughs)

I'll have more of that, Nilofer.

N: Wow, wow. You know what's really interesting, Katherine, was like about 2 or 3 years ago when I was going to do my tele-summit, I wanted to actually have the theme as 'The Greatness of Embodiment' and I was talking to one of the facilitator's and she said, "you know what, Nilofer, not many people get what greatness of embodiment is, so that won't really work for you." And then, I had a conversation with Gary and we actually chose 'Creation from Joy' and I'm wondering if that's what we and our bodies are not willing to step into and be aware of what greatness of embodiment is really?

K: Yeah. Not many people are willing to have the greatness of embodiment. It's not just the greatness of being in your body, but it's the greatness of being in your being and being aware of everything all around you. It's about seeing that there are a million choices to choose from all the time.

Our bodies love choice. They love choice. Right? It's like how many of you look forward to the idea of going to a buffet, where, you know, to give this analogy, you have 5 different buffets of gourmet sushi and gourmet seafood and you have every possibility that you could ever want on a buffet. Your body is like "yes please, yes please!" and then our humanness goes "oh my god, that's way too many choices. I think I'll over-eat. I've got to get it all in, in one sitting" versus "what would you like to play with today?" And so this idea of the joy of embodiment is giving your body permission to have infinite choice available. Right? When we're in judgment, can we choose? (laughs)

N: No

K: Right. Not from the space that we are talking about. I mean, you can make a choice but probably it's not your best choice. Right. And so for everybody…

N: Wow

K: Yeah, go ahead, Nilofer

N: There's a question, which I think might be like really – at this point of time – "My body and I, the being, are very grateful for being on the call. People often ask me 'how does one be?' So my question is, how would you address it, Katherine?"

K: Well, it's like if you are trying to be, you are doing. (laughs)

Whenever we are trying, there's this element and so being is that – how does one be? It's like when you are sleeping, you are not efforting trying to sleep. Right?

You just drift off into this infinite space. When you are walking, most of you don't effort walking. Right?

Or when you are breathing, you are not going "ok, I better inhale and then exhale." Right? You just do it and so anything that we are "doing" that there's no thought, there's no effort, that is the energy of being. It's like void of the judgment, void of questioning yourself and you know, simply if you look at a baby, right? And the energy of a baby when it's born, they are just like whoa! Wide-eyed and willing to gift anyone and anything. Right?

And I think this energy of being is willing to gift anyone and anything at any moment without requiring anything in return. Right?

Like the Earth is a perfect example of this. Give, give, give, give, give, it never actually expects anything in return but I get now that where we are with the Earth, we need to start to contribute back to it, so it can stay around for a few more hundreds of thousands of years. And I love that question that person asked, so it's like what I would say to every-body is what do you know about being?

Because each of us has a gift that I can't spit the answer out to but that only you know what that element is, like Nilofer, I love being on your series because you are so much space and you have this joy-like curiosity and also there's vulnerability to you that is such a gift and an invitation and you can't really explain the energy of that. It's just who you be. And each of us has that.

N: Yeah, just before the call I was just going through Facebook and I saw this video. And it's a video of a baby and this guy is giving the baby a massage and it's not like the normal massage that we do, but he was just like, he was tapping the baby, he was doing those little karate chop movements on the baby and the baby had such a joy in the body. It's like my body is looking at it and oooh, you know. (laughs) and I said "oh my god, that is so amazing."

And that's what you are saying it's the willingness to gift anyone and anything without requiring anything in return and I realized that's what the baby was doing at that point in time. Just gifting everyone that energy and I saw the number of likes and the shares under that video were like phenomenal! So like wow!

Would You Be Willing To Gift Your Body Anything And Everything At Anytime Without Expecting Anything In Return

K: Well, and here's a great question to include the body - would you be willing to gift your body anything and everything at anytime without expecting anything in return? (laughs)

N: Wow

K: Right? Most of us go, "ok, if I do this then my body will do this. If I do this, then I'll feel this in my body." Right?

But that's like a give and take Universe rather than gift and receive Universe. So...

N: So how do you get out of the give-and-take Universe into the gift-and-receive Universe?

K: Choice. (laughs)

N: Oh, Katherine! Give me a tool! (laughs)

K: (laughs) That's what Gary would say to you, "choice, Nilofer, choice."

So, choice, you know, and it's noticing if you are doing something with an expected outcome in return versus just doing it for the joy of it. Just doing it because it feels good, because you can, because your body is asking for water or to soak in a hot spring or to go for a run, not "oh, I'm going for a run because this is my expected outcome." Or "I'm going to eat kale for a week because this is my expected outcome." Right?

No, you do it from the joy of it and if stops being joyful, stop doing it, because then you are placing an expectation on it.

But when we gift – and this is where my own journey of my body, you know, getting out of no-judgment is still occurring every day. In this journey it showed me that when I was willing to get out of conclusion of this give-and-take Universe with my body. "ok, if I eat this many calories, then I'm going to have to do this much exercise" or "if I eat bacon, it's going to increase my cholesterol" or whatever it was, it was just constant calculation in my head that I didn't even realize I was doing. Right?

And so when I got out of that, I started doing things and eating and exercising from the joy because it was fun for my body. And when I started to do that, my body took on a shape that was really yummy, that my whole molecular structure of my body completely changed when I did that. And I got, you know, I had more awareness, I had more space for me, there was just this **possibility that I didn't even know I could function from.**

N: I love that. "Possibility that I didn't even know that I could function from."

K: Right! So how many doorways of possibilities are waiting for each of you with body, with the molecules of your body that you didn't even know you could function from? Like if any of you are out there thinking "I'm going to be in pain for the rest of my life" what if one of those doorways is you don't have to choose that anymore?

N: Wow

K: Yeah. And then what could you invite or what are the molecules of your body attempting to invite you into that you could begin to choose?

Everything that doesn't allow you to hear the subtle whispers of possibility, will you destroy and un-create it? Right and wrong, good and bad, POC and POD, all nine, shorts, boys and beyond…

Doorways

And I love your title "doorways" because it's like how many of us when a doorway opens, we are expecting it to be like this loud knock from the Universe and saying "here's your door! You just need to walk through it."

The Universe actually is whispering all the time with these subtle doorways, these subtle moments of choosing a greater possibility, of choosing more, of having more joy, of being more space, of just being.

N: And what would it take for those wisps of possibility to be so magnified that you could never ever miss them? I wonder...

K: Yeah. Well, can we do a 1-2-3 to make them more visible, more audible?

N: Yes

K: Yeah. So ask to expand out 100,000 miles. You guys are quick. (laughs) a 100,000 miles out in every direction, I love it. Quick beings, I love playing with quick beings. It's fun.

So we'll go 1-2-3. And lets do one more and actually because I was going to do it hard, but I got the energy of soft, so it's like doing a 1-2-3 but almost from the place of whispering it into existence. Yeah! There we go! Ok, so ready? 1-2-3.

Because it's like, truth be told, a whisper doesn't like to be shouted at. (laughs) A whisper probably likes being whispered back to. So we are doing a 1-2-3 from a whisper, yeah. How much more space does that create?

Choice As A Source Of Creation

N: So Katherine, talk about creations from this space.

K: Yeah

N: And how did that show up in your life?

K: Yeah, you know, one of the things that I've been talking about very recently is the idea that – and it was on the lines of an obesity tele-call Gary did, is that most of us use judgment as the source of creation. And so I asked him "what do you use as the source of creation?" thinking that his answer was going to be him and he said "choice" and when I got that, it was like wow! The Universe is asking us too just choose to be our infinite magical, amazing selves every day and we've got our head in the sand or we are like so focused on moving forward that we forget that at every moment we have infinite choice available to create.

I still use judgment as the source of creation without even knowing it, but when I stopped functioning from judgment as a source of creation in my body, I created a six-figure business, I created more joy in my body and I started to create a life and living I actually knew was possible.

I just didn't know how to choose it until I stopped judging myself and then I could start choosing it. So for me, I got to travel around the world, I now facilitate classes all over the planet, I have clients in a ton of different countries and some days, I'm just like "pinch me!" this is my reality because I wake up every day and I go "what can I create today?"

Some days, I'm heavy in my body. Some days I'm like "oh, this is uncomfortable" and then other days, it's like "wow, that was so magical. What would it take to do that again? What would it take to have more of that?"

Choice is the source of creation and when we give our bodies choice, because how many of us are truly willing to give our bodies choice from no point of view? Everything that just brought up, will you destroy and un-create it? Right and wrong, good and bad, POC and POD, all nine, shorts, boys and beyonds.

And I don't know if I totally answered your question, Nilofer...

N: I'm like, you know, blissed out. (laughs) This space of body...

(laughs) and my body and I, we got the energy of it, so thank you. And it's like I realize I'm trying to put "how to" to it, when it's just energy, the space and the consciousness. And that's what my body is showing me.

Body, Show Me The Magic

K: Yeah. And thank you for saying that, because here's the deal that I could talk you through it but it won't be the same as you getting it. Right?

Because how my body does it is totally different than how your body does it, is totally different than how Gary's body does it. It's totally different than how everybody on the call's body does it. Because each of our bodies has a gift and capacity that some of you may have begun to acknowledge, some of you may have totally acknowledged it, and 10 years into this journey with my body, you know, only 2 years into no judgment and I feel I'm uncovering all of the ways that my body is showing me the magic. And so each of you, it's not a "how to", it's more like *"well, what does my body know about this?"*

N: And I love that *"body, show me the magic."*

K: Yeah. *"Body, show me the possibilities. Body, show me all the molecules that have been wanting to play with me today and I've been too busy trying to do rather than be."* You know, *"molecules show me the energy of me when I'm being me."* And if you ask those questions enough, you'll live your way into being it.

N: Wow.

K: But you have to be willing to make the choice to discover what that is for you because nobody can tell you how to be you. Right?

Nobody can tell your body how to be your body.

You have to be willing to just be curious. To discover what that is for you, and when you unlock that magic, nobody can stop you from being who you truly be.

Except for you. (laughs)

N: Oh yeah, except you.

K: Except for you. We get in our way on a daily basis and it's just that choice. It's not about...

N: We are so brilliant at that, right? (laughs)

K: Brilliant. We are – if only we were as brilliant at constantly opening the doorways to different possibilities, I wonder what kind of world we'd live in?

Different Every Moment

N: Oh my god. Wow. Wow. So Katherine, what else do you know about bodies and being with the molecules and possibilities that nobody else knows?

K: Yeah, it's a great question. I know a lot, Nilofer. The thing is that I spent my whole life thinking that I didn't know anything. I spent my whole life hating my body, being in total judgment of me and my body and when I stopped, it was like oh my gosh!

I know that when I talk about bodies, they talk back and I love playing with all the possibilities. I know that I can never approach a body in the same way. Even if I were to work on your body today, Nilofer, I couldn't work on your body tomorrow and approach it from the same way as I did today. Because your body and your being is going to be different tomorrow than it is today. Right?

And know that everyday our body is changing and we sometimes forget to ask our – like I had the 'aha' today. I had been drinking coffee in the mornings without asking my body if it wants it, and I'm like "oh cute! I forgot to ask" because at some point, it wanted coffee and every day, it would start to be like "yes, please!" and now it's like communicating that "hey, we may want to shift concluding that we want coffee everyday."

And so I know that the Universe is desiring to gift you the magic of you if you are willing to play and be curious about how the molecules of your body could create the future.

N: So you know, as I was hearing you talk about coffee, I said, "oh my god, that's so many parts of my life that I'm going and I'm creating some conclusions and that's all so much" and I guess it's just starting, right?

It's just taking that one small step and then keep choosing to take more steps and more steps and more steps.

K: Yeah.

N: Wow

K: Here's the key that I love that you just opened for me. It's just like every step you take, you open new doorways, and every doorway you open, you open the possibility of a 100,000 more doorways revealing itself to you, you just have to choose to see it.

You just have to choose to acknowledge that they are there and be curious about how many are actually there. Yeah, and which ones you want to open, and not just opening one doorway, you know, opening a hundred doorways at the same time, what that would create?

I'll have more of that! (laughs)

N: I mean, all this amazing brilliance, I'm busy typing out. (laughs) I'm like I don't want to miss anything.

K: Yeah, and Nilofer, that's one of the gifts because each of you has this capacity to "function from doing" or what this reality would call doing and it's actually one of the gifts that you can be. Right?

And so everywhere where you are like "no, I have to stop doing and be", like I love to have 20 things on my plate at once and from this reality, most people are like "you are too busy" and I'm like "oh my god, if I wasn't doing this much, I wouldn't be being the gift of playing on this magical playground that we have to play on."

Yeah, and so how many of you love doing something or a hundred somethings? (laughs) and what if that could be a contribution to your being? What if that is you being?

N: Wow.

K: What if that's the way that your molecules play in space and possibility? Because if, like the concept that this reality has about being is oh, we just sit down and meditate or oh, we just lay on the couch and watch tv or oh, we just sit and wait for things to come to us.

No, we can actually be in action and the action is being. Right?

We just have to see where you are functioning from.

N: And I guess it's also, you know, when I look at what I do/be, it's always like I'm following the wisp of the energy, you know. It's like "oh, there's possibility. Let me choose that.

Oh, there's another one, there's another one, there's another one."

And it's like acknowledging that that's what we are being and doing.

K: Yes! Yes, and it's like I know that I'm being when I'm like active in 5 different things and I'm getting downloads of my future and possibilities and new tele-calls or new classes to create.

Like I know that I'm being when I'm doing and I still am receiving all this information in my Universe. So it's like if you are not receiving information or if you are not receiving your awareness, then you can go "oh, I'm doing. What would it take to be while I'm doing?" (laughs)

N: Wow, wow. You know I have these comments come in – "Wow, my body is loving this energy of allowance that this call is bringing. Thank you. How does it get any better than that? I wonder what reality my body, the molecules of my body and me can create from here?"

"Oh, wow, Katherine and Nilofer, you are rocking this call! Loving this call." Oh my god, it's like so amazing!

K: Yes,

N: Oh my god, wow! You know you've been such an invitation in this call to this space of no-judgment of bodies, to this space of vulnerability with bodies and I'm like going, you know, "I'm having that. I'm choosing that. I'm not buying into any of the BS anymore." Thank you so much. Thank you so much and this amazing call, wow! Wow.

I wonder what are bodies would like to choose? Wow.

K: Well, you are so welcome. It has been such an honor to play with you and to play with your yummy body and everybody that was on the call, and just like, thank you. It's been such a gift and yeah, when we acknowledge the gift that we are in our bodies, we gift the world infinite doorways of infinite possibilities and you never know where that doorway could lead.

You never know what you being, you know, the magic and space of you and your body could create for somebody else. And so I wonder what world, what planet, what possibilities we can create by truly choosing to remind ourselves every day that we have the capacity to choose the magic in our bodies, the magic in our beings and the magic in our lives?

And I'm so grateful to you, Nilofer, what a gift and I love bodies, so I'm like "Go bodies! Go play! Go play with each other!" (laughs)

N: Thank you so much, Katherine. This has been like wow. You can see I'm speechless. (laughs)

K: (laughs) Awesome! I love it.

N: So can you, I know we've gone a little bit over time and if you are okay, can I ask you one last question? (laughs)

K: Absolutely! Honored.

Bodies And Money

N: I'm wondering what you know about bodies and money?

Money Jar

K: Yes! I know a lot more than I thought I did. (laughs) And so when we invite our body and the molecules of our body to go create money or to go find money or to be the invitation of money, it's like, I mean, I'll actually share, so this December, I did a 30 day holiday series and on the first day, I got the energy that I needed to invite each of us to put away an amount of money that was slightly out of their comfort zone. So for some people, it was a dollar, for some people it was 5 or 20, for some people it was more. Right?

N: Sorry, sorry, so I didn't get this. What do you mean "put away an amount of money that was out of their comfort zone"?

K: So, in addition to 10%, we basically created – I've created a jar in my house. Right? A glass jar and every day, I put an amount of money in that jar, because most people during the holidays, they spend, spend, spend, spend, right?

And I was like "huh, I wonder if my body was willing to put away money to see what it could create for the future, not as part of my 10% fund but in addition." How my body would react and so it happened, every day I put away this money and then I'd ask my body to go play. Right? Like "hey body, go find more money."

And what happened this December, I probably had one of the biggest money months I've had in a really long time and I didn't have any classes on the books, I didn't have anything where I knew where the money was coming from. And so I say that because when we invite our bodies to go say "hey, molecules of my body, go find more money. Go play. What's truly possible?"

And so our energies are literally inviting us into the space of money and abundance and possibility all day long. It's what we talked about earlier, Nilofer, increasing us being able to hear the whispers. And so one of the whispers for me was to put money in a jar every day. And at the end of the month, I was like "oh my gosh! In addition to my 10% fund, I have all this money" and when I did that, what came into my business was like 10 times what was normal.

N: Wow

K: So it's like what does your body know about creating money and how can you take off the conclusionary reality?

Or how could you open all of the doorways that are waiting for you to open so your body can walk into all the money that it desires to have? Yeah. So it's like the molecules of our body, if we ask the molecules to go find judgment, it'll find judgment. If we ask the molecules to go find space and possibility, it'll find space and possibility. If we ask the molecules to go find money or create more money, it'll do that. You just have to be willing to allow it to happen in it's own time. (laughs)

N: Wow

K: Yeah

N: Oh my goodness. Wow.

K: Right. So, Nilofer, what does your body and what do you the molecules of your body know about creating and having and being the energy of money?

N: Oh, my body and I know a lot because I'm just acknowledging that it was my awareness that made me ask you that question. (laughs)

K: Yeah! Exactly! Exactly. And so what a gift and invitation that truly is because each of us has a magic with money that if we ask what our bodies know about money, it'll begin to show you.

So for each of you out there that wants to create more money – I'm sure no one wants more money in their life! (laughs) Right?

What does your body know about money? Everything that does not allow you to know, be, perceive and receive what your body knows about money, will you destroy and un-create it? Right and wrong, good and bad, POC and POD, all nine, shorts, boys and beyonds.

Anything that doesn't allow you to follow your body's knowing to have you go get the money, go create the money, go have the money, will you destroy and un-create that too? Times a godzillion. Right and wrong, good and bad, POC and POD, all nine, shorts, boys and beyonds.

Yeah, I'll just say this one last thing. This last month of December I was like well, most people go into fear and lack around the holidays and spending money, I was like "what if I out-create that?" So every day I woke up and I said **"what can I create today that will create more money right away?"** and I ask that question every day and every day, I force myself to get out of judgment of what that'll look like. So I'd just POD and POC it or I would use the energy of 'stop and walk away' and I probably had – I mean, I had this magical month of yes, money, but also like I had the best holiday season I think I've ever had because I was functioning from a space of joy and creation.

N: And you know what, Katherine, I think the most important thing that you said over there is you got out of judgment about that. You got out of that.

K: Yeah

N: Because you know, we get these tools about money and even in the call yesterday I received an email just before the call and it's like people are saying you know "I'm trying to create money and it's not happening" and it's that piece of judgment, it's that piece where you are continuously judging what you are creating that "oh my god, this should be this! And this is not showing up, so it's not working" instead of "what am I creating?" and you know, "stop this judgment, stop this judgment, stop this judgment!"

K: Yeah, and it was like, you know, it's like what you said Nilofer, it's so important to get out of the conclusion of what you think money showing up in your life looks like. Because your body knows how to create it. It just does. (laughs) Your body totally – and you know this, Nilofer. Right? Your body knows how to create money. Where we stop the flow from happening is where we conclude that it's not happening or what it'll look like.

"It's not blah blah blah." And that's where it's like – the body, if we don't judge it, if we don't put a timeline on it, it will create it. And it'll be beyond what you could ever imagine. So I wonder what all of you know about money, what your bodies know about creating it, and what your bodies know about having it so that it is an honoring of you and the magic you be.

N: Wow. Thank you so much, Katherine. Thank you. Thank you so much for showing me that space of allowance and being and magic with bodies that I haven't yet been willing to acknowledge. Thank you.

K: Oh, you are so welcome, Nilofer. I'm honored to play with you and create with you, and you are such a gift and I adore you and thank you so much.

"Can we use the money in the jar or is it like the 10%, not to be touched?"

K: So it's up to you what you would like to do with that money. Is it for your body? Would it be fun? You know, I had my 10% fund which I don't touch and so in addition, you know, the end of the month, I went, "wow, I have over a $1000. What do I want to do with it?" And I actually paid cash for a pair of skis because I've moved to the mountains and my body loves, loves, loves to ski!

Loves to ski. So I was like "This is going to be a contribution to creating my future" so the day that day that I paid cash to buy my skis, I got a new client up in the mountains from skiing that day.

So you just have to follow your awareness and you literally just have to see, well, do I want to keep the money? So I didn't spend all of it, I only spent half of it. But it was such a contribution that it created more.

So what does your body know? What do you want to do with the money? I would say don't spend all of it, because bodies like having. They like knowing that you are contributing to them. Right?

And what do you want to do with the money?

N: Absolutely. Awesome. Awesome. So thank you, thank you, thank you, thank you so

much, Katherine. It has been absolutely phenomenal and what else is possible now? Thank you.

K: What else is possible? You are so welcome and thank you. What else is possible?

N: Yeah. Thank you.

**Being You, Changing The World by Dr. Dain Heer
- http://bit.ly/2b2ggOL**

This is probably the weirdest book you've ever come across. It is written for the dreamers of this world -- the people who KNOW that something different is possible -- but who have never had the tools before. What if I told you that the tools exist? The possibilities you've always dreamed of are possible!

Being You, Changing The World by Dr. Dain Heer
- http://bit.ly/2b2ggOL

Being You, Changing The World - PACKAGE OF CHANGE II
- http://bit.ly/2aGFE8j

Being You, Changing The World - PACKAGE OF CHANGE 1
- http://bit.ly/2aHU61P

Being You, Changing The World - Processes From The Book
- http://bit.ly/2aVGwsQ

Being You, Changing The World - Audio Book
- http://bit.ly/2aVHepH

CHAPTER NINE

BE THE DOMINATRIX OF YOUR LIFE

By Christine McIver

TV & Radio Personality, Speaker,

Possibility Coach and Potent Creator of Magnitude,

CFMW

N: "The title 'Be the Dominatrix of your Life' and the word Dominatrix brings up a lot of energy for a lot of people. I am often asked what is the Dominatrix? How can it be a doorway to possibility?"

C: "Often when we hear the word 'Dominatrix,' what can pop up in our minds is the dominant role - or sexuality – or bondage – or submissive types of behaviors. The way I see it, it is about making that demand of myself. When you are making that demand of yourself, nothing – NOTHING – and no one can ever stop you. When you step into that energy, can you just get the energy of the Dominatrix? The strength? The 'I'm not stopping for nothing' energy?' When you BE that in your own life, you begin to create and demand more than you've ever had before. When we are willing to have our own backs – *truly* have our own backs and do whatever it takes to create the joy that we desire, we not only change *our* lives, but we change the lives all around us!"

"Nilofer, you've been doing that in your life. You are very different from me. All the people that you have on these calls are very different too, but each of these individuals – including yourself – have made the demand to change something. Fundamentally *change* it. No matter *what* it takes and you are doing just that!

Yet so many of us are looking outside of ourselves. We are looking to other people to find the 'how to do it right.' We look to the experts and often purchase many business bundle ups or business conferences. I've taken lots of different online programs, read lots of amazing books. Most of those are the 'How to' books. The 'How to' is for someone else, right? It works for them. So if I duplicate what they did, hopefully I'll come up with the same outcome. Sometimes a little bit of that works, yet often, it doesn't. I would take a nugget away from it, however, I still got to that point in my life when a lot of things weren't working.

Many people reach that point in their lives where they are like 'You know what? I'm too tired. I'm too worn out. I can't do it anymore. I've been trying so hard to create this life – to create the joy – to create the relationships – to create the body – to create the bank account – and I just can't do it!' You are ready to give up everything and leave, when you get to that point. I call it a 'choice point.' It's that point where you are either going to completely throw down your gauntlet and say, 'Enough! I'm out of here!' – or you're going to throw down the knife and say, 'I *am* doing this. Get out of my way!' I reached that point in my life two years ago. I didn't know which way I was going to turn. I had no idea what I was going to do, because I had been 'doing' everything that I thought I should do in order to create the joy in my life. Yet there was one huge thing that I was missing. I was truly missing *me* in the equation. I was missing 'checking in' on what was true for me and what *I* really did want. What was going to make the difference for me in *my* life and who was I being ?

What lies had I been buying up until that point that weren't creating the life that I desired? There's a lot of people in Access that maybe aren't as much of an extrovert as I am – and I made myself wrong for that, my whole life. I was made wrong for it as a child. When I really started to step into this, I have created my life where today talking is what I make my living from! Bringing my laughter and my joy and my energy is what is creating everything! I had been turning that down and doing what everybody else said would make me successful. That wasn't *me*, so how could all of that possibly make *me* successful? Does that make sense, Nilofer?"

N: "Absolutely! I love what you are saying. I'm listening to you and I'm going 'Wow' because that is what this reality really does…makes people wrong for being extroverts – and then you made yourself wrong for it, too! It doesn't matter who or what you are, we have this fundamental 'disease' of going into the wrongness of us, no matter what it is about. Wow!"

C: "Also I would say, Nilofer, that you're not as much of an extrovert as I am and there's nothing wrong with that either! People say to me, 'Oh Christine, I'm nothing like you. I'm not an extrovert. I'm not a big talker.' They say, 'I'm not this' or 'that' because they are looking at *me* and they are defining what success looks like *me*. I'm like, 'Wait a minute!' So Nilofer, let me ask you the question I ask them – do you like different types of flowers?"

N:" Absolutely! Love them."

C: "So tell me – name five different types of flowers that you like."

N: "Roses, lotus, petunia, gladioli, lilies…"

C: "Daisies, dandelions – I love dandelions now. Of course, that's the symbol of Access Consciousness. So would you look at all those other flowers and just choose one and say, 'You are all doing it wrong and this flower is the only correct one?' "

N: "No, absolutely not! I mean, literally that book, '*Would you Teach a Fish to Climb a Tree* 'co-written by Anne Maxwell, pops into my awareness!"

C: "Exactly! There is no wrongness in the Universe…*at all.* So when you step into that – when you really begin to look into that question – you will know this. I've been hearing the' doing it wrong' thing since I was a young girl, being raised Catholic like so many of us were. I wasn't a bitter Roman Catholic like many people are. It was an experience for me that I enjoyed, but there was a lot of heavy judgment there. There was also a lot of contribution for me. One of the things that I heard when I was just 17 years old and it has stayed with me to this day is, "God doesn't make any junk." God makes no junk, o k? Whether you believe in God or not, just that whole idea that there is no wrongness or junk in the Universe stayed with me."

"However, there was that voice in my head that was like, 'Well, if that's true, then why do I keep screwing up my life? Then why am I unhappy? Why don't I have the money? Why don't I have the joy?' That kept running through my head and one day, finally I was like 'Alright, enough of this! *Enough* of this! What in the world is going on?' When I started to claim, own and acknowledge that I created *everything* in my life, I stepped out of being the victim – I stepped out of blaming anything and everyone around me – and that's when things started to change for me.

When you are being the Dominatrix of your life, I want you to know that it's not usually comfortable. If you've created a lot of chaos in your life, getting out of that chaos may be uncomfortable, because when you've been doing something the same way, to change it means that you have to get uncomfortable. So if everybody would cross their arms right now in front of them, I would say 99% of you put your right arm over top of your left. Did you, Nilofer?"

N: "No, I didn't cross my arms."

C: "You are not behaving, Nilofer! I'm gonna have to get my whip out! Now, if you were a good girl or boy – and you did cross your arms – I now want you to do it the other way. Cross your arms the other way, putting your left over your right or the opposite. How uncomfortable does *that* feel? It's awkward. It's awkward for me. Right now, I'm literally flipping my arms back!"

N: "Yes, actually for me it's comfortable to cross the left over my right, so the right one was uncomfortable!"

C: "Yes, and you could play with this in other ways. If your haircut has bangs and the bangs go from the right side of your head to the left or the left side of your head to the right, I encourage you to change that and to feel comfortable. So change....change...knowing that initially change is always uncomfortable.

When you want something different in your life, that's where you can be the Dominatrix. Lean into your life and say, 'I don't care how uncomfortable this gets, I am changing this and I'm changing it now.' The only person – the only other being in the world that you have to make the demand of – is the one that you look at in the mirror. That's the only one. No one in the world is creating your life, but you. No one in the world can stop you, but you and when you begin to claim, own and acknowledge that you've created everything, there's so much power there. Everything that brings up for everyone, because that's really heavy right now, can we destroy and uncreate it all? Everything that is times a godzillion will you destroy and uncreate it all? Right and wrong, good and bad, POD and POC, all nine, shorts, boys and beyonds."

"When you claim, own and acknowledge that you've created all of the chaos – all of the anger – all of the unhappiness – all of the sadness – all of the lack – any part of *any* of that – please claim, own and acknowledge and *at the exact same moment* that you do so, you *can* change it all. When you really look at this, Nilofer, you go, 'Ok, I created this. Alright, there might have been other creators involved but I was creating this. Alright, cool. Look at how potent I was at creating that chaos. Ha! **What if I made the demand of myself to change it? What if I actually started working with the forces in the Universe? What if I actually started looking for something that was fun and joyful ? What if, I started to change and create anew?'** Now here's how my brain operates.

When I get to that moment when it doesn't seem that there is any choice left – there is nothing left in my bank account or my cupboards – or I just feel like I'm in a corner – I do what I call '**a check up from the neck up.**' It's kind of looking at the bare bones. What I would say is, 'Ok, do I have a roof over my head today? Check. Am I healthy? Check. Is there food in the cupboard for breakfast? Check. Are my kids Ok? Check. I'm O.K." In this moment, that's all we have, right? In this moment, in this time and space, I'm O.K. I'm OK.' So when we are not living in the past, and we are not beating ourselves up and judging ourselves for any of the chaos we may have created, and we are not projecting into the future that we might recreate that, but we're just here – right now – on this call with you, Nilofer and we just do a little 'check up from the neck up.' All is well. *All is well.*

From this moment, the clarity is when you decide to make another choice and to demand more in your life, you can create whatever you desire. That's it for me and that's what began to change my life, my joy, my happiness, my business and my bank account. When I began to be the Dominatrix in my life – for me – with me – sometimes kicking my own self in the butt – that's when I changed my life. And that's when it started to become joyful and exciting. That's when I saw all of the possibilities for me, completely and totally. And now, each and every day, I ask, 'What am I going to create today? 'What are the possibilities today that have never been there before?' "

Question: "How do I get the life I desire and be happy if I always feel unloved by the most important people in my life? How do I make them see my point of view? I want to be happy and loved."

C: "Well, you are certainly not alone and I believe that all of us want to be loved. We all desire deeply to be loved. However, if you're looking outside of you to have those people love you, what you are really doing is you are looking to them to fill something within you. I think that all of us have probably been at this point some time in our lives. I can tell you that for me, I'm divorced and there was a time during my marriage that I didn't feel loved, and that brought me to the point of really looking at this. I asked, 'If I'm not making this person my source for my love, then where is it going to be created? Where is it going to come from?' One of the things I absolutely know is, it begins with me – you – us. It begins with each and every one of us finding the things that bring us joy – that bring us love – because when you are being *that*, then you are being the joy, then you are being the love, and that's when you begin to attract to you other people in the same vibration, who will begin to enjoy you for *you*.

It's a really good barometer when you are unhappy with relationships… it's a really good time to ask, 'Ok, I'm unhappy with relationships outside of me, so what's going on within me that I'm not enjoying about me?' You know with relationships, people come in and out of our lives all the time – whether it's a lover, whether it's a friend, whether it's even a family member. There is no guarantee – whether you are blood relatives or not – whether you have a marriage or not – whether you've given birth to somebody or not – that the relationship is going to continue to be one that's a contribution to you. The *one* guarantee that you have is that you are always going to be in *your* life.

Now let's look at the second part of that question, about love from others and about being happy. Being happy is really looking at what *you* would like to have in *your* life. What would bring you joy and happiness? A different job? Starting your own business? Taking up a hobby? Finding new people to create adventures with? Maybe it's writing a book? Maybe it's playing with people all around the world? There's so many opportunities to create joy. Start writing something down. This is something that I often do."

"When my coaching clients get to this point, I ask them to go back to when they were a child and ask, 'What gave you joy? What was it in your life as a child that gave you joy?' As children, we don't have a point of view about what we should or shouldn't do – and we're not often judging ourselves around what we are doing. One of the things that I personally love to do, is swing. Get on a swing and swing! When I'm in a park, guess where I'm going immediately? I don't care who's with me, I'm going to that swing and I'm swinging because it brings back that energy of absolute freedom and joy. So if we look at the things in our childhood that brought us joy, we can just tap into what it was that gave us joy. It's not that you have to go on the swing all of the time, but what was it about that? How can you recreate those feelings, those energies in your life today? How can you start creating the joy that you desire from where you are now?"

N: "Christine, you know, it's really interesting you are saying this because initially when you were talking about 'I was looking for the joy,' I was actually looking at that part of my life when I was not so happy with my life. To be honest, I did not desire joy at that point in time, because I was so much into my own trauma and drama that I didn't even know that I could ask for joy and happiness. Now Christine, it's like, what if I were just being in the question: *I wonder how much fun I can have today? I wonder what joy and happiness is available to me today?* As you know, you will have things literally show up for you, which is going to give you exactly what you are asking for!"

C: "Those are some of the great questions of Access Consciousness. I also like: *'Universe, show me something fun today. Universe, show me somebody to play with today.'* When you are asking the questions of the Universe and you don't have a point of view about how they show up, you are going to be surprised at how things can show up so differently. As you know, I work from home, often working at my desk on my own and I *still* ask this of the Universe! So I might have a conversation with somebody over Skype or through Facebook or over the phone and sometimes I go out to the store to get food or whatever. Just having a laugh – having a conversation with the cashier at the store – can bring me fun and joy! It doesn't have to be defined and doing something extreme like skydiving (although skydiving is a lot of fun!) It can be something very simple. When we are not defining how much fun has to show up or how it has to look, we can begin to be the joy –

it's like gathering crumbs of joy, that can just build and build and build!

Why did we come here, Nilofer? So many of us in our lives are trying to get it right – we're trying to have enough money – we're trying to have enough 'experiences' or the right house or the right job. What's the point of all of this? If joy and fun and laughter are not at the heart of everything that we are creating, what's the point? What *is* the point?"

N: "Christine, do you see that that's a very different point of view than most people have?"

C: "Yes!!!!!!!!!!!!!!! That is because people are not looking to create joy and fun and laughter!"

N: "No they're not, because…they are trying to fit in and they are trying to be successful as defined by this reality, Christine!"

C: "Absolutely. Having fun and joy and laughter is not part of what success *is* in this reality! Right, according to many, many people! How many people in the world are sad and depressed and using some form of addiction to drugs, alcohol, shopping, sex or whatever (like having 70 cats) to try to create joy or to try to numb themselves to the pain of not having joy?"

Caller: "Hi, well, when Christine talked about joy and childhood, I remembered one afternoon I was feeling happy when I was two and a half, and that's it. I think it was after I won a fight against a smaller kid, which is not something I am particularly proud of. So I – but maybe, well, that's one issue."

Christine: "So, what *was* it about? What was the feeling you had after that fight?"

Caller: "My older brother had just lost a fight with the older brother of a bigger child, that was the brother of this one. So I felt like that I was – that I belonged and I had vindicated my brother. It was a very peaceful time. I don't know why the older brother didn't come in and take care of me?"

Christine: "So, was there a point where you felt like you were using your voice or you were standing up for something that you believed in?"

Caller: "Yes, I was successful in being loyal to my brother."

Christine: *"How can you create being supportive and bring in the kindness at the same time?" Everything that that's brought up for you, can we destroy and uncreate it all? Times a godzillion?" "Right and wrong, good and bad, POD and POC, all nine, shorts, boys and beyonds.*

It's just a really fun question to play with. So it's not that you want to recreate fighting with somebody but what if something that's brought you joy and you're curious about it like a child would be, and you start to look at the incident with the question, 'What was it about that incident that brought me joy?' You can begin to ask that question of yourself every day."

Caller: "Yes, I certainly feel very good like usually when I'm meditating."

Christine: "Cool, how does it get any better than that?"

Caller: "I feel even better…and I keep that feeling all during the day."

Christine: "What would it take to keep that feeling all day long?"

Caller: "Oh, giving up judgment of everybody beginning with myself."

Christine: "Yes and beginning with yourself and being in allowance of what anyone else chooses."

Caller: "Yes, when people judge me for not being confident, which there is some evidence of."

Christine: "I think you have a lot of laughter in your life right there!"

Caller: "Well, it's intermittent. I shut it off most of the times, like I shut off tears. Now that would be a miracle. What would it take for me to be able to not shut off tears when it's optimal? What would it be like to be really, really relaxed about laughing?"

Christine: "What have you judged about laughing?"

Caller: "That it's exhausting and that it's not serious. People will criticize me for laughing 'at them' or 'at the wrong time.' I've heard the phrase 'inappropriate laughter' more than once."

Christine: "Wow! So what if them judging you, would bring you more money? Would you be open to receiving more money?"

Caller: "Well, you know, that is maybe the real problem. No, absolutely not! "

Christine: "You don't want more money?"

Caller: "More money wouldn't be fair."

Christine: "You have a lot of points of view, my friend!"

Caller: "Oh well, I know what the right answer is, but I'm telling you what my subconscious says. Look at my life. No, receiving money is – well, there's something really wrong with it."

Christine: "What if you stepped back from all of these points of view that you have? What if you went up in a helicopter and you looked down at all these points of view and you were curious about them? You didn't say 'this is right' or 'this is wrong' or 'this is what I should be doing' or 'I shouldn't be doing that.' You were just being curious about your points of view?"

Caller: "Well 'curious' sounds like a great word and viewing from a helicopter sounds – well, I don't think I ever actually heard that question before!"

Christine: "Well, it is one of the tools that I use to bring myself out of something being significant. So stepping back from something and giving it a bird's eye view and really just looking at it and just being curious about it and turning it around and poking at it or pulling it apart. Go into that little child's curiosity that you still have with you and start looking at it. What is this? What is it about not receiving money that I've decided is right? What would actually happen if I did start receiving money?"

Caller: "Oh, I actually know some of those answers. What's right is that it allows me to get help from my friends, and in a tangible and clear way. What would happen is that I would have to decide what to do with it. I've had that happen. I work for myself so I get $3000 every now and then and then zero for quite some time. So when the $3000 comes in, 'What bills should I pay?' or 'what Access material should I consider buying?' "

Christine: "May I ask you a question?"

Caller: "Yes."

Christine: "Do you pay yourself first when that $3000 comes in?"

Caller: "No, absolutely not. It's just out of the question. I know that's a tool and it works for those who use it…"

Christine: " Here's something that will change – has changed – my reality and may just change yours. If you are willing to be dominant in your own life – if you begin to pay yourself 10% of that money, every single time, no matter what – and you put it into a 'having it' account, not a savings account, a 'having it' account…"

Caller: " 'Having it' sounds good – that's a new term to me. A 'having it' account…"

Christine: "Put it in a 'having it' account, and what you do is you begin to step into the energy of having money. So you are not going into this, you know, excessive amount of money and then lack money, because you always have money. When you begin to do that, the Universe says, 'Oh look at him! He's willing to have money! Awesome! It's time to give him more money!' "

Caller: "Well, I'm sure that works."

Christine: "Hey, wait a minute…hold on. You're sure it works? Are you willing to step up? Are you willing to be the 'Dom' of your life and do what's required to change this? Or do you just want to keep recreating the same thing?"

Caller: "Well, I haven't – I really haven't chosen. Actually so far I've chosen to keep on recreating it, that's obvious."

Christine: "Well, you've got a choice point with me right now."

Caller: "Yes."

Christine: "I'm going to do to you, what I do to my clients. Are you ready?"

Caller: "O.K."

Christine: "We're going to disconnect your line from asking me live questions until you make a decision. You're going to either step up completely and start making the demand of yourself or you can just keep doing what you are doing. Your choice. What do you want to do?"

Caller: "Make a demand of me or keeping doing what I… Well, it certainly feels lighter to make a demand of me to take control of my life. I got really tense on the second one."

Christine: "How much fun is that?"

Caller: "Keep doing what I… I mean, that sounds a lot worse than the last 14 times I thought of that."

Christine: "Kind of sounds boring to keep doing the same thing, doesn't it?"

Caller: "Yes, it's…I think I've done it long enough."

Christine: "O.K, so it sounds to me like you know a lot about the Access tools and you know a lot about the Access programs. How about you stop *doing* them and you start *being* them? No matter what – no more excuses – no more telling the story. No more. Enough."

Caller: "Start being it. I'm perfectly happy to not tell the stories, except when people ask."

Christine: "Wait a minute! I'm really glad you brought that up, because I'm going to bring in a personal story, O.K? So for probably twelve years, people would ask me questions about my life and I would go into this huge, long story of my marriage, how it ended, what occurred during that time and I would go into a lot of blame and blame and blame. I made all of that creation responsible for my present state of being. Finally, one day, I'm like, 'You know what? I'm tired of even hearing myself tell this damn story, let alone the energy that it keeps creating in me!' So I made the demand of me to not speak of it in that way again. So when people would ask me, I would say, 'I'm single. I've been single for a number of years – for these number of years. I've been working. I'm growing my business and raising my children.' I no longer had to go into this tirade. So you have choice, even *if* somebody asks you. Change the story – and change it now! Enough with this story! You know what? When you are not choosing the joy – or the creation of your life to something greater than it's ever been before – you are not contributing to the change in yourself and the world. So guess what? We need to change the world!"

Caller: "Yes, that's true."

Christine: "You are a vital part of changing the world, friend. Are you willing to take up that challenge?"

Caller: "I've been working on it, so… 'working on it' sounds a little heavy."

Christine: "Yes."

Caller: "I think I've been taking meaningful action on it, in the last day or so in particular."

Christine: "Ok, are you willing to turn that up a hundred times?"

Caller: "Turn it up a hundred times ?"

Christine: "Turn it up. Turn it up, friend. Turn it up!"

Caller: "That feels different!"

Christine: "Thanks for calling in. Wow !!! This is so much fun and I would love to see what else can be changed in your life!"

Caller: "Well, that sounds good and well. To me it seems like a difficult issue. I'm 68 years old."

Christine: "Hey, a girlfriend of mine said, 'Listen, you've been alive for 5052 years...I've been alive for 5048. Who cares?' "

Caller: " Yes, there's a lot to that. Yes, I'm tired of answering the questions myself and I got to learn that when people ask a question, maybe they are just being polite or maybe they, just want a very short, factual, relaxed answer..."

Christine: "Just ask yourself, "What would I like to share? What would be a contribution? What would change my life in this moment right now?"

Caller: "Yes, and 'What can they hear?' which may eliminate almost everything! Plus, 'What would be a contribution and what would change my life?'"

Christine: "Yes, because this is truly all about you right now!"

Caller: "Yes, it's me. There's nobody else literally causing this. Or I'm not..."

Christine: "You create everything."

Caller: "Yes."

Christine: "Thank you so much for your contribution. I really appreciate you calling in."

Caller: "Thank you so very much. I'm surprisingly pleased. Thanks."

Christine: "You're welcome! Keep laughing! Well, Nilofer, you saw a little bit of my Dominatrix program come out there with my clients."

Question: "The idea of Dominatrix makes me giggle and at the same time, I associate it with force. My question for Christine. Have I got this wrong?"

C: "Well, yes and no. The giggling first of all, is often a sign that there's something right about this for you. You heard the live caller laughing or giggling after I asked him questions when something was light for him. So there's something about the Dominatrix that's right for this person who sent in this question.

Often times, this reality associates being a Dominatrix as a force, so we're forcing something into it. If you are in a sexual relationship, so someone is a Dominatrix – and you choose to be submissive, so you know what that is in a sexual relationship? Where there's whips and chains and all the rest of it involved? O.K, if you don't know what that is, or everything that's brought up for everybody here, can we destroy and uncreate it all? Right and wrong, good and bad, POD and POC, all nine, shorts, boys and beyonds.

Even if you look at that relationship, the submissive one still has choice as to whether they want to go into that relationship or not. Ok? So, there's still choice involved with a relationship like that.

When you are looking at being the Dominatrix of *your* life, you still have choice. So it's not about forcing your choice onto someone else, it's about making the demand of you to change your reality and doing whatever it takes! Sometimes it requires heavy lifting as in, digging through your emotional baggage to move past it. Sometimes it requires you using these tools night and day to get past something that you've bought into that's been locking you and holding you down for a long time. Sometimes it's about 'leaning into' your life as if you are in a windstorm and you have to lean forward to move through it – because if you didn't, you could be thrown and you could actually be killed, right? So, you want to lean into your life. You want to keep moving in the direction of the creation that's going to bring you the joy – the laughter – the happiness – all the things that you desire and are available for you.

It really requires you making the demand of *you*. So many of us are looking outside of ourselves at what this reality is saying that we should be doing – how we should be doing it – who we should be doing it with – how long we should be doing it – and on and on.

Like this idea of retiring at age 65 just about makes me throw up! I don't even know what that means! To me that's like sit down and wait till you die. That's not me. This reality is forcing on us what it believes will bring us happiness – or it's forcing on us what or how it wants to control us. I'm the only one that gets to make my decisions for my life and I'm going to create the joy for me. What I do may not give anybody else in the world the joy that it gives me – and I'm ok with that!"

N: "Christine, when we began you said that there are a whole lot of people who are making a different choice, who are making a demand of themselves and changing. So, when I look at one point in my life that I went, 'I don't care what it takes, but this has to change!' it was literally like I stamped my foot and said, 'I don't care what I'm going to lose – I don't care what or who I have to give up – I'm going to change this.' When I look at that, there wasn't much force in it, though there was a very strong demand for it. Then there is this energy that shows up where I step into the change really easily and then there's this energy of resistance and reaction to that change that is coming up. I guess that's the point at which I'm trying to do force, to choose or not to choose. However, most of the time, it's just a choice – isn't it?"

C: "It *is* just a choice, Nilofer. I mean, that's the name of my business '*Inspired Choices*.' So, what's inspiring you that you would like to choose? What would you like to choose that'll inspire your life and inspire you to get out of bed every day? It *really* is just a choice and it doesn't always have to be force. Absolutely not."

N: "The other thing about it, is that you ask for change but you never know how it's going to show up. What has been true for me, is that sometimes I go into this resistance and reaction to how things are showing up instead of going ...Oh, is this the change I've been asking for?"

C: "Oh, absolutely Nilofer! When we are asking for a change in our life and we are asking to work with the Universe, we can ask, 'Universe, you have my back on this, right?' That is because a lot of times the way things show up is so different. When I started my business, I had expected that I was going to do just business coaching, and now my life is so different! If you would have told me three years ago that I was going to be doing body work, I would have said to you, 'Are you crazy? 'Now you know what? I absolutely love it! Doing the Access bars, and running Access Consciousness body processes and doing the Symphony of Possibilities work – oh my gosh !!! – it is so much fun. I enjoy it so much and guess what? I actually have a potency with it. Who knew? If I had only followed what I decided the way it should show up, how much would I have actually cut out of my life?

So, when we are asking for joy – when we are asking for a contribution – when we are asking and we leave it so wide open – when something shows up and you just look at it with curiosity (like a dog tilting its head and going 'huh') You begin to play with the possibility of it whether you choose it for five minutes, five days, five years, five lifetimes!

You just look at it with no conclusion – no decision – no right or wrong – no 'this is good' or 'this is bad.' So if it continues to be fun, you continue to choose it. As long as it's being fun and a contribution to your life in some way, what else is possible that can begin to come in? However, when we do this limitation, when we say it has to show up like this, it's like the Universe says, 'Oh my goodness, Christine, I wanted to give you that million dollars, but you've been deciding that you're only going to play over in the hundreds pool. You're not going to actually step up into the millions pool, because what you've asked for, the millions don't come in that package.' "

N: "Wow, yeah. So can you please talk about stepping up, Christine?"

C: "80% of people usually choose change out of pain as opposed to out of pleasure. So most of us have to get to the point where something is really, really awful before we will begin to change. When that begins to occur in your life, I would suggest first of all, don't go into the judgment of yourself – and if you do, I'd like to say book-end it. Say, 'I'm going to take today and be as miserable as hell for one day. 'Then tomorrow I'm going to wake up and go, 'Ok, what else is possible? I'm done with that. I'm going to begin to change this.' Just that choice – just making that one choice, Nilofer, is the first step to stepping up. When you are willing to be vulnerable with yourself or with others around you, you begin to step up. In this reality, we've been taught that if you're vulnerable, you're being weak. That's not actually true. The most vulnerable people in the world, the people that put up their hand and say, 'You know what, I need some help over here!' are willing to do whatever it takes. That's stepping up. When you are looking at people like yourself, Nilofer – and people like Dr. Dain Heer and Gary Douglas and all the other amazing beings that you've gathered in your summits, you look at them and say, 'You know what? I love what that person is creating.' What if you are willing to start asking the Universe, 'What would it take for me to create what that person's been creating? What would it take for me to have that?' That begins the stepping up."

"When you start doing that on a daily basis, as I said to the caller, you start being the question and you start being the tools of Access Consciousness. When you begin to do this and really make the demand of yourself with no excuses – no more excuses, even when you see, 'Oh, I didn't do it there. Ok, cool! Next!' – then that is the stepping up. Plus, when you haven't defined how something has to show up, you begin to receive in so many different ways. Since I have really been doing and being these tools consistently, Nilofer, everything in my life – everything! – has exploded exponentially! Before Access, I probably went on a vacation once every 10 years. Now I can't even tell you – I'd have to stop and actually think about how many places I have travelled to in the last year!"

N: "Christine, since just last year, I have looked at what you've been creating and it's been phenomenal – like you've stepped up!"

C: "Yes, I have. Thank you, Nilofer. All of the beings at Access have been such a huge contribution to this – and I kept saying every day, 'No matter what – no matter what it takes – this changes!' You can see in that demand that I'm not saying it has to show up like XYZ. I'm simply saying, 'No matter what it takes, this changes!' Plus I'm asking 'What else is possible?' When something comes, and it's really cool. It's like you get this peripheral vision and everything opens up when you ask. 'What else is possible?' With both curiosity and that energy of demand. 'What else? What else? What else?' No more playing small – no more waiting to be happy. 'What else?' What really starts to occur is that you start to receive but also you start to be open to more and therefore, more can come.

As I've been stepping into this energy, I've been connecting with other people and with other opportunities. I don't go into the 'yes-no' about an opportunity, I just go into the curiosity about it. So asking questions and being curious without a definition really has changed everything in my life in the last year – everything! It's so much fun because I've learned so many new things that I never thought I'd be doing, like being a radio show producer with a team of staff members and we work with all these brilliant Access people all around the world! I didn't have that going on in my reality even just two years ago, but what I did have was the desire to change whatever was necessary to create the joy and bring the possibilities into my life that I *knew* were available."

N: "Wow, Christine !! You know when you first started talking about the Dominatrix, I was looking at everything that you were saying and it was like, 'Yes, I have been that.' So for me the way it has shown up has been very different from the way that you are being with it – and it's going to be different for every person. It's just that choice to make a change."

C: "Exactly, Nilofer. When we are stepping up and making these choices for our lives, we can recreate ourselves in a snap of a finger! I am ready to bring these Access tools to the world and break them down to get them into your DNA, as I often say. That way you can be them and see how rapidly, rapidly, they can change your entire reality! Before Access Consciousness, I had a business of my own – I had clients and I was doing O. K. Today, I am a radio show host and producer and I'm going to own the radio station! I facilitate Access Consciousness classes and I do the energetic body work also. I'm working on my own book right now – plus I'm a business coach – I build websites – and I'm always doing so many things! So many creations have come my way and it doesn't stop, which is so exciting and guess what? Now I have total choice around everything !

I really want to bring this home before we finish, so I want everybody to listen to this. **You are the source of your life**. You are the source of everything in your life. You do not have to be at the effect of anyone else's choice, because you are a creator! You are the source to create everything in your life when you are willing to make that demand of yourself. No one – *no one* – can destroy you. Only you and when you know that – when you *really* know that – you can be willing to lose everything…because you know you can create beyond it!"

N : "You know what, Christine? What you are actually going to end up losing is all your limitations! Everywhere I've been making that demand of myself for the past two years, I've lost limitations while everything else has just shown up in a bigger – greater – more amazing way than I could have ever imagined!"

Question: "How do we change ourselves so differently if we have always been diplomatic and helpful and supportive of others and non-dominating?"

C: "You have to ask yourself, 'Do I want to change?' The desire to have more begins to be the catalyst to change this. I can tell you that, for me, I was always the helper. When I was a little girl and the 9th out of 10 children, I would baby-sit for my siblings. I would not only take care of the children, I would clean the house and the next time, I would clean the house plus I would do all the laundry and the dishes. I was always trying to be more for other people. That eventually becomes extremely exhausting because you are giving – giving – giving to other people… and where does it leave you?

When you are always helping someone else – or you are leaving you out of the equation – or you are putting you last – eventually what can begin to be created is resentment, anger and sadness, all of which can manifest into ill-health in your body. So you're at 'dis-ease' with your relationships – you're at 'dis-ease' with always giving to other people and you are creating that in your body! I can tell you that when you begin to say, 'You know what? I'm not putting everybody last – but I'm certainly not putting me last. I am putting me first' you begin to be the invitation for other people to do the same. Oftentimes when we look at someone and we've decided or concluded that they need help, we've bought into some lie that they can't do it for themselves. That doesn't change their life. That's like 'feed the man' or 'teach him to fish', right? It's more like 'Let's teach other people how to fish by how we do this. Let's step into taking care of and creating our life of joy and abundance and we will teach others to do the same.' I use this saying: "Sometimes saying 'yes' to me, will mean saying 'no' to you. It's an honoring of me, not a dishonoring of you."

N: "Christine, is that actually putting yourself in the computation of your life, where you were not there anywhere?"

C: "That's right, Nilofer. We've been taught if you're a good little girl or boy, you'll consider others first – you'll put everybody ahead of you. That's a lie. That's a lie to keep us controlled in this reality. This is not about being unkind to anyone and this is not about not being a contribution to other people. Putting yourself last because when you do that you are saying, 'I don't matter.' It's about the most unkind thing you can do in the world."

N: "You know, Christine, I have an amazing process for this.

'What is the value of never being unkind to others?' Everything that is will you destroy and uncreate it all? Right and wrong, good and bad, POD and POC, all nine, shorts, boys and beyonds.

When I first heard this as part of the Creative Edge of Consciousness, I said, 'I don't think that applies to me.' Then Gary said that when you start running this process on yourself 30 times a day for the next 30, 60, 90 days or however many days it takes, you are going to unlock you from being unkind to you."

C: "*Oh, that is brilliant Nilofer and everywhere that anyone has bought into putting themselves last, making themselves wrong for what they desire and require, can we please destroy and uncreate all of that now? Right and wrong, good and bad, POD and POC, all nine, shorts, boys and beyonds.*

Ask yourself right now, 'Would an infinite being truly put themselves last?' No – never!

If you ever wonder about that, look at children, especially under the age of five, who are such brilliant examples of being – really being – infinite beings! They choose for themselves – always! And they are happy – playful – curious – and nothing is significant. *Nothing is significant.* They are just being. What would the world be like, Nilofer, if we all stepped into just BEing, playing and creating? How much joy and laughter would we all have in our lives and how much would that joy and laughter actually heal the Earth?"

"*So everywhere that you've been refusing laughter and joy in your life, can we please destroy and uncreate all that? Right and wrong, good and bad, POD and POC, all nine, shorts, boys and beyonds!*"

"Joy and laughter are two of the most fundamental things that can change everything. I'm an extremely hard-worker – I love creating – I'm going at it for hours and hours each and every day – and there is joy in that for me! There is laughter in that for me! Creation is fuel for me and when we get out of what it's supposed to look like and we just keep following what is fun, what is a contribution, what is joyful for us, our bodies and our beings, we can change the reality around us for everyone!

Remember, you can choose for you! What choice is everyone willing to make today that will change their reality? What choice? *What choices can I make today that will change my reality?"*

EARTH THRIVING

Have you ever acknowledged the gift this Planet is to YOU? And have you ever acknowledged the gift that YOU are to the PLANET?

You could use the tools, exercises and questions to open up a totally different way of BEing and communicating with this planet.

Would you be willing to join in creating greater possibilities on, for and with the EARTH?

Get this telecall with Aditi Iyer at
www.whereismydoorwaytopossibilities.com

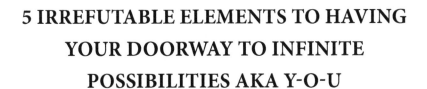

5 IRREFUTABLE ELEMENTS TO HAVING YOUR DOORWAY TO INFINITE POSSIBILITIES AKA Y-O-U

By Rhonda Burns

Mentor, Intuitive Wellness Facilitator, Speaker

Atom Bomb of Consciousness

R: Let's play! Let's get this party started. I would like to invite everybody wherever you are, if you can safely, I'd like for you to close your eyes, and I'd like for you to really take several deep cleansing breaths, as deeply into your body as you can get. Down into those cute little toes of yours. And if you have the ability to put your hands on your face, on your cheeks, or on your forehead – whatever's comfortable, please gently touch your skin.

And I really want to bring you, your brilliant being and your body together with me, with all of us at this time. If you can't close your eyes, you can still breathe deeply, you can **be – here - now**. I really want you guys here with me and present. And then I'm going to ask you to lower your barriers. And for those of you who are new to the body of work called Access, who may not understand what a lot of this is; please trust and know that as soon as I ask you to do it, you are already doing it. It's not about knowing how. So I'm going to ask you to lower your barriers some more. These are all the energetic walls and barriers and things that we surround ourselves with in order to not receive all the information.

So we've connected with our breath, we are lowering our barriers, and now I really want you to expand your energetic depth and breadth as far, as wide, as deep, and as high as you can go. Could be the size of your room. Again it's not about how. It's THAT you are and can. You can expand your energetic field out to the size of your city…to your state…to your country…to the planet, to the Universe. Keep breathing. Now I want you to open your eyes, and I don't know about anybody else, but I'm in a really soft space. I'm smiling. I'm content and I'm also here. I'm very present to all the energies that I am perceiving.

IRREFUTABLE ELEMENT# 1: BE PRESENT IN YOUR LIFE

R: We are talking about the **5 irrefutable elements to having your doorway to possibilities** – that is number 1. And I am not a big list person, but these are 5 key for people to really having what they desire and number 1 is **being present in your life**. And that's a great way just to start. It is to learn to be present in every moment. And usually it takes us slowing down and making a demand of ourselves to be here now, no matter what's going on around us. So we just got present. How does it get any better?

So, I think people know by now if they have listened to any of the previous calls, there's no magic doorway that's going to make anybody happy, or it's nothing outside of us. There are lots of things that can contribute to our happiness, contribute to our possibilities, but *we are the source*. So the doorway of infinite possibilities, it begins and is, with us. And so when I was thinking about the topic I wanted to speak to, it was like "Wow! What is that? And what does that look like?"

I am this presence. I have this energy to me and I wanted to really hone and craft that in such a way that I showed up in the world being everything I knew I was here to be, and I kept finding areas and pockets that I was lacking and that stuck me, or tripped me up.

I have worked really tenaciously in not only these 5 areas – there are a lot more than 5 elements – but these 5 that I'm going to share tonight are the ones that were key to me having truly liberated myself from the limitations, for me stepping up into a space of potency that I knew was possible, but I wasn't quite sure how, and once I stepped into this space and chose it, I haven't looked back. And yes, life has exponentialized. Things get more fun. There's more ease; there's more joy. I have brilliant, amazing, beautiful friends that contribute to me. I can't complain. I mean I can, but I don't want to, because life is really, really good.

R: In coaching and facilitating, usually when people come into a new body of work and are so trained to respond along the lines: "Ok, you are asking me to do something, but I don't know *how*." We are always looking for the 'how', because no one has actually ever informed us, encouraged us, let us know that we are so fast, we have tremendous capacities, we are so potent, and we have such amazing abilities. Nobody has ever told us this, so we go around saying, "Well, how do I do this? How do I do this? Well, I can't do that because I don't know how." I'm going to ask everybody to suspend their need to know 'how' and start to tap into trusting THAT we are capable of anything. Now we may require tools, tips, some new processes, perhaps information we may not have yet, but there is nothing we cannot create, have and generate if we are willing to choose. Does that make sense?

N: Yes, if we are willing to choose.

R: That's the key – *if you are willing to choose*. I have people that like to call for coaching and they complain and they just like to keep retelling their story repeatedly and I ask, "Do you really want to change this? I'll keep taking your payment, but I really do like to affect change." But again, it's just choice. There's no right or wrong. But people, who know me, know that I am willing to change anything. I am willing to look at everything. I get to it when I get to it, I change it when I'm ready, but it's just choice.

IRREFUTABLE ELEMENT# 2: TRUST YOU

R: This is based on my experience and what I observed when I look at Dr. Dain, when I look at Gary, and I look at other facilitators, or I look at people in the business world. I'm a very watchful, observant person; I pay attention. **Trust** – so we've got presence started and then trust comes next. In looking at this…as I would listen to calls, or watch other people facilitate, I would observe how quickly and easily they would ask a question, or they would get awareness around a subject, and they would follow a line of thinking that was spot on target. And I kept beating myself up. "Wow, I'm not that fast. Wow, what makes them so special? How are they able to do that?" I had that conversation with myself for a while.

And then I got sick of it and I said, "You know what? I'm done. I'm absolutely done. I'm not going to do this anymore. What would it take for me to trust myself so implicitly, undeniably, that I'm willing to know what I know, to ask the questions that need to be asked, to be, to show up and be everything I'm here to be?" That's the energy of a demand. So I asked myself the question, but then I also said, "I don't care what it takes, I am going to trust me, *no matter what.*" And let me tell you, Nilofer, within literally an hour, I was – not tested, but something came up that I had to choose to trust me, and when I checked in on a question that was asked, the awareness that came up was instantaneous, and I caught myself getting the awareness, having it be instant and then actually trying to find an answer. And I looked at it and I went "Whoa - crap!" That's what we do. We tend to be so fast and get awareness and information so quickly, instantly, that we refute it because it's too fast, because it's usually too easy.

How many places and spaces are you denying the instant awareness that you have and that you be? Everything that is, and everything that brings up, can we please destroy and un-create it all? Right and wrong, good and bad, POD and POC all nine, shorts, boys and beyonds.

Trust That You Know What You Know

R: How many of us have never been given permission, or invited to trust what we know? That's what I was really made clear of is most of us are humanoids, most of us are super-fast, most of us have these abilities that are beyond this reality and we grow up in this normal human reality and we're not acknowledged for that brilliance. We're not acknowledged for that speed. We're not acknowledged for all the gifts that we are here with. So I heard initially in the body of work, to 'know what you know', but then to trust what you know? Well, trust was a huge issue for me. And I had a hard enough time to keep my trust in other people and then it was actually harder for me to trust myself, which was really unfortunate.

Everything that is, and everywhere anybody is not willing to consider that they CAN trust themselves, no matter what it shows up like, no matter what it looks like , can we please destroy and un-create all that? Times a god zillion. Right and wrong, good and bad, POD and POC all nine, shorts, boys and beyond.

And everything the word 'trust' brings up, all the misidentifications, mis-applications, all the projections, expectations, separations, rejections and judgments, let's POC and POD that too. Right and wrong, good and bad, POD and POC all nine, shorts, boys and beyond.

So again, this is a process.

If you are willing to choose to be present, number 1, to trust you, number 2 – *no matter what* - POC and POD anything that comes up that makes you think you can't be the demand that you are going to trust you...watch what happens. Watch how things start to shift. How you start to show up differently. How the questions that you ask start to be really potent and get to the meat of the matter very quickly.

R: Before I go into the next elements, a lot of people don't really know my background, or about me. They might see me in social media and they don't really have a lot of history and again, I don't tell the story to perpetuate anything, but it's really more for clarity and growth, and it's interesting because as I got to the space of playing with this; all of it ties into personal potency. And I love the way that Gary Douglas, the founder of Access, defines potency in foundation class as *the ability to change anything.* That's cool! And when I really tap into that – the potency, I'm like wow! I have always been this really potent being, and many of us, we were made wrong for it while growing up.

We were these big energies, we had all this enthusiasm and we had all these creative bursts however it showed up for each and every one of us. But I was raised in an average, normal, mainstream household in middle-America, here in the United States, with my step-dad who was an Air force pilot and then he left to go to the Episcopal seminary, so then I was a church kid. I was raised in religion. I was raised in very much what we call the "status quo", which is "you do what everybody else does. You don't rock the boat. You don't make waves. You make like everything is perfect. You show up and you smile whether you're miserable or not". That was the way I was raised. I was conditioned and entrained so very well, and I got to a point in my life where I had all this success, I had a six-figure income, the career, the money in the bank, the cars, the toys, all the trappings of success, and I had my son, who is now almost 10.

Back in 2006, I was looking in the mirror and I literally said to myself out loud, "If this is all there is, I'm out. I'm done." I was at this cross-roads, this precipice of "change or die". I mean those were my options at that moment, because I could not go on doing what I had done, the same way I had done it. So it was either step up and change it, or die. Well, obviously I am not dead. So, in that moment I had no idea how I was going to change it, what it was going to look like, what it was going to cost, who was going to be in the picture. I had none of it. But it didn't matter, because I knew it had to change and I knew I wasn't ready to check off the planet. It just wasn't on the cards for me then.

So through just that demand of "it's changing now!", I was able to start putting one foot in front of the other and I would – this is before the tools of Access – but I was asking questions and I was following the energy and I would go to this seminar because it felt good, and I would go to this class because it felt good; I would read this book because it made me happy and through that, well, I'm no longer married, I'm a single mother, I left corporate America, I own my own coaching practice; everything has changed. Nothing is the same and I am so grateful that I had the moxie to just do what I had to do. The reason I share this story is because I was so steeped in the status quo and in "normal, average, real America" - in this reality, that when I found the body of work of Access, it freaked me out, but in such a way that on one hand, it turned me on and it lit me up and it spoke to every molecule of me, and yet I had this sensation that it would slap the face of society because it flies in the face of what most of us have been raised with.

Normal, Average , Real- What's That?

So I was at another crossroads. Ok, so I have this crazy set of tools and this crazy body of work that works so fast and so effectively that you can change anything, *everything* and it stays. It doesn't have to go back the way most work does. Or I could go back and kind of dabble, kind of – no, I actually made the choice that I'm willing to be as weird as I need to be in order to be happy and if people want to judge the work, if people want to scoff at it, if they think it's too far out there, that's fine. That's their choice. But this body of work – the tools of Access, the classes, the processes, everything about it, is the most effective, fast, fun, crazy body of work I've ever played in and I just – well, who else wants to come play? Who else would like freedom in their lives? Who else would like to have all of them, perhaps for the very first time? And actually live a life of joy and playfulness and light? That's what I'm down for, I don't know about anybody else.

What creation are you using to invoke and perpetrate the necessity to be normal, average, real, mundane, mediocre, the same as everybody else, rather than the magical, undeniable leader of a totally different reality that keeps you tethered, chained, tied and locked down for all eternity? Everything that is and everything that brings up, can we please destroy and un-create it? Right and wrong, good and bad, POD and POC all nine, shorts, boys and beyonds.

R: One of the things that I absolutely adore about Gary Douglas, when I first found him and the body of work, I would listen to him and I would watch him in class, and you know, you can vouch for this too, Nilofer, how tenacious he is about word choice, because it's based on the energy that he is trying to stir up to clear the most. Sometimes he'll create a process and he'll be like, "No, change this word and change this word," and if you hear him facilitate, when you listen to him speak, he's so present and he is so tenacious with this language use because he wants to address and match the energy the greatest. I love language. Like words turn me on. It's always been my thing. So that was so cool for me to experience. I would sit watching or listening and I was like "what is he doing?" at the beginning. It's funny to me now because when I create a process, or I ask somebody a question, because I'm reading the energy, a lot of times the words that come out don't make any sense, but they are absolutely spot-on the energy that we need to clear it, so it's really cool. I'm beyond grateful for Gary for showing me that possibility and allowing me to step up into that capacity to read the energy and to create from that space, that which will change the most.

I just see people so much that are floating along, they're on auto-pilot, they are in the mainstream.; they're not wanting to make waves; they're not wanting to stand out and that's mundane and mediocre to me. That's my point of view. But when I look at them, I see how much energy it takes them to keep that locked down, to keep the brilliance and the magnificence of themselves, to keep it locked down at that level, and it's exhausting. And I know, because that's a space I used to function from. I was exhausted all the time because I was keeping this powder keg under wraps. And it just didn't work for me anymore. So I'm here to invite anyone who's willing and ready to explore the possibility of starting to allow whatever part of you would like to show up to do so. It's simply choice. And it usually never looks the way you think it is.

Mis-step, Or Lack Of Presence?

Caller: I've been on an amazing spiritual path and growing exponentially, but then in the past 6 months, I have fallen twice. Once I passed out and let my nose break the fall, and I fell down a flight of stairs. I didn't break anything, but I sprained my shoulder pretty good. Is there a block or something that I'm perpetuating, or not seeing what's creating these?

R: Truth, in those 2 instances, were you actually present and in your body?

L: Probably once yes and once no.

R: Yeah, there's some heaviness in some way, shape or form. So everything that is, I'm going to ask you to destroy and un-create it all. Right and wrong, good and bad, POD and POC all nine, shorts, boys and beyonds. So let's look at the one where you weren't in your body. Can you discern which one that was?

L: Yes.

R: Which one?

L: The first one.

R: Ok. So truth, where were you? Makes me want to laugh. It's super-light.

L: I don't know.

R: Do you get the energy? You don't have to tell me. You don't have to know the words, but can you get the energy?

L: Yeah, it was heavy.

R: It was a heavy energy?

L: Yeah.

R: Ok, cool. So everything that is, I'm going to ask you to destroy and un-create it all. Right and wrong, good and bad, POD and POC all nine, shorts, boys and beyonds. We have the capacity to be with our bodies and in other places, so truth, do you have a capacity that you have not yet acknowledged?

L: Yes.

R: Ok, would you like to acknowledge it now?

L: Yes.

R: Ok, beautiful. Everything that doesn't allow it, I'm going to ask you to turn it up a little bit more, step into it a little bit more. Nice. Right and wrong, good and bad, POD and POC all nine, shorts, boys and beyonds.

Rather than making it a wrongness – yes, falling down, hurting your-self doesn't feel good, but usually there are different things that could be and there's an avenue I could go down, (I don't know that I'm going to go down it tonight) but the first thing that we tend to do when that happens is we make it wrong, and that's why I say, ok, truth, do you have a capacity in some way, shape or form with this? We've now ac-knowledged that you do. So the one, when you fell and you were with your body, truth, what was that?

L: A misstep.

R: Pardon me?

L: Just a missed step, kind of.

R: I guess my question would be if you are truly being present in every moment, would you ever have a misstep?

L: No, true.

R: So everything that is, let's destroy and un-create it all. Right and wrong, good and bad, POD and POC all nine, shorts, boys and beyonds. I catch myself now, let's say if I'm cooking something in the kitchen and I drop something, or I'm walking and I trip, what I now know is in those moments I'm not actually in with my body.

L: Right.

R: I mean its snap instant. Its ten seconds of unawareness. Its 2 seconds of unawareness.

L: Right.

R: So I wonder how much more you can play with truly being aggressively present in your life, in your daily routine, in every moment, and then if you have these things that show up, you can check in and say "Ok, what was the value of not being aggressively present? What was going on in those moments?" Right?

L: Right. Definitely.

R: Cool. So what else? Is there something else there? Are you making any of that wrong?

L: Not wrong per se. I'm usually so healthy and everything, that I am just trying to make sense of it, kind of.

R: Right.

L: And you know, medically – like the first one, I completely just passed out and broke my nose, but, I tried to make sense of conditions that led to it. Instead maybe it was as you said, me not completely being present in my body.

R: So, truth, "When you just passed out and broke your nose", truth, were you the only one in or with your body at that time?

N: What she means to say is, "Truth, were there any more beings in your body?"

R: "Truth, how many beings were with you in that body at that time?"

L: Oh. Well, I just keep getting that it was 5.

R: Ok cool. So what do you know about entities? Have you heard us talk about entities in Access?

L: I mean I know there are all types of entities.

R: Ok cool. Entities are simply – as Shannon O'Hara explains, who's to me the queen of talk to entities here in the Access body of work, it's an energy that's defined. That's the English language definition; energy which is defined. So you're an entity, I'm an entity, Nilofer's an entity, music is an entity and so on. Non-physical entities are what I'm talking about. So these are beings that no longer have bodies or perhaps never had bodies, and what I've come to work with and know lately, I have a capacity with entities and there have been times in my life, in my son's life that when we are either hurting ourselves, bumping and falling down, we're not the only one in our bodies at the time.

L: Ok.

R: *So in that instant, when you fell, were you the only one in control of your body at that time? So everything that is and everything that brings up, can we please destroy and un-create it all? Right and Wrong, Good and Bad, POD and POC, All 9, Shorts, Boys and Beyonds™.*

I'll share a story. I got to a space not too long ago. I kept having this thing going on with me and my body where I would ask it a question, I would get the awareness, but it didn't feel quite right. Long story short, I don't know if you have ever heard of walk-ins and original occupants, but I wasn't alone in my body and it was a really huge turning point for me. I had gone through all the Foundation level 1 and upper level classes, I had cleared entities and I got to another level, and I determined that I wasn't the only occupant in my body. And it freaked me out! But once I stepped up and said, "Ok, what's it going to take to change this?" Now I'm the only one in my body and the level of freedom and presence and potency and everything that I've stepped into – the me that I've known was here, but it was kind of muddled for a while, is here in full force now. Yes, so there's nothing to be afraid of with entities, there's nothing to shy away from. Most of us have a capacity with them, or have them with us and we don't usually know it. So, that's my story.

N: So, I have a question for you.

Would you like to be the only occupant in your body?

R: Good! Great place to begin!

L: I'd like to be as light and happy as the two of you sound. Yeah, definitely.

R: So, "Truth, today, right now, how many other beings are in your body?"

L: I got 3 immediately.

R: Ok cool. Let's play with the 3. So, "Truth, who are you? Truth, who were you before that? Truth, who were you before that? Truth, who were you before that? Truth, who were you before that? Truth, who were you before that? Truth, who were you before that? Truth, who were you before that? Truth, who were you before that? Truth, who were you before that? And truth, who will you be in the future? Thank you. Take all your magnetic imprinting and ex-printing with you and go. Right and wrong, good and bad, POD and POC all nine, shorts, boys and beyonds." Truth how's that now? Are there any still remaining with you?

L: I have 1, but…

R: Is that you? Is that you, or somebody else?

L: I don't know now, but what's there is making me smile. Let's put it that way.

R: Hello! Welcome to your body! THAT is YOU! It's that simple. It's really that simple. Now you get the sense of the lightness and you're smiling and the ease. That's you the being.

L: Right.

R: So anytime you start to feel not that way, or a little funky or – I mean there's a lot of other tools we have to use, but once you've identified that you do have a capacity with entities, they come in your body, you've allowed it, you've played with them for a while, you can always just check in. "So, truth, am I alone here?" And it's that simple to clear. That's one step of clearing entities, but it's that fast and it does create more space for you.

L: Can I do it?

R: Go ahead.

L: On my own?

R: You certainly can. I do it all the time. My son who's almost 10 does it. You also learn that in Foundation if you take a Foundation class.

L: Right.

R: Shannon O'Hara has lots of stuff available for free on www.access-consciousness.tv. There are facilitators out there that specialize in entity work, and it's a really fun topic.

N: And Shannon has a book called <u>Talk to the Entities</u> which you can get and have more information about entities.

R: Yes. And it's short, it's an easy read. It's really cool. One more thing is that I'd like to invite you to be the dominant energy and dominant entity in your life and in your body. And basically, when you make that demand of yourself, and you basically proclaim: "This is my space. You don't need to come in here. I got this. This is mine", you start to hold the energy and the space that they are not going to come in.

IRREFUTABLE ELEMENT# 3: GET TO KNOW WHO YOU ARE

R: Ok. So we talked about presence and trusting you. If I didn't trust me, do you think I could have done that? Nope. So I just showed you guys what it's like when you can trust you. **Knowing you**, you have to **get to know *who you are*.** When we cleared those entities and she said "I'm smiling", that's the knowing of what you feel like, the sense of who you are and your space. We are infinite beings who chose embodiment and we are beings of light. We like joy. We like laughter. We like fun. We like ease. So when we are not being that, who the heck are we being? What are we doing? And usually we are doing a lot of things, because we are really good at it. So really getting to know you, your essence, your vibration, whatever you want to call it, your vibe - **you have to get to know who you are**.

And most of us have gone through this life, wearing everybody else's ideas of what it's supposed to be like to live. So I really invite and encourage people to really get to the space of, "Gosh, who am I?" We have the question in Access – "Who am I today and what grand and glorious adventures will I have?" Well, I say break it down. "Who am I? Body, who are we? Universe, show me my contribution." You really do have to get to know who you are, so that you are not playing somebody else's role. That's the next element.

Who Am I Defending For And Against?

I was sitting in a mastermind and this speaker was on stage speaking what I, in that moment, deemed as "against everything that I know is real and true". He was boldly, in our faces, speaking against everything that I coach for, and I was mad. I was sitting in my seat just fuming and getting really angry. I managed to stop myself and I said, "Wait a minute, if I'm too busy defending my point of view, I'm going to miss what's in this for me." And because I *knew*, *I knew* that I was called to be at that particular mastermind that weekend, I knew there was information for me there. I had to stop defending my points of view, or what I thought were my points of view just because someone else had their point of view and was really sticking to it. In that moment I dropped my barriers like we did at the beginning of the call, I expanded my energy out as far as I could go, I breathed deeply, I got really present and I said to myself, "I can trust myself to know who I am in every given moment, but this guy has information for me and I have to receive it." Now what I do with it was my choice, but in that moment I knew I was capable of receiving his information and still being me, because I knew myself.

N: I remember you posted this on Facebook, Rhonda, and I looked at it and there was something like that going on in my Universe and I was judging somebody and I looked at that and I went "wow" and I just lowered my barriers and I said "What contribution is this person being that I am not acknowledging?"

And it just opened up, this whole, you know, space and energy in my world.

R: Doesn't it? And it's that fast. So the quote that I think I posted with that is "If you are too busy defending your point of view, you'll miss what's in that for you," something to that effect. So yeah, what would it take for us to just trust that when we are in a situation or with someone, receive the contributions. Some of it is more enjoyable than others but there's a contribution in it if we're willing to receive it. And you can still get to be you; if you know who you are, you trust who you are and you are being present.

IRREFUTABLE ELEMENT# 4: PLAY

R: **PLAY. Play, play, play**. We make things so significant and so serious in this life and people with their word use of Facebook and social media and they are trying to be proper and business-like. It's like, you know what, there's somebody that's going to be on your summit later on, George Ira Carroll, who I adore, Nilofer, because that man will throw down a gauntlet with words and he will stir things up faster than anybody I know and I love it! Because he's playful, because he makes me laugh, and I know he stirs people up! What would it take to be more playful? And you don't have to do it George's style and you don't have to do it my style, you don't have to do it Dain's style, but like what would it take for us to be more playful? Because joy and play and laughter - that's the stuff. So if you don't know what is fun for you and you don't know how to play, you need to reach out and I'll ask you some questions to stir that pot.

IRREFUTABLE ELEMENT# 5: CHOOSE YOU

What's the 5th one? What wants to be the gem tonight? Oh, how about **choosing you**. So, this element of having your infinite doorway to infinite possibilities, having all of you, *you have to choose you*. Just because you choose for yourself, doesn't mean you are choosing against someone else. They may think it, they may want to try to make you feel bad, but when you choose for you, watch how your life changes. Watch how people step up in their lives. Watch how people respond to you. When you honor you and choose for you in every moment, that's what it's all about. And it may not always be comfortable – I'm not going to lie – I am so aware of other people's discomfort, I'm so aware of other people's stuff and so when I choose for me, I get that download. But guess what, that's their stuff and I'm going to give myself permission to choose for me, which then allows someone else the permission to choose for themselves. And why would I deny them being able to choose that? So I'm choosing to show up and I choose me.

QUESTIONS

"How does one get clearer on what we are supposed to be as a contribution?"

R: It's not about 'what' we are supposed to be. When you choose to be here on this planet as the love and the kindness and the caring and the nurturing and the presence and all that you be, and I don't care where you are on your walk right now, but if you are willing to just BE yourself, which Dain's platform of 'being you changing the world' is all about, if you are willing to be yourself, that is the greatest contribution to this planet and the people on it, than anything else. Because we have a willingness to be different, to be the kindness and the caring that most other people aren't willing to choose. So it's not a 'what'.

I don't know how to answer that any differently than to invite you into the energy of choosing to play with these elements, to choose to keep knowing you more intimately. Know who you are really and what's really vital and important to you, and then you are going to start to piece this together.

N: The other thing is, I've also heard Gary say that just by your presence on the planet, you are a contribution.

What if you were to go to this question – *"What contribution am I being that I'm not acknowledging?"*

And use it like every single day. This is a question which changed so much for me. I started getting awareness' of everywhere that I was being a contribution and that just moved my world.

R: Many of us like the external validation, the external information, and I do this. Sometimes when I get to a space and I'm just kind of stuck and funky, I'm like, "Universe, would you please show me the contribution that I am?" I know it but sometimes I just need to be reminded of it. And it's funny, it's getting so fast now. The last time I asked that, I had 3 people sign up for a class within an hour of me asking. I said, "Thank you Universe, I got it." And I got off my boo-hoo box and got out of my pity-party. So ask and you will receive.

Additional Thoughts On Being A Contribution

- It's not about "what" we are supposed to be. More of "Who am I and what can I contribute to the kingdom of we?"

- "Universe, show me my contribution, please."

- Truth, what am I here for? If I chose to be here....what's my contribution to be?

- What would be fun for me? How could I play in the world today that would be a magnanimous and phenomenal contribution to all?

- What energy, space and consciousness (esc) can me and my body be that would allow us to be the space of magic, space, change, contribution, invitation, inspiration, presence, allowance, gifting, receiving, joy, playfulness, wonder and the infinite kindness, caring and honoring we truly be?

- Truth, WHO am I? Truth, what is my contribution? Truth, what legacy would I like to create and leave behind? Truth, what's truly vital (important) to me?

"What tools can I use to expand my business and money flows exponentially?"

R: Get past the point of view that it's about money, that it's about business; this is non-linear. This is so energetic. I used to focus on "Oh my business isn't growing fast enough. There's not enough money coming in." When you can get to the space and the true potency, as a being that you be, and you start showing up in the world like that, when you get really clear on what your business is about and you would be willing to die for it – this is called your 'why', your point of view – then that starts radiating into the world and people find you in ways you could have never formulated before.

Money, money, money

- Be the demand, "I don't care what it takes, I'm HAVING money."

- "I AM money. I love money & money loves me."

- How many ways can I tap into the infinite Universe of endless money and have it come play with me with total ease, for all eternity?

- Know how much it costs you to live each month and make the demand of yourself that you're never going to bring in less than that amount, and you'll bring that in at a minimum whatever amount feels light.

- Know that it isn't about the money. Everywhere we make things significant, it sticks us.

- Who knows more about money and has such an ease with it that you can duplicate their energy, ask them questions, read their books and choose to be that type of ease with money?

- And where can you go and what can you choose that would allow you to have, receive, create & generate absurd and obscene amounts of money from anyone and anywhere at any time with total ease?

- Start honoring you with 10% of everything you bring in.

- Start carrying an amount of money on you that you feel "rich" people would carry. Don't spend from that stash. Just HAVE money.

- Listen to everything you can pertaining to money, do the How to Become Money workbook, get clear on what your POV's about money are so that you can clear them and keep asking for all the ways you can have money come to you.

It's so confusing about just "Be you, no matter what? What if someone is being unkind? Does Access promote that?

- Poc/Pod all the "confusion" for all lifetimes.

- Return to sender with consciousness attached all the "confusion" talk.

- Get to KNOW you intimately and get to TRUST you. If you're not crystal clear on whom you are then how do you know if you're being you?

- Being you and being kind doesn't mean you're a doormat. It doesn't mean you have to allow people to treat you badly or unkindly.

- We teach people how to treat us. If you're willing to be the true potency you be (Yes, kindness is a potency - think about Dain), and you maintain that level of potency and presence all the time, others will not be able to match that and those that may want to be unkind will gravitate away from you more and more.

- Access doesn't promote unkindness. Access' definition of consciousness is that EVERYTHING is included, but nothing is judged. Does kindness exist? Yes. Does unkindness exist? Yes. The more you CHOOSE kindness, caring, potency, your capacities, and be the demand for phenomenance and greatness, the more you will be that and the more of it will show up in your Universe. Be the vibration that magnetizes all the extraordinary things you KNOW are possible. It starts with you. (If there are further questions on this, or they want further facilitation, please let me know).

So does choosing me mean it doesn't matter if my choice affects others in a way that isn't a contribution?

- Contribution means the simultaneity of gifting & receiving. EVERYTHING is a contribution. Some is more enjoyable than others, but everything contributes and creates more awareness.

- If you are choosing to be conscious and aware, and you're functioning as an infinite being, you will choose what will always create the greatest (It's the brilliance we already are). Even if someone else has the point of view or the conclusion/judgment that it's not a contribution. They are functioning from this reality and wanting things to be the way they want them to be. Doesn't mean they are being conscious.

- Some of the biggest "wake ups" I had were as a result of people choosing for themselves and my initial reaction/response was to make them wrong. But when I looked at it, asked myself questions, cleared my points of views and really got present to the contribution, I was grateful for all those moments.

- Choice creates awareness. How much awareness are you denying by not choosing for you? And even if you get to the other side of something and you have the awareness that your choice wasn't the most expansive or generative, guess what...you can apologize, or make amends, or make another choice, or whatever else might create something greater.

- Use IPOV (interesting point of view I have that point of view, they have that point of view)

- POC/POD all the pov's (points of view) and decisions, judgments, conclusions & computations (djcc's) you have from any lifetime about what it means to be a contribution, what it looks like and what it requires.

- Ask, "If I choose this..." (Is it light and expansive or contracted and heavy)? Start to get tapped into energy of what your choices will create.

- We've been conditioned and made wrong so long for being ourselves, for choosing for us, for allowing our brilliance to shine in the world that we tend to automatically want to think that no matter what we choose, it will be wrong for someone else. There's no right and wrong, just choice. Gary says so in the Bars video! :-)

The ELEMENTS to having your doorway (YOU) - undeniably are:

1. **Presence** - at all times in all places; really start to get clear on where you're not present or where you check out.

2. **Trusting you**, no matter what; make the demand to trust you and your awareness no matter how uncomfortable it might seem.

3. **Knowing you**, no matter what; get to know YOU and what you "feel like", what your senses are and how they show up, etc.

4. **Choosing you**, no matter what; choosing FOR you doesn't mean you're choosing against someone else.

5. **Play and Playfulness** with everything; get lighter and have more fun, lose the significance and heaviness of everything. PLAY!

6. **Language**, be aware of the words you use at all times; flip your script constantly and watch how things change.

7. **Gratitude**; the more you be the space of gratitude, the more it grows and even if things get sticky or tough, if you can be gratitude for something, anything, then you can change the energy.

8. **Intimacy**

9. **Vulnerability**

10. **Allowance**

11. **Receiving**

12. **Laughter** - it changes things faster than anything, including tears.

Hi, I'm so frustrated. I seem to attract people who I end up having to speak up about something that is uncomfortable and it ends up they go away and blame me, and I feel much shame. I do my best to not judge myself, but I used to isolate and hide and it had been years of isolating. Then I took the step to go to Access classes and now don't know where to turn, as I attract the same people........my heart is aching.

- "Everything is the opposite of what it appears to be, nothing is the opposite of at it appears to be". (10x in the morn/10x at night) for 30 days

- Shame is a distractor implant (There are 16). Poc and pod everything holding the distractor implant in place and for EVERY distractor that shows up in you or someone else you're dealing with, poc/pod it and everything holding it in place.

- All the lifetimes you committed to being the "whipping boy or girl" for everyone and everything, and the eternal wrongness, so that everyone else can maintain their eternal rightness for all eternity, , will you please revoke, recant, rescind, renounce, denounce, reclaim, destroy and un-create all the oaths, vows, fealties, comealties, commitments, covenants, promises and binding contracts?

- Truth, what do I love about _____?

- Truth, would you be willing to acknowledge others discomfort and still BE you anyway? Just because you are aware of something doesn't mean you have to do anything with it. It's just information. Every time you try to judge you, or it or them, poc and pod it!

- "I don't care what it takes, I'm changing this!" (Energy of demand). Get the energy of the type of people you would like to have more in your life...generative, kind, caring, nurturing, present, conscious, willing to be an enjoyable contribution, etc.

- The more you choose to be the potency you truly be, the more you will magnetize the generative people in your life that will contribute enjoyably to you.

- As stated above, we teach people how to treat us. If you're vibrating high and you maintain that higher vibration, the lower vibrations won't be able to come in with ease or as frequently.

- What's the value of me re-creating this? What do I love about _____? (If something keeps showing up, we usually have a value in it we've not yet acknowledged).

- Truth, what's it going to take to change this?

- What energy, space and consciousness (ESC) can my body and I be that will allow us to be the aggressive presence, the aggressive kindness, the potency and the infinite being of magnitude we truly be?

I know my body and me have capacities. I can sense people's thoughts. So when some people are doing drama and having so many judgments about me, I do barriers down and it doesn't have much effect. Need your facilitation about what to do with continued awareness of their mental chatter about the situation; about me, etc. It's like I am having a fun moment and this awareness comes specifically when they are angry and doing the arguments energetically. These particular moments are not fun for me.

- How do I use this wonderful capacity in a way that is fun for me?

- It's a new muscle that takes practice, practice and more practice. We've had how many lifetimes doing it one way and now we're trying to make the changes and the difference like overnight. KEEP GOING!

- Make the demand that no matter what, you're going to be the energy, space and consciousness required for yourself to BE with all that with total allowance.

- Consciousness isn't always comfortable. In fact, the more you are open, vulnerable, aware and choosing to have all the information, you're going to get it all! It can be INTENSE! Be willing to keep playing in the intensity and see how much more ease you can have with it.

- 'WHO DOES THIS BELONG TO?" Do it for 3 days, 6 days, and 10 days, etc.-constantly! I guarantee you'll see that all of it is someone else's.

- And cool, isn't it great that they're choosing to live from such limited and finite points of view? Now, what would be FUN for me to choose? What can I create and generate today? How many more things can I add to my plate to keep me from playing in everyone else's Universe?

- And if it's fun for you in whatever moment, acknowledge that. The not so fun parts demand to be and do whatever it takes to change that.

- What's the value of me re-creating this? What do I love about _____? (If something keeps showing up, we usually have a value in it we've not yet acknowledged).

(If there's more to be tapped into or facilitated, let me know and let's have a conversation. Sometimes email facilitation isn't all that! That goes for ALL these questions!)

What else is possible?

What else is available to us that we've not yet considered or imagined?

What will it take for us to be the phenomenal potent creators of a totally different reality beyond this reality for all eternity?

R: *You are the change*. You are more potent and capacitive and phenomenal than you may have ever been given acknowledgement for and I would like to do that right now. Thank you so much.

4 Special Being You Classes (Money, Body, Relationships & Future)

Dr. Dain Heer's unique and transforming points of view on bodies, money, relationship and creating the future transcend everything currently being taught.

http://bit.ly/2aBkgER

CHAPTER ELEVEN

CREATING BEYOND THE IMPOSSIBLE: THE MAGIC OF CHOICE

By Heather Nichols, MSW

Certified Access Consciousness Facilitator

Transformational Coach, Speaker, Teacher

I have always refused to see that anything was impossible--even as a kid. This reality is so based on limitation and what you can do and what you can't do, and as long as everybody stays within that box, we're told that everything will be ok. I've just always been somebody who has refused to believe and buy into that. Once I found Access Consciousness, I realized that not everybody saw things the way I did, and I started coupling the tools of Access with my tenacity for creation to create way more than I ever had before. The greatest tool for creation is choice. Choice is one of the widest doorways to possibility, and it's so much easier than we think, or that we sometimes even want it to be.

I have heard a lot of people ask, "Yea but, how do I choose?" Gary Douglas, the founder of Access Consciousness, will say (with so much ease), "Just choose!" I know that moment of: "Arghh! But there has to be something more! It has to be more complicated than this!" And yet, I've played with "just choose" enough times to know that it really works.

Six years ago, I realized that the life I was living was not the life I could be--and desired to be--living. I was in an 'ok' marriage, with 2 small children, and I was choosing to function from so much limitation. I knew that if I chose to get divorced, that it wasn't just a choice to get divorced. It was a choice to totally recreate my life. I had a 1 year old and a 3 year old, and it was not the most convenient time in the world to get divorced! But I had an awareness of so many possibilities that I just couldn't ignore.

I think we all have had that sense of a niggling awareness—that awareness that, once you have it, doesn't go away, doesn't leave you alone, and keeps popping up, tickling you every once in a while. It gets stronger and louder and more difficult to ignore—and at some point, it becomes a change or die, choose or die situation—and you've got to jump! I knew that if I didn't follow the strong pull in my world to take my life apart, I would wither away...and I wasn't willing to choose that. I didn't have the tools of Access Consciousness at the time, but I knew how to listen to my 'gut' and follow the energy of what I knew. I knew that the Universe had my back, that I was going to be ok, and that it was time to create a different reality for myself in every area of my life.

At that point, I committed to me and my 2 little babies. And as I stepped into the change, I had no idea how I was going to create what I knew I could create. Looking back, I see that I was willing to choose the life that I knew was possible then, but in that moment, I just knew I had to make a change. And really, what I did was say "Yes". And now I am living the life I knew was possible 6 years ago when I took my first step. I just keep asking, "how does it get even better?" And it does!

So many of us want to know there is going to be this safety net there, and the 'how' is the computation, decision, conclusion, and judgment that we think is going to create a safety net. In reality, trying to figure out 'how' actually just limits our capacity to receive the awareness that is required in order to create what we would like to create. Judgment, which is basically just any sort of decision, computation, or conclusion about how anything is, is actually just a barrier. Anytime we use our mind, it's a barrier, and we are literally putting energetic walls up around us. When you function from the barriers of your mind, it eliminates you.

You have a choice every time you make a judgment, every time you have a computation or a conclusion about something. In those moments, you can choose something different. You can clear it, you can call a friend and get a little facilitation, or have somebody ask you a question. You can ask "what else is possible?" If you acknowledge: "Ok, right now, I'm in judgment. Right now, I'm looking for the conclusion that I think will allow me to actually choose", then you have the possibility for change. It's choice itself that gives you more information and more possibility.

A great question to ask in these moments is, "If I could choose anything right now, what would I choose?" Sometimes, what changes things is simply the choice to say "yes" to an energy in your life that you are aware of, that you've been unwilling to choose because you don't know how you are going to get there. When we make whatever it is we would like to have in our lives that significant, we eliminate the possibility for play. What if you function from, "What fun possibilities are there for me to play with as this energy?" And then you can receive from it, become it, and choose it. That opens up so much more space for play than: "I have to create this and if I don't create this, I'm going to die!"

The Universe Has Your Back

This idea that the Universe has our backs is so foreign to so many people, and it's one of the things that creates the space for greater play with choice. The Universe isn't a solid thing that you can see; it's an energy, space, and consciousness. Right now, start to perceive that energy. *The Universe has your back.* If you don't have even a tiny sense of that, what do you imagine it would be like if the Universe *did* have your back? Allow that energy to come into your world; and as you place your attention and your awareness there, expand it as a possibility in your life. Let it become bigger, more real, more substantial--in your body, in your being, in your Universe, in your life, in your reality.

This is one of the ways that you can play with the energy of the Universe having your back--even if you don't believe it right now! If there is a tiny glimmer of a possibility of something in your awareness, the more you are aware of it, the more you cultivate it, the more you be it and be with it--the more you strengthen that as your reality.

Being, knowing, perceiving and receiving that the Universe has your your back is just a choice, and there are moments when that choice takes a lot of courage. It can feel like an impossibility in your world. Yet, at some point, what 'has been' stops working and if you are truly going to create, you must start to demand something totally different. This is when you have to step outside of your comfort zone. To function & create from the space where the Universe has your back can require a huge step out of your comfort zone!

The choice for a more expanded space of being can sometimes just be your willingness to say: "I'm having *that*. I have no idea how, but I am." And when you choose it, new awareness will start to show up. This is one of the 'tools' from Access Consciousness – choice creates awareness. It's so opposite of how we've been trained to function. Maybe you've heard that and you've rolled your eyes at it, played with it a little bit, or even a lot. And yet, how much more can you know, perceive, and receive about how choice creates awareness? How much more can you know, perceive, and receive about your capacity to choose your way into greater awareness every 10 seconds by making choice after choice after choice? And the funny thing about that is, it sounds like a lot of choosing, but we make unconscious choices all day long. What conscious choices can you make now? What consciousness can you bring to your choices? How far outside of your comfort zone are you willing to go to create a different reality for yourself and the world?

Children

Children have that knowing that anything is possible. So many of them know that if they make a demand strong enough, they can create anything. Yet kids are 'educated' out of their tenacity of choice and creation. My kids are incredibly magical, creative, brilliant creators and they create instantaneously all the time. And every time they do, I do my best to acknowledge it.

My 9 year old asked me when he was 8: "Mom, can 8 year olds have a million dollars?" I said, "What do you know about that?" He said, "Yes they can. So, how do I create that?" I said, "I wonder what questions you could ask?!" And he said, "I'd like to put my allowance in my bank right now." He was willing to choose, and to just start with the $20 that he had! When he chooses to have money, he creates it instantaneously and with so much ease. It's how he creates everything he desires. It's what is possible for all of us.

Relationships

Another area where we tend to eliminate our choice is relationships. What have you made so vital about possessing happy relationships that keeps you in the constant elimination of you? Everything that is, will you destroy and uncreate it?

One of the things that Gary Douglas talks about is the willingness to lose everybody and everything. When I first heard that, I thought, "Yeah, I'm willing to lose about 95% of everybody and everything." But there was that last 5% that hooked me! Whatever it is that you are not willing to lose, if you are making it vital, you are making it a source for your existence, for your life, and your livelihood--and you are believing the lie that you can't live without it. If there are people in your life that you are not willing to lose, you must create your life in defense & protection of those relationships. Somewhere you decide: "If I choose this, it'll eliminate that person. If I choose this, it will create disharmony..." and you start dynamically limiting your choices. The possibilities that you are willing to see get extremely narrowed. And what does that do for happiness, when you feel stifled with your choices and with the possibilities that are available? Most people I know get grumpy when their choices are limited! And yet we create that for ourselves all the time!

I've seen that, when I really do get to that space of the willingness to lose something or somebody, what actually happens most of the time is that the relationship gets greater! When you're willing to jump into that space, you actually lose the limitations in the relationship. If it's no longer 'vital' for you to have it and keep it; you have total choice and total freedom. For me, when I've been holding on to something so tight and then I choose to let go of it, it becomes so clear that I was hanging onto the limitations and not the possibilities.

There is this absolute magic that can show up with you being the space of allowance, possibility, and choice that is a totally different invitation than most people have ever seen or perceived before. It doesn't exist in this reality. And that alone – the energy, space, and consciousness of you being you -- is such a dynamic invitation into something more for people.

The other part of relationship is that you also have to be willing to create it. We live so much in this ideal of "If I find the right person, then I'm going to have that perfect relationship, and I'll have the white picket fence etc." and then we get into the relationship and we realize, "I don't want this!" But rarely do we actually even consider that we can create whatever it is that we would like to have and beyond. Choice and asking questions are a huge piece of perceiving what else is possible in relationships.

Problem Solving

In this reality, we're entrained to look for the problems and go about finding the solutions to those problems. We turn what is actually an awareness of a different possibility into a problem. It's almost like we turn 180 degrees and say: "this is the problem!" so that we can actually create a solution. So, what stupidity are you using to create conclusion as the solution to the problem you cannot solve are you choosing? Everything that is, will you destroy and uncreate it?

Solving problems is not a creative process! It's not about possibility. And problems are what we fabricate when we bastardize our awareness of possibility. What if, instead of that, you tapped again into the aware-ness of the Universe having your back? What would you like to choose and create from there? Does an infinite being have problems?

So, instead of problems, what can you create? What can you choose? What are the possibilities that you've never perceived before? What would be fun for you? Are you willing to choose in a way you never have before? You can create whatever you would like to create, and choice is where you start! What do you know that nobody else knows? What possibilities do you see that might be choices only you can make? What choice is available to you that's not available to other people?

What if you were willing to play with this totally different possibility? What if you tried on, as your reality, the total magic that choice cre-ates? Even for an hour or half a day or a day? What if it was just a fun game where you could actually just start to allow yourself to receive new energies and see what you can create? It's the choice or choices that you're refusing to make that limit your possibilities. Are you will-ing to be that powerful and potent in your own life? Are you willing to be the creator of your own life? How much fun can you have with it?

Vulnerability

Vulnerability is one of the 5 elements of intimacy; my point of view is that when you have intimacy with you, that's actually what creates everything. Vulnerability with you is the willingness to tell yourself the truth about what your choices truly are and what they aren't, what the limitations are that you are attached to and what you are willing to go beyond. If you don't bring awareness to those limitations, they can unconsciously run your life.

How can you include your body in receiving, and in vulnerability with you? How can you include your body in choice? Your body is brilliant! It has so many gifts to bring and to contribute--and when your body is included, you get to be so much more of the greatness of you.

How much play can you bring to all of this? How much joy? How much wonder and peace? What if you could function from "Hey, Universe! Show me what you've got!"--and know everything is actually going to show up greater if you're willing to have the vulnerability of not knowing and of being out of control with receiving. It allows for the space of true creation in ways that control and computation never will. "What energy, space and consciousness can your body and you be to receive in totality every day?" Everything that doesn't allow that to show up, will you destroy and uncreate it?

What if you choosing to be you, and to be different, is one of the greatest contributions that you can be to a different possibility & a different reality on planet Earth? Are you willing to be that? Are you willing for it to be that simple?

WRITE A BOOK

Do you have a book in you that would like to be written and published?

Would you like to write, publish and make your book an Amazon Bestseller?

From coaching on getting started, to helping you with the publishing process to getting your book to be an International Amazon Bestseller, Nilofer offers it all. Contact her to explore the Infinite Possibilities with your book - nilofer@illusiontoilluminationsummit.com

CHAPTER TWELVE

BEYOND THE EX-FACTOR

By Ritu Motial

Strategist, Writer, Behaviour Change Specialist,

Speaker, Long-distance-full-time mother,

Writer, Documentary Filmmaker, Content Creator

Access Consciousness Facilitator

N: Very early on in my journey in Access, I made a demand of myself that if I'm going through some interesting stuff called CRAP, I'm not going to wallow in it for very long. I'm going to reach out and ask for help, and Ritu is one of my friends to whom I reach out whenever I'm in that really interesting place. And, it is so amazing to have someone who has your back. Thank you for that, Ritu.

R: And thank you Nilofer, for having my back, and you know, I always go to you. So thank you so much, and really I must thank Gary and Dain for the wonderful tools. It has brought so much ease into my life and what else is possible?

Beyond The Ex-Factor - Parenting With A Twist

N: Ritu and I have had this conversation before. One of the things that I really, really look at, Ritu, and I admire, is how much of a parent she is even though she's been away from her sons for – how many years now, Ritu?

R: 12 years.

N: Wow. So do you want to talk about that? I know we were going to talk about it at the end, but let's begin the conversation from there.

R: This is one aspect of the Ex-Factor conversation. After my divorce, I went through a situation where the boys were growing up with their father and I was away from them, and so I've looked at the whole concept of parenting and I've also looked at - is distance really a parameter when I'm in a parent mode?

The awareness was that distance really doesn't matter. That's been a totally different awareness of parenting. Also, I've always followed the 5 elements of intimacy with my boys. There's been an openness, there's been allowance, there's been a huge amount of gratitude for the two of them because really, through all that I went through, it was the boys who said, "Mum, just carry on," and I'm just hugely grateful for that.

N: So would you share with us some of the tools that you actually used when you were away from your sons, and how was that for you?

R: Sure, let's look at what relationships really are for each of us. So what does that particular relationship really mean to me? I kind of looked at the whole definition of parenting, what did parenting really mean to me, and so whatever point of view I had at that time of course, I had been destroying and un-creating all the conventional points of view that people have of parents. That parents should always be there. That parents should be strict. That parents should be blah blah blah. So I looked at the whole thing and what was going to be a contribution to the boys' life and living, and asked, how can I allow that to be a contribution to me? That was one thing.

The other thing that I looked at was that I did not choose to go into guilt. Did I really need to beat myself up that I was making a choice to be a different kind of a parent? I didn't have to do that. I actually was in total allowance of myself to begin with and in total gratitude for myself for choosing a different possibility. What it has brought about is a lot of openness. One thing that came through was the kind of relationship I have with my boys, not many parents can enjoy even though they have lived with them throughout; the openness, the honesty, the allowance. The allowance factor is so huge. Today they tell me, "You know what, we don't want another mother. We are just so happy to have you as a mother because what it has done for us is given us a respect for women, for people and for being a person, someone who has different possibilities with what you would call a conventional relationship. So I think that has really been a very critical factor in our "relationship."

N: Ritu, I remember, when I met you for the first time and you told me this thing about, "I'm a full-time long distance parent" and I was "wow!" The energy of that itself was like so amazing for me, and I could really perceive the joy and the happiness and that communion you had with your boys.

R: Yes, I always say, "I'm a long-distance full-time mother" with total joy!

What definitions do we have of relationships? When we will look at any relationship, and we all have a certain definition, could we just destroy and un-create all of those definitions? Right and wrong, good and bad, POD and POC, all nine, shorts, boys and beyonds.

Relationships And Its Godzillion Definitions- Hmm, What's The Value Of These?

How many definitions and parameters do we have in place to create a relationship? Everywhere you are in a relationship, whether it is as a husband and a wife or ex-husband and ex-wife or as a mother and a parent and a child, would you please look at all the definitions that are defining those relationships and holding those relationship positions, and could we destroy and un-create it all please? Times godzillion. Right and wrong, good and bad, POD and POC all nine, shorts, boys and beyond...

Wherever we operate from a definition of a relationship, would we you please destroy and un-create it all, times a godzillion? And all the oaths, vows, fealties, comealties, blood-oaths, swearings, promises, contracts and bindings we have to keeping that definition of that relationship intact, would we now please revoke, recant, rescind, renounce, denounce, reclaim, destroy and un-create it all? Right and wrong, good and bad, POD and POC, all nine, shorts, boys and beyonds.

N: Would you explain about the oaths and vows and fealties and comealties? What is all that exactly and how is that sticking people in relationships?

R: Let's look at the Ex-Factor that we've been talking about, and I'm really looking at the E-X-Factor. So When you have a husband, so there are those little promises that you have and all the attachments that you have that are associated with a husband. So we say "A husband is supposed to look after us. And I'm a wife, I'm supposed to look after my husband. I'm supposed to look after the house." The kind of promises we make, "No, I will always look after you" or "you should always be there with me", we bind ourselves with all the promises and all the oaths that we've taken. "I'm going to be with you till death do us part." So does that truly give us choice? Or does it become a have-to situation?

N: It becomes like a necessity.

R: When it becomes a necessity, how much do we truly enjoy doing that or being that? It's a duty. It's something that you are supposed to do. It's not something that's joyful for you any longer, and this have-to position creates no-choice. I couldn't stand up and say, "You know what, today I just don't feel like cooking for you." And it was like "No, no, you are supposed to do this. No, you are supposed to do this." There's this constant chatter that continuously happens. You're a wife, therefore you should do this. You're a mum therefore you should do this. You're a blah blah. It doesn't give me freedom of that total choice.

Now when I'm in that situation, am I really being in allowance or a contribution to me? It took me a while to realize that until and unless I wasn't a contribution to myself, I couldn't be a contribution to anyone else around. We negate ourselves or obviate ourselves from that the entire equation and we're only looking at it as "I'm a mother so I should do this. I'm a wife so I should do this."

All of those oaths, vows, and fealties that we have taken in any lifetime, or in this lifetime, in any dimension, or in this dimension, to be brought into the form and structure of that particular relationship, can we revoke, recant, rescind, renounce, denounce, reclaim, destroy and un-create it all, times a godzillion? Right and wrong, good and bad, POD and POC all nine, shorts, boys and beyonds.

If you could just move past the have-to's and say "hey, it's not fun for me to wake up in the morning. It's not fun for me to, you know, to be cooking" then I have a choice in this matter. Am I also not giving a choice to the other person to be what is fun for them?

If I'm giving them that the choice to be them, is it not a more expansive Universe that we are creating? Rather than limitations where it is always, "Eh, now I have to get up and cook for my kids. Eh, now I have to throw a party for my husband. Eh, now I have to do this."

Now look at the Ex-Factor. My relationship totally underwent a change to the extent that from a husband, he became an ex-husband. So, when you look at an ex-husband, what it is that you have? When you are looking at an 'ex' situation like it's passé, there is so much bickering, and there's so much, "this guy did this to me, oh my god, this guy did this to me, oh my god." When I started moving into that space, a conscious choice which I made was that I am not going to let any of this affect me at any point in time and I'm not going to let it affect my children at any point in time.

I started looking at what could I create with the Ex-Factor. What could I create with my ex-husband? One of the tools which I use very regularly is to destroy and un-create my relationship with my ex-husband. Another tool which I use is ***What energy, space, and consciousness can I be to get my ex-husband to contribute to my life and living with total ease, joy and glory?"***

It started opening up doors, it started opening up awarenesses. I looked at that, "Hey, I never allowed him to contribute to my life. What would that contribution be, if I would just allow?" He's actually gone from being an ex-husband to – I just joke with him, I say, "you know what, my parents have adopted you now." I'm so grateful for the way he has looked after my parents in my absence.

Can we then have a different reality with the Ex-factor? How many barriers do we have to totally receiving from that? Whatever that may be, his bickering, his love, his affection, him going with somebody else and whatever that may be.

All the barriers that we have erected to totally receiving from whatever the relationship be, would you please destroy and un-create all of that, times a godzillion? Right and wrong, good and bad, POD and POC, all nine, shorts, boys and beyonds.

Contribution- What Else Is Possible That I Have Not Even Looked At?

N: So I was just listening to one of the classes by Gary and Dain. Dain was talking about how somebody created a class in a town he was going to do a class in and he could perceive their energy and they were functioning from anger, hate, fury and rage, and right then, he said, "How can all of that contribute to me? And how can I out-create all of that? And how can I have fun with all of that?" and I was like "Oh, we can use anger, rage, fury and hate also and even that can be a contribution to us when we have no barriers to it!"

R: Absolutely! I'm so glad you brought this point up because one of the things I've been saying is "How can I out-create my ex-husband?" That's it, and suddenly you realize that we have such points of view about what out-creating means. So am I out-creating him financially?

Am I out-creating him in the space he occupies in this Universe, in the terms of the name, fame, etc., etc.? Or am I just out-creating him at a very basic level? So I kind of looked at it and I said, "Oh wow." I mean, if I look at what my contribution has been and I'm not negating his contribution at all, he has opened up so much space for us to have this conversation. So when I look at that whole space of out-creation I have looked at, not that today he is earning let's say X amount of money and I have to earn 2X, it's actually how much more peace and gratitude and kindness I have for myself. So could that not be an out-creation?

How many definitions do we have about out-creating? And wherever we are not getting to the energy of out-creation, would we please destroy and un-create all of that, times a godzillion? Right and wrong, good and bad, POD and POC, all nine, shorts, boys and beyonds.

N: I was just aware that this energy of out-creation. We are out-creating with each and every call that we are doing (in the summit), there are no words for it, it is not a linear thing. It is not that it has just one energy. It has so much. So if you were to go to question – "I wonder what out-creation means?" How would you perceive out-creation? Like that class I was listening to of Gary and Dain, they spoke about out-creating. What if you could wake up every morning and out-create your monetary reality every day? And I said "Absolutely. I never thought of that." Out-creation can be in so many different ways.

R: Absolutely. And when Gary says that you be that question, and ever since I've gotten into that being that question, when you live as a question, you know, you start looking at "Oh, this could mean this also. This could mean this also. What else is possible out here, which I haven't looked at and I'm not even willing to look at?" Now am I willing to look at it? So what is it that is stopping me from truly looking at whatever that out-creation for instance could be, or the meaning of that relationship, or the definition of that relationship, and you really go back over it. It opens up so many different doors for you, it's incredible! You are just looking at it and saying "Wow! I never thought that this was a possibility. What else is possible here?" Like when you were talking about operating from anger, rage, hate, and fury, one thing which Gary always talks about, which I find amazing is that, "If YOU don't operate from a distractor implant, you can use others' distractor implants to your advantage."

It makes so much sense when you are in the question of "what would that be for you?" How much are you not looking at Ex-factor and going "What is the distractor implant here? So what is really important?" and you realize that half the time people are operating from a sense of guilt, or doubt or just the need for validation, so how do you use that to your advantage? What is it that you are looking for? And how can you be a contribution to them so that it is a contribution to you as well?"

N: When you are speaking of contribution, it's that simultaneity of gifting and receiving, so not only are you expanding your own Universe but you are also expanding their Universe.

R: The way we are brought up, the way we grow up, for us contribution is "oh, what can I contribute to expanding other's Universes?" Ok, buddy, what about making a contribution for me as well?

Another thing, I just find I've been playing with this word 'contribution', and looking at "what else is possible with contribution?"

Recently I was in Lucknow where my parents and my ex-husband live, I was in the question of, *"What energy, space and consciousness can I be to be a contribution to my relationship with my ex, and bring more joy, ease and glory there?"* Suddenly I realized that it is not only that I have to be nice to him in terms of talking politely, talking well, but there are times when just being that intensity is also a contribution. So if I step up into my own space and say "Only this much and no more," it opens up a door for him as well, "There is another possibility here. So far I was just walking over her, and now she's not going to take shit anymore", and he starts looking at a totally different reality.

What does contribution truly mean? Everywhere we have created a definition for contribution and you we are operating from that, please destroy and un-create it all times a godzillion. Right and wrong, good and bad, POD and POC, all nine, shorts, boys and beyonds.

What Is Right About Me, That I Am Not Getting?

Caller: "Hi. Please help. Feeling desperate and truly fucked up with people using Access to be superior over others. I've worked diligently on myself. Thought I was wrong. Found Access that tells me that I'm not wrong, yet seem to have superior bitches showing up in my journey in Access. It sucks big time. Can Access people do whatever they please and never have to take responsibility for their unkindness and never have to apologize? It's truly sad as it is getting really twisted weird out here with some Access people. and How are we supposed to navigate this and encourage others that Access does work?"

R: That's a fantastic question and I'm glad you brought it up because I've also been asking this question.

Everywhere we are making Access significant or Access insignificant, would we please destroy and un-create that? Right and wrong, good and bad, POD and POC all nine, shorts, boys and beyonds.

Everywhere we are making being an Access facilitator or practitioner significant and a measure of "oh this person is totally aware", would you please destroy and un-create it all, times a godzillion? Right and wrong, good and bad, POD and POC all nine, shorts, boys and beyonds.

Wherever we are not able to look at ourselves and the contribution we truly be, would you please destroy and un-create that as well? Right and wrong, good and bad, POD and POC all nine, shorts, boys and beyonds.

Now if you were to just go past and look at people who are using Access tools; so which space are they using them from? Are they using the tools from the kingdom of we, or are they using it them to make themselves superior bitches? This is where the whole thing of that 'what's right about me that I'm not getting?" really worked for me. If I'm operating from that space of *'What's right about me that I'm not getting? What are my contributions? What can I be? What energy, space and consciousness can I be to be a contribution, beyond my imagination?'* When you and really start looking at that space of being, you would probably realize that everybody is in their own zone, so you can actually use that to your advantage.

N: The other thing is, "For what reason are you choosing to be an effect of other people's reality?"

All you have to do is "you know what, I'm not choosing this anymore. I'm not going to be at the effect of any other person's reality" and sometimes, it's just as easy as making the choice of not being that thing.

The other thing that I've found really works well for me here is to use this clearing "What energy, space and consciousness can my body and I be, to be the kingdom of We, we truly be for all eternity?"

I was seeing this a lot in my own life and I said maybe I'm not being the kingdom of We and maybe I'm not being a contribution, so I literally started running this clearing 20-30 times a day. What I began started to notice was how much I was being that energy of the kingdom of We and all those people who I was perceiving to be doing competition or meanness, I started to see a shift and change in them. It was so amazing to watch that. I started including myself in that energy in the computation of my life.

R: Another question I've really been using a lot is "What's right about me that I'm not getting?" As humanoids, how much do we truly have gratitude for ourselves? And just how kind are we to us? And how much do we judge ourselves continuously? So if you are in that space where you are constantly judging yourself, can you have a look at yourself as someone who can contribute? You are constantly looking at "oh my god, they've done so much. Oh my god!" So another thing which I would always ask was "Show me the truth of others and show me my truth." So it's working both ways and then you are totally in allowance of "ok, so what? You fucked up, you fucked up. Big shit! Ok? Now what can I create?" So when you are being that level of allowance, what can you truly create then? And it really doesn't matter when you are looking at someone else's truth and it may not really be what you thought it was, and then you are in allowance of it. "Ok fine, wow, that's interesting. Interesting choice. And wherever I've stuck myself with that, POC and POD that."

Am I Significant Or Insignificant?

Everywhere where you are making you significant or insignificant, and others significant or insignificant, would you please destroy and un-create it all, times a godzillion? Right and wrong, good and bad, POD and POC all nine, shorts, boys and beyond.

I ran this clearing statement continuously for me, and I realized that when I'm looking at 'oh, this one did this to me' or 'this one is greater than me'– am I not making myself significant or insignificant? If I be the unique contribution, can anybody be my competition? Not really, right? So in that space, am I not making myself insignificant? Correct? So we either make ourselves too significant "Oh my god, this person is doing this to me!" You know, what if it could just be that they be that. It's not that they are doing it to you. They are not running behind you and doing it to you. You are making yourself so significant in that situation. Or it could also be "Oh, I did this and used this tool and I cleared so and so for them." What about people's choices in that situation who came to you? What it did was, it suddenly started showing me my reality and where I was not putting me in the computation of the whole reality. You know what you said the kingdom of We, so the minute I'm making myself insignificant or I'm making myself significant, there is a distance that I'm creating.

Am I operating from Kingdom of We or am I operating from Kingdom of Me, or Kingdom of them? So there is a judgment all the time. But when I'm truly operating from Kingdom of We, what is the significance of others or significance of me? Right and wrong, good and bad, POD and POC, all nine, shorts, boys and beyonds.

What do I love about beating myself up? Everything that is, times a god-zillion, would you please destroy and un-create it all, times a godzillion? Right and wrong, good and bad, POD and POC, all nine, shorts, boys and beyonds.

Not only do we judge ourselves, how much do we really beat ourselves up? "Oh, she did this. She is so much better than I am. He is so much better than I am." Well, what he is, he is. What she is, she is. What you are, you are.

Caller: Hi. What you've been speaking has been really touched me all over. What seems to be going on in my life is like I'm unplugging from the matrix and these people there want to put their plugs back in. It's really fascinating because these two people don't talk to each other or nothing and they probably don't even remember each other. It's been long since they saw each other, but they both tried to make me worry about my son and then, and it was like really fascinating because I told one person I'm going to bed and then she texts me at midnight telling me that Shane, didn't come over to her house, and can she buy fur coats for me. So really what she wanted to do was make me worry about Shane, you know? And then the other person Facebooked me and asked me about my son, and I was like "wow! Isn't that interesting that these two people are so connected in what they are doing but they don't really even know each other?" That make any sense? I'm really not taking it personally and I'm really just kind of like standing back and looking at it and POD and POCing some, but if I ever finally start getting sucked back in it again, then

R: I'm going to stop you and can I ask you a quick question? Truth, are you a finite being or infinite being?

Caller: I am an infinite being.

R: If you are an infinite being, who has the potency?

Caller: Well, the one with the most awareness, from what I understand.

R: Would you please POC and POD that point of view. Right and wrong, good and bad, POD and POC, all nine, shorts, boys and beyonds. If you are an infinite being, you have potency, total awareness, right?

Caller: Yes

R: When you say that someone is sucking you into the worry, are you being potent?

Caller: No

R: And are you an infinite being?

Caller: Yes

R: So can you ever be sucked into someone else's point of view unless you choose to do so?

Wherever you are allowing yourself to buy other's trauma and drama as yours and not question 'what's this? What can I do with it? Can I change it? If so, how do I change it?' will you now please destroy and un-create that? Right and wrong, good and bad, POD and POC, all nine, shorts, boys and beyonds.

Everywhere you are making the whole situation significant and trying to attribute "oh wow, this has happened. What's that? There's got to be some meaning." All of those justifications and significances and the stories that you've created around it, would you please destroy and un-create it all, times a godzillion? Right and wrong, good and bad, POD and POC, all nine, shorts, boys and beyonds.

What if somebody calls up and says, "You know what, Shane needs this." Another one says, "Oh how's Shane?" What if it could just be that insignificant, and what if it was no big deal? Maybe you just have to pick up a phone just and check out "Shane how are you doing? Cool, great. Ok."

Wherever you are making it extremely significant or marginally significant, would you please destroy and not getting into the question of it - would you please destroy and un-create it all, times a godzillion? Right and wrong, good and bad, POD and POC, all nine, shorts, boys and beyonds.

If you are an infinite being, do you have total awareness?

What creation are you using to create the lack of infinite awareness you are choosing? Everything that is, times a godzillion, would you please destroy and un-create it all? Right and wrong, good and bad, POD and POC, all nine, shorts, boys and beyonds.

What Is The Other Ex Factor?

N: You spoke a lot about the Ex-factor which is to do with the ex-relationship. Can you speak about the other Ex-Factor?

R: The Ex-Youth and Ex-Glory?

In my life I've looked at a situation where I was married to this gentleman who was extremely rich, and I had a staff of 10, I had cars and blah, blah, blah. And after my divorce, I came to a point where it was interesting living and interesting choices that I had to make. Now in that situation, do I go into "hey, you know what, this is all available to me, or Oh my god, what do I do now? Ok, fine, that happened. Now what do I create? Now what are the choices available to me?"

I find a lot of people going into the trauma and drama of having lost a job, having lost money, having moved past what you call their prime youth and just putting an end to life after that. Their life after that just crawls. I have a 23 year old son and I am 50. Do I look at that and say, "Oh, I'm so old. Do I stop?" No, I have been in this question "What does age mean to me? Is age a number?" Age is just a number. Does age actually signify anything? Nothing.

How much is age controlling me? How much is this whole situation of no money controlling me? And how much am I letting it actually control me?

Everywhere we are letting the numbers control us, whether it is age or money or the number of servants or the number of houses that we ever had, would you please destroy and un-create it all, times a godzillion? Right and wrong, good and bad, POD and POC, all nine, shorts, boys and beyonds.

Wherever we are looking at numbers as a very significant part of our life and living, could we please destroy and un-create it all, times a godzillion? Right and wrong, good and bad, POD and POC, all nine, shorts, boys and beyonds.

Wherever we are not choosing to go beyond the numbers and are only getting attached to the numbers, would we please destroy and un-create that as well? Right and wrong, good and bad, POD and POC, all nine, shorts, boys and beyonds.

What could I choose and what could I create and who and what could I create me as right now? What more magic can I create? What more magic can I be?

I found that with this tool infinite possibilities opened up, and today, I look at "oh, I choose to create this. Now what else can I create? Now what else can I create? Now what else can I choose?"

There is a full-time job that I do, there are the Access workshops plus I'm working on my own book, plus I've just finished writing a script for a documentary. Now if I had let that thing – if I had only stopped at that point, "oh, I'm divorced and I don't have a job anymore" I probably wouldn't have moved into this space.

Everywhere we are letting our past hold us back and keep us going back into a loop, would we now please at the count of 3, destroy and un-create all of it? 1-2-3. 1-2-3. And 1-2-3-4 for a future that we create from a totally fresh space. So at the count of 4, 1-2-3-4. Thank you.

Caller:"Any clearings to completely wipe off the energy of all the exes in relationships, jobs, deals and all failed or successful health plans and to start off anew?"

R: *"What energy, space and consciousness can I be to live life as now, in the now?" Totally enjoying now.*

"What energy, space and consciousness can my body and I be to out-create my past with total ease, joy and glory? And everything that doesn't allow me to do that, I now destroy and un-create it all, times a godzillion. Right and wrong, good and bad, POD and POC, all nine, shorts, boys and beyonds.

Wherever I am making my past more significant than my now, I destroy and un-create that? Right and wrong, good and bad, POD and POC, all nine, shorts, boys and beyonds"

Caller: "I have been divorced with my son's dad for 16 years and my son is 17 and he never contributed financially. He did really little and I wonder what can I ask him to contribute to my son even though he is almost 18. What else is possible? And thank you, I never thought of him until you had this. So grateful to you both."

R: *Truth, are you good at receiving? And how many barriers to receiving do you have? Everything that is, times a godzillion, will you please destroy and un-create it all? Right and wrong, good and bad, POD and POC, all nine, shorts, boys and beyonds.*

All the barriers you have erected to receiving, would you now destroy and un-create it all, at the count of 3? 1-2-3. 1-2-3. 1-2-3. Right and wrong, good and bad, POD and POC, all nine, shorts, boys and beyonds.

Wherever you are not willing to receive from your ex-husband, would you destroy and un-create that as well? Right and wrong, good and bad, POD and POC, all nine, shorts, boys and beyonds.

What energy, space and consciousness can my body and I be to receive totally from my ex-husband with total ease, joy and glory? Everything that doesn't allow that will you destroy and un-create it all? Right and wrong, good and bad, POD and POC, all nine, shorts, boys and beyonds.

So if I'm going to say "oh, you know what, he hasn't contributed?" How much am I judging, how much should I really step in and say, "Mister, come on, you haven't contributed a dime. Get on with it!" Are we really willing to ask that question? Do we totally honor ourselves? Do we recognize that we deserve it or are we getting into this "oh I don't deserve it. Oh maybe I can't ask him." Why not? That's his son as well. Isn't it?

All of those stories that you have sold yourself, and you've bought in wholesale, would you now please destroy and un-create all of them? Right and wrong, good and bad, POD and POC, all nine, shorts, boys and beyond.

R: There is another question which Gary actually had spoken in a couple of classes. He said **"What energy, space and consciousness can my body and I be to get the fucker to do exactly what I desire with total ease, joy and glory?"**

Whenever you are making life so serious and so dramatic, would you please destroy and un-create it all? So what fun can I create with him? Anywhere you are not willing to be that space of fun, would you please destroy and un-create it all, times a godzillion? Right and wrong, good and bad, POD and POC, all nine, shorts, boys and beyonds.

I actually found with my ex-husband that a lot of teasing and having fun with him just puts him in "What the hell is she on about?" and it's great fun to watch him doing that because then you can just go have fun with him. If you know what I'm talking about and what I mean. It's great, because then you are getting out of the wrongness of you. When a relationship breaks or goes sour, how much do we judge ourselves and hold ourselves responsible for it?

Everywhere you beat yourself, you curse yourself and you've beaten yourself up with that stick of self-flagellation, would you now please destroy and un-create it all, times a godzillion? Right and wrong, good and bad, POD and POC, all nine, shorts, boys and beyonds.

What Other Fun Can You Have With Your Ex?

What comedy can you have with your ex-husband? Or your ex-boy-friend? And wherever you are not willing to be that, would you please destroy and un-create all of those traumas and dramas and go boom!? Right and wrong, good and bad, POD and POC, all nine, shorts, boys and beyonds. Times a godzillion.

N: I'm just laughing because you brought in this energy of the ex-boy-friend. How many people are there who make the ex-boyfriend or ex-girlfriend significant. "Oh my god, they left us" and all that.

R: *All the stories, so truth, all of you guys out there, and all the stories you have sold yourself, so truth, did you really want them? And wherever you are not willing to look at that, would you now destroy and un-create it all? Right and wrong, good and bad, POD and POC, all nine, shorts, boys and beyonds.*

Because, if you truly had wanted that person in your life, you would have done something different. Did you truly want them? Haha! And all the stories we've told ourselves that how we really wanted them but they cheated on us, would you please destroy and un-create all of those stories? Right and wrong, good and bad, POD and POC, all nine, shorts, boys and beyonds.

Beyond The Ex-Factor

Once you go beyond the Ex-Factor, you're getting into the creative mode. You create yourself. So what could you create? What would that brand new you be?

N: Thank you Ritu, that was really amazing and what is one last thing you want to leave us with?

R: For me what really has been is looking at this whole space of how many whole definitions I have of me and what if I were totally defini-tion-less? What could I create then? What would my life be then? And so I've been really destroying and un-creating me and that includes, me as a mother, me as ex-wife, me as whatever that is. And then the that question of *"what more can I create? What more can I add to my life? What more fun can I have?"* So that whole thing of creation, when we look at creation, is – am I creating fun or am I creating something which is from somebody else's point of view? For a very long time, I did not think of me as being valuable because I was not doing X number of workshops or because I was not doing X number of sessions or because I didn't have X level of a job. And it's only in the last year, ever since I've been really, really using these tools of Access to just get into this whole space of "what's fun for me?" and "what would that create for the possibilities of this world and beyond?" So here's an invitation for all of us to really look at that. What's really fun for you and what could that create? (Rather than creating based on somebody else's point of view about what we really should be creating.) Would that be fun for everyone?

N: Wow. No, I'm sure that wouldn't be fun. It's much more fun to do what other people expect of you. (laughs)

R: (laughs) Absolutely. *So wherever we are making that important, would you please destroy and un-create it all? Right and wrong, good and bad, POD and POC all nine, shorts, boys and beyond.*

Need and Tug Telecall Series

This class is based on the book, The Place, and how the character Jake manages to ask of the earth in order to find gold. He asks based on a point of view of need, and shows us how you can pull from need instead of how you make a problem from need.

Most people go "Oh, I need this!" but it's not an energy of invitation it's an energy of rejection. So this is the place where you use how you "need" in your life to get the universe to support you.

http://bit.ly/2aEysdC

CHAPTER THIRTEEN

WITCHES AND WIZARDS

By Julia Sotas

Certified Facilitator of Access Consciousness

What Is A Witch?

J: When I was a little girl, my mom was a Reiki Master. Today I was cleaning up my computer and I came across this cartoon and it was a picture of a man lying on a massage table and this woman going at his back with a rake – like a big, sharp rake. And he's like "Huh, this is so interesting; I could have sworn that Reiki was about something else!" (laughs) Oh my god, I just love that cartoon! I think it's so funny to look at the man's face. And that's how people look at me when they think that I am a witch. I've been doing magic my whole life and since I joined Access Consciousness, it has just amped up quite a bit. Using the tools of the questions has just really, really helped my – let's just call it witchcraft, magic, whatever you want to call it.

There's a lot of judgment around what it means to be a witch because in history the women who were witches – and I'm just going to talk about women for a little while here because that's sort of the connotation of a witch - women who were witches were strong threats for the public, to the government, to men, to all of these different institutions that were very powerful. So you would be called a witch if you were a powerful woman and burnt at the stake. And when I came to Access Consciousness, I got a lot of clearings on what it meant to be a witch and all of the different lifetimes in the past that I was burnt at the stake and that really helped me amp up my powers because I was scared to do things – almost wouldn't admit to myself what I was doing and was being able to clear it and being able to clear the different lifetimes in which I swore I would never do it again. I've been able to amp things up unbelievably. So that's been fabulous.

"All of the lifetimes in which you were a witch, a wizard, an emperor, an empress of social level and you were killed for it, raped for it, robbed for it, destroyed for it, your family was killed for it or your money was taken away for it, all those place, times, everything that is, will you revoke, recant, rescind, reclaim, renounce, denounce, destroy and un-create all of that, times a godzillion?" Right and wrong, good and bad, POD and POC all nine, shorts, boys and beyonds

That's a building block for me and brought a really big sense of freedom. Going out of wrongness of being a witch. I have lot of close friends who are Christian, it's a worry for me because I wonder, am I doing something wrong? Or is this wrong? But it's not a wrongness, it's just a choice and it goes against everything that has been institutionalized and made right and so it's important that we know who we are and what we are actually creating in the world. And to be it is not wrong, it is all just a choice.

So anywhere you judged yourself for your magic to the point that you couldn't do it anymore, you shut it down, you closed it up, you put your wand in the drawer and wouldn't let anybody know where your wand was, will you destroy and un-create it all and go back to the drawer and get your wand out? Right and wrong, good and bad, POD and POC all nine, shorts, boys and beyonds.

N: There is this weird energy I perceive around wands. Can you talk more about that?

J: What does a wand mean to you? What comes up, what judgment?

N: It's more of this energy of something outside of me which creates the magic and I know that is not true.

J: It's a total lie that magic can ever be outside of you.

Everywhere that you've bought that your magic was outside of you, will you destroy and un-create all that? Right and wrong, good and bad, POD and POC all nine, shorts, boys and beyonds.

Perhaps the wand is not the magic but the person behind the wand and how they choose to use the wand. Everything that is, will you destroy and un-create it all? Right and wrong, good and bad, POD and POC all nine, shorts, boys and beyonds

Relationships And Magic

A relationship is something people usually use to destroy their magical powers, capacities, abilities, all those different things. It's not that a relationship is wrong, it's just that sometimes, like when you meet somebody, you see them across a crowded room and you see this beautiful, incredible being and that's the being they truly are. All their magic and all their potency and all their beauty, and we look at them and we go "Wow! Like I would really like to be with that person." What happens if you do end up being with them is that you start cutting off different pieces of yourself in order to be with them and then at some point, you know, because you want to accommodate them, you want to compromise, you want to make sure that they like you, you want to make sure that you don't lose them because they are so incredible, and they do the same for you. And what happens is that we usually shut off our magical capacities in order to be with somebody else. And I've seen a lot of couples, a few couples that actually their magical capacities are amped up by being in a relationship because both people are willing to be the magic. But for the most part, I haven't seen that to be true.

Everywhere that you used relationships as a way to destroy your magic, will you destroy and un-create all that? Right and wrong, good and bad, POD and POC all nine, shorts, boys and beyonds.

N: We all are witches and wizards, so what if we choose to acknowledge this and play with this 24x7? So what would it take to live as magic every second of every day? So I wonder what would that be like and how is that for you, Julia? How does that show up for you?

J: Well, that's a good question. It's different and most days I'm feeling like magic but it's been a long journey to get to this point. I think that there's so much judgment about what it is. Gary Douglas on the Global Bars day said something that really helped me and touched me. He said that it usually takes people 5 years to start using the tools of Access Consciousness in every single area of their life if they really dedicate themselves.

When I came to Access, I was in University, and so I looked at Access Consciousness as sort of a second university degree and I looked at it and I thought, "you know what, I'm going to dedicate 4 years of my life full-time to this, and see what comes out the other end." So I didn't do it as a peripheral thing. I actually stopped going to the university and started doing Access full-time and it was a really, really difficult journey at the beginning because it was so different than anything that was expected of me and so different than anything anyone had ever seen of me before and also I was going through clearing so many different things in my life so quickly that all my stability was gone and the only person I had to rely on was myself.

I like the way that Dain and Gary facilitate because they do so in such a way that no matter what you do, you can't look to them as gurus or depend on them. You have to depend on yourself and I am so grateful for that. Because I'm at a place where I totally trust myself and I have my own back and I don't have to look outside of myself for anything. I think that was some very skillful facilitation on their part. So for me, being a witch or wizard is not necessarily something that happens overnight, but if you commit to that journey and you commit to every area of your life, to be something that works for you using your magic, it will show up. It will show up. It works a 100% of the time.

You can't use Access Consciousness and it not work if you are actually using it. And it takes discipline and it's super-uncomfortable, like agonizing. I mean I went through times where I was suicidal and at the same time, some days at that time were amazing and incredible and it was just different days and it was just a journey of ups and downs. Now that I've got through some of my darkest demons, things are a lot easier. And every day they are getting better and better and better and better. And some days I'm like "Oh my god, can it actually get better than this?" And it's always trusting that it will get better and better and better, until you are living in your own reality, in your totally own magical world. And it's not a fairy tale; it's not a fantasy.

I was giving a talk on Saturday to a group of people at an Expo and they were asking "Isn't what you are talking about sort of just a far off fantasy?" And it's not. If you actually look at what you would like to have as your life, and don't look at it as a fantasy, you can start to create it, because what you call your fantasy is a life that you could actually have and it takes magic to get there. You can't do it without magic.

What Is Magic?

N: What is magic and the place that you were speaking from, that alchemy, that capacity to change anything and it doesn't necessarily mean that you do "poof" and something disappears although all that is included in it. But magic is way beyond that. Right?

J: For me, magic is the ability to change anything in my life, into something that works better for me or that's more enjoyable. I'm sure that a lot of people on the call have heard about the nine trannies? And if you haven't heard about the nine trannies, the nine trannies are these 9 things, these 9 ways that we can change anything in our life. And this to me is kind of the Access Consciousness definition of magic.

And there's trans-migration, which is moving from one place to another without actually doing it physically. Like getting somewhere before you are actually meant to get there. There's trans-mutation, which is actually changing the physical structure of your body, structure of your body into something else. There's Trans-location. Trans-literation, which is when you change language or you can understand different language than yours.

This helped me a lot when I was in Costa Rica. I haven't gotten to the point – and I know that there are people on the planet who have gotten to the point where things actually move in front of your eyes and you can actually walk through walls. That is possible. I have not done that. I can't wait and I am working towards it every day. From the time that I was like 5 years old, I was like "I would like to fly", nothing else matters to me other than flying. Literally with or without wings, with my body, actually defy gravity and lift off into the sky and fly. And that has been my life's mission and I was very lucky to have very kind parents and a very kind upbringing and so none of that was ever knocked out of me, like there were things that tried to knock it out of me and I just wouldn't let it. For me, it is my right to fly. Why would I not be flying?

I was driving on an icy hill because I live in the middle of the frigging Arctic, it was 35 below Celsius, or 40 below Celsius where I live. I live in the coldest city. A city that's 2 hours away from me is the coldest city in the entire world, with a population of over 50 thousand. We can beat out any place in Russia, any place in the world. It's cold here. So I was sliding down this icy hill and I just about to hit the car in front of me. I was going pretty fast and I was just about to hit this car and I said "Ok, this is not happening" and instead of going into the reaction of "Oh my gosh!" I told my car, "No, car, don't! No!" And it stopped sliding and actually flung backwards. My car went backwards up the icy hill rather than sliding forwards into the car. And it was right before I hit the car. It went up the icy hill and stopped there. And I was like "Oh awesome!" But that's normal. That's the way it should be. That's the way we should be living. But most of you will only do it in an emergency situation.

Everywhere that you've only been willing to have your magic in an emergency situation, will you destroy and un-create all of that? Right and wrong, good and bad, POD and POC all nine, shorts, boys and beyonds.

So by the same token, if we can change the movement of our car and make it go backwards and go against physics, why can we not lift off the ground and fly away?

N: As you were talking about your situation, I had this awareness of me when I cross the road in India in the middle off the traffic, I just look there and I put up this wall of energy and it's like "no, you are not touching me. I'm going to cross this very busy road here!"

So the thing is, each one of us has done that kind of stuff.

Everywhere that you have done that stuff, would you be willing to acknowledge the magic that you be and the magic that you have created? And everything that doesn't allow you to perceive, know, be and receive that, will you destroy and un-create it all? Right and wrong, good and bad, POD and POC all nine, shorts, boys and beyonds.

The first time that I read Gary's book 'Magic – You are It and Be It', he says acknowledge the magic that you've created, I sat down with this pen and paper and I started to list down all the magic that I had created. And at that point of time it was all the big things that I had done. But now, when I'm doing magic, it's those little things that pop up. There's moments of magic which fill my day. It's like that point of time when my son is throwing a tantrum and I go, **"What energy, space and consciousness can I be to change this right away?"** and in 2 minutes he is ok and he is playing. That is magic.

And then I'm about to go out of the house and I go "Maybe I should carry my umbrella" and I pick out my umbrella and I go out and it's raining. That is magic. It's those little moments that we are creating magic all the time that would you be willing to acknowledge that? How much magic can we read about today I wonder?

Hiding Your Magic

J: *"Everything that you have done to buy into other people's judgments of what magic is and of your magic, will you destroy and un-create it all?"*

Right and wrong, good and bad, POD and POC all nine, shorts, boys and beyonds.

One of that places that I find to be not very much fun is a hospital because the colors on the walls are like pale yellows and pale creams and these pale ugly turquoises and it's just disgusting. I hate those colors and to me those are the colors of this reality.

What have you made so vital, valuable and real about possessing the pale hospital walls of this reality that stops you from using the paint brushes and magical wands that you be, that you as a being are, to create a totally different reality? And everything that is, times and godzillion, Right and wrong, good and bad, POD and POC all nine, shorts, boys and beyonds.

What have you made so vital, valuable and real about possessing the pale hospital walls of this reality that stops you from being the magic, the possibility and the potency that you truly be? And everything that doesn't allow that to show up, everything you've done to stop yourself, will you destroy and un-create it all? Right and wrong, good and bad, POD and POC all nine, shorts, boys and beyonds.

Caller: Years ago, I was doing some magic, I was experimenting and something happened and came back and bit me in the tush.

When you were mentioning about when you were driving in the car, you said "no, car!" yet what would you say to do magic without having to be in an emergency situation?

J: Day to day there are certain things you can do to ask the magic to show up, that level of magic, where you are actually moving things or moving the car. The first thing that I would do is to just start asking for it to show up in your daily life. We have to remember that nothing ever happens to us ever. Nothing has ever happened to you in your life. You've created absolutely everything. So if you look at it from that perspective of "What have I created thus far? Ok. Cool." And acknowledge that, acknowledge the magic that you've created, acknowledge that you are a crazy person and I'm a crazy person and Nilofer is a crazy person and probably if you've all come to this call, you are crazy too. And that's so exciting and what a gift to be a crazy person. The conversation will look different for absolutely everyone, but it's like waking up in the morning and going ***"Ok, I know I can create magic in emergency situations"*** and then asking the question of ***"What would it take for magic to show up not only in emergency situations?" What other areas of my life am I willing to have that level of magic when it is not saving my life or not getting into a car accident or not having a tragedy?*** Because usually we are willing to prevent tragedy but what we are not willing to do is to create a better life.

What stupidity are you using to create the necessity of magic only under distress are you choosing? And everything that is, times a godzillion, will you destroy and un-create it?" Right and wrong, good and bad, POD and POC all nine, shorts, boys and beyonds.

That's an awesome clearing to use. What I was saying before about the conversation and asking the question, sometimes we hear facilitators give the tools, give the questions, give the clearing statements and we just repeat them the same way that the facilitator has repeated them and what I challenge you to do is to actually have a conversation of ***"What's it going to take for me? What conversation do I have to have? What questions do I have to ask the Universe? What questions do I have to ask myself? What do I have to change in my life in order to have magic in all areas all the time?"*** It is your right to have that. It sounds kind of political when I say that but this is who we are, this is who we be, this is the sparkle in people's eyes. Why not take that sparkle and use it everywhere? And the whole world is set-up to knock it out of us. So the fact that you are asking the question and that you are reading this book is absolutely phenomenal. And you are 90% of the way there to having it. And what else is possible?

I don't want to give you anything too concrete. Use the clearings but just start asking starting different questions of yourself and the Universe about what will it take for you personally? What's going to have to change in order for that to show up? And don't answer the questions, just put them out there.

Caller: I feel like in this lifetime besides other lifetimes I've been an alchemist, doing really magical things but when I mention it to somebody, I know they think it's not just the crazy factor but it just seems like there is not anybody to talk to or play with and do that.

J: Right. But it's not something you say to someone at a cocktail party to become friends. What if you started asking the Universe this question. I had a private session with Gary 3 years ago and he gave me this question. I go through phases where I ask it and when I don't ask it and it's really shown me some pretty incredible things of how you can have people to play with wherever you go in the world. I live in a very small town and I have so many playmates. I make playmates. Everybody looks at me like I'm this crazy magical thing and they just want to get more magical when they are around me. And I look at some of my friends, they are this crazy magical thing and they make me want to be more magical. So the question is – *"Universe, who can you bring me today that will keep me on my way?"*

Caller: I asked today "What energy, space and consciousness can me and my body be to receive in totality every day?"

J: I would be careful with that question. That is a good question but there's also may be an energy of assumption that you are not already receiving in totality. Because you are. You just haven't acknowledged it yet.

Caller: Yes. That's the part that – there are certain things I am more aware of and that I am acknowledging now and I look at myself and I go, "Wow, I created that. Wow. I did that!" and it's fun to see yourself changing.

N: And the other thing I've noticed with magic is don't make it significant and don't be attached that you say, "Oh my god, I have to create it." When you are playing with it, it's that energy of just playfulness. In how many more ways can I create magic today? What else can I do?

I remember when I went for my first Level 2 and 3, there was this clearing that Gary ran, *"What energy, space and consciousness can you and your body be to be the nine trannies 24x7 for all eternity?"* I started running that clearing every day and even if I said it just like once a day, my whole day was magical. I was aware of so many of those moments of magic. Take any of those clearings. You could run something like *"What energy, space and consciousness can I and my body be to be the magic I truly be for all eternity?"* and just play with it. See what shows up. Just have fun with it.

Caller: A couple of years ago, I designed a recipe for a really amazing chocolate cake and I said to myself "I wonder if I could really make some business with this cake, you know" I asked the energy of the cake, "What would you like to be called?" and it said "The Chocolate Magic Cake". Well, I'm going to follow that and see what happens and where it takes me from there.

J: That's an awesome idea. I'd like to share with you one of my personal favorite magic trick for building a business. I put on a big expo on Saturday and there was record enrolment. It was our first year and we had more people than had been in any expo in that building before. It was a wellness expo called the Westman Wellness Show in Brandon, Canada.

A friend and I put it on and we are both Access facilitators and every time we would go into "Oh my gosh" like for you "Can I really make this cake? Is it a silly idea? Is anybody going to buy this cake? How much work is it going to be to make this cake, to bring this to fruition, branding and all that stuff?" Anytime that you go into a contraction or into your logical mind of "This doesn't make any sense, why am I doing this," expand your energy out, bigger than the Universe and start pulling energy through the energy ball of the business. And keep pulling energy and pulling energy through that. I've realized that if you just use the one tool of pulling energy, you can create any kind of business you would like to create and you can also put the energy of you being the magical being that you are, you can put that in the energy ball as well and just pull energy through that every morning.

I noticed that pragmatically whenever I was like "This is too big of a job. I can't do this. Why are we doing this? Nobody is even going to show up." I would just put my barriers down and pull energy. We were on the front page of the newspaper, we were on every radio station, we were everywhere and this expo was a huge success. So what can you pull in by pulling in energy? Who can you pull in to be the baker? You be the baker. Who wants to do your branding? I got things for free like crazy. That's a form of alchemy. Changing the energy of the whole business or entity and just use that alchemy and pull in whomever you require.

Magic Diary

J: I had a notebook. It was a little angel notebook that my Auntie Diana had given me. Every day I would write 10 questions that started with the words "What would it take…"

What would it take for me to have my own private jet?

What would it take for me to have a million dollars?

What would it take to get the gift that I am? I had no idea. I just thought I was like a pathetic little girl.

What would it take for this guy to ask me out on a date?

What would it take to change the world?

What would it take for me to actually like my life when I get up in the morning?"

What would it take to travel the world?

What would it take to go on one trip every month?"

I filled the whole notebook. It was the month of December and that December every day I would write and it filled the whole notebook.

Just filled with questions. And I closed the notebook and put it away in my drawer. I found the notebook 2 years later and started reading through the notebook. I burst into tears. Because every single thing that I had asked for in the notebook, I had got. Absolutely everything except I haven't got the million dollars but I am joyfully on my way to that.

N: Can I ask you a question?

J: Yes.

N: Have you created a million dollars in your lifetime?

J: Um, that's super light.

N: You have right?

J: Yeah.

N: So maybe you just want to change your question to "What would it take for me to have a million dollars every year?" (laughs)

J: Oh, thank you! Ok, thank you so much! Duh!

N: I just heard Gary say that somewhere! (laughs)

J: Oh I am so glad! Thank you for saying that out loud. Oh, I'm so cute but not so bright sometimes. (laughs)

J: I created this notebook and in this notebook were all these questions. When I found the notebook, the guy that I had asked to ask me out, who didn't even know I existed, he was just a random boy in the university, he and I had dated for 4 months and we had a beautiful relationship until he moved away and it was incredible. And the time he moved away, I was ready for that.

The private airplane… now my 2 best friends, or my best friend that I do Access Consciousness with, the one I did the expo with, she and her partner just bought their own beautiful airplane so now we fly everywhere together. We are flying around the world in this airplane.

Probably once a month, I started travelling every single month to a new Access class to Australia, to Costa Rica, to wherever I may go, every single month.

It was just everything that I had asked for 2 years before was my life 2 year later. And I think that it brings us to that point you had made earlier Nilofer, of not making it significant. Not using these questions as a way to prove to yourself that you are good enough. All I was trying to do was get a better life. And so I wrote the questions down, I put them in a drawer and I didn't look at them for 2 years. I didn't ask them repeatedly, I didn't go "Oh is this going to work?" I didn't answer the questions, I didn't do anything. I wrote the questions and I put them in a drawer. So it's a really fun exercise and it has created so much magic in my life.

N: Oh my god, I love you Julia. Thank you, thank you, thank you for saying this! I am going like, my body is going "Eee, when can we start? When can we start?" (laughs) I'll probably write a hundred questions today! (laughs) That is awesome!

J: (laughs) You won't be sleeping. Your husband and your son will find you furiously scribbling in a notebook. (laughs)

N: No, but it's 5 am here. I mean it's 4:50 am here so I'm not sleeping anyways. I might as well not sleep back today. If you look at me I'm like this little girl that's jumping up and down in my chair and I just have my magical little boy who has woken up, who has come here. (laughs)

J: Yes, the possibilities are completely endless and I just like having it written down. I like notebooks, it's fun for me, I have my fluffy pens and it's really fun.

J: Life is so easy if we let it be easy and is it going to be all changed, and easy and perfect tomorrow? May be. But you've probably been through 4 billion years of shit so it might take a little time to get over it. It might take a year or two and I know that I was on Nilofer's call last year and

I am a completely different person than I was a year ago. I was like scared out of my chair to be on this worldwide tele-call last year and now it's exciting and fun. So just make choices and choose to be you and choose to be uncomfortable and choose to be a witch and choose to be a wizard and choose to be the crazy person because people aren't even watching you anyway. People may judge you for a second but they are so self-absorbed in their life, in their own problems, they don't care.

Judgment isn't even real. Everything you've done to make judgment more real than your power, your potency and your creative capacities for creating a joyful life beyond anything you or anyone else has ever seen, will you destroy and un-create it all? Right and wrong, good and bad, POD and POC all nine, shorts, boys and beyonds.

Other people's judgments of you are not your business. They absolutely have nothing to do with you and if somebody is not choosing magic that is so awesome because then you just have the chance to mess with them. And that's really fun. Everything that brings up, will you destroy and un-create it all? Right and wrong, good and bad, POD and POC all nine, shorts, boys and beyonds.

The world is just a playground. Look at the world from the perspective of "Who can I mess with today?" and "How much fun can I have messing with them?" If everybody was totally conscious and totally perfect, didn't judge you and you danced around the meadows all day, that would be fun, but this is pretty freaking fun too! It is so much fun to live in this world and to grab life by the horns and to do things that you never imagined that you could do or create by using your alchemy or using your magic and your power and your potency.

N: You can do magic 'Just for me, just for fun, never tell anyone' and you can keep expanding yourself so much that people won't even notice that you are doing any weird stuff.

Keep in the energy of question rather than you think what you create is an end in itself.

J: *All the judgments, conclusions, computations, significance, linearities, forms, structures, anything that you have made solid or real about magic – forget about being real, none of you are real - will you destroy and un-create all of that? Times a godzillion. Right and wrong, good and bad, POD and POC all nine, shorts, boys and beyonds.*

Magic is something that you know should be possible and if you actually are willing to commit to it, it's a commitment to yourself. If you are actually willing to commit to the magic above everything else, it'll work. Since I was a little girl, i knew, I'm going to fly. I will not die without having lifted off the ground and flown through the sky. And not in an airplane and not with a hand-glider, I would just love to fly. And that's the truth of who I am and I committed to that at a young age and I have taken every step towards that. And sometimes, I'd be away from it, sometimes I'd forget about it and it brought me to Access Consciousness and I wonder where else it'll take me. Get clear about what's the truth of you and the magic that you are and commit to it. It's a commitment.

J: I wonder what all of us are going to be in 3 years because of this call and because of hearing this. I wonder what the future will be now that we've had these conversations.

Magic With Teeth

Caller: How do I use my magic? My teeth started deteriorating some time ago. They are doing better now but the dentists said that they would just want to pull them all out.

Julia: I used to be a kid who had like 9 cavities. I used to go to the dentist and he'd be like "you have 9 cavities" "you have 7 cavities" so I know how you feel. Have you ever heard of Access Consciousness body processes?

What you are going to want to do is stick your hand in your mouth on your teeth and say the words "Demolecular manifestation" and "Molecular demanifestation" and then run the clearing statement. Right and wrong, good and bad, POD and POC all nine, shorts, boys and beyonds.

The molecular manifestation and demolecular manifestion is a process in which we put our hands on our body, on different things, on wine, on food and we change the physical structure. We change the molecules of the objects to create a greater possibility. It can change your teeth if you do it every night. You put your hands on there every night and run it for about a month and just keep asking, "what else is possible?" If you do that for a month, I wonder what results could show up.

I use this MDDM (Molecular Demanifestation Demolecular Manifestation) process a lot. It's taught in the Foundation class that comes after Bars. I use it on everything. People just use it on food, they put their hands over their food to change the structure of their food. I go way farther than that with it. I had a sweater that I didn't like, I was like "oh, why did I buy that sweater, it's an ugly sweater. Oh, I'll just change the molecules of this sweater so that I like this sweater more. So I just put my hands on the sweater and said "Demolecular Manifestation" and "Molecular Demanifestation". Right and wrong, good and bad, POD and POC all nine, shorts, boys and beyonds. The molecules changed and now it's my favourite sweater.

You've got to think outside of the box with these things. I have a friend, after I told her that I did it with my sweater, her couch was uncomfortable so she put her hands on her couch and she's like "Molecular Demanifestation" and "Demolecular Manifestation". POD POC POD POC. And her couch is now comfier. So don't just think of it in the terms that Gary tells you to do it, with all your tools, just go way outside of the box and play with it.

Commit To Your Life

Caller: I have denied my gifts and the magic, so what process can I run to have that magic back?

J: What if it wasn't a process? What if it was a choice to commit to your life completely? Sometimes we want a process for certain things and there's not really an energy there to clear but more of a choice. I was talking about flying. I will fly. It's completely insane. There is no physical reason that I should fly but it's my right and I will fly. It's more of that energy and waking up in the morning and saying "Ok, I am not denying my magic anymore" and these are the conversations that we have to have with ourselves.

It's not fair to you or to anybody else reading this or to me to be an Access zombie, just asking the questions, that means the questions that we were taught or having these conversations. It's energy for you. What is it going to take for you to not deny yourself anymore and just say to yourself "I will commit to being everything that I can be. I commit to not stopping myself anymore." And just being that energy of demand. Usually, people don't like to answer when I say that because they want a magic clearing!

N: Thank you Julia. This has been like such an amazing, wondrous creation. Thank you so much. Oh my god, I'm just waiting to sit and write down my questions. (laughs) the molecular demanifestion, what else can I touch, what else can I touch? (laughs)

J: Yeah, exactly, exactly! Like anything, and even like we are oh, this is the same thing I was talking about with the magic under stress. Like if something's broken, you use molecular demanifestation to fix it, but if we like something, why don't we use molecular demanifestation to make it even better?

Question: At times creation takes a second and at times even months are not enough. I do have magic I know, what am I missing that keeps me from creating in some areas magically?

J: Where are you making yourself stupid, that you are actually brilliant? Who projected at you your whole life that you are stupid? All of this abuse, will you destroy and uncreate it all? Right Wrong Good Bad,

Pod, Poc, All 9, Shorts Boys Beyonds.

What would happen if you were out of control with your magic? Everything this brings up will you destroy and uncreate it all? Right Wrong Good Bad, Pod, Poc, All 9, Shorts Boys Beyonds.

Question: My body has capacities more than I can name. It is not fun if happening all time. Like I am enjoying a meal and my body is telling me about pains of others in their back or knee etc. Killing the joy of what I am being and doing. I'm telling my body thank you body now show me how my energy feels like etc. Clearing? Or guidance? I do love my capabilities, just want to have more fun with them than all the time " What's sad around" awareness?

I would repeatedly ask:

What do I love about being a martyr? Everything this brings up will I destroy and uncreate it all? Right Wrong Good Bad, Pod, Poc, All 9, Shorts Boys Beyonds.

THE MAGIC OF CHILDREN

Get the transcript of an interview with Anne Maxwell –
The Magic Of Children: What Are They Telling Us?
Visit www.whereismydoorwaytopossibilities.com

CHAPTER FOURTEEN

MY CRAZY KIDS AND HOW THEY DROVE
ME CONSCIOUS

By Louise Derksen

Access Consciousness Certified Facilitator,

Mother Extraordinaire,

Intuitive Life Coach

Kids And What They Contribute To Our Lives

L: I have two sons and when I was pregnant with my second son, my older son was diagnosed with ADHD. He'd been having a lot of what everybody else would term difficulties. The day-to-day operations of getting dressed, eating, brushing teeth, etc, he needed somebody full-time to follow him around and prompt him on everything he was required to do to get ready for the day. At school, he was rolling around on the floor and had a lot of kind of classic symptoms of autism and/or other diagnoses. He either wasn't completing his schoolwork during class or just not starting it at all.

We brought him up completely natural, organic, healthy lifestyle. No sugar, he wouldn't watch TV, he wasn't immunized, he loved a plant-based diet. We had a lot of different modalities that we were using with him and it got to a point where he was coming home and asking to die. He just didn't want to be here at all. So, we chose to try medication. We were at the end of our rope and there was nothing else that was available for us at that time, so we tried for 2 years on different medications. That was a complete other set of nightmares that added to everything.

He started having rages. Yelling and throwing himself around and trying to get his hands on anything he could break or destroy. He was totally out of control. When the rages passed he would be so sorry and confused. He didn't understand what was going on and why he did it. My son is not violent and had never been before taking these medications. This was behavior that was so out of character that I knew the medications were not working to add to his quality of life. He didn't have friends when he was on these medications; he couldn't interact with others, didn't know how to laugh and was very unhappy. He was getting more work done at school and the teachers didn't have to supervise him so much but did his grades improve? No.

And then, fortunately, I had a conversation with my Dad. I told him that nothing was working for my son and he said, "Well, you need to get in contact with Gary Douglas and make an appointment with him." And so I looked up Gary online and thought; "Oh my god, he's going to be $400 an hour. I can't call him every 2-3 days when everything just goes completely mental and breaks down at home." Then I saw that there was a class we could take. So, my son and I went out to Vancouver. We completed an Access Bars class and that was instantly amazing. Within 2 weeks of running his bars and continuing to run his bars, he jumped in the car after school and said to me "I have my happy back, mom" and I just remember crying all the way home. Before this he would get in the car and be angry. He would not talk no matter what I said to him. It was just such a huge difference and he hasn't gone backwards.

His tutors and his teachers have mentioned that he has a sense of self that not many children have. He has a sense of himself, has a sense of humor, he's a happy kid. He's different, but he's so okay with being different. And we use the tools every day with him. And if we hadn't,

I don't know where we would be. It's just been amazing, absolutely amazing.

In the mid-90s, when Gary Douglas was offering classes in New Zealand and Australia, my Dad went to his classes. And I didn't know at the time, I was travelling around New Zealand at the time and I can recall him using some of the tools and the questions with me. When I mentioned Dad to Gary he remembered him, and that was cool. Now I get to share tools and questions with my Dad.

When Gary says that once you start using the tools of Access it changes your family, it really changes your family. Like my dad attended classes in the 90's and it changed me without Dad ever POC and PODing me or telling me what he was doing. Now it's third generation. My kids are using it on me.

N: Wow. I find that just incredible. I was just talking to my sons the other day, they just got their report cards and in our Indian culture or I would say, the Asian culture, there is such a strong sense of competition that you have to out-do this one and you have to perform and you have to blah, blah, blah, blah. One of his friends' mother called me and she said, "Did you see the marks in English? And have you seen how badly they have marked the kids? And the teacher is not good."

And I said, "You know what, I haven't seen the report card and I can't really comment on it. When I see it, I'll call you and talk to you."

When we looked at the report card my son also had not done well and I could see this kind of contraction occurring in his world and I just let him talk to me and then, at the end of it, I asked him, "So what do you know about getting really great marks?"

So he looked at me and then it's almost like a light bulb went off in his head, and he went, "Oh, that's really easy!" It's the way he said it, the energy of it.

I said, "Ah, so you know about getting really good marks. So don't worry about it."

I had this awareness of how this woman's energy, had impelled him even without him or me choosing that. Just by asking him that one question about what he knows, it just got him off that, and I realised, wow, these tools are so amazing!

L: Yes, we are very aware of the projections, expectations, rejections, separations of others.

On the way to school I run with my son, *"All the projections, expectations, rejections, separations the teachers have of my children or of me, (I go to the school to talk with the teachers) and that we have of them, that my son has of the work, that we have of grades, that the other students have of him, that he has of the other students, and everything else to do with this, will you please destroy and un-create it all, times a godzillion? Right and wrong, good and bad, POD and POC, all nine, shorts, boys and beyonds.*

Also destroy and un-create all the projections, expectations, rejections, separations that are designed to destroy, how often do teachers have to be right.

N: Oh, all the time.

L: All the time. *And the students are very much into being right with each other, whether it's about schoolwork or about what they know and how often are children trying to be right with us? They have to be right with us, right? And how often do we need to be right? Everything that is, will you please destroy and un-create it all, times a godzillion? Right and wrong, good and bad, POD and POC, all nine, shorts, boys and beyond*

Every year I have 2, 3, 4 meetings with the school and they are not 15 minute parent teacher meetings. These are 1-2 hour meetings with 4 or more teachers at a time. Everybody has their way of dealing with my son and if it's not with my son, it's with the label, the diagnosis.

He's has a designation a learning disability. I pursued that assessment privately; it gave him easier access to resources at the school. After asking the principal a lot of questions I found out that he would have to fall behind 2 years in his grades before that they would get him tested for a learning disability. That means they would only look at him as having "attention problems" rather than "hey, he can't do what you are asking of him, what else is possible?"

If you have children that are struggling or suspect they have learning disabilities or anything else, I really encourage you to get private assessment. To wait for the school to test your children is not a good idea. You can get resources and access to what's called an individualized educational plan by having a Psychological Education test.

That's what we did with our son, the schools just don't have enough resources to test every child with "disabilities". Getting my son tested made a huge difference. Now he has support available to him. The teachers adjust the way that they teach with him, so that they have to present their class material in a completely different way.

I talked to my son about the label and I've said "It doesn't mean that that's you. It's something that we use to get people to be different and to get people to be willing to ask questions about how you learn."

N: I love that.

L: It's recognizing or being willing to acknowledge there's a system or structure in place with schools, with grades and with learning and being willing to take a look at it.

Ask all the questions you need to ask. I was with a principal at an elementary school for half an hour about the process of a child having a learning disability. When they would get tested? How many children are tested through the school? He gave me a lot of information and awareness of what steps to take that worked for us. What created a lot of awareness for me was there are only 6 spots available for children for each school here in our city. The school recommends and refers a child to Psychological Educational testing. There are approximately 500 students in each school. The waiting list to be tested after being referred is 2 years. So my son would have to fall back two years in his grades and then he would have to wait 2 years for an assessment. I knew that would not work for him or us.

The more questions you ask, the more you know about how that structure operates and that will give your child a better chance to use that system to his or her advantage. And if you have a designation, it can give you access to resources. It can also get people to ask questions about how your child learns, if they learn really differently.

N: Wow. I love that. So Louise, can you talk about what really started to happen when you started running your son's bars the first time that you found Access, or you went to the bars class?

L: The biggest difference for me was all the mind chatter of "What do I do? How do I get him to go to bed tonight?" Every single night with him, it had to be different. I couldn't put him in a routine because by the third time that I had presented that same routine, he would have figured it out and he would said flat out "no".

My son was – I'm not going to say challenge, but I had to get creative with him. He's super-smart, he had everything figured out before the third time I used that technique. For example, one parenting suggestion is that you show your child two pairs of pajamas, you give your child choices. You don't mention bed-time, you just say, "Would you like to wear these ones to bed or this ones to bed?" That is a great way to get them to move forward.

They make a choice and then you say, "Would you like to read this book or this book?" and then you've taken them another step.

"Would you like to read it here or there?"

"Would you like to brush your teeth here?"

You give them choices that keep them moving them forward towards bedtime. "Would you like to listen to this music or would you like to listen to this music?"

You ask them to choose within the premise of the next step.

I would do this with my older son and the first night, it was incredible. We had a miracle big time. He got into bed, read stories. It was amazing. The second night, he had this very suspicious look on his face as soon as he sees the pajamas and then I start with the choices. He is looking at me like "mmmhm, something's going on here." He went to bed, but it was slower and not as much fun as the night before.

 On the third night, he just looks and me when I ask "Which pajamas would you like to wear?" and says "No".

He's already got it figured out, he knows it's a manipulation, and there's a choice there, but there's no choice for him, it all heads in the same direction. He just says flat out "No!" This is how it would be.

We did sticker charts with him and by the third time, he's figured it out and there's no way. He wants nothing more to do with it. Anything that was a disguised choice.

I had a lot of different ways to deal with or be with children, get them moving forward and have them do what I would like them to do. With my older son, he had it all figured out and that was it. I had to start using games, laughter and silliness. I used spontaneity and was totally present in the moment with him. I couldn't have a time projection or agenda with him.

N: Wow. No time and agenda with him, talk about that.

L: I don't know how long it's going to take for him to go to bed. We all set bedtime for our children. Good parents do that, keep the children on a schedule, that is what we are supposed to do. I started to fire myself from all the jobs of being a parent who does everything right. I fired myself from meeting that goal because I had made up my mind or had a judgment of this is the way to be a good parent and bring up my child.

All the points of view that we have, and all the judgments, and every-thing that we've bought about what a parent is and how to parent your child, and what is best for your child and what is best for you, can we please destroy and un-create all of that, times a godzillion? Right and wrong, good and bad, POD and POC, all nine, shorts, boys and beyonds.

This is not about my children choosing their bedtime, it's me not put-ting a time limit on it. So some nights it's going to be really, really quick and some nights it's not.

N: So it's basically like both of you together choosing what works for him?

L: Yes. Every single night is different. *It's the projections, expectations, rejections, separations of what this is going to be like tonight, or how he's going to be, how he's not going to be, how I'm going to be or not going to be, and what any of this is going to look like. And everything that is, times a godzillion, can we please destroy and un-create it all? Right and wrong, good and bad, POD and POC, all nine, shorts, boys and beyonds.*

The more I was willing to fire myself from having to put him to bed at a certain time, that it had to look a certain way, that he had to eat at a certain time, to fire myself from all of those jobs, he found his own routine.

N: Wow, wow. So it's almost like you cannot be unconscious around him.

L: No. There's a presence that is demanded and being in the present. You cannot have an outcome. You have to be totally in the question. As soon as I go and put an outcome or an expectation then he gets a sense of that. His awareness is off the charts.

N: Yeah, and then he fights you on it.

L: He fights me on it or he shows up like that judgment I have of him. If

I have an expectation that this is going to be difficult, that he's going to resist, that he's going to fight me. What happened last night was a huge blow up and it's going to happen again tonight, then that's what he'll be. He'll get a sense of that.

You know that tension before you go into something? This is where I was functioning from before I did Access, before I started getting my Bars run, that tension in my body and the projection and the expectation I had of everything, of how difficult it would be or he was going to be a certain way. He would receive all that information from me and be that.

N: Wow!

L: Yes. *How many projections and expectations and rejections and separations do we put out into the world or put into people's Universes before we even start anything with them? And everything that is, can we please destroy and un-create it all? Right and wrong, good and bad, POD and POC, all nine, shorts, boys and beyonds.*

Including the ones we have of ourselves, or how we are going to be? I would be hanging on for dear life to be a calm parent when in actuality I just wanted to blow. Which is not appropriate, it's not in this reality; you are not allowed to blow up. That's considered bad parenting.

Everywhere you are unwilling to be a bad parent, will you please destroy and un-create it all, times a godzillion? Right and wrong, good and bad, POD and POC, all nine, shorts, boys and beyonds.

There is a level of intensity that occasionally will show up with me and my son, which is required for him to be present with me.

N: So how does that show up?

L: It's almost like he's not quite here and he has his own agenda or he is in somebody else's reality. If I ask him to do something and I ask him again and again and I've pulled his energy, I've used all the tools and he's still not willing to be present. Sometimes he is choosing not to hear me or choosing not to do as I ask him rather than not being present. First, I take a step back and ask, *"Okay, is he choosing not to do what I'm asking or is he not present right now or is he incapable of doing what I'm asking?"* When he's choosing not to be present and his body is in front of me but he's off somewhere else, then I will be an intensity of being here and being now.

I'm not the laser intensity of energy; it's very broad banded. There's a space for him to be like "Oh, okay, you want my attention."

The second questions I ask is *"Okay, where are you?"* I ask where he is energetically. Yes, his body is in front of me or on the couch, I am asking for where his being is, his energy. Then I ask myself to go to where he is, to expand to where he is. For these children to be in and down in their bodies is very uncomfortable for them. They are these huge infinite beings and a very small space of a body can be very uncomfortable and they are quite expanded so you just ask "Where are you?" and then go to where they are. Then ask for them to be where they are and also be aware of here and now.

If any of you have children right now ask where they are. Now ask yourself to expand to where they are. Often I get this sense of this warmth or my son's happiness and that's when I know I have expanded to where he is. Children have a lot more expansiveness than what we do as adults. So that's their gift to themselves, to expand to where your children are, is a huge gift.

N: Wow!

Energy Pulls

L: Yes. I also talked about the pull energy which is pulling energy from all over the Universe through their body and then through your body and out the back of you. And they will start feeling more awake. If you have a child that seems to have a hard time thinking or disengaging from something, it's a really amazing tool.

When I first started playing with these tools, I asked my son to turn off the computer and he didn't hear me or was choosing not to hear me. And so I asked him again, so by the time I got to about the 4th or 5th time, I was like "Okay, so where are you?" Okay, I'll expand out to where you are. Okay. And then I asked myself to pull his energy and then I thought the words "Could you turn off the computer?" and he sighed and turned off the computer. I was ecstatic, "What! That was easy!" (laughs) That was fantastic. I was like "Okay, I didn't even need to say the words! I just thought them or put a picture in his head of him closing the computer."

N: This is what I've noticed with my kids, it's so much easier to think things at them and then communicate telepathically rather than talk to them.

L: Yes, yes. They are talked to all day; they are told what to do. Absolutely.

The other day he said; "I don't have words. I can't say anything to them." He's talking about the teachers, that he doesn't know how to say what he would like to say and I said, "What if you use pictures?" You can use pictures with people around you. I asked him, "Did we communicate with each other more with pictures than we talked verbally since you were a baby?" He says "Yeah."

"Well, how do you use that to your advantage?"

N: Yeah and the other thing is that, you know, can they receive what he has to say?

L: Yes, and that's true. Most often teachers are not interested in listening to their students.

N: Yeah

L: Yeah. Another part of the tools was the question. Asking questions. Every morning, straight after breakfast with my son, he would end up on the floor. We couldn't get him up off the floor. He would just roll around on the floor and once, I did the bars class and started asking questions, what I did was instead of trying to get him off the floor, I took a step back. I asked, "Okay, so what is going on here?" Most of what they are showing up as, is an awareness that they are having. So I was starting to be willing to ask the questions of "What is going on?" What is actually going on? What is he aware of? It was the second day; I caught the school bus going past the window, which stops down at the corner. I'm like "Huh, that was interesting." The third day, he hit the floor and I stood there and I watched the school bus go down past our house and I'm like "Hey! Zen, are you actually aware of all the kids on the bus that don't want to go to school?" He lifted his head and goes, "Huh?" I go, "Well, you hit the floor every morning and then the school bus goes past." He says "What?" I go, "Are you aware of the kids that do not want to go to school today?" He goes, "Oh, yes." That was really light for him. And then I ask him, "So where do you start receiving that information? Is it when the bus is at the corner or is the bus two blocks down?" And it's like we kept asking where it was. Three blocks down, 4 blocks down, 5 blocks down, 6 blocks down, 7, 8. It was the 8th block down that he started receiving all that information.

N: Wow!

L: And he didn't even ride to school on the bus because he couldn't. It was too much for him. I drove him every morning. He would start receiving all the download of all the kids that day. Another place where he was; "I don't want to go to school" was as we pulled into school for the drop off. We asked questions about that; "When do you download your day?" Most kids download their day before they even start their day.

You can use that to your advantage. If you have a schedule, for example, you have all day with your child and you have certain things that you would like to get done that day at certain times. You can ask to energetically download that information to your child and you may notice that it goes a lot quicker and easier; they already have the information that they require to know what's going on that day.

I would ask my son, *"When do you download your day? Is it at this point before you get to school? This point? This point? And this point?"* and it's a good half hour or so before he gets to school. He has downloaded all the teachers, all the students, everybody's moods, everybody's emotions, what's going on at home for all of them as well and who's where and in what kind of mood. He already knows what's going to flare up in different places in the school at different times whether or not he is present there or not. Then he'll start trying to shift and change things because he cares that much about everybody at school.

N: Wow!

L: They have a huge capacity and if we start asking questions about what is going on for kids, not only does it open doors for them but it opens doors to start going, "Okay, so what am I doing here?"

There are three questions or that create ease with all of the awareness and information they receive. The very first one of them I asked every day after school, whether it was in my head or verbally. I would run, as we drove home, **"What did you facilitate today that wasn't received?"** and at first, it was huge. It was this big, huge, great, big, heavy bag of like 'not received' and then we would destroy and un-create all of that. Right and wrong, good and bad, POD and POC, all nine, shorts, boys and beyond.

"What did you facilitate today that was received? At first, it was a very little, a pin light. It was like this little light that was received of what he was facilitating and *"Everything that doesn't allow you to acknowledge that, would you please destroy and un-create it all? Right and wrong, good and bad, POD and POC, all nine, shorts, boys and beyond"*

I would run this every day and I found that over a period of 2-3 weeks, the heaviness of what was not received shrunk, he started knowing what could be received and what could not be received. Then I found that the 'what was being received', expanded. It was unexpected and really cool to watch. Those questions are amazing for parents to run every day for themselves.

N: Yeah. And what is the third question?

L: The third one is *"If I were a superhero, what did I just do?"* *Everything that doesn't allow you to acknowledge that, will you please destroy and un-create it all? Right and wrong, good and bad, POD and POC, all nine, shorts, boys and beyonds.*

There was one time my son got in the car after school and I put my hand on his knee and said "How are you doing?" and I just got this flash of anger. He didn't do anything physically or say anything, there was nothing on his face, there was just an energetic anger. I thought to myself "Whoa, what was that?"

I started driving for a while, asking questions, and asked him "Hey, was someone really angry at school today?"

He said "Huh, what are you talking about?"

I said, "Well, I don't know. I just kind of perceived some anger and I know that's not you. You are not angry like that. I was just wondering if someone got angry at school?"

He's like "No, no, it was fine."

We sat there for a little longer, driving along and then he said, "Oh, oh yeah, one of my friends. There was this boy that was teasing him because he knows that my friend's going to get angry. He started to get angry and when he gets angry, he hits people and I knew that if he was going to hit this guy, that he would be suspended."

I said, "Well, did you pull all the anger from him so that he didn't hit the boy?" He goes, "Oh. Ok."

I said to him, "Ok, so your friend, he won't ever change it if you don't just allow him to perceive that his anger is a problem for him. That is doesn't work for him. So could you just return it all to sender with consciousness attached."

And he did, and then he was fine. He was absolutely fine.

The other part we had to work out with my son was everywhere he was trying to fix everything. I asked him "What if you are the energy and the space and the consciousness that you could be that would change that rather than pulling all the anger, all the drama, all the trauma and all that unhappiness from people."

N: Yeah, thank you so much. This has been like wow! I just have a comment come it – "Love you and your transparency, dear Louise. Behind that awesome strength and generosity of spirit, the rock of Gibraltar energy is so obvious." Wow.

L: Thank you.

N: "How often do you run his bars? And usually how long do the sessions last?"

With children, Bars sessions are really short. So ideally 20 to 30 minutes. The best indication is to hold the implant bar for 1 minute for every year that they are and then 1 – 2 minutes for the other Bars after that. Tell the children "Let me know when to change my hands." They can tell you verbally and if they are not telling you verbally, watch their bodies. My son will start squirming. He would want to get off the table. That means I've gone too long, I need to switch. As soon as I switch, his body will change. Other children I found that they will put their hands together and I can just gently say, "Is it time to change my hands?"

Watch their bodies, if they are not verbally telling you, their body will. Something else that can help is watching a movie or show. They can stay there a little longer. You don't want to overdo it. You want the Bars session to be enjoyable. You would like them to walk away going "Hey, that wasn't so bad. I can do that again." If you try to do it for too long, then they won't enjoy it and then they won't come back.

How often? At first, everybody got their bars run as often as possible.

Now I wait for him to ask. He knows. He knows he requires it and so it's a total choice for him. I noticed that before school starts, and I don't mean for the day, I mean for the year, he finds that when there's a holiday that he'll ask to get his bars run every day or every second day coming up to starting school. He is aware of things that start coming up, not only for him, for the kids and teachers as well.

I do a really cool little manipulation that makes everyone happy. I don't pay my children any allowance, I pay them to run my bars or run body processes on me. So they get a session as well as...

N: Give a session.

L: And then I'm so happy, I'm so willing to pay them and they get money and they are happy. I find my kids will generally ask. They will go for quite a period of time without asking for anything and then all of a sudden they'll ask me. I leave it up to them.

N: "Dear Louise, I'm so grateful for the call. It has given me a lot of ease for dealing with my son."

The conversation that we are having and the places we are going with the way she has been with her kids is so amazing. After your older one, how was it with your second child?

L: He's really different. Again I had to completely change how to parent him. He would appear to be a normal child but between him and I, we know he's not.

He doesn't require a lot of the facilitation. He's really interesting. If I ask him a question, he'll say "I don't get it." And then I'll ask him another question. "I don't get it, mom. I don't get it." For me to use the tools with him it doesn't work the same way as say with my older son. I can say to my older son, "Hey, who does that belong to?" or "Who are you doing that for?"

When I first started using "Who does it belong too?", with my older son, he would yell at me. "It's mine!" and I thought I would have to change or show him no, it's not actually yours. I would try and convince him that it's not. After a while I realized as I asked him a question, he would perceive that it wasn't his but he still was choosing to say "it's mine". So I would just ask him the question and then continue what I was doing, if I was just walking away, I would keep walking. He would come back to me about 5-10 minutes later and go "Hmm, Mom, I didn't know who I was being."

With my younger son, if I ask him, he knows all the tricks. I ask him "Who does that belong to? And who are you doing that for?", you cannot change his mind on it. I have to completely again fire myself from the tools. It's not about always using the tools. I found with my younger son to acknowledge that he's already got it. That he doesn't require facilitation.

I'll say things to him like "What do you know?" It's more of an acknowledgement with him. I'll say to him "Are you just really smart?" The other thing that works with him is the opposite. Saying the opposite will create that opening of the door that question. When you ask a question it opens up an energy? I say to him "Well, you can't" or "Don't worry, it's yours. There's no way you can't change that" then he will instantly open the door himself. Or I'll say nothing or in my head, I'll run distractor implants.

My younger son has a tendency to get stuck and repeat things over and over again. I'll run "All the distractor implants of anger, rage, fury, hate, blame, shame, regret, guilt, addictive, compulsive, obsessive, perverted points of view and all the rest of the distractor implants creating this. Right and wrong, good and bad, POD and POC, all nine, shorts, boys and beyond"

He'll have doubt and he'll have fear, I run; "All the distractor implants creating any and all of this, Right and wrong, good and bad, POD and POC, all nine, shorts, boys and beyonds"

With my younger son one time, where I said to him, "Why don't you just energetically ask Gary?" I had nothing more to ask. He was in repeat "I don't get it." But he wanted to know what it was but he didn't get it when I said anything. I said to him "OK, expand out to where Gary Douglas is. It's not about finding Gary's body, it's the energy of Gary." I said, "Ask him the question." He totally did. And he's like "Oh, I'm just really smart, Mum!" When he doesn't get it, he really is being whatever that is. If that makes any sense, whatsoever.

N: Oh, it does. As you are talking, I'm looking at my sons and the way they are being and they are both so very different and thank you for really giving me a different way of being with my sons. My sons are going to be really happy that I talked to you today.

L: We also have this assumption, or we've taken on this job as a parent to fix something. This was something that I realized that why my mother's and my communication broke down was I didn't have a problem for her to fix. I would have to create a problem for her to parent me, to fulfill her job. We assume we have to fix things with our kids rather than acknowledging they most probably already know and they most probably know more than what we know.

All the jobs that we've taken on to fix or to rescue, to save, to correct something, all of those jobs to do with how children don't know and how we have to show them how to do something, or that they have to learn something, can we please destroy and un-create it all and we revoke, rescind, recant, reclaim, renounce, denounce, destroy and un-create everything we aligned and agreed with and resisted and reacted to, that allows us to exist. Right and wrong, good and bad, POD and POC, all nine, shorts, boys and beyonds.

When we have a purpose or job to fix a problem, then there has to be a problem for us to fix. This can create a problem in the first place. This is where I had to fire myself from so many different jobs. Our children are infinite beings. They have a smaller body. They already know. We don't have to teach them anything. If we ask them questions or ask them -

"What do you know? What are you aware of?" then they learn – or not 'learn', we're opening doors for them to have their own awareness and knowing about the world. We do not need to teach them anything. Everything that is and everything that brings up for everyone, will you please destroy and un-create it all? Right and wrong, good and bad, POD and POC, all nine, shorts, boys and beyonds.

N: "My son is in high school and is having a hard time interacting with others. He feels judged and unwelcome often. What would you recommend?"

L: Ask him; "Are you really aware of other people feeling judged? And are you trying to change it so that they don't feel that way so that you can inter-react with them?" How aware is he of how everyone else is? All the judgments everybody has of themselves?

The expansion tool, where you expand as big as the room you are in, as big as the house. Expand out to the edge of the city, to expand out across the continent, across the planet in all directions, expand through the solar system in all directions. Do that every morning and then ask him to do it during the day, then he may find that he doesn't have so much of that going on.

Ask him questions about what is he aware of. Is he aware of everybody else's stuff? Who does it belong to?

N: My son is just 5 and an half years old and he just doesn't like to go to school to read and write. It stirs his world so much just that his school is starting. At the same time, once he goes there, he stays too long and doesn't want to come back home after the school is done. What is this about? And what questions can I ask?"

L: My older son was the same. He would stay after school and get all his work done. Everybody is gone. Who does it belong to? Is he actually aware and is he downloading his day before he gets to school? And by downloading his day, is he downloading – how many children in his school would like to be at school? And then, how many teachers would actually like to be at school that day? Would it be a little, a lot?

N: (laughs) No one.

L: The teachers are just as unhappy as the kids are about being at school. Everybody's gone, is there a really nice space for him to just be him there? Asking questions for him to start being aware that he's really aware of what's going on with everybody around him. Who does it belong to? What are you aware of right now? When did you start getting information about all the kids? Before you get to school? Before you get out of the car? 2 blocks before we get to school? Heavy and light is a really amazing tool for that too.

N: "Louise, thank you so much for addressing this subject. Can you comment on how to be the invitation to have children contribute to the creation of a nurturing home? My teenage daughters do not contribute to any cleaning, cooking, maintenance or laundry. It is as if I'm living with the grandparents in the Willy Wonka movie. They lay around in bed like gorgeous mermaids or cats. So they are willing to work together as a team to resist me. This does not work for me and I have not been able to out-create this. Any tools or processes you would suggest? I do feel 'get me out of here' energy and 'get them out of here' energy. What else is possible?"

L: See how many I can give you. One of the first ones is tell them they are doing a really great job. They are teenagers and their job is to drive you nuts and to torture you and tell them they are doing a fantastic job. See what shows up. It puts a question in their Universe and you may find they smile when you ask. The other one is to be "interesting point of view, I have all these points of view about what they should be doing."

POC and POD all your points of view you have about what they should or should not be doing. All the projections, expectations, rejections, separations. They'll pick up on that tension and that charge. The more space that you have about asking them to do something, there's nothing for them to push against. Another process that I've been running recently was "What stupidity am I using to create the … ?" and put my son's name and my husband's name and everybody else's names, whoever I can think of names, not all at once.

I run *"What stupidity am I using to create the (my son's name) I am choosing. And everything that is, times a godzillion, destroy and un-create it all." Right and wrong, good and bad, POD and POC, all nine, shorts, boys and beyonds.*

I'll add in the alphabet soup and apple pie soup. Which are the connection points, the stability points, incarcerations, artificial intelligence, automatic response systems, the crushed automatic response systems, the projections, expectations, rejections, separations and all the ones designed to destroy. Everything that is, times a god zlillion, destroy and uncreate it all? Right and wrong, good and bad, POD and POC, all nine, shorts, boys and beyonds

The other day, my son came upstairs and I asked him to get in the shower. This is a huge sticky point for us. He doesn't want to get in the shower and there's a huge argument. When he is in, he doesn't want to get out and then he'll forget to wash. I had been running for a couple of days that stupidity process and I asked him to get in the shower and I perceived his energy trying to find where the resistance was and it wasn't there and so he was like "Huh" and he turned around and got in the shower. I was like "Okay I've got to keep running this one. This one is really working for me." It's almost like they'll find where the charge is in your Universe, where your resistance or where you have a projection or an expectation that they are not going to do it or how they'll do it, and then they will push on it.

N: The ones that I've been doing a lot is "everywhere I'm aligning and agreeing with this or resisting and reacting to this which allows it to exist." And that is working so well for me. At one point I had this intensity of energy in me and it's like "you know what, this has to be done, and I can't do it on my own." I was this intensity of presence with my kids and broad banded it, "This is what you have to do and you have to do it" and they got that. "This is not a place I can mess around with Mom, so I better do it." And they did it

L: Yes, and when that comes up, you haven't asked a question about "is this going to work?" It comes up. All of a sudden, this intensity, you can start being this intensity and it's not shutting down the intensity by going "Oh that's not how we're supposed to be as parents." As I said earlier, recognizing sometimes that intensity of presence is required to get somebody to keep moving forward. It's a kindness. There's a kindness to you and them with it.

N: The other thing which showed up for me was yesterday, my son came home from school and in my body I had this intensity. My son comes in and says; "So Mom, what can I eat?" I told him what was there and he said "Eww!"

I looked at him and I said, "You know what, I'm really not feeling well. Would it be okay for you to just eat this today? Just for today." And he looked at me and he said, "Okay".

Instead of doing trauma and drama, I just presented him the energy of what was going on for me and he got it and he was so willing to just contribute to me at that point of time.

L: Yes, and a huge part of that is acknowledging you are not asking a question beforehand about what works, you are just being really honest about "Hey, here's an intensity right now. This is what's coming up for me." or "Hey, this is not working for me. I'm not having a great day" or using the other tools.

Trust what comes up, what pops up and just follow the energy. *All the judgments that you have about being all these different things. This reality likes you to think that you have to be consistent. That you have to be a level-headed, consistent parent. Everything and everywhere you are trying to be what this reality would like you to be or a level-headed, con-sistent parent and that you are mono-parenting, can you please destroy and un-create it all, times a godzillion? Right and wrong, good and bad, POD and POC, all nine, shorts, boys and beyonds.*

Everything that doesn't allow you to follow the energy for you and for them, which, truth, will that create a greater possibility? Everything that doesn't allow that, will you please destroy and un-create it all? Right and wrong, good and bad, POD and POC, all nine, shorts, boys and beyonds.

N: Wow. Ok. I mean, oh my god, this call is just opening up so many doorways. I have more questions coming in. "Thank you so much for this call. A different energy than other calls. I have my son at a Waldorf school in Byron, Australia. I thought this would be as good as it could get, so I stayed in this judgment even when it couldn't deliver what I thought I was creating. This is so helping me with where I somehow failed him. My thinking this is not creating what I wanted for him. I can now be aware of my interesting points of view and use some of these great tools. Even at this stage – he has completed school now. So thank you so much for this great call."

L: So welcome. If you are willing to let go of your points of view, he would have had a totally different point of view of Waldorf. *If you de-stroyed and un-created all your points of view of his school would that allow him more space and allow him to receive more of the contribution that it could be for him? Everything that doesn't allow that, Right and wrong, good and bad, POD and POC, all nine, shorts, boys and beyonds.*

We used the tool heavy and light this year about what schools for the boys. We chose what came up as really light after asking the questions "What would my son's life be like in 5 years? What would my life be like in 5 years? What would our family's life be like in 5 years if we choose this school? If we don't choose it, what would my son's life be like? We chose a totally different school. We didn't have a reason. My son told his friends, "I don't know why we are changing schools." We chose to follow the energy and that has improved his grades.

We didn't know what we were choosing. We were just willing to follow the energy of what would work.

N: It's like my second son, he was doing okay in school. Not too bad, not too good, just doing okay. This is a gift really my mom gave me. She is okay with both of us, my sibling and I, doing whatever we were doing and she left us and she never really made us study or things like that. This is a gift I've passed on to my kids and all of a sudden, last year, for no reason, my son changed. I haven't changed anything in terms of the "things that we do" but all of a sudden last year, he started getting full marks in all the exams and he got the academic prize and the only thing which is different was, I was attending all these Access classes and I was listening to all the Access classes all the time at home. Whatever you do, please don't do that.

L: Nilofer, I'm curious, did you start asking your son questions about what he would like as his life?

N: I didn't ask my son any of those questions but I had been asking this question for myself. What would I like to create my life as? For the last 2 years. And in asking that question, I guess it has really changed things for him.

L: It's in your Universe and then they get it as well and that's one of the things we do with our son. He spends more time than I like on the computer and so I ask him "What would you like to create as your life? How will this make you money? What can you create with this? What would you like your life to look like in 5 years?" Asking him questions with no agenda attached to it, it started opening doors for him to start seeing what he can create with what he enjoys.

N: I asked Gary this question in the first Level 2 and 3 I was in. I said, "Gary, my sons are spending all their time on computer." and he said, "That's great! You have a built-in electronic baby-sitter. Just let them do what they are doing." And I was like "Really?" It still was a judgment in my Universe and I eased off on that. Yesterday, my younger one, who is also called Zane, he comes to me and says, "You know mom, I know a way in which I can make money off YouTube. I have to do this, this, this, this and this." And I was like in the middle of having my dinner and I said, "You know what, Zane, I know I can help you and I can show you the system of putting all of that in place but can you please let me eat my dinner right now?" He looked at me and went, "Ok, fine. Eat your dinner, then I'm going to get you and we are going to do this." And then he went away. In the time that I was eating dinner, he had figured out a way in which he could get so many likes on his YouTube video and by the time I had done dinner, he was like "Mom, I've got 60 likes on my YouTube video."

L: Yes, they are faster than us, they get it faster than us and it's just opening those doors to say, "Hey, what are you going to create with that?" You know, it's just fascinating. My son has a group of friends that's what they do. They make money off YouTube. He comes to me and says "Mom, I need a bank account. I need somewhere to put the money."

J: I was in Bars class one time and you know how you were talking about how you feel when I'm running somebody's bars. There was this guy I was running the bars and I just kind of got tired. Even though it hadn't been very long, and he was already asleep. He was knocked out and so I went to the bathroom and came back and what I was reading was I hadn't run his bars long enough. What is my question around that? Is it when you feel kind of like you are tired? Is that another sign that you've run their bars long enough?

L: Sometimes when you feel what can seem like tired is you being the space for them to receive. Gary has talked about having a pillow there that you can rest your head on or people who run each other's bars sometimes the gifter will fall asleep. It's just a space. The other question to ask "Have I got to where this all they can receive? Or "Is this all I'm willing to be?"

J: Can you say that again? "Are you willing to be?"

L: Yes, you are asking; *"Is this all they can receive? Or is this all I'm willing to be?"*

J: Oh. Is this all I'm willing to be? I am willing to be, not them. Okay.

L: Yes, you can ask, if it shows up that this is as much as you are willing to be, you can destroy and un-create everything that doesn't allow you to be whatever is required for this person to receive. Everything that is and everything that brings up, will you please destroy and un-create it all? Right and wrong, good and bad, POD and POC, all nine, shorts, boys and beyond

You are asking a question about the person that you are gifting to. Is this all they can receive? It's not to give them anything more than they can receive. And also check in with yourself to see if you are willing to be something else so that they can receive something greater.

J: Okay, am I willing to be something else so they can receive something greater?

L: Have I reached the limit of what I can be?

J: Okay, I have another question. My granddaughter, they live next door to me but I have this awareness that she's really doing what my daughter wants her to do, by you know, dilly-dallying and all that stuff. She's really doing what my daughter wants her to do. How can I assist her energetically? Maybe sending pictures? She gets contracted, she'll like put her head down and she'll just walk like she has been rejected or dejected and her back hurts and her head goes down. Is there anything I can do for her energetically? Maybe in my mind?

L: Can you run her bars?

J: It's iffy, my daughter is kind of weird around this Access stuff. I'm not really allowed to be around her by myself too much. If that makes any sense. Okay, so how would I?

N: *What energy, space and consciousness can you and your body be to stop protecting your granddaughter for all eternity? Everything that is, will you please destroy and un-create it all? Right and wrong, good and bad, POD and POC, all nine, shorts, boys and beyonds.*

When we go to protect, rescue, save, protect or try to heal somebody, that person has to, for you to have that job, they have to require protecting. She could be really, really aware that you have a job to protect her, so she has to show up as with a problem for you to continue your job. What if she was an infinite being?

J: She is. She's very vital. She's very good at actualizing things. She has been since she was a little, baby really, and I'm aware of it, but still I've been trying to protect her. Do I just keep running that?

L: Is what she's being actually working for her?

J: No, I don't think it is working for her. When she was choosing to be happy, no matter what was going on, that seemed to work for her. There was a time when she just chose to be happy, no matter what was going on and that seemed to work for her better than what she's doing right now. That's light.

L: What if you send her the picture of her being happy no matter what?

J: Me seeing a picture of her being happy, no matter what?

L: Yes. When you are around her imagine in your head exactly what you just said.

J: Oh. Okay. Then that releases me. I felt a release when you said that! That's awesome! Thank you.

N: As I've been listening to you talk throughout this call, and also having seen you parent your son, especially when we were in Venice last year, what I'm really aware of how much you are living the tools and you are being the tools all the time with your kids and as I was listening to you, I was going "What would it take for me to be that?"

R: Hi Nilofer and Louise. I just love all these answers you are giving. I thought I would ask rhetorically is there any part of this that wouldn't apply to dealing with myself and with other adults?

L: Absolutely, use these tools with other adults as well. The only thing that maybe different between children and adults is with adults, they have a lot more points of view. You could ask an adult a question and it won't open a door like it will with children. With children, you can ask them a question and you don't need to say anything more after that. They will let you know or they have opened a door wider and bigger than you can ever imagine or have access to and it's such a huge gift to you as well. You perceive or receive that door opening and absolutely use this tool with adults. One huge gift that Access Consciousness has given me is to sit in a room of 4 or more teachers and be able to facilitate something different for my son by using these tools.

N: Thank you for your question. Wow, Louise, this is like phenomenal. Thank you so much. I'm so much more present to who my children be right now and wow, thank you.

L: You are so welcome, Nilofer. They gift. They don't even realize it, they will gift even when things seem difficult or the challenges, the troubles and the resistance that show up will, if you are willing to use a question. Whether you ask them a question or you are willing to ask yourself a question, like "What job am I trying to have here." You know, you can create so much more for yourself.

Questions -

N: Thank you.... I can sense this duality in my child's world.... I am all about he knows and look for what is he good at...(sometimes I lose my peace and calm) and my husband believes that as dad he needs to teach him lot of things and his duty to make him a good person... or as a teenager he will be spoilt. What ESCs can I be to change this??? Talking to my husband hasn't worked and when next time my son throws tantrums (he is just 5.5 yrs. old) my husband uses that as a proof that he needs to handle him his way...and I see myself trying his way .. I just want to change all these.... HELP!!!!

Hello N,

Here are some questions you can ask your child when you have a quiet space to do so:

"Did you chose me and your father?"

"What do you know about your father?"

"Would you like this to change"

"What energy, space and consciousness can we invite to change this?"

With "temper tantrums" you can ask:

"What is truly going on here?"

"Is this someone else's"

"Is he validating other people's realities with this?"

"If so, is he willing to change it?"

"If so, how do we change it?"

If you do not have "words" come up for these questions, ask if there is an energy that comes up that doesn't have words. We do not have enough words in any language to describe all the energies that make up this Universe. You can destroy and uncreate the energy that comes up.

Being You, Erasing Fear Once and For All Call + Processes

Is it time for you to stop living from fear?

What if fear isn't real for you? What if it is a construct? Could you imagine what your life and future would look like if you had no fear? What would you choose? What would you allow yourself to receive and be? What could you create and generate? What if what you call "fear" is actually … excitement?

Using a completely different way of looking at this age-old subject, this is a 1.5-hour teleclass with Dr. Dain Heer that can LITERALLY change your whole reality around fear.

http://bit.ly/2bawwxv

CHAPTER FIFTEEN

❖

THE ARTLESS ART OF ALLOWANCE

By Bhagyalakshmi Murali

Access Consciousness Facilitator,
RRFY & TTTE Facilitator, Certified Life Coach,
Speaker, Healer

Most people on hearing the title are curious why 'allowance' is referred to as an 'artless art'.

It is because allowance is actually very simple. It is natural and it is effortless. Now, I know there may be many people who would find this difficult to believe, but it is true.

When we are willing to perceive it outside of us, we know that the Universe, the planet and everything in nature is evidence of total allowance. However, most of the time, most people choose to neither perceive nor acknowledge it.

Interestingly, we are made of the same elements that are there in the Universe, so the knowing of how to be in allowance is deeply embedded in each one of us. Our bodies are in allowance too. We overeat, don't eat, starve ourselves, don't drink enough water, drink too much (not water), don't get enough sleep or sleep too much, don't get enough exercise, or override the body's need for rest and force it to exercise and it is still in allowance of us. Sometimes it even kills itself for our sake.

If that is not allowance, what is? So we do know how to be in a state of allowance.

To be in allowance or not is so very often the question because of the fear that it may be misinterpreted or misidentified as weakness. The energy of allowance has nothing meek or weak about it. There is a space and a presence that is very potent.

The allowance we are talking about is not what this reality tells us it is. According to this reality the word allowance means many different things. So let's take a quick look at what allowance is definitely *not*. If one were to check the internet for the word allowance, one would come up with the following; *none* of which I am referring to, when I talk about allowance.

What Allowance Is Not

It is **not** the allowance given to children at regular intervals, often times controlled by parents, to teach children money management early in life.

It is **not** the travel allowance given to employees.

It is **not** the mitigating factors or circumstances taken into consideration to pardon/excuse/tolerate/accept someone or something.

It is **not** the recommended daily allowance of antioxidants.

It is **not** the free/checked baggage allowance on flights!

It is **not** the monthly allowance three quarters of men in Japan get from their wives!

It is definitely **not** a synonym for doormat.

It is never about being someone who is always walked all over, humiliated, taken for granted, submitting meekly to domination without complaint.

Myths About Allowance

Now that we know what it is not, let us also bust some myths about allowance.

Allowance is not possible in this reality.

Allowance is being a doormat.

If we are in allowance we are weird.

Acceptance/forgiveness/surrender/patience/tolerance are synonyms for allowance.

Allowance is something that comes with age.

Change is possible without changing one's points of view.

Self-judgment, judgment of others, criticism of self/others results in improvement.

None of the above happens to be true.

So...What Is Allowance?

"Allowance is 'interesting point-of-view', without judgment", according to Gary M Douglas, the Founder of Access Consciousness,

It is where you choose to perceive everything as 'just an interesting point of view', where you neither agree and align with people, their ideas or beliefs, nor do you resist or react to them. You really have no point of view about anyone or anything. You allow people to choose whatever they would like to, while you hold the right to be and do so, too. It can be a choice in every ten seconds, just for 10 seconds. What if, we were to live life in ten second increments?

So allowance is choosing to function from a space where everything is just an interesting point of view. It is always the way out of everything. It allows one to be the source for all creation and all change. In fact, it is what ensures rapid change. Allowance is being the rock in the stream. It makes it possible for one to be aware of other people's thoughts, feelings and emotions without being impacted or affected by them. It enables one to be so empowered and so aggressively present that one does not become the effect of anybody or anything. Allowance is what makes it possible for someone to allow things to be as they are until they show up differently. Allowance is empowering and makes a difference to everyone and everything. Most importantly allowance is just a choice.

If it is as simple as I know it can be, why is it so difficult to be in allowance of oneself and others? Our judgments, conclusions and fixed points of view make it difficult for us to be in allowance.

Allowance As A Doorway To Possibilities

So how can allowance be the doorway to possibilities? For this door to open for us, some other doors must be closed first. If taken in the alphabetical order, it would be something as follows.....

We need to close the doors on which **'Anger'** is written. Being angry cancels the possibility of being in allowance. We need to close the door on which **'Aversion to change'** is written. It does not allow us to change anything. We need to close the door which forces us to **'Agree and Align'** with others, no matter what our own knowing is.

We need to close the door that says **'Blame'**. As long as we are playing the blame game, there can be no allowance. We need to close the door that says **'Competition'**, which this reality promotes. In a world where everyone is unique, with a very distinct and special contribution to make, can there be competition? Absolutely not! Another door we need to close is **'Conclusions'**. Jumping to conclusions never really helps in any way. Then we need to close a door that marked **'Doubt'**.

It distracts us from following our awareness and being in allowance.

We need to close the door named 'Envy', which does not allow us to be the infinite beings that we truly are. Some of the doors we really must choose to close are 'Fear', 'Guilt', 'Hatred' and 'Helplessness'. Would an infinite being ever choose any of these? We have to close the door that is marked 'Inadequacy', "I cannot be/do this, you know, it is not possible for me. I don't have within me the wherewithal to BE/DO that". Inadequacy does not allow us to the be potent creators we are. We have to close the door named 'Immortal Soul', which keeps us in a loop of karma, repeating the same patterns again and again.

Two of the doors we must close are 'Judgment' and 'Jealousy', neither of which offers any scope for being in allowance. Another door we must close is called the 'Kingdom of ME'. There is no such thing as 'ME'. It is just 'WE'. We have to close the doors of 'Lack' and 'Limitations'. We have chosen to embody in an abundant Universe where there is no such thing as lack. The only limitations are those we buy into. We have to close the door marked 'Mimicry' because we tend to mimic our parents, our elders, our teachers, our ancestors and others.

We have to close that door so that we can BE who we truly are. We have to close the door which says 'No Choice' because there is always choice. Another door we have to close is called 'Obsession'. As long as we are choosing to obsess about something, what can we change? Nothing! One of the biggest doors that we must close is 'Perfectionism' because it keeps us judging ourselves/others all the time. It doesn't allow us to be in allowance.

We have to close the door that in my world is called the 'Quitter's Refuge'. Quitting is NEVER an option! The other doors we must close, are the ones marked 'Rage', 'Resistance', 'Reaction' and 'Regret'. If we stay in any of these rooms, they will keep us from being in allowance. We have to close the doors of 'Separation', which is a myth, if we are choosing oneness. We have to close the door marked 'Shame', which is also a distractor implant.

We have to close the door named **'Tolerance'**, because it is another word that is NOT a synonym for allowance. Then we have to close the door marked **'Unconsciousness'** that keeps us in a way that we are not present at all, so that we can be in allowance. The door named **'Validation'**, needs to be closed as well. What would it be like to never want or seek it from others? We have to close the door on what is called **'Victim Consciousness'**. As long as we think we are victims, we will create situations where we will be victimized, because it is like a neon sign above our heads, telling the whole wide world who we are choosing to be, namely victims.

We have to close the door marked **'Worry'**. If we are worried all the time, that does not let us be in allowance at all. Another door we need to close is called the **'Whiner's World'**. Always whinging and whining about things from the past, does not allow us to be present and in allowance. There is another door we must close, which I refer to as **'The X-Ray Approach to Life and Living'**, where there is always the need to analyze, to figure out, to look for something wrong. Wanting to find out the details, like taking an x-ray to 'see' everything, that is not visible to the naked eye. We have to close the door on that as well.

We have to close the door on what I call **'Yarn Spinning'**. We are so full of yarns that we spin, that we continue to recreate the same things over and over; so we cannot create change or be in allowance of something greater, something more magical and miraculous coming into our lives. The last door we must remember to close is the one that says **'Zero Allowance'**.... so that we can be in total allowance of everything and everyone, including ourselves.

Opening New Doorways

If we close all these doors, then new ones can become accessible to us, like the door marked **'Abundance'**, which allows us to perceive the **'Beauty'** that is all around us. We could access the door that opens up **'Choices'** for us that we never knew existed. We would be able to open the door that allows the Universe to contribute to us, and to allow us to be a '**Contribution**', as well.

We can open the door of '**Delight**' and '**Fun**'. We accessed these door-ways so very often as children. We need to get back to opening them again. The doors to '**Empowerment**' and '**Enthusiasm**', will then be accessible to us, which will allow us to function in a totally different way in this reality. We can open another door marked '**Freedom**', and choose total freedom. We could open the door marked '**Gratitude**' for whatever is, so that we can have more to be grateful for.

We could open the door to '**Happiness**', which is actually our natural state. Most people put off happiness in the present as something that may be possible in the future, if and when 'some goal is accomplished'. We could open the door to '**Impeccable Relationships**', that allows us to be in communion with our self and others. We could open the door-way named '**Joy**'. What would it be like to live joyous lives?

The doorway that says '**Kindness**', can be opened too. What would it be like, if there is more kindness in the world? We could open the door marked '**Leadership**', that allows us to be the leaders that we truly are and be catalysts for infinite greater possibilities. We have to open the door that says '**Magic and Miracles**' which abound in the Universe and which we so often miss perceiving, knowing, being and receiving. We have to open the door which says '**No Point Of View**', which al-lows us to live with the knowing that everything is just an interesting point of view.

What would it be like to open the door that says '**Oneness**', so there is no separation? So, if there is someone you want to judge; you wonder whether you are noticing that because you were that sometime, maybe not in this lifetime. So do we need to clear that time, space, dimension and reality? We do. We have to open the door to '**Possibilities**', that allows us the potency to live phenomenal lives. It would be very ben-eficial to open the door to '**Questions**', that would allow us to see the infinite choices available to us, the possibilities that are there and the contribution that we can be. We could choose to open the door to the

'**Riches**', that the Universe so desires to gift us.

We can open the door to '**Simplicity**'. This reality has so complicated our lives and tied us up in so many knots about how difficult life is, that we have forgotten what we came here knowing; that life could be simple and one of great ease. So when we open that door, The Artless Art Of Allowance becomes very easy. We have to open the door to '**Truth**' because deep down we know what the truth is. We have to open the door to explore the realm of '**Unconditional Living**', where we do not compromise on anything and do not expect anybody else to do so either.

We have to open the door named '**Valuable Inputs**', that allows us to receive contributions from everyone and everything. The door to '**Wisdom**', allows us to know, that we know, that we know and that we have not come here to 'learn'. We have come here to know that we know everything. We would benefit tremendously from opening the door that would allow all the '**X-Men and X-Women**' (Access Consciousness parlance) who have chosen to embody in this reality, to help facilitate the change that this world so requires at this point of time. What would it be like to open the door marked, '**YES**'? Wouldn't it be amazing to be able to say, "Yes. Whatever it takes to be that contribution to consciousness, I'm in allowance of all of those possibilities opening up for me when I open the door to '**Yes**' ". When we do that, we realize that there is '**Zero Trauma and Zero Drama**'. It is just total allowance.

How wonderful is that!

As long as we are functioning from our thoughts, feelings, emotions, beliefs and fixed points of view; we are in reactive states which leave no room for allowance. **So this is where we have to be very present, so that our awareness never exceeds our allowance.**

What would it be like to be in the space of total allowance at all times? What if, we could clear some conscious or unconscious blocks that do not allow us to be in allowance?

Here are some clearings that may help.....

What can you be and do different today that would give your allowance muscles a workout like never before? Everything that does not allow that shall we destroy and uncreate it please? Right and wrong, good and bad, POC and POD, all nine, shorts, boys and beyonds.

What energy, space and consciousness can you choose to function from that allows you to have no points of view about anyone, including yourself? Everything that does not allow that shall we destroy and uncreate it please, for now and all eternity? Times a Godzillion, right and wrong, good and bad, POC and POD, all nine, shorts, boys and beyonds.

What would it be like if your allowance could always exceed your awareness? Everything that does not allow that, shall we destroy and uncreate it please? Right and wrong, good and bad, POC and POD, all nine, shorts, boys and beyonds.

What if you could choose to be so present that allowance becomes a way of life for you instead of an exercise you must practice? Everything that does not allow you to choose that shall we destroy and uncreate it please? Right and wrong, good and bad, POC and POD, all nine, shorts, boys and beyonds.

What would it be like if others could perceive you as the embodiment of total allowance and know that they can choose to be the same too...if they so desire? Everything that does not allow that shall we destroy and uncreate it, please? Right and wrong, good and bad, POC and POD, all nine, shorts, boys and beyonds.

What if you could realize that being in allowance is simpler than being in judgment? Everything that does not allow you to realize that with ease, shall we destroy and uncreate it please? Right and wrong, good and bad, POC and POD, all nine, shorts, boys and beyonds.

What if, all that is required of you is to remember that everything is just an interesting point of view? Everything that does not allow you to remember that shall we destroy and uncreate it please? Times a Godzillion, right and wrong, good and bad, POC and POD, all nine, shorts, boys and beyonds.

What if being truly in allowance is so empowering that nobody and nothing could have power over you? Everything that does not allow you to be that shall we destroy and uncreate now please? Times a godzillion, right and wrong, good and bad, POC and POD, all nine, shorts, boys and beyonds.

What if you could remember that every point of view you actually own, owns you? Everything that does not allow you to remember that shall we destroy and uncreate it please? Right and wrong, good and bad, POC and POD, all nine, shorts, boys and beyonds.

What would it be like to step out of judgments and step into knowing instead (knowing that allows you to be in allowance)? Everything that does not allow that shall we destroy and uncreate it please? Thank you. Right and wrong, good and bad, POC and POD, all nine, shorts, boys and beyonds.

What if you could acknowledge that total allowance equals total freedom? Everything that does not allow you to acknowledge that shall we destroy and uncreate it please? Right and wrong, good and bad, POC and POD, all nine, shorts, boys and beyonds.

What would it be like for you to choose to be in so much allowance that you become a catalyst for change and infinite possibilities? Everything that does not allow you to choose that shall we destroy and uncreate it please? Times a Godzillion, right and wrong, good and bad, POC and POD, all nine, shorts, boys and beyonds.

What would it be like if you were willing to be exactly who you are, without making other people's points of view and judgments relevant, so you allow yourself to have total choice? Everything that does not allow you to have total choice shall we destroy and uncreate it please? Right and wrong, good and bad, POC and POD, all nine, shorts, boys and beyonds.

What would it be like to thrive in your 'total choice Universe' instead of the 'no choice Universe', that most people believe is their reality? Everything that does not allow you to thrive in your Universe of total choice shall we destroy and uncreate it please? Times a godzillion, right and wrong, good and bad, POC and POD, all nine, shorts, boys and beyonds.

What if allowance is just a choice? Everything that does not allow you to remember that it is just a choice in these ten seconds, would you be willing to destroy and uncreate it all? Right and wrong, good and bad, POC and POD, all nine, shorts, boys and beyonds.

We are at a very critical juncture in the history of this planet. What if we could reach the tipping point of at least 10,000 people functioning from total consciousness, so that the planet can thrive like it was always meant to. What would it be like to reach and exceed that target now?

What if **'The Artless Art Of Allowance'** is one of the doorways to such a Possibility?

MAKE YOUR BOOK AN AMAZON BESTSELLER

Have you written and published a book? Are you writing a book? Do you have a book in you that would like to be written and pub- lished?

Would you like to write, publish and make your book an Amazon Bestseller?

From coaching on getting started, to helping you with the publishing process to getting your book to be an International Amazon Bestseller, Nilofer offers it all. Contact her to explore the Infinite Possibilities with your book - nilofer@illusiontoilluminationsummit.com

---

CHAPTER SIXTEEN

AARGH!! MY DOOR IS CLOSED!

(also known as.... Alrighty then, now what?)

By Rachel Silber, CFMW

Access Consciousness® Facilitator, Speaker, Adventurer,
Change Agent, Loves to Play with Possibilities

Aaaargh! My Door Is Closed!!!!

Have you ever been there? Have you looked around you and seen no way out? No way through? Just barriers and obstacles everywhere you look?

And when everyone else speaks of possibilities, have you wondered if there are any there for you?

When Nilofer contacted me to invite me to participate in her telesummit, I had just chosen to come out of hiding. Literally. Hiding, you might wonder?

Yes. Hiding. Just so.

Hiding behind any door, peeking through cracks, being camouflaged or better yet, invisible, and in short being addicted to the wrongness of me. Does that sound familiar, my friends?

For years, I lived life as the perpetual fly on the wall.... blending in.... staying safe.... and no one need know I even exist. I lived a life of conforming and compromising, a life of not making waves, a life of pleasing everyone and living for everyone else.

So when Nilofer contacted me, I balked.... I breathed.... I stepped into the discomfort.... and I accepted.

And then she shared the title with me - the Doorways of Infinite Possibilities!

Those beautiful doorways are fine and dandy for everyone who actually sees them, who opens them...., but what about me and others like me, the people who don't even see a door? Or if they do see one, what if the door is locked? And barred? And blockaded?

Do we give up? Do we give in? Do we quit? This is where I went when Nilofer asked me to participate in the telesummit. What if there is no door? Yikes! Aaaargh! Now what?

So let's see this about this elusive doorway. Whether it is there or not, will we let that be the thing that stops us? If we just knew there has to be a way, even if we do not see it clearly, or see it at all, what else can we do?

A Late-Night Locked Door Adventure

When I was a teenager, I went to a modeling program (yes..... me) so I would learn to carry myself with more poise and even learn a few beauty tips (you should see me now). All the parents were invited to attend our final presentation - a runway show. At the end of the evening, my parents and I were just about the last people to leave the building. The elevators were not working so we went down several flights of stairs to a door that led outside the building.

Except the door did not open. At all.

And as we walked slowly back up the next flight of stairs, that door would not open either. Nor the next.

That was a massive "Aaaargh!" And hence the title of this chapter. What do you do when a door does not open? Do you bang on it? Do you shout? Do you call for help?

We did. All three. And no one came.

So my father, bless him for always being prepared, took out his pocket knife and began to dig a hole in the sheetrock wall. He broke through to be able to reach the door-handle on the other side and that's how we finally left the building.

Years later, I saw a similar doorway and on the opposite wall was a button that said "*press here to exit*" and memories of that night-time adventure flooded in. It seemed so familiar - déjàvu all over again. What if there had been a button like that all along and we just never noticed it? One click on that button and we would have been free to step out with ease: no struggle, no effort, no sweat and no broken walls. How much is truly available when we are willing to take off our filters and look around us? How much of what can be ease and joy and fun do we refuse to see and to acknowledge?

That was the very first image that popped into my head when I heard 'doorways to possibilities'. What came to mind was my father with the knife, breaking through no matter what - even if it means going through the wall.

Never give up. Never give in. Never quit.

Not that we have to make anything difficult either. We can choose to have ease just as easily. When we are willing to take our blinders off (yes, I am referring to those decisions and conclusions we've already come to about how hard something supposedly is...) we can see other possibilities.... many of which we've never even noticed before.

What Color Are Your Blinders

How many decisions and conclusions and judgments and definitions have you come to that keep you stuck? How many points of view are you making greater than you? Where have you given up being you to please everyone else? Have you judged how you see the world as all good (white) or all bad (black)? What are the colors and possibilities you are not noticing?

When we refuse to see all the possibilities (or at least a few of them, eh?), we stay contained and stuck in our own jail or box - a container of our own making.

Sound familiar? Have you ever been there and done that?

Here are some of the ways I defined myself and created my very own limited world:

Being the good girl.

Being the good daughter.

Being the good student.

(Notice a pattern?)

Being good in general.

Getting married and being the good wife.

Being the good mom.

Keeping the family together.

Doing everything for others.

Living a life according to other people's expectations and just going with the program.

And there is so much more! I won't bore you with the details. I'd just like to ask you to become aware if you do that in your own life.

So what have you defined yourself as?

How do you begin to step out of the trap you've created - that locked, though possibly beautifully decorated cozy jail cell? Where is your doorway or for that matter, the exit sign? First of all, please be aware that there are infinite possibilities available to you when you begin to ask questions, and they may not all look like doorways. Would you be willing to notice any opening that shows up like windows, and gateways, escape hatches, cracks and openings and even "press here to exit" buttons? What if nothing ever looked the way you thought it "should"? So look around you and begin to ask questions.

Questions invite in the magic of the Universe, whereas conclusions.... conclude! Become aware of and celebrate the rightness in your situation. There is a silver lining if you are willing to acknowledge it. Ask "What is right about this I'm not getting?" and "What is right about me I'm not getting?" as often as you can. Notice I did not ask what is wrong with you. If you are anything like me, you've been there already, at least a few times. And really, what if there is nothing at all wrong with you? To get out of where you are stuck - begin doing something you have never done before. Will you give up going to the wrongness of you as an automatic response to life? Great! Thank you!!! And perhaps you might begin to notice even more things that are 'right' in your life! What do you admire about yourself?

Life In The Coffin Zone

Do any of those definitions and expectations we mentioned earlier make you feel light and expansive and tingly and yummy all over? Hmmmm...... I thought so.... me neither. Living a life of complacency, normalcy, conformity, stability, and 'following the program' is living in your comfort zone or as I like to call it, your coffin zone. That's one heck of a self-containment unit, isn't it?

That coffin zone is your very own custom-made box. Once you acknowledge the magnificent container you've created to trap yourself, you can begin to see how to take it apart by choosing something different. Yes, your comfort zone may be cushy and comfortable. Yes, it is familiar and stable and solid and real. It is everything you've defined and everything you have allowed to limit you. But what if there is more?

How much have you locked away from your life by thinking you've al-ready 'got it right?'

Everything you are defending for and against in order to maintain the stability in your life, will you destroy and uncreate it all? Right and wrong, good and bad, POC and POD, all nine, shorts, boys and beyonds.

So consider this your invitation. You can stay inside of your favorite coffin or you can open it and peek out. You can look around you, open the door a crack, and make a choice. Just a choice. Not the choice of a lifetime. Not the one choice that rules all choices. Just a choice. A choice for a few seconds. A choice that invites you to play. A choice that invites you to wonder. A choice. What if what's on the other side is not scary (or even what you've pre-determined that it 'should' be)? What if it is simply what it is? And guess what, you lucky duck you? You get to choose again. Your choice will bring up awareness, a knowing, in your world. So will you choose?

The awareness you get follows the choice that you make. When you choose, you might fall flat on your face or get a skinned knee. You might fail miserably, or even gracefully, and then you still have the freedom to choose again. Imagine yourself standing before a series of doorways. You can look at all of them and begin to choose, opening them one by one. What if you choose to open a door that has a lion roaring behind it? Quick! Shut it! And recognize that you can say, "Whoa! Yikes! Next choice!"

Every choice you make creates awareness. What that means is that first you choose, and then you perceive what that choice will create in the world. When you choose something... you get a subtle ping, a whisper of awareness, and if that ping is light and tingly, it's a great choice for you. If it is heavy and contracted, you just might consider making an-other choice.

Ease On Down The Road

The awareness of what is true for you, what is light and expansive, is your GPS system, your inner personalized tour-guide to your life. Just keep choosing what is light and joyful and fun! That's what is true for you! Sometimes you might over-ride your GPS and wander about a little lost until you get back on that light and expansive yellow-brick road. And hey... what if you would enjoy the off-road adventures as well? You can pick the wildflowers and look up at the clouds... as long as you keep choosing every few seconds. So what if you get lost? Will you cut yourself some slack? If you've gotten off the road and created havoc for yourself, guess what? You can ask a question and choose something else. Ease on down the road again.

Do You Allow Yourself To Fail

What have you decided failure is? How much have you used your decisions about failure to stop yourself? How many times did Thomas Edison fail when he invented the incandescent light bulb? Wasn't it over nine thousand times? Would you have given up before then? I probably would have! Yet Edison carried on. He was willing to be a doorway to a new possibility and I have gratefully enjoyed sitting in a brightly lit room when it is dark outside. I don't even have to figure out how electricity works, I just flip a switch and enjoy it because Mr. Edison didn't give up. He found lots of ways that did not work, he learned a lot, and he kept going till he found something that did.

What have you stopped yourself from creating because it wasn't as fast or easy or smooth or direct as you thought it *should* be? How much have you stopped your creations by being unwilling to fail? What gifts has the world missed out on by your giving up? So will you allow yourself to fail? To be wrong? To screw up? To make a less-than-glorious choice that... well... just does not contribute to the life you'd like to have? And are you in allowance of you? Because you know, my friend, you can always choose again.

Begin With Wonder

Are you willing to be curious? Questions are truly wonder-ful! Real open-ended curiosity-inducing questions bring up a wondering and a willingness to receive awareness. Most of the questions we've asked our whole lives do not involve any wonder. They are glorified answers with a question-mark attached onto the end for good measure. When you decide, pre-judge or answer - it is already concluded, finished, caput - no energy to follow, no adventure to explore. Every question within it has a quest... an ad- venture that unfolds as you choose. If something isn't working in your life, what if you could ask a questions? How about "What question can I ask that will change this?" or "What can I be and do different that will change this?" My favorite is "What else is possible here I've never even considered?" When you truly wonder, so many more doorways begin to open up in the world for everyone.

So when you ask a question, will you be present for whatever energies come up? Whatever they are, just BE with them. Notice them. Be present with them. Acknowledge them. Be grateful for them. In some way, they have served you and now you can release them with no judgment, desperation, or resistance. You can destroy and uncreate (POC and POD) each point of view and you can also choose something different. It is just a choice.

What energy, space and consciousness can we be to fail, to fall, to experiment, to play and soar whenever we please with total ease? Everything that doesn't allow that times a godzillion, will you destroy and uncreate it all? Right and wrong, good and bad, POC and POD, all nine, shorts, boys and beyonds.

Would you be willing to let go of how you think anything 'should' show up? All those lovely projections and expectations that keep you 'shoulding' all over yourself, will you let them go too? Change never looks the way you think it will look, does it? It just is what it is. It is not right or wrong. It just is. And change is not nearly as big or as bad or as scary as you think it is. It's not all lions and tigers and bears, oh my. If you are willing to get over your point of view... you just might surprise yourself!

There's a whole new world of possibilities available to you! These possibilities could show up as a door, or a window, a little path, a garden-gate, a little crack, a mouse-hole, a little light that's shining through that lets you know there is something there and suddenly, things don't seem so solid and heavy and real. Are you willing to be surprised? What grand and glorious adventures can you have today? What possibilities can you now perceive that you've never allowed yourself to perceive, that if you'd perceive them, would change all realities?

What Are You Unwilling To Be

If you give up, and never be all of you, what would the world be missing? Yup, you got it - the gift and the presence of you.

We've been and done everything already – so what is the value of stopping yourself? What have you defined as failure? What have you decided is wiping out and falling down? What have you deemed is wrong about you? What are you unwilling to be? Where have you judged yourself as failing? What would you do if you knew you could not fail?

Everything you are unwilling to be locks you up and limits you. What would change when you would be willing to BE whatever you've refused to be? Might it change your whole reality?

A few years ago (or was it months?) I was very unwilling to be silly. Very! My stick was shoved so high up my butt it that it practically served as an antennae above my head. Silliness and fun had no room in my life (or were only available when I played with animals or with kids.) I valued being taken seriously and being respected. Being silly would mean that I was an outright failure because no one would receive me – or so I thought. If I were being silly, did it mean that I couldn't also be seductive or inviting or intellectual or aware? It seems that's what I decided. Being silly (and the aftermath of being silly - not being taken seriously) was failing in my world. Call it what you will – that judgment was not fun. It wasn't giggles and ease. It was a mix of shame with a dash of "I'm not willing to receive all that judgment of me. So I'd rather nobody notice when I mess up." And in trying to be perfect, I became invisible.

Every day, that is changing. I'm now joyfully 'messing up' in public big time! I am speaking out more. I am willing to grate on anyone's ears with my bastardized Spanish (I live in Guatemala). I am willing to have my classes in any mix of languages and throw in impromptu songs as well. I am fa-SILLY-tating people! I'm willing to be the energy of "Hi! Want to have some fun?" which invites other people to play and to let down their barriers too. We don't have to be everybody's cup of tea. What if we didn't have to walk a tight-rope of expectations? What if we could twist and shout, or twirl and swirl, and slip and slide being us? Those who would like to have that energy in their lives will find us.

Did you know that the 'failing,' that stumbling along and finding our way, though unstable, doesn't have to be hard? It can include lots of laughter and giggling! It can become a whole new dance! One and two and three and four and step and slide. Now step and stumble, and step and tumble, and step and twirl, and step and soar. What if we did not make falling or failure very significant? How many times can we fall down and how much fun can we have falling? Where have we tried to make our life so right, that we've locked ourselves right out of it?

Everything we resist we solidify and create more of in our world. Between Suzy Godsey and Blossom Benedict of Access Consciousness, I think I received the wedgie of a lifetime during a 'Right Voice for you' class when they said, "Oh, Rachel! She's so sweet yet she's like a mite. You know, invisible and annoying." And I thought, "Holy Moly, Guacamole! Me? Really? Oh my goodness!" and I went into the wrongness of me for about an hour (or was it more?) and then I said, "Well, ok. *What energy, space and consciousness can I be to be the most invisible, most irritating, most annoying, most pesky, most mighty little mite on the planet?*" Within a couple of weeks after I began running that process, Nilofer contacted me to participate in the telesummit, so what else is possible? How does it get any better?

When you are willing to be everything with no judgment and without resistance, you have total choice. Do you know the adage "What you resist, persists?" Maintaining a resistance to something takes a lot of energy. This is energy that you could be using to create something generative instead. What if you no longer resisted? What if resistance is futile? (Thanks, Star Trek!) Where are you in the computation of your life when you resist? When you begin to be playful and relaxed and open, and you are willing to experiment with everything, there is total space and freedom.

That's what I love about the ESC (energy, space and consciousness) clearings. Embracing all of you by being willing to BE any and all energies and not resisting and reacting to anything is really easy to do. Just ask *"What energy, space and conscious- ness can I be that would allow me to be the_____ I truly be?"* Fill in the blank whatever is coming up in your world and have as much fun as you dare. Here are a couple of examples:

What energy, space, and consciousness can I be to be the magic that changes everything around me with total ease? Anything that doesn't allow that, will you destroy and uncreate it all? Right and wrong, Good and bad, POC and POD, All 9, Shorts, Boys and Beyonds.

What have you decided that you absolutely and utterly cannot be? Let's play with that.

What energy, space, and consciousness can I be to be as terribly and horribly wrong as I truly be? Anything that doesn't allow that, will you destroy and un-create it all? Right and wrong, Good and bad, POC and POD, All 9, Shorts, Boys and Beyonds.

Doesn't that one put a smile on your face? What else could you explore?

You Are The Chief Engineer

Maybe you haven't been willing to be all the energy and all the joy and all the exuberance and potency that you truly BE. Maybe you were told to stuff it as a kid. Maybe you were told that you were too much or asked that lovely question – "Just who do you think you are?" Or maybe you were told you can't be too happy or that you have a problem. I was.

I lived most of my life according to everyone's expectations and desires for me to have the life they couldn't have, and the life they decided was ideal. None of it really worked out well for me. In college, I was diagnosed as bi-polar and medicated regularly. I married my college sweetheart right after graduation and not surprisingly, divorced after a few short months of marriage. I lived reacting to everything around me, rather than recognizing how much of my life I truly do create. Then I discovered Access Consciousness and I have not looked back. Recognizing that I create my life gave me immense freedom and the choice to change anything and everything.

When we begin to acknowledge how much of our life we create, new possibilities begin to show up. What could we create without our self-imposed limitations? Who would we be without our past? Without our decisions and histories and definitions of who we are (or aren't) and everything that we believe is real and true about us?

When we judge ourselves, we lock ourselves in our jailhouse (or box or coffin…) with no apparent way out, until we begin to ask, "Is this real? Am I really trapped? What else could I choose here? What if there is no box or jail or coffin? What if this was not a problem – what else could it be? Who would I be without this limitation?" It is amazing how we brilliantly lock ourselves up in a box for which only we hold the keys! It's the perfect trap! What if we could acknowledge that the box is there because WE ever-so-carefully built it up with every choice we made and every story we told? So will you now let go of everything that makes your box of limitations more real than your capacity to create something different? If those limitations are not as solid and real as you thought... what can you choose now? This is worth repeating: We create everything in our life - including the barriers and obstacles to stop us - and then we are frustrated by our struggles. We complain about our situation and think how powerless we are! Cute, isn't it? If we created it, can we not also uncreate it? So what can we change? What if we would turn a blank page and begin a new story?

What if we are more aware than we've acknowledged? As aware beings, able to perceive so many people around us, whose points of view are we holding on to and creating our life from? Who are we being when we say our door is shut? Or that we have no choice? Once we shine the light of awareness on every point of view we've held on to or every story we have told, we can see the limitation and choose something different. What if changing is as easy as choosing? Are you willing to be in allowance of that and of you?

Property

Question from a caller: "Ok, I just saw an ad for a very beautiful villa, which feels so expansive and happy and has all the elements I was look-ing for in my ideal next house. I don't have that kind of money which is required to pay the rent cheques. What can I do? I don't see a door so how can I at least clamber in through the window to have it?"

Response: I love that! Yes, you can clamber in through the window. First is the desire. You've seen something that you would like - you've chosen it. There is a demand you are making in your world to have that energy in it. Now begin asking questions and choosing what is ex-pansive. Like a two-step dance - choose, follow the energy, and choose again. Our choice creates awareness. Nothing will change if we don't ask and get the Universe and quantum entanglements in motion. There are a lot of people who've never even allowed themselves to see the villa. They've never allowed themselves to consider that there may be something greater for their future. Maybe they've decided they are not worthy of it or that only other people can live in a beautiful villa, but they cannot. Essentially, they exclude themselves from having it.

By admiring the villa and desiring it, declaring "Ah, I'd like to have that," you've already begun creation. Creation does not come from referring to the past nor the logic of what is currently in your bank account, using that as a reason and a justification to make yourself small. Creation does not come from conclusions. It comes from wonder and the questions and choices that you be. So begin! *"What would it take to live in a house like that or an even better one?"* Don't limit yourself to just that house. What might turn up is something completely different, and much more expansive for you. *"What will it take to live in a place that will contribute to my life and would be totally joyful for me? What can I be or do different today that will begin to create this in my world right away? Hey Universe, what is the place for me?"*

When we attempt to create out of a decision, out of an expectation and a conclusion about how and when and from where something can show up, we've slammed the doorway to possibility shut rather than opened it wide. So begin by asking curiously. If you don't have a point of view defining what you would like to receive - that it has to be this particular villa or that particular car or this particular relationship - things begin to show up in the most amazing of ways.

Nilofer: What if you did not buy into everything you've learned from metaphysics about having to be very specific about what you want? What if it was just the energy of what the house is giving you? Like the house that I'm living in right now. Three years ago we were actually looking for a house to move into and I went with a friend who was also looking for a house and stumbled across this one. I came into the house and the moment I stepped in, my energy just went "whoosh!" It just expanded out and then when I looked at everything that the house had, it had everything that I didn't even know that I was looking for. But it was perfect. It was "Oh, I wanted that! Oh, it has this and I wanted it. It has this and I wanted this! And it has this and I wanted it." So what if it was just about the energy and what if it was just following the energy and choosing from there?

How many doorways of possibilities are we missing when we are so dedicated to looking for something specific? (Hint: Concluding again, are we?) We don't recognize that there's another doorway (possibility) just next to the doorway (possibility) that we've been focusing on, but there is another way around or even a 'press here to exit' button we can press that would totally change things, if we were willing to take our blinders off and notice that there are infinite possibilities in the world.

What are we refusing to perceive by distracting ourselves with conclusions, reasons and justifications, that if we'd be willing to look beyond them, would allow us to create far greater than we've ever dreamed possible? Anything that doesn't allow us to be aware and willing to receive everything, can we destroy and uncreate all of that? Right and wrong, good and bad, POC and POD, all nine, shorts, boys and beyonds.

The other energy in this question is "I would love this but my bank account doesn't allow me to have it" and "This would be wonderful.... just for other people." What if that's not true at all? Whose points of view are those? What if the Universe is so abundant that it will give to us everything we ask for and desire? What if living is not about surviving like so many people choose to in this reality, but thriving beyond it?

And if you are having financial strains recognize that's from previous choices and acting from points of view that may not even be yours. Since your point of view creates your reality, are you willing to say "Ok, I screwed up. Not my brightest moment. Cool! That was then. Now what can I choose?"

What can I do today to create and generate more money right away, for now and for the future? Anything that does not allow that, can we destroy and uncreate all of that? Right and wrong, good and bad, POC and POD, all nine, shorts, boys and beyonds.

It might seem as if you are surrounded by barricades, impenetrable ones, and they will begin to shift and change.... until they just entirely disappear. Now what will you choose to be and do different to create your reality? Notice some other possibilities around you?

Fire That Judge!

Response to a question about Judgment: Everywhere someone is judging you, what if who they are really judging is themselves? What if the things people say to you give you a lot of information about them and how they function in the world? What if their judgment has nothing to do with you? What would it be like if you didn't take personally the judgments, the definitions and even the projections directed at you? Are you willing to receive the judgment and just let it flow through you, as if you were a wide-open window? When someone judges you, your being in allowance of their judgment while being yourself, invites the judgment to dissipate and opens the door to a new possibility. What contribution could you receive from their judgments?

What would it be like if you would turn it up in the face of judgment? What does that mean? It is being you, no matter what anyone else says. It is being aggressively present in your life and never giving up, never giving in and never quitting. I've been accused of trying to be the center of attention – which is kind of funny considering how I was told I'm invisible and irritating as well. Rather than taking the accusations to heart, I keep choosing what is light and expansive for me. I often ask a) What contribution can I be in the world? And b) What can I choose to create something greater?

What energy, space and consciousness could you be to flow through your day with more ease, without having your dukes up and defending yourself from everyone else? If you aren't defending for or against anything or anyone, how much freedom would you have in life? What could you create if there was nothing to prove?

Now imagine when we allow ourselves to choose something other than judging ourselves and our past and our choices, how many possibilities we can invite people to exploring? How much joy could they have being themselves? That is rare in this world! So rare that most people don't even consider that as a possibility!

Where are you unwilling to receive judgment? How much fun can you have receiving it? How wrong are you willing to be? How goofy? How obnoxious? When you don't need to be right, you can be free. That is a priceless invitation! Are you willing to acknowledge the potency of receiving everything - including judgment? It can be a huge contribution in your life.

So everywhere you are aligning and agreeing and resisting and reacting to receiving judgment, will you destroy and uncreate it all? Right and wrong, good and bad, POC and POD, all nine, shorts, boys and beyonds.

What energy, space and consciousness can you and your body be to receive judgment with ease for all eternity? And everything that brings up, will you destroy and un-create it all? Right and wrong, good and bad, POC and POD, all nine, shorts, boys and beyonds.

What if there's nothing outside of us that can stop us? The only thing that can really stop us is what's between our own ears. That's it! What if we fire that little chatter-box? What possibilities can we become aware of without the limitation and meaning our inner-judge places on us? What if we're so much more magical than we have never imagined? What if we can create a whole new reality beyond this reality? Yes, we might have been living as a mite until now, being irritating and invisible and small, blending in and camouflaging so we don't get hurt or even seen.... That was then. What if we let that go and begin to let our light shine? Even one little candle light in a room full of darkness changes things - no more darkness.

JOB Is The Joy Of Being You

Question: "I knock, knock, knock, applying to jobs and wait patiently for the recruiter to notice it but after 5 years doing it, I haven't had anything on hand. Now I realize I have to change my course of action for a different reality. What particular question or clearing can you help me with and those in similar situations because in terms of job hunting especially, what can a candidate do after sending the resume? Isn't it the recruiter who has to come back to me?"

Response: Well, there are a few different things that you can do in that kind of situation. When you send your résumé, remember these people are receiving tens or hundreds of different résumés for the same positions. What can you be and do different to have your picture and your résumé stand out more?

What if you asking a question like *"What capacities do I have? What contribution can I be for their business?"* And please be aware of what their business is, rather than sowing your wild oats by randomly mailing out hundreds of job applications at once. *"Ok, so if I were working for this company, what contribution could I be for them? What can I be and do different that's going to change things there? What could create more expansion and contribution, both for the company and for me?"* That will change how you present yourself both in the résumé and in the job interview.

The way you walk into an interview, present and confident, makes a huge difference. My husband has a call center and he recruits people on a regular basis to provide customer service for companies in the United States. I remember being at job fairs to help recruit and looking at the people. There were lots of people applying, some confident and some... not so much... and it is easy to notice the difference. When you begin with confidence, you don't walk up to a person who is recruiting with an apologetic air of "Oh, excuse me, I'm so sorry to bother you.... but you know, here I am with my application and I really do hope you notice it." You are present. You strut in with ease, willing to acknowledge the greatness of you: "I'm a gift in the world and can be a gift in your organization. When can you fit me in? When can I begin?" It's a totally different energy. There were those people who would come up to me, to give me their résumé and apply for a position. They would reach out to shake hands and their handshake was like holding a dead fish. Does that inspire confidence?

When I filled out my application for university, I just did it to please my parents. I had my heart set on attending the University of Texas and my uncle came and spoke about a college I'd never heard of, Brandeis University, and said, "You know, this is a wonderful university in the Boston area. You should fill this application out." I said, "No way! All my friends are going to University of Texas in Austin and that's where I'm going." No question or other possibility in my world, right? My mother grounded me until I filled out the application for Brandeis. So I filled it out - in crayons with lots of different colors and doodles all over the application. I didn't think they were going to take it seriously, and they accepted me because I was me. Look at the energy. I wasn't trying to impress. I was just being me and I did not worry about what they thought of me.

When you are afraid to be you, you blend in with everybody else, and who can find you then? If you are more worried about being appropriate and right and exactly what they are expecting, is there any room for the gift of you? You are already unique and different, would be willing to express it? What can you add to your application that will make it be more memorable than anything else they've ever received? What if you would send in your résumé via email with a little video of yourself? Or with an audio recording inviting them to call you? Or asking them a question, in the email or in the résumé? "How does it get any better than that? How can I contribute to making your company more innovative?" They might look at you as if you are the strangest person who's fallen in their lap but they will notice you. There's bound to be humanoid in there somewhere who hears you.

Another tool I love playing with is the energy pulls. If you know the recruiter's name or even just the name of the company, lower your barriers and pull energy from everywhere in the Universe, and expand and pull even more. Pull energy through the name of the company, pull it through the name of the person that you've sent the application to or the committee you'll be speaking to about being hired, through the position, through the company, through you and back out again and keep pulling and pulling and pulling. Keep pulling until you feel your heart opening up, and then begin to send little, tiny, trickles of energy out to everyone and anyone in that company, that can contribute to your having the job you desire. What if you could use this way beyond a job? What if it could be one of the tools for creating your life? Send those little trickles out to anyone and everyone who may or may not have heard of you yet, may not have looked at your résumé yet, and the moment that they do, ask for that flow to be equalized, so the moment that they call you, the moment you walk into their office, the moment that they open the email that you sent them, they feel an "Ah, alright! This is somebody who feels like a part of our team, someone who is right for us."

What if you were willing to be the choosing one, as Steve and Chutisa Bowman (co-authors of Benevolent Leadership) suggest? What if you live proactively choosing, not reactively waiting to be chosen? What if you would be the one interviewing to see which job you would like to step into? What if you would choose?

What energy, space and consciousness can you and your body be to be the choosing one for all eternity? Everything that brings up, will you destroy and uncreate it? Right and wrong, good and bad, POC and POD, all nine, shorts, boys and beyonds.

What if we would choose not from logic, not from desperation, not from need or obligation, just from "What would I like to choose next?" Just for the next 10 seconds, it doesn't have to be a lifetime choice, just for the next 10 seconds. If you open this door, if you send your résumé out to this place, what would your life be like in 5 years? Would it be light? Would it be joyful? Would it be expansive? Cool. Go for it. And you can proactively call the company and be the choosing one. Call them and say "Hi! I know I'd sent in my résumé, and perhaps it wasn't on the top of the list yet, but I'd like to ask, how can I contribute to your company?" You choose them and show them how when they have you on board, their life will never be the same again.

When you follow what's generative and light, it contributes to you, it contributes to the company, and it contributes to the way your future is created. It's more fun to create from lightness than from stuckness, right? How does it get even better? What can you choose that will be greater? Who would be the most fun to work with? And to which would it be most generative for you to apply? Rather than doing a blanket mailing, ask some questions and get to know the companies and how you could contribute to them. This way you are not waiting, you are creating. Most companies don't meet many proactive people like that. What if you were willing to be different and be totally present? It might scare some people off, but how many more doors will it open?

It Is Not The End

When you are willing to fail and fall and be grateful for the experience, getting up and dusting yourself off and smiling anyway, you can be the invitation for someone else who is seeking change. Rather than saying "Oh, life is just terrible. It's the end of my life, the end of my rope, the end of the way," what else could you choose? There's not one person who survived childhood on this planet unscathed. It's not about the past. That's who you were, not who you are now.

I was abused when I was younger and as a result I said yes to abuse quite a few times in my life. I also abused myself... it was such a familiar energy and I made myself wrong for it. Now, what if you didn't make yourself wrong? What if you did not punish yourself incessantly for your past? What if you were willing to be kind with yourself and be grateful for your choices? After all, they have brought you to where you are right now. There is no need to dwell on why you chose what you chose. It is part of your experience base. Will you let it define you or determine your future? Who can you be without your story? And if you did not see the situation as the end that defines you, what if it could be a new beginning? What is the gift that is there? Change how you see things and everything you see changes.

Keep asking, so what? Now what? What can you be and do different? How can you let life roll off your back, shake it off and step up? There's the story of a donkey that fell into a well and the owner of the donkey got several neighbors to come and help him fill the well and bury the donkey at the same time. In their minds, there was no other option. Now the donkey was aware. Every time they would throw a shovelful of dirt on him, he would shake it off and step up. Shake it off and step up. Shake it off and step up. Pretty soon the level of the dirt floor in the well was rising and rising until he was able to easily step up and out of the well. He did that by just shaking off whatever landed on him much to everyone's surprise. What if you would be like that donkey?

What if you don't let the outside world weigh you down? Sure, you can make it significant and choose to have a lot of frustration in life, or you can shake it off and choose again. You are not a victim. You are magnificent! What can you change in your world that will change things? Would it be lowering your barriers? Or expanding your being out 500 miles in all directions? Taking a deep breath? Asking a question? What if nothing that you were, nothing that you have experienced, nothing that is around you now, no box or container or jail that you have constructed is greater than the next choice that you can make? What if YOU are the doorway to a new possibility?

Being You, Living Beyond Judgment Call + Processes

There is nothing rewarding about judgment... well, other than the fact it keeps you small and gives you plenty of excuses not to change or receive anything. Who do you judge the most? Well, YOU of course! But do you really know what judgment is? Did you know that everything that makes you heavy has some kind of judgment in it -- whether it is positive or negative?

If you're willing, this 1.5 hour telecall facilitated by Dr. Dain Heer can give you the tools to start getting out of judgment of you and everything today!

http://bit.ly/2aGRwXS

❖

CHAPTER SEVENTEEN

VULNERABILITY & GRATITUDE: KEYS TO DOORWAYS OF POSSIBILITIES

By Pratima Nagaraj

Author, Speaker,

Coach - Lifestyle, Business and Empowerment

Nilofer: It's so wonderful to have you on this call, Pratima and also the topic that you have chosen - Vulnerability and Gratitude. When I started using the tools of Access, for a long time I did not really get Vulnerability. I just knew it was such an important element but I didn't know how to be that. So let's just jump into it and see what this is.

What Is Vulnerability?

Pratima: I totally get what you are saying because I have been using Access tools for almost 3.5 years and I thought that I got it, but it's only recently that I realized I actually got it! I felt like I knew what vulnerability is but it's so much more than what I had imagined it to be. When I started exploring this deeper and choosing to be more vulnerable, I noticed how my life completely shifted gears.

It's interesting that when you invited me for this summit, I was playing with these tools in my life and I thought *"Why not talk about this?"* I know that this topic is not very common and not many people have explored in-depth and to be honest (and this is me being vulnerable here) – when you invited me to speak here, I thought "Oh my god, this is my first summit. Can I really do this? How many judgments am I going to receive? What if I am not perfect?" I literally had to be vulnerable, lower my barriers and be open to receiving everything with no point of view and then say yes to you!

One thing I noticed is that there are many myths and misconceptions associated with vulnerability. I looked it up in the dictionary and the definition of vulnerability is:

'being susceptible to physical harm or damage' or

'being open to emotional injury' or

'being susceptible to an attack or criticism'.

And that's exactly what we know about vulnerability. Nothing beyond it! But hey, what if everything that you have heard about vulnerability, you've been told about it, is a lie? That's what we are here to explore today, that vulnerability does not mean to be weak or submissive but it is in fact the courage to be yourself. It is about being YOU without subscribing to other people's points of view or opinions and being without any barriers or walls around you. So it's literally like being naked out there in the world. When you are naked out there, you are more susceptible to receiving judgments from people but when you are there without any barriers, you can receive it with no point of view. The more I have been practicing it, I have noticed many more opportunities and possibilities have started showing up in my life.

How To Be Without Barriers?

N: So how do you actually be that? How do you be without barriers?

P: (laughs) Like how to breathe? Yeah, I know, I get it, because that's a question I have asked myself, so many times and, you get it when you get it! What's worked for me is to be very aware of when your barriers come up for you.

Is it when someone judges you?

Is it when you ask something from someone and they say no?

Or is it when you actually go to speak in front of a group of people?

Or is it in a relationship?

So it could be different things for different people, so what really helps as a first step is to notice when those barriers come up and then it is a conscious choice to lower those barriers. Notice I don't say "push those barriers down" because pushing required an effort and for me, vulnerability is totally effortless. I just close my eyes, I expand out and then lower those barriers all the way down and then I am open to receiving everything. Basically, when you have no barriers, you literally have no projections, expectations or judgments about YOU or other people. You have no reason to go into the wrongness of you and you are completely in allowance and willing to be seen as who you are. When you have no barriers, you are being authentic, being YOU.

N: Does it mean that if you are in the space of judging you or judging others, you could go "oh, I have my barriers up!" and just lower them?

P: Yes, absolutely. The moment you notice you are going into judgment, say "interesting point of view I have this judgment" but even before that, notice first that you are going into judgment and you have your barrier up there! You have an invisible wall that's got erected because that's like your defense mechanism so that you don't get judged. What's the best way to stop it? By putting up a barrier around you! So, notice it and then lower it.

Being Grateful For You

P: Another thing I would add here is – you can actually receive all judgments with more ease when you have gratitude for yourself and others. Which is why I chose this topic where vulnerability and gratitude go together because for you to be vulnerable, you also have to be grateful for yourself, grateful for your existence on this planet and grateful for the contribution you be to the people around you and even a contribution to YOU. Something that works for me very well is being grateful for ME.

N: When a person starts from a place of not being grateful for themselves, how do they start? Where is the start of gratitude? I know it's a really simple thing and you have so many people who talk about gratitude but how do you start?

P: Yeah, I can connect to that very well because I have been there, done that! When I became a certified facilitator and started facilitating classes, people gave me feedback about how awesome my classes were, how much they got out of it and how grateful they were for me. But I was judging myself as to how crappy I had done the class and how I could have done it way better etc.! After I heard this, I went wow, here's everybody who is very grateful for the contribution that I am being and I'm that one person who is so ungrateful for me! That really hit me hard. Until that moment I didn't realize how ungrateful I was being for ME. I then made a conscious choice to look at and acknowledge the contribution I am being to people around me and to this planet. That's been easier after I started choosing to be more and more vulnerable because you cannot show gratitude to someone or to YOU by staying behind a barrier.

Vulnerability With You

We talk about vulnerability with others but there is also an aspect where you be that vulnerability with YOU. What does that mean? You are literally being with you with no barriers. When you lower your barriers to yourself, you are in allowance of the good, bad and ugly about you and you have no judgment of anything about you and that's when you can start looking at the contribution you are being and how valuable you truly are, and start thanking yourself. It's easier to be grateful when you have no barriers and which is why I would say the first step is to start lowering your barriers to yourself and then it becomes easier to see what a contribution you are being.

N: It's also that we are very willing to judge ourselves and see where we are wrong rather than seeing where we are being a contribution.

P: Yes who does that belong to? Are those judgments even yours? Because 99% of the judgments don't belong to us. When we are born and as an infinite being, we literally come with no points of views. We are only energy, space and consciousness. So where do these judgments come from? It's something that you perceive from other people, either they may have judged you or they may have just projected on to you. You being psychic, pick up on those judgments and lock it in as real and true. So judgments are not real. If you look at resolving it, you are stuck in a loop. Instead be aware that it is not yours.

N: This is so true, because I would have done anything to avoid judgments. All my life I was trying to fit into what other people wanted me to be and I would have done anything to avoid those judgments. To have the tools of Access has been such a gift for me.

P: Yes I agree because I was someone who hated being judged, being rejected, being criticized that I literally cut off so many of my talents, abilities and capacities so that I could avoid those judgments! I would build invisible walls, locking me up, thinking it is a safe place and then hiding myself behind those walls so that I am not seen. I'd also start judging myself way before someone else judged me because I had this stupid and insane point of view, "before you could judge me I have already judged myself. So it doesn't matter whether you judge me now or not. I judge myself more!"

N: So it's not going to hurt me so much to have you judge me!

P: Exactly. What an insane point of view!

N: So when you don't have barriers, what happens to the judgment?

P: They just dissipate and melt away because when you don't have barriers, you are actually being more space. Barriers make you more solid and you contract. You can't be space and also have barriers. Imagine you are expanding and then you come across a fence that's like a barrier around you. As you expand more those barriers are down, because that space you are occupying is literally melting those barriers. So, no judgments can stick you when you are being the space you truly are.

N: When you have no barriers, when you are being totally vulnerable, does this mean people are going to stop judging you or more like you are not going to be the effect of their judgments anymore?

P: People are never going to stop judging you! That's probably not going to happen but yes, you are going to stop being the effect of other people's judgments because you no longer buy into it as true and you can begin to create your life the way you desire. That's why for me, vulnerability is the source point of creation. Vulnerability is the space from which you can create phenomenal things. When you are truly willing to be vulnerable, you are willing to be seen and heard in the world. There is a risk of more judgments coming your way when you are seen and heard but you will have so much more ease in receiving those judgments that they no longer matter to you because you are now focusing more on generating and creating your life and having fun.

Being Vulnerable Increases Your Awareness

N: There have been times, Pratima, where I have been lowering my barriers and I perceive these judgments and even with barriers lowered, something about the judgment is sticking me. Can you talk more about what goes on over there?

P: When you lower your barriers, things become more intense, because when you become vulnerable, your awareness grows exponentially. So what's happening when you are lowering those barriers is that you are perceiving those judgments even more, it's 100 times more intense than it was before you put those barriers down. So you may feel like the judgments are increasing and sticking you more, but what's really happening is you are just being aware of it more intensely. You are also aware of the space the other person is functioning from because usually when people judge you, it is more about themselves and not about you. People judge you for what they themselves do. So how much awareness are you receiving when you have lowered your barriers and how much of that have you acknowledged?

N: Yes, it totally makes sense. When I receive that awareness, I am trying to fix things there instead of asking "Is this even relevant to me?" I have been sometimes intensely aware of judgments that I have received in relationships, for example, and the more I lower my barriers, the more intense the judgments seem to get until I asked "Is this even relevant to me?" I got a NO and I said, "never mind, I'm not choosing that" and then everything just lightened up for me.

P: That's a great question. "Is this relevant to me?" A lot of things dissipate when you actually be that question. Most of the times we are picking up so many things around us which have nothing to do with us and then we try to do something about it without realizing that awareness is just awareness. You really don't have to do anything about every awareness that you have!

N: Also when I would lower this barrier, I would have this awareness of a place that the other person was functioning from. For example, I was doing a business deal with someone and I would lower my barriers and I would be aware of the contraction in their Universe and I would perceive how that contraction was going to affect me and the business deal that we were creating together and before I actually realized what it was, I would immediately buy into that contraction. I know that "my point of view creates my reality", so my reality would start getting created from contraction which existed until I went "Oh, so they are functioning from that contraction and now how can I use this awareness to my advantage? And how can I out-create their contraction?" That would open up the whole energy for me.

P: That's amazing. One thing that I realized when you started talking about this is, how when you begin to choose vulnerability, it can actually change other people's world as well around you. One of the aspects about vulnerability is also to intensely receive the pain of the other person who doesn't want to acknowledge it themselves. So the other person is going through something, they have judgments about themselves or they are contracted. So it is about intensely receiving all of that without trying to fix anything for them. And when you lower your barriers to it, you are just being able to perceive all of that and be with it, receive the awareness of how much insanity/contraction/ hurt/ pain they are choosing. Also sense that place where the other person feels that they are probably not being received for who they are being. So when you are able to be that intensely present and vulnerable with somebody, they will actually begin to feel received and will get that space where they can make a different choice. The other person can choose something different because of the vulnerability and allowance you are being. That's ultimate caring.

The other aspect is, you don't subscribe to their point of view. You don't buy into it and you ask "how can I out-create that?" I love that question because then you don't have to buy into anybody's insanity. And for me, these 2 aspects have created wonders, especially working with people who I thought were difficult to work with and I saw how me choosing to be in allowance gave them a space to make a different choice.

N: Wow, great. So Pratima, we have a live caller who wants to ask a question.

Vulnerability In Action

Caller: Hi, I really appreciate this conversation. There's part of me that's getting it and there's part of me that's saying "what's right about this I'm not getting?" I've heard Gary Douglas mention about receiving judgment and how I guess if you receive the judgment how that can turn into more money for you, and I'm hearing and I'm going to obviously listen to this again because it's really deep and I really appreciate that you are addressing this but can you give us some real examples of what is going on in your head and what you are actually saying to yourself to cultivate that ease?

P: What I'm really saying to myself is that these judgments are not about me. For example, if someone is telling me that I am not social or I'm dominating or I'm selfish it is actually about them. It's got nothing to do with me. And the second aspect is, I don't make it a wrongness. I say to myself "so what if I'm not social. I really don't enjoy talking to people so much because it's just my choice to have the space that I'm in." I really don't make those judgments into a wrongness and I'm literally willing to receive it and go "that's an interesting point of view that somebody thinks that I am dominating." And I'm just there without a barrier to it and being grateful for who I am. I'm literally being grateful for me, including good, bad and the ugly of me. So it's not just being grateful for the nice person that I am, but it also includes being grateful sometimes for the mean person that I be, because when I have been mean or rude to somebody and later I've realized "wow, that was a really crappy choice to make. So what can I choose different now? That's not something that I would like to create in my life, so let me just choose something different without having to go into the wrongness of anything. Did that make sense?

Caller: Yes and I've been playing with it more deeply in the last couple of months and noticing judgment of myself.

P: Have you asked who does that belong to? Are those judgments even yours or is it something that's been projected on to you for like years and years or lifetimes? Because when something doesn't belong to you, you really can't change it because you haven't created it.

Caller: Yeah, it is not mine

P: Yes you may be mimicking somebody else's points of view and judgments. So who or what are you mimicking when you are actually judging yourself? Whose judgments are those?

Caller: Boy, how did I get so lucky today?

P: For me using the tool "who does this belong to?" is very helpful and it's been the most effective. It's one of the basic tools in Access and I love going back to basics every single time. There are times where I have indulged myself being crazy, cranky, upset and after few hours I realize none of that is mine!

Caller: I'm really enjoying this conversation so thank you both, ladies.

P: Thank you for this question because this is one place where almost all of us stick ourselves, which is judging ourselves and that's where vulnerability really comes into play. For me, even before choosing to be vulnerable with others, it's all about being vulnerable with myself and it's only when I started lowering barriers to myself, I noticed how much I judge me. And yes, I did mention that most of the judgments don't really belong to you, but judgments can also become like an addiction. It could become like a thing that you go to in order to distract your-selves from creating something greater in your life. So, another thing I would look at is, "where am I using judgments to distract myself?" I would use judgments to distract myself from creating stuff, whether it is creating a class or creating more money or creating my life, I would instead go into judgment because that's a way I can ensure that I don't create what I desire. So that became like an addiction. So any place you go to in order to cut off your awareness becomes an addiction.

Caller: Yeah, I've noticed that I've done that myself and I'm glad you are bringing that up.

P: *Everywhere you are using judgments as an addiction and to cut off your awareness, can we destroy and uncreate all of that? Right and Wrong, Good and Bad, POD and POC, All 9, Shorts, Boys and Beyonds*

Everywhere you made being different and being YOU wrong can we now destroy and uncreate all of that? Right and Wrong, Good and Bad, POD and POC, All 9, Shorts, Boys and Beyonds

When you start giving up your judgments and being you, you are so different from this reality and that is seen as a wrongness too, so we buy into a point of view that "I'm actually different. I'm being me and that's a wrongness."

Caller: It is insane. But it does take time to keep at it and you just sort of go there automatically. Is there any kind of clearing for that or?

P: For me what helped is I would spend a couple of minutes every day just closing my eyes, lowering all my barriers and just willing to look at all the worst judgments I have about me. You can do this exercise now.

Exercise:

Close your eyes and just look at all the barriers that are there around you. Perceive all the barriers, all the defense systems, all the walls that you have erected as a way of protecting yourself. Now go ahead and lower all those barriers down, all around, 360 degrees. Just lower them down, even further. All the way down. And just when you think that you have lowered all your barriers, go ahead and lower them down even more, and expand out 100,000 miles in all directions and now just become aware of the worst possible judgment you have about yourself. Allow it to come up. Allow that energy of those judgments to come up and just look at it as an interesting point of view.... just observing it...without trying to analyze it..... now expand it. Expand it even further. Now occupy a space as big as the Universe and allow those judgments to just dissipate in the space that you are being. And if you still sense a solidity with that judgment, go ahead and turn it 180 degrees. Flip it again, turn it 180 degrees, again, and again and again until the charge around it completely melts away and keep expanding ......and as you expand, any barriers that you encounter, just allow them to dissipate in the space that you are occupying. And what patterns of harmony can you truly create and be with yourself now that would allow you to choose more gratitude and vulnerability with yourself? And what energy, space and consciousness can you and your body occupy to create a phenomenal future from this space? And everything that doesn't allow that, just destroy and uncreate it all. Allow it all to dissipate. And whenever you are ready you can open your eyes. Just bring your awareness to your body.

Caller: Thank you. That was really good.

P: Thank you for asking that question because that's what got this energy up. I'm really grateful for it.

Caller: Yeah, I think I started to go out there and look for a judgment, I'm not sort of getting any.

P: (laughs) That's the fun part.

Caller: I tried to dig and "no, I'm not finding anything" and I thought "Ok, I'll just be okay with that." Thank you so much. That was great. Much appreciated.

N: Ok, we have another caller.

Caller: Hi, I don't really have a question, I wanted to say that was awesome! I'm more of ME right now. I'm totally ME and it just rocks! And you helped me achieve that you people are awesome!

N: I love it! Thank you!

P: Thank you!

What's The Value Of Having Barriers

N: Let's look at some more questions that have come up.

"What question can I ask so I can lower my barriers to myself? And what questions can you ask to lower your barriers when you are in the midst of fear and judgment?"

I guess you handled that one. Or do you have more to say?

P: Well, for me, more than asking any question, I would look at the barriers coming up. Have you seen X-Men? Where his knuckles just spike out at those moments of danger? So it's like that. Any time you actually perceive those walls going up, you have to literally go "ok, walls up" and lower them down. It is a choice you have to make. Many times we get stuck in fixing something that is not working rather than just make a different choice that would work!

Also a question that I would play with is *"What's the value of having these barriers?"* because that would get you to look at what you love about having barriers because we only hold on to something that we get a value from. So is it because you don't want to create your life? Or is it because you don't want to be seen in the world or you bought into the lie that you need protection or something else?" Whatever comes up just destroy and uncreate everything.

Vulnerability As Courage, Strength & Potency

N: Wow. That's amazing. Next question.

Can you talk about how vulnerability is also about courage, strength and potency?

P: Yes. That's what it is and that's something none of us acknowledge. I came across using vulnerability as a courage when I watched a TEDTalk by Dr. Brene Brown called '*The Power of Vulnerability*'. When you are willing to be vulnerable, no one can control you and you literally have no need to control yourself. So you are willing to be present in the moment and choose what works for you. It's a lie that we need barriers to protect ourselves. In fact, for me, since a kid, I am the only child for my parents so having been in India and being the only child and that too a female, I was brought up in a much protected environment, and I was told that there is danger everywhere. I need to be extremely careful, I need to be aware of protecting myself. So I had trained myself to put barriers up because I thought I needed protection, but really, it's the opposite. It's when you have your barriers down, you have that potency and ability because you are literally willing to be aware of everything around you and you can make a choice based on your awareness. So vulnerability is the greatest form of protection because even if there is danger around you, if you are truly willing to trust your awareness and receive that awareness, you can make a different choice so that you don't have to actually go through it.

N: Do you have an example for it?

P: Personally, choosing to be vulnerable gave me the courage to be seen and step out into the world. For example, making my videos. I was someone who was petrified of filming videos and sharing it out in the world because of the judgments I would receive. I know I was doing that from behind a barrier and I realized how much of my business I was limiting by choosing to have that barrier. So it's just been about a month now. I lowered my barriers and I said "ok, I'm choosing to be vulnerable here. What would be the worst possible judgment that I could receive? That the video is crappy? That I'm not good enough? Fine. So that's an interesting point of view." When I chose vulnerability with me and I created the video and I destroyed and un-created all those points of view I had about those videos before I posted it on social media, I saw how much my business expanded! There were more registrations for my classes. My website list is growing and I have more clients and more money coming in. All that was possible because of the courage that vulnerability gave me in making that choice. It allowed me to truly use my potential to the maximum, because I knew I had an ability to connect with people through these videos. So having barriers didn't give me the courage, lowering the barriers gave me the courage to choose what I wanted to choose.

N: Wow. And did you notice that people actually didn't have any judgment of you? (laughs)

P: I know! Here I was for many years functioning from a lie that I'm going to be judged. In fact people sent me messages saying how much they loved the video. It is such an insanity how we create all these constructs in our head, put up those barriers and think that we are protecting ourselves!

Vulnerability And Receiving

N: Let's talk about a different element and that element is about receiving and barriers.

P: You literally cannot receive anything with a barrier. One of the elements of vulnerability is 'Receiving'. When you have a wall, can you really pass through it? Can there be any kind of an exchange between two people where they have a wall between them? NO. So when you erect barriers, you are cutting off your receiving in every area of your life and that includes money and your business, your health, your relationships. We assume that these barriers are meant to protect us and we hide behind it thinking it's a safe space to hide ourselves. Those barriers not only block the receiving that flows towards you but it's blocking the energy flow in both directions. So you cannot literally receive anything from anyone and you cannot contribute to other people either. By having these barriers you are cutting off your receiving and cutting off the contribution you can be to this planet. What if you lowered those barriers and realized you being YOU can actually change the world! What a contribution you can be with your talents and abilities to people around you!

If I had chosen to have my barriers up, I wouldn't be here speaking on the summit today and I wouldn't be doing anything about vulnerability or the things I have planned. So what contribution would I have been cutting off by avoiding all of this? So there are both aspects of it. You cut off your receiving and you cut off being a contribution.

N: When people acknowledge you or are grateful for you, like in your case you started receiving emails or people meet you and they acknowledge what contribution you are being to them, can you receive any of that if you have barriers?

P: No way! Also when you don't receive it, that's like saying to those people "Hey, you are stupid for acknowledging me. You are stupid for saying that I'm good. You are stupid that you think that I'm being a contribution." Is it really honoring those people when you don't receive their gratitude for you?

N: Yeah, for a really long time I would receive all these emails from all over the world, people would come up to me at different events and just tell me how much of a contribution I was being and I was like "so what? What's the big deal?" It's only when Gary Douglas said something to someone in a class, it made me realize "Oh! I'm not receiving any of this acknowledgement!" so from that day I consciously lower my barriers and I receive that and it has been such a contribution in my life, my living and my business to be able to receive that contribution from people.

P: I completely agree. We tend to ignore that aspect when someone compliments or acknowledges us. It's so easy, it becomes like an automatic response to ignore it.

N: Yeah, and it's so insane because on one hand there is all this acknowledgment and gratitude and you are not receiving that and on the other hand, you are trying to get validation for whatever work you are doing!

P: Yeah, that's the conflictual Universe that we create. We would like that but then we would like to be validated but not truly be grateful for the acknowledgement we are receiving.

The simplest clearing for this is "*What stupidity am I using to create the conflict with me that I am choosing? And everything that is, I now destroy and un-create it all. Right and Wrong, Good and Bad, POD and POC, All 9, Shorts, Boys and Beyonds*

You can receive all of the acknowledgements with total ease only when you are willing to receive yourself. So where are you creating the conflict that you are not willing to receive yourself but then you are looking for someone else to receive you? Because the relationship begins with YOU. So it's only when you are willing to acknowledge yourself and be grateful for yourself, when someone else acknowledges that you will notice it and you will receive it with gratitude.

Have you ever been around people who have been truly vulnerable and receive the gratitude you have for them and receive you? Have you noticed it is such a joy to be around such people? I have been lucky enough to be around such people and especially men, because men are told not to be vulnerable in this reality, but it's really a joy to be around someone who's willing to receive your acknowledgement, receive you and receive everything with no point of view. So what would it take for you to be that?

Vulnerability Is Natural & Effortless!

P: Being vulnerable is not an effort. We are all born vulnerable. Vulnerability comes naturally to us, so it actually takes more effort to not be vulnerable than to be vulnerable. Because our bodies for example, are naturally vulnerable. They are receiving information all the time from everything and everyone around us and we talked about how receiving is one of the elements of vulnerability. So our bodies are receiving information all the time, which means our bodies are vulnerable, but we put in a lot of effort to actually cut off all the awareness that our bodies are receiving and put up barriers to not be vulnerable and that takes a lot more effort than to be in allowance of it.

Also you look at kids, have you seen how vulnerable kids are? Because it comes naturally to us at that age. As an infinite being, vulnerability is that energy that we be. It's inherent to us. As kids we are so vulnerable, but then what happens as we grow up? We are taught that we need protection, we need barriers, we need to safeguard, judgment is wrong, and you cannot receive it and so on. So we learn the process of putting up barriers. Putting up barriers is a learnt behavior and it's like an implant and it does not belong to us, whereas vulnerability is something that's natural to us.

What would it take for all of us to truly acknowledge the vulnerability that we be and embrace it completely to open those doorways to possibilities?

When you choose to be YOU, which is the natural state of vulnerability, opportunities just fall into your lap and literally, that's what's showing up for me, especially in the last couple of months. I was truly surprised by it, it bowled me over, because when you told me the theme of the summit, which is **Doorways to Possibilities,** that's when I realized that ME choosing to be vulnerable is what's creating these possibilities! People who I thought disliked me have been approaching me with business deals and opportunities. Money has doubled and tripled in the last 2-3 months, and all of this with total ease, literally there has been no effort from my end, except for just choosing to be more of ME and choosing to be without barriers. How does it get better than that?

Being Brutally Honest With Yourself

N: What else do you have to say about vulnerability, about gratitude?

P: One key aspect about vulnerability is to be brutally honest with yourself, something that I was not willing to be all my life!

N: I've seen a lot of people who speak about brutal honesty, but people use that as creating more judgment of self in their life, so can you talk about the difference between being brutally honest with yourself and judging yourself?

P: Well, the thing about being brutally honest is to just be present with yourself as an interesting point of view but also to know what is it that you truly desire in your life? When I started being honest with myself, I noticed that I'm being very ungrateful for me. Now, I could have gone into judging myself more for it or I could go "wow, I'm really ungrateful for me and what else can I choose differently? It's an interesting point of view that I'm choosing to be ungrateful. I wonder what would it create if I actually choose to be grateful for ME?" So it's more of the space that you be when you are being honest with yourself and you literally have to be in allowance of you. You have to look at it as an interesting point of view, that's when you can't go into judgment because it's only when you are trying to solidify everything that is coming up, it sticks you. But if you are expanding out and being the space of allowance then it won't affect you.

And also you don't have any expectations or projections that when you notice something when you are being brutally honest, that you have to change it. Like when I saw that I'm being ungrateful, I'm not willing to step out, I'm not willing to create videos, the first thing I realized was I was not willing to choose it, because I was honestly not willing to create my life as bigger and greater as I thought I wanted and that hit me hard because I realized I have been lying to myself that I want to step out there and create a greater life but I really don't want to! It's not necessary that you have to have an expectation of you that you have to change it immediately. In fact, I was being with that energy for a couple of months before I actually made the choice to change it and start creating videos or to start being grateful for me. So being brutally honest also includes that you don't have an expectation that you have to change it because you are not looking at whatever you are choosing as a wrongness but it's just a choice that you are making and you can change it whenever you desire to change it.

N: Wow. I want more, more, more, more! Do you have anything more?

P: When you are willing to be honest then you don't have to make yourself wrong. Because now you have the awareness of a space you are functioning from, it's like "ok, so I'm functioning from a space of no gratitude" and from there you can start asking questions to change it. The purpose of being brutally honest for me is to really look at the space that I'm functioning from so that I can change it when I choose to change it and that's when different doorways to possibilities open up and different choices start to show up in my life.

KEY ELEMENTS:

It's just amazing what these two elements can create for you. To sum it up in 3 key points:

1. Vulnerability is easier to choose when you truly love yourself and you are grateful for YOU.

2. You don't have to beat yourself up if you are not choosing to be vulnerable because vulnerability is a muscle that you build. It's something that we've kept dormant for many years, so it takes practice and you have to keep using it, being it, in order to make it stronger.

3. The rewards of vulnerability are immeasurable. It's amazing when you start seeing the possibilities that open up and you choose more and more of it and that's what's become a driving force for you. I'm seeing what's being created in my life and I'm like "I'm having more of this. I'm demanding more of me to choose this." You get to experience true oneness with everyone and everything because you don't have barriers and you are open to receiving everything.

Be aware that when you choose to be vulnerable your intensity of awareness increases which most of us are not willing to have, so you actually feel like there is more crap in your life when you choose to be vulnerable and you have to realize that crap is not yours, you are just so much more aware without barriers that you are perceiving all the crap from everywhere around you.

Here are a couple of clearings to play with.

What vulnerability are you refusing that you truly could be choosing that if you would choose it and be it, it would change your entire reality, life, living, relationships, money and business and create the patterns of harmony that you truly desire? And everything that is, are you willing to destroy and un-create it? Right and Wrong, Good and Bad, POD and POC, All 9, Shorts, Boys and Beyonds

What are you refusing to perceive, know, be and receive that if you would actually choose to perceive, know, be and receive it, would actualize as total vulnerability and gratitude for you and as you? And everything that is, are you willing to destroy and un-create it? Right and Wrong, Good and Bad, POD and POC, All 9, Shorts, Boys and Beyonds

P: I am extremely grateful beyond words to this amazing man Dr Dain Heer, who is full of magic and phenomenance personified and truly embodies vulnerability to such a degree that you can perceive it in every molecule, every pore of his body and being. Just by being that, he changed my world and has been and continues to be a huge inspiration and invitation for me to step up and choose to be more vulnerable and more of ME. I was able to know what vulnerability truly is only because he showed me what it is like to be it and how by choosing to be it, you can actually change the world.

N: That was amazing. Thank you Pratima and thank you everyone for being on the call

P: Thank you! Grateful to have been here.

TELESUMMIT WITH NILOFER

To get an invite to Nilofer's next telesummit full of tools and clearings from Access Consciousness,
visit http://www.illusiontoilluminationsummit.com

CHAPTER EIGHTEEN

WHAT IF YOUR LIFE IS A PIECE OF ART?!

By Kalpana Raghuraman

Internationally acclaimed artist seduces people
to choose possibilities and change
with her capacities to create 24/7

Nilofer: Hi Kalpana, welcome. I'm so happy that you could contribute your energy to the summit.

Kalpana: Wonderful. Thank you.

Caller: You speak of the energy of art and I make it artless. If this is not infinite possibilities, what is?

K: I am an Access Consciousness Facilitator and I'm also a choreographer, a dancer and an artist. I've been busy with the energy of art all of my life and as I was driving today I was thinking about this call and about what made me come up with this title. If I say, "a piece of art" what comes up, what energy comes up or what words come up for you?

N: It's interesting you ask me that because when you talk about a piece of art, what actually shows up is just, me.

K: Awesome. What else is possible?

N: I am a piece of art.

K: Yes. What would it take for us to always choose that and perceive that also for ourselves.

And I was thinking of what a piece of art means. For a lot of people it's something outside, right? Like a piece of art that you go and buy. What if it's you and what would you then choose if you have that energy?

If I think of a piece of art I always get this really juicy, expansive energy. I would think of Picasso. I imagine him, how he was painting and if he wanted to add something to his painting. Everything would be from that space of juiciness and yumminess and choice.

What if we chose that every day? If that was our life, how beautiful, magical could we make it? That is something that I feel for me, has been a really interesting space to live from. For some people when I say "a piece of art", they contract because they think that it has to be beautiful or it has to be pretty or it has to look good. We go into judgment. A question that I would like to ask you all is, "What does art mean to you?" What comes up for you?

N: For me, it's like a blank canvas on which I can paint all the possibilities of my life.

K: *Everything that doesn't allow you to do that times a god zillion, would you destroy and uncreate it? Right and wrong, good and bad, POD and POC, all nine, shorts, boys and beyonds.*

What if your life was a piece of art? Wouldn't you be looking for the most fabulous colors to paint with? The most wonderful tools to play with? Everywhere you are not choosing that all the time, do you want to destroy and uncreate that, times a godzillion? Right and wrong, good and bad, POD and POC, all nine, shorts, boys and beyonds.

All the limited points of view about what art means and what a piece of art would look like and what that would show up like, will you destroy and uncreate all of that, times a god zillion? Right and wrong, good and bad, POD and POC, all nine, shorts, boys and beyonds.

Awesome. It is really that energy of art that is so expansive.

N: I was in a 'Right Voice For You' class, which is facilitated by Blossom Benedict and so many brilliant facilitators all over the world. One of the things that we actually do in the 'Right Voice For You' is that we become okay with creating not-so-perfect art. And how much are we actually trying to create our life as perfect?

K: Exactly. Thank you so much for bringing this up. That is beautiful and it's so poignant here. It is said, that looking for perfection is something like a curse for artists, because then they have to judge themselves.

That is what we have put on ourselves all the time to do. What if you don't have to do that anymore? That is exactly what I love about what Blossom brings to the class and what 'Right Voice For You' really is as an energy.

What if we don't have to use those masks of perfection? To me, perfection is a way to hide behind an idea. What if you can take away that mask of perfection and you just say, "Here I am, this is what it is." A blank canvas or a very filled one.

What if it is okay, whatever that might be? What if it is okay, whatever turns up and shows up, even more brilliantly as you then? Everything that doesn't allow that times a god zillion, would you then destroy and uncreate it? Right and wrong, good and bad, POD and POC, all nine, shorts, boys and beyonds.

N: In the 'Right Voice For You' class, Gary asked us to draw something and literally, what I ended up drawing was like this wiggly little line on the paper. I looked at it and I was judging it. He actually gave us some words and you had to draw something. I went, "Oh my god, how dare I not create a masterpiece from these 2 words that he has given us!"

K: Yes, how much do we do that all the time? It's perfect that you say masterpiece because I totally recognize this. When I work with dancers and I ask them to do something, exactly like Gary gave 2 words and asked you to draw something, I give tasks and then I always say, "You don't have to make a masterpiece." This idea of a masterpiece is a heaviness and is such a contraction. If you don't have to do that anymore, then what will you choose? If it doesn't have to be perfect anymore, what would you choose?

Nilofer, could you just look at that line that you drew, could you bring it in front of you now and could you not judge that?

N: *I'm still judging it.*

K: *Exactly. Everything that is, will you destroy and uncreate it, times a god zillion? Right and wrong, good and bad, POD and POC, all nine, shorts, boys and beyonds.*

Is it perhaps, because we have such a limited idea of what it should look like and if it's not one of those few things then it's totally judge-able?

N: It's more like, "Okay, so what are people going to think when they look at this, and they are going to judge me so before they judge me, I'm going to judge me."

K: "Before they can judge me, I'll judge me - so I'll trump them at it." Right?

N: I'll trump them at it and I won't feel so bad.

K: Yeah, what if you could just say, "Hey, this is what I brought up right now." And that's it. What if you could receive those judgments and go, "Okay, I have another chance. I'll do something again." What if that's okay? That whole place where we go "What will they say about me?", that's where we stop the flow of possibilities.

Everywhere that piece of drawing reflects you and a very limited you, will you destroy and uncreate that, times a god zillion? Right and wrong, good and bad, POD and POC, all nine, shorts, boys and beyonds.

If you could do that same task again and if you would draw from the energy of you rather than from the words of the task? From the energy of the task instead of the limitations the words of the task bring up for you? If you perceive that energy and then you go, "Okay, this is me. The totally magnificent, expansive me", and then draw, what would come out then?

Every time we don't choose that, we actually choose for this reality.

N: The funny part is that, I have seen some of these abstract paintings, which are supposed to be great masterpieces, which are like a few little squiggles.

K: Exactly. What would make one piece a masterpiece and another piece not a masterpiece? It requires judgment. If you just perceive the energy of it, that space that we are, that we always can choose and then we do whatever we do, it's such a different way of doing it. It's not a forcing and it's not a judging. Wow.

That's a beautiful gist of energy. What if we can start choosing that space of not-forcing now? Everything that doesn't allow that, times a god zillion, will you destroy and uncreate it please? Right and wrong, good and bad, POD and POC, all nine, shorts, boys and beyonds.

What have you made so vital about forcing yourselves to do that which keeps you from being? Everything that brings up times a god zillion, will you destroy and uncreate that please? Right and wrong, good and bad, POD and POC, all nine, shorts, boys and beyonds.

What if you don't have to judge yourselves into doing anything? Everything that is, will you destroy and uncreate that, times a godzillion? Right and wrong, good and bad, POD and POC, all nine, shorts, boys and beyonds.

This space is always available but we just forget it or we just choose not to do it. We just don't choose it. Can you perceive how soft and smooth this space is?

N: Yeah. And I almost couldn't hear what you were saying. "What did I miss? What did she say? What did I miss? What did she say?" What is the energy of art, again?

K: For me, I would call it an expansive space where everything is possible and this action of the molecules moving and us choosing and creating from that space.

You draw from a space of contraction because you have to do it perfect and you are going to do a task. If you do it from the energy of art instead of judgment of perfection, it's something completely different.

When I'm creating with my dancers in the studio or with myself in the studio, I ask the molecules of the space to contribute to me and to play with me. For me, this is so much the energy of art. The conscious choice of involving, asking and receiving the contribution, not only of the space that we are, but also the molecules around us. Everything is part of that moment and that moment becomes eternal as a painting, a dance, a sculpture, a written work or any other art. If you think about a painting, say a Van Gogh painting, he drew this piece and it is an eternal contribution to the Universe because we can all go and see it and it is being a contribution to so many people. The fact that he drew that and that it's still here and it's contributing energetically to us, makes it so dynamic and makes it so alive. For me, that's just amazing and also the energetic of art. Nothing is dead. It's always moving. It's always contributing, we just have to choose that and we can choose to receive this contribution or not.

N: Oh wow. Talk more about functioning from this energy of art. From and as the energy of art.

K: *I've really realized this word 'art' can be so heavy for people. It does not have to be. As soon as I step into this energy of it, it is such an orgasmic space. It is such a generous space. It is such a generous space that it is really this oneness and by calling it the energy of art, it helps me, to choose that beauty, to choose that expansion. I destroy and uncreate that too, because we don't want the definition to limit us. Everything that is, will you destroy and uncreate that, times a godzillion? Right and wrong, good and bad, POD and POC, all nine, shorts, boys and beyonds.*

When I'm working with a creation and I go into the studio, I really take a moment before going to the rehearsal space. I'm doing lots of clearing. I'm talking to the piece and I'm having a conversation with the artwork and with the space and the energy. When I come into the studio, I have already worked with the energy and I'm choosing as an energetic interaction and play that is already being created. That is like preparing the soil for the seeds. This very conscious interaction and conversation really helps me to also choose this communion with this energy of art.

When I don't ask for the energy of the creation of the art, I can find myself sticking myself with all the limited ideas of how I should do it, how I'm not doing it, why it's not working, why this thing should have been perfect but it's not yet, all the limitations come up. If I don't choose this expansion then I often choose limitations and crap. As soon as I do that I go *"Hey, wait, what is this energy? What can I choose?"* And as I ask what I could choose for, it shifts again.

This brings me to the question of curiosity. The energy of art is a curious energy. It's the energy of curiosity. How curious can I make myself about all of this? How curious can I make myself about my life, my living? This curiosity for me is this space that I don't go into conclusion, I don't go into decision of what I want to create or what I think it should look like. When I step into the space of this child-like wonder and curiosity, I'm always asking questions, I'm always ready for more and I'm always ready to say "Oh, it's not that, maybe it's that". This curiosity, for me, is very much a space that is connected to the energy of art. It's a great source of creation and an awesome source for possibilities.

N: I'm wondering when you are going to your studio, what are some of the questions you are asking to get that juiciness and that yumminess going?

K: That's a great question, Nilofer. It's not the same every time but I destroy and uncreate my relationship with whatever I am creating. I ask a lot of energy, space and consciousness questions.

What energy, space and consciousness can I be to perceive, know, be and receive what _____ requires of me, what the creation, requires of me?

I ask to be in communion with the piece. What energy, space and consciousness can my body and I be to be in communion with _____?

I also really, really ask for the energy of non-judgment of myself.

What energy, space and consciousness can my body and I be to be non-judgmental me and everything I'm creating?

The way we are taught to create is very much from a space of judgment. Access has been a great liberator in that way because it's never felt right to create with judgment.

I've always chosen to create differently. The way we are taught is so judgmental and artists are always killing themselves and judging themselves, destroying themselves with their thoughts about their work. It's a struggle and it's painful. The awareness of creating from judgment that Access has brought to me, always was with me because it never made sense – "I would think why would you choose that?"

So I destroy and uncreate all these points of view every time, all the conclusions I have about what I'm creating, I really have a conversation.

I say "Okay, I want to work on this piece today, let's see what comes up." I'm thinking about that scene. I wonder what else is possible?

I also ask questions about destroying and uncreating everywhere I don't choose to know before I go into the studio. There are moments that you are working in the studio and suddenly you are like "Okay, what to do? What to do? What to do?" I go into the space of question.

I say "Okay, what do I know here?" and click, it comes.

If you work with other people, destroy and uncreate your points of view about them. I destroy and un-create and clear points of view of what I think is possible and is not possible or should not be possible.

I involve the tools, the things that are connected to the creation. If you are a painter, I would also suggest you involve your paint, your brushes and the canvas. Everything is energy and everything is a contribution, we just have to be willing to receive it. Destroy and uncreate all your relationships with all those tools. Ask them to contribute. It depends on the situation; these are the kind of questions I ask when I'm going towards to creating, when I'm driving towards the studio.

N: Wow. Wow. I mean, I'm listening to you and I'm going "Why didn't someone teach us this while we were in school?"

K: I know! It's so true. I know that it's an energy I am with my dancers. I'm asked often to give master classes, for example, I was just teaching at the university for theatre students and I was telling them, "Ask questions." I don't know why nobody taught us that but please go for it, and it's such a different space you step into if you choose that and I wish I had learnt this when I was younger. How does it get any better than that? At least I know now, and I can choose it now.

N: How does it get any better than that? I look at even my kids and both of them express themselves so beautifully through their artwork and they are always so much in judgment about themselves because that's the way they have been taught.

So much so, that my son, who is 16 now, stopped drawing a couple of years ago because he was like always judging himself. "Oh, I don't enjoy it." The reason why he doesn't enjoy it is because there is so much judgment piled on him about that.

K: Yes, all the judgment he is probably aware of around him, right? Of others who are judging their own stuff?

N: Absolutely.

K: *How much judgment have we taken on from our art teacher, from our art peers, from people around us about what art is and what it should look like and how it should be judged? Everything that is, will you destroy and uncreate it? Right and wrong, good and bad, POD and POC, all nine, shorts, boys and beyonds.*

It was really funny, I was just speaking to my friend and she was saying, "Yeah, my son, you know, his art teacher is always giving him such horrible feedback. He hates drawing now. I really work with him, trying to make it fun because otherwise he just hates it because he gets judged all the time."

In a way, a lot of people don't choose these tools, they choose Art with a big A, because it is connected to judgment. *All the energy of judgment that we have connected to art, can we destroy and uncreate that now, times a god zillion? Right and wrong, good and bad, POD and POC, all nine, shorts, boys and beyonds.*

That is also when I said "your life as a piece of art" or if we step into that contractive mode of what art could be looked at as then our world becomes so small and if we can bring up those very limited ideas of art and destroy and uncreate them we create possibilities. Then we can look at it and say "Okay, now what is possible and what would my life look like now?"

If I see art as a space, that we really experience, this yummy, sweet, sensual, very nurturing space, what could we create? What could we do also in terms of sharing these tools, so that our children don't have to judge themselves and we can show that there is something else possible, there's just not that much around. I feel that choosing to function from that space is a beautiful invitation really, a beautiful invitation to help others choose it too.

Magic

K: Yes the magic! For me, all of this is very connected. I love when you said "... a piece of art, that's me." Magic, I call it the undefined path of possibilities. It's this space that everything is on. The molecules are humming and everything is contributing and you are in that space. It's so connected to the energy of art for me because it helps you step out of that limited, very contracted space and then you choose that magic.

When you very consciously choose that, the things that show up are just magical. If you had asked me when I was young what would be possible with my art, I could never have thought of what I am doing now. I'm a full-time artist, a choreographer, dancer and performer. Right now, I travel all over the world and I would not have dreamt that and yet, I know that it is connected to my choice that I always kept on asking questions and I really invited the energy of magic into my life and into my art. The energy of magic for me is also very much connected to this communication with the molecules and this space where you just know.

It's connected to knowing and this knowing, that has been turned off so often for a lot of us that we are not allowed to hear. This knowing that we're not allowed to know because it doesn't make any sense because it's not defined. *If we can choose to be in that undefined space, I wonder what could turn up? What possibilities can you create and choose?* This is where the fun starts.

N: For most of us we go to knowing, we use it as a tool to define something. It's really interesting that you are saying knowing is undefined because if you look at knowing, it's just an energy which shows up and it need not have those cognitive words to it. It's that energy of knowing that shows up and you start to create from there.

K: Exactly. If you allow that knowing to be as undefined as possible, it is actually a sea. It is this limitless space. It's beautiful what you just said and it's beautiful because as soon as you choose it, you can find it. That's what we always say and it's also with the knowing. If you can allow yourself to keep it as undefined and then play with it, it becomes really magical. If you contracted into, "it's this and it's this and it's this" then you limit it again and that's where you shut off the magic, that's where you shut off the possibilities. It's really space and choices.

I would say, daring to have fun, to get on the path that has not been walked on. I always call it the 'pathless path', this path that doesn't even exist yet. In a way I have to say my life has been that way because of the work I do as an artist. I'm the only one in the whole country who does exactly what I do and I've actually been a pioneer and I've really embraced this choice of stepping into and playing with this undefined path. If that can be a space of knowing for you always, then wow! How much fun can you have? How many realities can you turn upside down?

N: Wow, I love that.

K: It's really funny, I was in India and I was getting a lot of interviews and people were saying, "You do that in Europe? You do that? You do this?" and it was just they were like waah! They didn't know what to make of me. "And you travel around the world with this?" They couldn't understand because there is no path, there is no example, there is no model, no reference.

Everywhere we feel we need a role model to do something so that we know how to do it, and how to create this art and how to create this life, living and reality, will you destroy and uncreate all that, times a god zillion? Right and wrong, good and bad, POD and POC, all nine, shorts, boys and beyonds.

There's no model, there's no path, there's just choice of stepping and choosing, this knowing and creating magic with it and possibilities. Wow!

N: I have comments coming in. "This so eloquently expresses what I have tried to teach in art classes. This is brilliant. Beautiful and powerful questions to circumvent huge judgments people have of themselves and others to protect themselves and their precious expressions into the world and their knowing." I'll have what she's having.

K: Please do! Love it! Wow! Now what this person says is so exquisite because we often judge others so that we can hide –let me use something very practical as an example of that. I'm preparing to perform in this huge dance festival and all these people are all creating their new work and I can sense this big-ass judgment they have of their work and they have to cover it and they have to protect themselves and they have to hate other people's work so that they can feel good about their own work, they don't feel good because they are judging it and so on …

There's so much of that happening all the time and it's so unnecessary and if we can just see that and say "Hey, there is another choice. I didn't even know it was possible before, but it is!" If we see that we do not need to go there, if we see that we can choose differently….wow!

People often tell me "Oh, but it has to be hard. It's normal that you judge yourself." In my head I just say, "No, it's not." It's a way of surviving in this reality, but then who wants to just survive, instead of thrive? In the world of art or this energy of art, it's so connected to judging yourself, let alone others. If we can move that, if we can shift that, then it has nothing to do with judging, it is not an expression of your limitations rather it is an expression of your unlimited limitless infinite being. How much freedom would that give to people?

N: Wow. Wow. Absolutely.

K: Then how much contribution would that be? If you don't have to do that part, the judging, how many more people would choose that? There is another possibility available. I'm happy if that can tweak somebody's Universe who then thinks, "Hey, can I look at what I'm doing in a different way?" "Can I do it in a different way? Can I be an invitation for something else?"

Often, it's like what I was saying about the painting always being alive. With a performance you go and see a theatre piece, you go and hear music, you get touched. You are never the same again after that. That piece keeps working on you, just like a session keeps working on you. Just like when you have a session, it doesn't end when you get off the table.

If you have an experience of a beautiful music piece it keeps working on you, it keeps shifting things and it's only our unwillingness to receive this that stops it from doing what it can do. It's also this invitation. It's more and more surprising me how much it's connected to receiving. Something that I never thought was connected but it's so connected to receiving. Also to receiving judgment, being open to that and opening it up to receiving everything as well.

Caller: Good evening and thank you. I'm an artist and I don't do that full-time at this time, I used to. I notice I do painting and design jewelry. I noticed that I create something and it's so nice or so beautiful and yet I really want to sell it but then part of me wants to keep it. Everything is one of a kind and sometimes because I'm also very intuitive with the natural crystals and gems that I put in my pieces, that sometimes I select them and then they don't want to leave me.

K: Hmm. Can I ask you a question?

C: Sure

K: Just now you were saying that when you are creating that and you are selecting them. What I sense is that you are selecting them for you, if you would wear it.

C: Well, actually most of the stuff I wouldn't wear. It's just I like to design things for all different kinds of people. Most of the stuff I would not wear but I buy it for the quality or the colors or the style or whatever it is.

K: It seems to me that there's this love, that there's this energetic thing that occurs between you and the stones or whatever you are selecting and I would wonder what would happen if you would have a conversation with them as you are making them? You could say "Hey, I'm starting to make this and this and this. *What do you want to look like? Who would you like to buy you because you are not going to stay here forever.*" Have this conversation with them. How would that be? What does that bring up for you?

C: Yeah, I can definitely do that.

K: Somehow I feel they fall in love with you, to be really honest. They are just like "Oh my god, she treats us so well. Why would we ever want to leave?"

C: I think that's going on because when I make something or design something, I don't just bam-bam and put it together. The simplest pieces take me hours and hours and sometimes days and then I wait for them to tell me that it's complete, it's ready or the stones are a match with each other. They get along with each other. They were meant to be together. I go that far in a sense and I love what you are saying.

K: *What if you could also destroy and uncreate all the significance you might be attaching to it that makes your products kind of un-mobile? Everything that is, will you destroy and uncreate it? Right and wrong, good and bad, POD and POC, all nine, shorts, boys and beyonds.*

C: Should I destroy and uncreate my relationship with them?

K: Should you? For sure! It's an invitation. I have seen that the weirdest things limit us. We have a relationship because we create conclusions and stories.

Oh, another question that I always ask that I didn't add to the list - all the conclusions, expectations, considerations and past references about whaterver it is you are creating, I destroy and uncreate those times a god zillion.

That is such a killer for the energy of art and creation. That could be something for you to look at as well. I would invite you to consider it or to play with it. It seems to me it's this love affair that you have with beautiful items. If you could destroy and uncreate it, it's new and fresh every day.

C: Do I do it with each piece or I could just do it as a whole?

K: Whatever works for you. There is no recipe, it might be just the whole bunch one day and the other day you want to have a specific clearing with a few of them. Please play with it. Please see what works. For example, sometimes I work with 30 dancers then sometimes I'm like "Okay, I'm really tired to name each and every one of them" and

I say "these dancers" and sometimes I pick out a few and clear them all, and I just play with it. See whatever is required. It's also really the energy of what is required and allowing yourself to know that. "Hey, what is required of me here? What would work? What would give more ease?" Then you go for it. Please play with it and see what is bringing you ease and bringing you space.

C: I love that.

N: Can I add to that?

K: Of course. No! I had to say no, right?

N: Then I have to do the humanoid.com thingy.

K: Exactly (both laughing)

N: When you were actually describing how you create your jewelry and how "I select this piece to go with this" I would say listen to the recording and write down the words that you used. What if you went in a totally new direction with your business and what if you started designing custom jewelry for people? Offering it to people upfront and people came to you and they said, "Okay, I'd like you to design this piece for me."

K: That's amazing.

N: What would that be like for you?

C: I've done some of that but not as much and I've sort of like slowed down in my business. I'm not doing as many art shows as I used to. I've sort of I guess got bumped out and disenchanted with some of it. I don't really want to necessarily do it that way but I would love to be able to get out there in a different way and I love it when somebody says "Can you make me something?" or I have "Can you design it into something, I have this. I got this in Hawaii, can you make this?" I'll make some kind of cool creation out of it. I like that.

K: *All the disenchantment, all the energy that came up, would you like* to destroy and uncreate that? *Right and wrong, good and bad, POD and POC, all nine, shorts, boys and beyonds.*

All the connected conclusions and decisions you made, and expectations and projections that you might have still, will you destroy and uncreate those as well? Right and wrong, good and bad, POD and POC, all nine, shorts, boys and beyonds.

The awareness of how much that can limit us or stop us has made me choose to do a lot of clearings around that.

What energy, space and consciousness could you be to create the kind of business and art that works for you? Everything that doesn't allow that times a god zillion, will you destroy and uncreate it? Right and wrong, good and bad, POD and POC, all nine, shorts, boys and beyonds.

Everywhere you are comparing it to the way it is done and standing for or against it, will you destroy and uncreate it? Right and wrong, good and bad, POD and POC, all nine, shorts, boys and beyond.

What undefined path can you show us and what if there is no one right way? What if there is only your way?

I can perceive that you have created a lot and what if there is a new space for you available and you could create anything you like and whatever makes you jump. Whatever makes you happy and excited? Whatever is a contribution for you and for everybody else and this planet? Everything that doesn't allow that to show up times a god zillion, will you destroy and uncreate that please? Right and wrong, good and bad, POD and POC, all nine, shorts, boys and beyonds.

It is also this awareness that all these creations are a contribution. They are a big contribution and if you can acknowledge that, then they can be even more and you can be even more and with more ease as well.

C: Hi Kalpana, because it is conscious art, the zones are conscious, the paintings I started to work on haven't sold yet. I start to put them together and there's like a different element of consciousness that goes into them. Some of them have like symbols and holograms inside the paintings and different things like that and there's a part of me, I think it's because I've been like a witch before and I still probably am…

K: Probably…

C: I'm afraid to say what I'd really like to say about the pieces and it's not so much somebody's going to make me wrong, but in a sense I guess I'm worried they are going to think I'm really super-weird.

K: Yeah, which you are…

C: Which I like…

K: Which you are…So what's the problem? Is it true?

C: Yeah.

K: Or are you just not choosing it?

C: Probably both.

K: Both?

C: Yeah.

K: Hmm, there are a few things here. *Everywhere you are not choosing it and you are creating the stories around why you are not choosing it, will you destroy and uncreate it, times a god zillion? All the 'becauses' why you are not choosing it, would you destroy and uncreate all that? Right and wrong, good and bad, POD and POC, all nine, shorts, boys and beyonds.*

You know what I often say when I coach artists, I say "Nobody changed the world by doing the same thing."

Everything that brings up, would you like to destroy and uncreate that times a god zillion? Right and wrong, good and bad, POD and POC, all nine, shorts, boys and beyond.

What if there is no reason to do it or not to do it but it is just choice? And you being the beautiful, crazy, wacky witch that you truly be, why the hell are you here, lady? What if you could embrace that with a lightness that you also have? I can perceive it, you send very strong pictures, so I see you working and you love it and why do you want to deprive us from that?!

C: Yeah, thank you so much that you really opened up a great deal of things for me to perceive, know, be and receive.

N: Thank you. Wow. Oh my god. There's a comment which has come in, "When I have poured so much of myself into a piece, it is an act of vulnerability then to launch it into the world. Great to have questions, especially about significance. Thank you, thank you, thank you!"

K: Vulnerability is a big thing. I really work with it very consciously when I'm creating or when I'm performing and it's true. If you choose that consciously, things can shift and become more ease and fun. Artists often say, "This piece is my baby! I have to show it to people!" and if you can just bring your barriers down and say "Hey, this is just what I have to share. If you don't like it, okay, you can choose not to. You don't have to buy it, you don't have to watch it and you don't have to look at it. It's just a choice. This is what I chose to create. This is what I have to contribute."

If you can choose to stay that vulnerable, in my experience, it just makes that space even more magnanimous, even more expansion. Which then exponentializes the space even more if you really choose to stay vulnerable with it and not with the 'becauses', all the reasons, all the justifications for why.

Sometimes people go "Oh yeah, but you know, I wasn't done yet", or they start to give you already reasons why you might not like it, so that they show you that they saw it too. If they stay vulnerable, there's nothing to hide and there's just this is it. There's nothing. It's just totally open and I feel that is also very much the power of art and the power of choosing, creation that way.

What I am giving you is an invitation to stay in that space of vulnerability every time because what if our life is a piece of art and we choose to be vulnerable all the time? And bring our barriers down all the time? Keep them down, keep them down. What if you don't only do it in a certain moment rather you choose that all the time consciously? Choosing vulnerability all the time has been a beautiful ride with so many surprises and so many small beautiful moments of people just coming to me and saying, "Thank you for your smile". I know and I choose to keep my barriers down and somebody can receive it. Oh my god, that is such a gift for me as well. What if we can extend that and not only the moment in the studio or the moment when you are in the gallery? What if that is always a choice and always something that you can choose?

N: Wow. Let's talk about out-creating.

K: Yeay! Out-creating. Yes, out-creating is very much looking at also going beyond what you think you want to create in a way. It's about going to this beyond space and that's also the tele-class I'm starting in April. 'Out-create your Reality.' Out-creating, when the first time I heard Gary say it my whole body just got so excited! It was like "What's that?" In a way as soon as we have an idea of "I want to make this", already there is an idea, if you out-create even that, and if you can out -create yourself, you can go beyond any definition, any story, anything that you know and go to that unimagined space. What else is possible? If we can look at that, oh my god, how cool! That is something that really always excites me. Right now too, while I'm talking about it. It's a very juicy, close-to-orgasmic space for me, a very yummy, yummy, yummy space and it's something that I'm very diligently looking at.

N: "Interesting. This energy of 'I don't know' is coming up when it comes to what it is that I would like to create, but deep in there is also this energy of 'I'm here to create something marvelous'. What is this about? What questions can I ask to get aware and choose what is that I can create and contribute? Thank you."

K: Awesome. I would ask that person to destroy and uncreate what 'marvelous' means, because that is a judgment. It stops them or stops this person. "I don't know" - so if you did know, what would it be, would be my question. "I don't know" is something we've learnt to say and use. We say it for everything. "What do you want to eat?" "I don't know", "What do you want to create?" "I don't know."

What is underneath that? What potency are you hiding behind that "I don't know". Is this the time to step out of that and step into what you do know? It doesn't have to be defined, like I said. It can be just a whiff, it can be a space. I would definitely ask you to destroy and uncreate that marvelous, amazing thing that you know you are here to create, because it can also be a limitation. If you could take that away, then what is possible?

You were saying that you know that you are here to create something and that it's something marvelous. Everything that is, would you like to destroy and uncreate it, times a god zillion? Right and wrong, good and bad, POD and POC, all nine, shorts, boys and beyond.

C: Yeah, it's more than marvelous. It's like something, something, but I don't know. Something like that.

K: Is it that you don't know because you cannot put a word to it?

C: Yeah.

K: *Everywhere you've made the verbal expression of it more important than the energy of it, will you destroy and uncreate it? Right and wrong, good and bad, POD and POC, all nine, shorts, boys and beyonds.*

Everywhere you feel that only words can express your knowing and therefore you don't know, will you destroy and uncreate it? Right and wrong, good and bad, POD and POC, all nine, shorts, boys and beyonds.

What if it's okay? Ooh, what's that?

C: It was another layer of 'I don't know'.

N: Can I ask you a question? What do you love about not knowing? Say "I don't know" 3 times.

C: I don't know. I don't know. I don't know.

N: *All the SHICUUUU implants and explants keeping all of that in place and everything underneath it, keeping it in place, will you now revoke, recant, rescind, reclaim, renounce, denounce, destroy and un-create it all? Right and wrong, good and bad, POD and POC, all nine, shorts, boys and beyond.*

Every time you say you don't know, you have actually turned off your knowing.

C: Yeah, it's half light and half heavy.

N: What is half light and half heavy?

C: Every time I say, "I don't know. I have turned off my knowing", it is half light and half heavy.

N: *Yeah, so what do you love about "I don't know"?*

C: That I may not express what it is.

N: *Everything that is, will you destroy and uncreate it all? Right and wrong, good and bad, POD and POC, all nine, shorts, boys and beyonds.* What do you love about "I don't know"?

C: It's a good reason to hide.

N: (laughs) *Everything that is, will you destroy and uncreate it all? Right and wrong, good and bad, POD and POC, all nine, shorts, boys and beyonds. What do you love about "I don't know"?*

C: More about, I'm not getting the words but I'm sensing something.

K: Yeah. I'm getting the energy of it.

N: *Everything that is, times a godzillion, will you destroy and uncreate it all? Right and wrong, good and bad, POD and POC, all nine, shorts, boys and beyonds.*

K: *Everywhere you have decided you have only one turn, so you can only decide once what it is that you want to create, that you have to do it right, perfect, correct, can you destroy and uncreate that please? Will you revoke, recant, rescind, reclaim, renounce, denounce, destroy and uncreate everything that is and everything you've decided, concluded and promised to yourself? Right and wrong, good and bad, POD and POC, all nine, shorts, boys and beyonds.*

There seems to be this pressure that I can perceive about getting it right, what it is?

C: Yes, yeah, it's one time, one life. And one, one, one, one…

K: Exactly. And "otherwise I'm so fucked." What about 10 second increments? What if you could just choose and then if it doesn't work, choose something else? Nothing is written in stone and everything is possible. Always. Now what do you want to choose? What do you want to create?

C: There is a sense of like bits and pieces works better than one big creation. Then I'm not creating anything really. It's like try this, try that and just…

K: Bits and pieces, did you say?

C: Yeah. Like the 10 seconds, in my world it goes to like "Okay, try for 10 seconds. Doesn't work, move on". I'm not really creating anything big there but trying too many new things.

K: Okay, it's not that you just only do it for 10 seconds. If it's working for you, you can stay in that space, right? *Everywhere you are making your life into bits and pieces, will you destroy and uncreate it? Right and wrong, good and bad, POD and POC, all nine, shorts, boys and beyonds.*

Everywhere you have an idea of that big project and whatever that is, all the conclusions, projections, rejections, expectations, limitations, judgments, will you destroy and uncreate all of those, times a god zillion? Right and wrong, good and bad, POD and POC, all nine, shorts, boys and beyonds.

Everywhere you've created something in another time, space, dimension or reality that destroyed people, will you destroy and uncreate that and revoke, recant, rescind, reclaim, renounce, denounce, destroy and uncreate all of that, times a god zillion? Right and wrong, good and bad, POD and POC, all nine, shorts, boys and beyonds.

C: Wow. That was big.

K: Yeah. How is that now?

C: Interesting. The project seems light now.

K: Awesome! *Everything that project means to you, will you destroy and uncreate it? The energy of what that means, will you destroy and uncreate it? Right and wrong, good and bad, POD and POC, all nine, shorts, boys and beyonds.*

Wow, that's really shifting. Cool. What would it take for it to be fun for you?

What energy, space and consciousness can your body and you be to be like a child with it? To play on it, to climb on it, to go underneath it, to suck on it, to bite it, to lick it, and what else could you do? Everything that doesn't allow you to choose that, will you destroy and uncreate it? Right and wrong, good and bad, POD and POC, all nine, shorts, boys and beyonds.

N: Oh wow, that was superb. That was a brilliant way to end our call today. Thank you so much Kalpana. I had so much fun and it's like wow! You know, this whole energy that you be of being undefined and of being like the pioneer and all, I'm having all of that.

K: Yeay! How does it get any better than that?

Deal & Deliver

This 1.5 hour call is about how to get clarity when you are making any kind of deal with someone. This can be in regards to your job, your business, your relationships, finding roommates and baby sitters, and anything where you're working with other people.

Pragmatic, practical and straigh forward, this call gives you Â the kinds of questions you should be asking and the information you need to create what you would like in life.

http://bit.ly/2bafHDV

CHAPTER NINETEEN

SCHOOLS OF CHANGE

By Simone Padur

Access Consciousness Facilitator,

Educator, Illustrator, Author and Artist

N: Simone, what are schools of change?

S: It's funny it's changed since I last talked to you. I did a hangout lately called 'Living Voluptuously' and I had such joy creating it. It was so easy and fun and lots of people signed up. I was looking at that energy and wondering, "Wow, this doesn't happen with the Access classes that I do about kids, school and education." Then I realized how much of myself I had cut off to "be a teacher". That's the first thing I would really like to look at how much do we cut ourselves off in order to fit in the box of teacher or parent or student? If we were willing to not do the box thing, what else would be possible?

N: I have two boys and I'm looking at how much they try to fit into the box and if that box weren't there, what would be possible?

S: I realized that I wasn't willing to do that outside of my classroom. In my classroom I'm very comfortable at being outside the box and doing things differently. Outside the classroom I was very worried about being judged as unsuitable or questionable. When I look at teachers that inspired me they were often the troublemakers, they were often the ones that were willing to step out of the box and say, "Hey, there's a different world out there. Hey, what if we looked at this differently? What if we asked questions?"

Every hair is standing up on end as I talk about it and what if we could be that? What if just by asking questions, "Who can I be to inspire me today?" If you are willing to inspire yourself and go out and be you, that is when change can occur.

There's this wise man, I believe his name is Dr. Dain Heer, and he wrote a book called 'Be you. Change the World' That is truly it, if you are willing to be you in school, what change could you create? That would be my question.

N: Wow. I was just thinking about my son. He is pretty laid back most of the time, he is about 16, and he has this, I would almost say, threshold of accepting things. He will just tolerate a lot of stuff going on in his Universe. There were these so called friends of his, who were being unkind to him, they would throw gum at his clothes or pour juice over him and things like that and he was not doing anything about it. Then yesterday, he just said "no". When someone did do those things, he gave it back to them and he comes home and he tells me, "You know what, mom, we were planning to go out in the evening because it's the weekend to hang out together and I know that now they are not going to invite me to go with them but I don't care. I'm not going to take this nonsense anymore."

S: Wow. How cool is that?

BULLIES

N: How cool is that! How often do we assuage ourselves because we want to just fit in with who our friends or what society is telling us to be? That brings me to one of the questions that our listener has sent in and they wrote, "Hi, what can one do about bullies showing up? I don't realize this until it's too late. Can you talk about that Simone?"

S: So, bullies. Is this a parent writing in or kid or...?

N: I actually have no idea.

N: Let's talk about kids and bullies because it's about school.

S: Definitely. People often think that bullying is a really straightforward thing, much like abuse. There is a strong belief out there that if someone is bullying they are wrong and the victim is right. People don't always look and see if the victim is involved in perpetuating the bullying.

Sometimes, a kid is different and they will get picked on because they are different. However, there are also kids that might look for somebody to pick on them. I see this in classrooms; the little guy would pick on the big guy in the classroom because he knew that the big guy wouldn't get him. As soon as the class was over that big guy would get the little guy outside the classroom. It can become a game that can get out of hand. That's something to look at. I can also run a clearing here.

What stupidity are you using with the bully you are choosing? And everything that is, times a godzillion, would you destroy and uncreate it all? Right and Wrong, Good and Bad, POD and POC, All9, Shorts, Boys and Beyonds.

Ask, "Ok, so what other awareness do I have here?" I know for myself, I was bullied at school and I wasn't really willing to be aware of how mean people could be or manipulative. I was constantly blind to what people were actually doing and their actual intent because I wasn't willing to see meanness.

What if you could just look at that? It's not always something easy to look at. Oftentimes we'll look at these people in our lives, they are so-called friends, and we'll go, "Oh, I would never choose to treat anybody like that. I would never make that choice." That doesn't mean that somebody else wouldn't. Some people say, Oh, it's because they had a tough childhood or because they didn't get this or whatever it is. What if it was a choice? What if it was a choice to choose to be mean or not? That's something else to be aware of.

The curious thing about this is, when you are willing to acknowledge the mean people in your life, you can go, "Oh, so they are mean. Now I can make a choice here." Not only that, the mean person also starts to be acknowledged for who they are being. You don't have to acknowledge them out loud, because maybe that is not your best choice. If you just acknowledge in your head, "Oh, you are mean." Or, "Oh, you are being a jerk." Then they have a chance to change. It has happened so many times where, "Oh, this kid isn't very nice" and then I just go, "Oh." I have no point of view about it. That's just who they are.

Look at how people change in different situations, being aware of when they are like that and when they are not is an honoring of them for who they are choosing to be at what moment in time. I don't know if that was convoluted or answered that question, please let me know.

N: No, it's brilliant. What I love about the Access tools is that they are so weird and they work.

S: Exactly! Yes. They really give you access to what's actually going on.

N: And you know the part you said, "I would never do that!" But you know there are other people who would do that and that's the place that most of us stick ourselves the most. (Laughs)

S: Yeah, definitely.

N: We look at other people in relationship to what we would choose or not choose and then it surprises us when somebody makes a very stupid and different choice.

S: That's true.

Being Different

N: I have a caller who sent in this comment, "Thank you so much. I'm looking forward to the call. I was in the academic field for almost 20 years and I'm different in the way I go about my work. So, weird, they must have labeled me. Thank you. Simone, how are you different in school?"

S: How am I different? I'm pretty much willing to talk about anything. If a kid asks me a question about something, I will talk about it. If they are studying somebody and they want to know about their life, did they have a tough life? If they ask me a question, I'm willing to talk about whatever they are willing to hear.

That's another tool that's very useful as a teacher, is only telling a person what they can hear. Sometimes I forget to use this tool, but more often than not, I ask, "Okay, what can this student hear? What can they receive?" That means you deliver only the amount of information that student can take in at that time; which allows them to stay engaged in the lesson. It does take practice using this tool so please, play with it and see what happens.

That's a great thing about using these Access tools, is that your senses become so keen that you can catch your students before you lose their attention. It works as a teacher, or as a parent or anybody that works with kids. You can start to sense it. All of a sudden, you feel that shift of energy in the room, when your kids are little and all of a sudden it gets really quiet. (Laughs) You are, "uh oh". That ability to perceive that shift in energy is heightened. It's similar in the classroom, they zone out, their bodies are still there but they have left. I've had that in classrooms where I'm like, "Uh oh, I'm losing them". I immediately switch gears or I stop talking. I realize that I've either said too much and they are overloaded or they've had as much as they can hear or I've over explained a concept to them and they are now bored and getting ready to leave.

That's one of the things I do different, when I'm in a classroom. It's like a lot of other people you've talked to on the show Nilofer, we all have those areas where they are more of themselves than in others. Obviously, that is changing more and more and we are being more of us in all areas. For me being in the classroom, I'm all of me pretty much all the time.

What Is Conscious Education?

S: That's a great question! It's funny with this call coming up today, it's amazing how things show up when you have something scheduled like this. There's a discussion at school this week about whether or not people should eat meat and if it was ethically right to do so. I looked at this and was, "OK, that was an interesting conversation. I don't really have a point of view about whether people eat meat or not and what else is possible?"

I started asking myself, "What are all the sides to this conversation?" It occurred to me what Conscious Education for me is, at least thus far, it's the whole picture, a sense of wonder and the continuous thirst of discovery. "Ok, let's look at this from every angle. What if we included everybody in this equation? What would that create?" For example, with this discussion about whether to eat meat or not I looked at; What is the animals points of view about being eaten? What is the plants' point of view? What about the Earth? What would work for everybody? What about big business? What about the government? Let's look at all of this and what are we aware of? What feels light? What if we looked at everything? To me that is what Conscious Education is, looking at all possibilities and continuing to ask questions.

Part of looking at the whole, in my point of view, is being willing to challenge our own beliefs or points of view. I'm having fewer and fewer points of view about anything, which allows me to ask more and more questions of myself and my students. Conscious Education is cultivating the culture of questions and possibilities in my classrooms.

N: I had heard Gary, the founder of Access Consciousness®, talk about Conscious Education and somebody asked him, "Gary, what would Conscious Education look like?" He said that Conscious Education would be a place where the teacher starts off a day by asking the students, "So what would you like to learn today?" Once they come up with a topic, then you go out and find all the material about it; find books or search online or things like that. Then you teach the students to be aware and you teach them the tool of what's light and what's heavy, so they know what is true and what is not true about the information?

I said, "Wow! That's such a different way of looking at things".

In India right now there's a new government and they are changing all the textbooks. They are changing the history and they are changing all kinds of things and maybe they have done this in the past. We read what is going on and think it is the truth. If you give them this one tool of what is light or what is heavy, your children can really be aware of where they are being lied to.

S: Yes definitely. That is the easiest way to teach. Many times we are like, "This is the way it must be and this is the curriculum and that is what I have to follow and blah, blah, blah." If you ask your students questions, you can do it in your head or out loud, which allows your student's interests. This makes teaching often fun and ease for everyone involved.

I have this big file of lessons that I have collected over a long time and I open it up and I say to the lessons, "Okay, please talk to me. What would be fun for the kids? What would be fun for me? What would like to play today?"

I do this because a lesson is an entity and has a consciousness of its own, just like we do. It's energy with an identity. Every time I use this method, not only do the kids enjoy it but, there's this magic that happens in the class. It's very cool because it's the students directing where you are going and it's amazing. Amazing!

Tools

N: Simone, would you like to share a few tools for parents, for teachers who are just starting off with this way of being in schools or this way of being with education and their kids?

S: Asking questions is a great tool, especially with little kids. For instance I was teaching kindergarten and I had a little boy who came up to me and he said, "Miss, Miss don't know how to draw a fish." I said,

"Well, what if you did know how to draw a fish?" He looked puzzled for a moment and then went back to his desk and he drew a fish. He came back to me and said, "Miss, Miss, I know how to draw a fish!" Questions, especially with the little ones, work brilliantly as they are often still so willing to know what they know. It's trickier with the teenagers, but I find having a sense of humor really helps with that age group.

I use the light and heavy tool a lot. For example, in my classroom, if a kid comes in and they don't know what to do that day or they don't know what kind of project they would like to start I say, "Ok, what's fun for you? What sense do you get? Do you feel like light in your body? Is it exciting? Or does it feel heavy and you don't want to do it?" That's how I use the light and heavy tool.

The third tool is a really good tool for parents, and you might want to ask 'truth' in your head before you use this tool. (The 'truth' tool is something I will mention in a minute). Let's say a child is feeling overwhelmed with their homework, you can ask that child to ask the different assignments, "Truth, now?" or "Later?" to know which homework to start with first or when to start their homework. Often times we pressure our kids (or ourselves) with, "You have to do this now." We are probably worst with ourselves, and then we judge ourselves when we don't do it at the time we thought was appropriate. Whereas, if we ask, "Ok, so what requires my attention now?" This gives you a sense of what needs to be handled and end up being easy. That's a great tool for anybody really. It gives kids an ease with doing homework or projects or anything else they would like to do without getting overwhelmed.

The fourth tool is the 'truth' tool. This is a great one for teachers and parents and hopefully, your kids won't get a hold of it, otherwise you'll never be able to lie to your children again! Basically, when you ask a question, and you say this in your head, you ask "truth?" Then you get a sense of whether the kid is lying to you or not. "Truth, homework, now or later?" You'll know if they are lying and saying later.

Using questions and the 'truth' tool is also really effective with class-room management. It allows you to truly know what is going on. For example, if a student comes up to you and he's says, "Miss, Miss he hit me!" You say "truth" in your head you will find out if they are lying or not. Either the child will mistakenly tell you the truth or what they are telling you will feel really heavy. A lie always feels heavy. That's a tool that I use a lot, a lot, a lot.

Getting The Most Out Of School For You And Your Kids

S: First of all, I would ask yourself a question and your kids a question, "Is this school working for us?" You can also ask, "What is this? What can we do with it? Can we change it? How can we change it?" For any-thing you don't feel is working about your school, for you and your kids. First of all, you want to ask, "Can we change this school? Iif we can, now or later?" If it's a school that can't be changed, sometimes that happens, then you want to look at, "Ok, what is going to work for us? What school would work for us?"

If it is that the school can change asking those question is magic. What if asking questions as a student, a teacher or parent could change things? It doesn't even have to be aloud it can be in your head. What if just by being you, you could change your whole surroundings?

I went on this crazy walk today, I had heels on and I really wasn't plan-ning on going for a walk and I went all over the neighborhood. I just was going with this sense that I needed to walk this way and that. I had no idea why and yet, I got the sense that as I was walking, I was changing things. Change what? I'm not really sure. That is yet to be seen and there's a possibility that I might not actually ever cognitively see it. How cool is that that you can change your environment just by walking around in it?

What Would It Take For School To Be A Nurturing Place For Our Kids

S: That's a big topic. First of all, this is something that was suggested to me years ago was to ask the consciousness of the building, the consciousness of the Earth, the consciousness of the paper, of the stationery, of the desk to start contributing me and students. What if it was as simple as that? *As simple as asking; all the things that have consciousness to start contributing to changing the school and making it more nurturing. How overjoyed would the school be to be able to play with everything that was willing to play? What are the possibilities?* Does that make sense?

N: Wow. I'm writing down everything you are saying!

S: Just as we are talking about this I can sense the molecules are already starting to hum, everywhere.

N: I wonder how many schools we're sitting here and changing? Can you talk about what to do as a parent when the teachers don't function in the way you are speak of?

S: One of the things I would do actually is destroy and un-create all the projections, expectations, and conclusions any one has placed on your kids. I know Gary often did this with his own kids so that they wouldn't be affected by any judgments that teachers had of his kids. That is one tool you can use, because teachers have a huge impact on their students. I didn't realize the full extent of that until I started teaching. It is crazy! Teachers spend almost more time with kids when they are school aged than their parents do.

Another tool you can use is putting like a bell jar over your kids (not a literal one an energetic one) while they are at school. You can just be like, "Ok, get your bell jar on." (Laughs)

Bell Jar

N: Simone, talk about the bell jar and what does the bell jar do.

S: Sure! It just allows the kid not to be impacted by any or all judgments, projections, expectations and conclusions that anyone puts on them. They just ping off like water off a ducks back. You can also put the teacher in a bell jar as well if that's required; just ask. In fact, that might be even more of a contribution because then they are not inflicting themselves on other kids as well. With people that are place in a bell jar any judgments and projections they have just smack back at them instead of impacting others.

N: Would the bell jar on the child work if, for example, they were having their friends do meanness to them and stuff like that or judge them or stuff like that? That would work as well, right?

S: Well, what do you know, Nilofer?

N: (Laughs) Yeah. I'm wondering do you put the bell jar on all the time or just when they are in school?

S: Well, what I would ask is what is required here? Just be aware of what your kid requires. You could even ask, "Ok, so whenever they require the bell jar, let it be there for them please." It could be as simple as that. I think sometimes we worry about, "Oh, did I do the bell jar today? Or didn't I?" Especially, if you're like me because I don't remember anything. That is an easy way to have it done without having to really worry about it.

N: Awesome.

S: Yeah, what else? I feel like there's information I'm missing here. Here's one, I think there are some mean teachers out there and in my interesting point of view, maybe they shouldn't be teachers. One of the things that I would do for somebody that is really, really nasty and shouldn't be maybe in the school system is –

Exposé

Everything that doesn't allow them to be exposed for who they truly are, and everything that doesn't allow their truth to be told, destroy and uncreate it all; and then you just POD and POC everything that doesn't allow that.

- 391 -

Very quickly, that person can no longer hide the meanness that they are. That's a very potent tool.

I always ask the question, *"Ok, if I do this, what will this create?"* By asking that question, you'll either get sort of a light feeling or a heavy feeling and you can also ask, "Ok, so if I do this, what will this create in 5 years, 10 years and in 500 years?" Then you get the sense of the long-term effect of what your choice might be creating and continue to ask questions as that may change.

That way you are inclusive, you are working from the Kingdom of We, everybody is included, rather than just you or just you and your kid. The other interesting thing about that process that I just gave you is, that once that person is exposed for the meanness that they truly are or for whatever it is that they truly are, it then gives them the choice to change. As long as they stay hidden from what's really going on they don't have a choice to change either. Does that make sense?

N: Absolutely. You know I ran this process on someone. I heard your interaction with Gary where he gave you this and I ran it on someone. This person is a figure of authority in a particular institution and they were impelling their points of views on the different members and a lot of people were in that no-choice Universe where they could not make a different choice. Just as you were saying that, I just realized what I've noticed is that person is no longer impelling their point of view.

S: It's a process that is incredible. I've used it numerous times and it's really good for bullies. If your child is being bullied at school it could contribute to having those bullies exposed. There are some kids that are really sneaky about it and they get away with a lot. That's a great way of getting them caught out. (Laughs)

N: "Hi, can you give me some questions for the students to ask from a teacher's point of view? Like what would you like the students to be asking for them to be a contribution in the classroom?"

S: Ok. She's asking if the kids can give the teachers some questions?

N: I'm not exactly sure what she's asking but the way I perceive it is. Hi Caller, can you clarify it? It's a bit unclear for both of us at this moment. I'll just wait for you to respond.

"Hi Simone, I have nearly a 6 year old son who started his Year 1 now. I get a huge opposition for everything I say. When I ask my son to get ready for school, to eat his food, to get ready and go out for a walk or play in the park, anything. I have been asking him questions, giving him a view of what it can create. What else can I be or do to change all this? It really drains my husband's and I energy so much. Thank you for all the awareness."

S: Well, I know Gary had something similar with his kids. They would take so long to get ready in the morning to go to school and he finally said to them, "Look, I don't mind taking you to school in your pajamas. I don't have a problem with that". (Laughing) He said they were never late for school again.

N: (Laughs) I love that!

S: Number 2, is I would ask him, "What do you like about fighting? And do you realize that when you fight, the person you are fighting most is yourself?" I've heard Gary use that a number of times with parents and kids and stuff like that, that's a huge one. The other thing I use a lot when I ask a kid a question and I feel like my question hits a brick wall is, I will ask my barriers to go down. What you do is ask, "Ok, all of my barriers go down". It is from that space that I then ask the question. Sometimes for some kids, and it might be that they've had a hard time, you never know what they are coming from. They come into this world, you don't know what they've lived before and you might not know what they experience. You can just put your barriers down and just ask. The intensity of kindness that you are being can seem to them as intensity and they may not know the difference between intensity that is meanness and intensity that is kindness. This is a way of being that space where they don't have anything to fight against. If you are willing to be that space, there's nothing for them to hit against. You are just like a big marshmallow. It's one of my favorite tools.

N: There's one tool that I use with my kids which I find just works so incredibly. What I do is I will look at some of the really stupid choices that they are making, it's like when 'my question hits that brick wall', what I will do is, "Ok, so whatever it is that they are choosing, let me contribute to their choice."

S: Oh wow, that's a great one!

N: For instance my elder son who's 16, he's into this bodybuilding. His friends are telling him, "You have to eat only protein and this is the workout you have to do and that is the workout you have to do and blah, blah, blah".

In the beginning when he started this whole routine, I was getting so triggered by it all, it was not funny. The first thing I did was I ran this clearing on myself.

What energy, space and consciousness can I and my body be to stop protecting my kids for all eternity?

Every time I would have that intensity come up like, "Oh my god, I have to stop him from doing this stupidity to his body", I would run that on myself. The charge dissipates and then I go, "Ok, so he's making this really interesting choice. How can I contribute to him?"

For the last 4 months, he has been going to the gym every single day for two hours and he's been really abusing his body and I can perceive that in his body. Then suddenly, he comes in this week and says, "You know what, mum, I'm not going the gym anymore because it's really boring to go all alone. Instead I've found this workout that I can do for 45 minutes at home."

For 2 days, he's been doing this workout and he was just telling me last night, he said, "You know what, mum, I love this workout because there's all this breathing in the workout and there's this stretching that he leads us through. After I did the first workout, I thought my body would be really sore, but you know what, my body feels so good because of all the stretching that I've done."

I realized, wow, I've been contributing to his choice and he's like, "Well, ok, never mind, been there, done that, had enough, let me choose something different." (Laughs)

S: I love that, *"How can I contribute to this?"* That's amazing.

N: It is amazing. I am so in awe of the tools and especially when I can get out of having a vested point of view about what things should create.

Let me read a comment, which has just come in, "There is such a dearth of teachers who really are there for children in a way that adds value to their lives. Simone, what an awesome teacher you are. May your tribe increase." (Laughs)

Okay, let's take a live caller.

Caller: Hi. You were just answering my question right now. You were talking about the fight. I have asked that question, and my son goes, "Yes, I want to and I want to fight myself." I say, "Okay, what's the point of fighting for everything including you?"

S: So, does he give you an answer when you ask that question?

C: Yeah, sometimes he gives an answer and sometimes he just gets more angry, he is like, "Why are you trying to take me out of it?"

S: Right. Well, I would definitely not play with Nilofer's question. (Laughs)

C: That was a huge contribution, definitely.

S: I acknowledged the other day that I picked a fight with friend of mine. This made me realize, that I really love to debate and argue. I was never really willing to acknowledge that about myself. It's fun for me. My whole body like revs up and there's like this "zoom". I was on this great tele-call with Nilofer, called the 'Horse Whisperers' with Melanie Clampit and what I realized was that I wasn't willing to acknowledge that I loved watching other people explode in anger. I wasn't willing to explode myself, not necessarily in anger but just being willing to be out there and to be the controversy, to be different. I wonder, with your son, how much is he willing to actually be different from his peers?

C: Hmm, that's a very less point. (Laughs). I mean, it seems very less to me.

N: Is that your conclusion, dear?

C: Ah, yeah, let me POC and POD that. (Laughs)

N: And how much are you trying to be a good, perfect, correct parent here?

C: A lot.

N: Yeah, and what if you gave that up? I have an awesome energy, space and consciousness clearing for you.

What energy, space and consciousness can you and your body be to be the worst possible mother for all eternity?

C: Yeah, that's so light.

N: Whatever you do, don't run that one. (Laughs)

C: Yeah, I think the same goes with his resistance to eating. He can go a whole day without eating. He just doesn't want to eat.

S: Well, you might want to ask...

C: If you feed him, he's okay but he doesn't want to eat by himself. He doesn't eat at school. Sorry, sorry, I was... Continue.

S: Does his body not actually want to eat most of the time? How much food does his body actually require?

C: I keep checking and giving. I don't force him every time, but the minimum stuff. I've left him for a month not eating, I didn't force him. I let it go, but he went too skinny, like the body who has never eaten.

C: He had started feeling sick and all and then I had to start putting him back in routine.

S: There is something about that that I'm just remembering from a call I did lately and it was almost, "How many lifetimes was that part of his religion or that it was closer to godliness, to not eat?

S: Does that read for you and him?

C: It's a little light but there is something more.

S: Okay, so what is that? What are you aware of? That right there, what's that?

C: Sometimes it does come that he doesn't like this place very much and he doesn't want to stay here more.

S: *Everywhere you are not willing to allow him to choose that, if that would be his choice, and I know that's not the thing that a parent wants to look at necessarily, or to deal with. Everything that doesn't allow you to acknowledge that that might be his choice, and everything that doesn't allow you to be in total allowance of that choice, would you destroy and un-create it all? Right and Wrong, Good and Bad, POD and POC, All 9, Shorts, Boys and Beyonds.*

C: It was so weird, the moment I was saying "yes" it was now he wants to oppose that. It's like, you say yes, he'll say no. You say no, it's yes, with a contrast kind of a Universe.

S: I've noticed with myself working with kids, as soon as I'm in allowance of whatever their choice is, and it's that contribution thing that Nilofer was talking about again. If you are in total allowance of their choice and don't have a point of view about it then they will choose with more ease rather than choosing out of resistance to you. They might still choose the same thing, and at least you know it's been their choice. It gives them choice whether they want to be here or not. Have you had that conversation with him? Hey would you like to be here?

C: Not really, but once I had, probably couple of months back but that was in anger. It was an anger response.

S: Maybe when you are calm. Ask him again and also ask him, "Is that really your point of view?"

"What are you perceiving? Are you aware of all these other people that don't want to be on this planet?" How much is he taking that out of those other peoples' worlds? A lot or a little? Everything that doesn't allow you to acknowledge that, would you destroy and un-create it all? Right and Wrong, Good and Bad, POD and POC, All 9, Shorts, Boys and Beyonds.

It may be that he is trying to change the world by taking stuff out of other people. That might be something you would ask him, "Are you doing this to change things and what if there's an easier way? What if you don't have to take this out of people? Is it the people's choice to have this? Even though you sense it and you say, god why would you choose that?"

C: That is his question actually to me. He keeps asking me why all these things happen in the world? Why can't it be easier?

S: Because people are stupid.

C: (Laughs) Ok, got you. I have a better sense but I don't have words, but thank you.

S: You are very welcome. Thank you for your question.

N: Wow, that was awesome, Simone. How often is it that we don't acknowledge other stuff, which is going on?

Learning

S: What else can we talk about? Something that just came into my head was learning, learning in schools for kids who struggle with learning. I know this is an issue for a lot of parents and kids out there. One of the things that pops into my head is concentration. A lot of people are trying to get these kids with ADD and ADHD to focus to concentrate, which rarely successful. If you have a kid that has ADD and or ADHD, they actually need to be doing multiple things rather than "focusing".

I know I've taught kids who need to have the television on, the radio on and they need to be doing their math homework and also dancing on the spot. I'm exaggerating a little bit but they need to have multiple things going. That is something to be aware of as a parent and or teacher. Fortunately, I teach art so generally they are doing multiple things at one time rather than having to concentrate on one. I rarely have that going on in my classroom.

Another thing to be aware of is kids that get overwhelmed in class with questions asked of them, it may not actually be overwhelm and it may not be that they are going blank. When you ask them a question, they have so many ideas downloading, that they may not be able to answer. If you can ask a more specific question that can really assist them and you.

Also if you ask questions that relate to a student's experience, it gives them a starting point. It's like putting what they are interested in back into their world. The moment you have their interest, its gold in your hands. You have them and they'll take their lesson or project to some crazy and phenomenal places once they are interested.

N: My younger son who is 12 years old, he has this really weird energy. He likes to play on the PS4 and one of the games he plays is FIFA, the football game. When he goes to those higher levels of difficulty and he is not able to get it and when that happens, he gets so upset about it, he screams and he shouts and he starts wailing and crying. I tried different things and it doesn't really work. I wonder if you can shed some light on this? I've seen this happen in other areas also. I think he has this judgment of "I cannot do this but I have to do it" and then he goes into a contracted Universe with some of his projects at school and things.

S: There are a few things going on. First of all, I'm going to address the football because that seems to be different than the other thing. The football, I would actually ask, *"How many lifetimes has he been an incredible sportsman, all the DJCCs, which are decisions, judgments, conclusions and computations he has, that he had made over that period of however long, destroy and un-create all of that? With this school stuff, is it the same energy for everything or are they different things going on?"*

N: Some of the school stuff where he forgets to do his homework. Then he'll wake up in the morning and he has that small amount of time to complete the homework. Even before he can do it, he has to sit and cry and literally just create a big trauma and drama around it, instead of just doing whatever the work is.

S: Can I ask you a question? Is he really, really fast?

N: He's very fast, absolutely, really fast.

S: Is he so fast that doing it the night before or when he has more time and is that not very exciting for him?

N: Probably not. (Laughs)

S: What if this is a way to be down to the wire, the trauma, the drama, the blood, the sweat, the tears, "Will I get it done? Will I not get it done? Will I get it in on time?" (Laughs) It's of course, not a humanoid trait. I personally never did that! (Laughs)

N: I never did that too. I was always way ahead of time, right? (Laughs)

S: One of the things you might look at is, does he need to add more things to his life? If leaving things to the last minute is his entertainment, maybe he needs a few more projects. Maybe ask him, "Ok, so what if you added more to your life? What if you could show me how fast you truly are? I wonder if you really are that fast? (Laughs) That's one thing you can look at. That 'down to the wire thing', that's a humanoid thing. If we have enough projects then time goes away, that's what I find. Is there anything else there?

N: It's not – so it's still that trauma and drama bit which he chooses to go into. I wonder if there's something I can do to snap him out of it when that comes up with him at that point of time?

S: I'm kind of bad at that, because I will actually do the trauma and drama beside them, which I find funny and it's not always my best choice and sometimes they just get more angry at me and sometimes they see how funny they are being.

N: Yeah, I've done it too. Sometimes I'll just sit there and I will scream and shout, "Oh my god, I can't do this and blah, blah, blah". He just gets angry at me and he wants to beat me up. (Laughs)

S: I'm thinking of what Gary usually says if somebody goes into that 'Woe is me my life sucks.' You can say, "Your life does suck. I don't know how you deal with life. I would stop breathing. I think I would just lie on the floor and give up." That might be another thing you might want to play with. (Laughs) How would you react to that?

N: Yeah, let me play with it. I will for sure let you know what happens the next time. (Laughs) I'm finding it so funny!

Choices With Future

Okay, Simone, can you talk a little bit about this? When you have teenagers and they are making choices about their future education or life, what are some of the questions that you can ask or you can give them?

S: I often ask what's light and heavy for you? Gary talks about all the time; "What do you do with such ease that you have never realized has a value?" Really looking at not only what they do academically with ease, but also who they be with ease that would be a contribution not just to them but also to the planet. That's something to look at because it might not necessarily mean they are going to university, it might mean that they go and apprentice somewhere. There are lots of different ways to get where you'd like to go that will be joyful for you.

While we are on the subject of teenagers, this is one of my favorite things to do. If you have a grumpy teenager in your life and they come into the room looking like the world has ended or you know they stubbed their toe, some teens are like that. Not all of them however. Just look at them and say, "You know, I am so grateful for you. You just light up my life and you bring this sunshine in, that just makes the darkness disappear." It's amazing, if you can say that with no barriers and no point of view, it seems to jolly them out of it. All of a sudden, it's really hard for them to hold that misery in place because you really are being grateful for them. It's fun, so I do it a lot. (Laughs)

N: (Laughs) Oh my god, I can just see my son coming home grumpy from school. I'm going to play with this one for sure.

N: I have this interesting thing, which happens with my son and he is always asking me questions about factual information. For example, he will ask me things, what is the population of this city and other information. I get irritated with that. It's why does he want encyclopedia information from me? Can you just facilitate me on that, Simone?

S: That sounds like my everyday world. If you have kids say: "Well, what is that?" or "How do I spell that?" or "What does that mean?" I always say, "There's a dictionary right there or there is an encyclopedia online". Or you could say, "Wow, that would be a would be a great thing to Google. You should Google that." Make a game out of it. "I wonder how fast you could Google that?"

If you do have the time and you are in that space where you can just play with this. You could have a phone or he has a phone and ask, "Ok, who can Google it first? Who can get this? I wonder what could you find out about this?! I wonder what you know that I don't know? I wonder if you know more than I do?" It becomes a sense of play and less of an irritation for you. It also empowers him to be able to discover the knowledge for himself.

N: (laughs) Thank you for that one.

S: No problem. What if we can have a sense of play with all our kids?

They manipulate us all the time. What if we could start manipulating them back?

N: (Laughs) Who me? I could never manipulate my kids.

S: (Laughs) No, you are too weak, pale and interesting for that one.

N: (Laughs) Absolutely. I totally do it. One of my favorite manipulations with my grumpy teenager is, "I know it's your job to drive me crazy. Do you know what my job is?" I'll say it so innocently. I'll say, "My job is to embarrass you in front of your friends." And he gets the chills when I say that. (Laughs)

S: (Laughs) Oh that's fun! Oh boy, that's really good.

N: That's my really good one.

"Would you talk about your points of view on screens for kids – TV, video games, etc.?"

S: That's a great question. What I would look at is how is your kid using the screens? Do they have choice in the matter? If they don't, what is that? That's a great area for the questions; "What is this? What can I do with it? Can I change it? How do I change it?" You can ask that with 'We' instead of 'Me' as well.

Maybe your kid does need that time to just veg out and there are lots of people that require that. It allows them to sort out what's going on during the day or just a time-out to sort things out in their heads. There are some kids that become addicted to screens and can't really walk away them. That's a huge discussion in many schools and amongst many parents. Many people suggest that gaming or watching screens is addictive. I wonder if they are necessarily addictive or if there's something else going on. My personal point of view is it's a symptom of something else going on.

If your kid is OCD it's a great way to dumb down his awareness because he's hyper focused on something. There is often repetitive motion with their bodies that gives them that sense of peace or calm that they might not get if they are bombarded with a lot. Something you might want use with your kids, to give them a sense of space, is taking them out into nature. I know some kids are "Ah, I don't want to go for a walk!" What if you could find something that everybody enjoys that involves being in nature?

There's is another exercise you can do which is simply have them put their feet on the floor, feel their butt in the seat and then expand themselves as big as the room, as big as your town, as big as your country, as big as the world, and that also gives them a sense of space. It lets them know that they can be that space whenever they require or where ever they feel they are being impacted by anything around them or their day. If you operate at 300,000 miles of being that space in every direction, then you are not impacted by everybody's thoughts, feelings and emotions. My perception is that more and more kids require that space and so nature or that exercise are two ways of getting that.

N: That's brilliant. I have also seen this with my son. For example, he'll come home from school really grumpy and then he will just switch on the television and his body will just calm down and relax to a degree, which is phenomenal. The other day he came home after a school activity and he came home literally crying and wailing; "My head hurts, and this hurts and I have all this homework that I have to do and why do they have to give me this homework on a day on which I have after-school?" I just went, "Ok, so if you didn't have this homework, what would you do?" and he looked at me and he went, "I would watch TV." I said, "Come, let's watch TV." I switched on the TV, I made him sit there and then he just relaxed. He watched TV for half an hour and then he just completed whatever he had to do, which was quite amazing.

S: You not having a point of view about it is a huge gift to him.

N: When I first went for my Level 2 and 3, I asked Gary the same question because I had a point of view of this reality of; "Oh my god, they are addicted to their games." I asked Gary, "Gary, what about when kids are addicted to their games?" He said, "They are your electronic baby-sitters. Let them play. They will be out of your hair for hours." I going, "What?" (Laughs) I stopped having a point of view about it after that. Okay, Simone, one last question and then let's wind up.

Our caller writes, "What will be a stress-free alternative education for kids, if home-schooling is not a possibility?"

S: There are alternative schools that are more student-led. There are some where kids have more choice. There's everything from where they can choose the subjects they would like to do or free-schools or democratic school where kids can actually choose to go to lessons or not. There are also other schools like Reggio Emilia out there that do cater to more play, more of a free sense of being. Allowing the kid to be a kid, to run around and have fun and really start to choose for them. You might want to look into that. Ask your kid what they would like to choose. What would work for them? Go and visit some schools and ask, "Ok, so what's going to work for you? What's going to be fun for you?" That's what would be my suggestion.

N: Wow, Simone, thank you so much. This has been such a brilliant conversation and we really went so many different places here. Thank you so much, it's been such a contribution.

S: Thank you! I had no idea we were going to go all those different places!

SESSIONS WITH NILOFER

Would you like to have the magic of Nilofer touch you, permeate you and turn your reality on it's head?

Here are some possibilities -

SOP Sessions (Available Online)

Verbal Facilitation on any topic under the sun
(Available Online)

Right Voice For You Sessions (Available Online)

Bars (In person)

Bodywork (In person)

Contact: Nilofer@illusiontoilluminationsummit.com

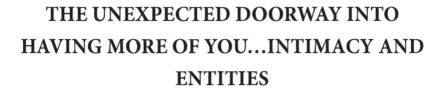

CHAPTER TWENTY

THE UNEXPECTED DOORWAY INTO HAVING MORE OF YOU...INTIMACY AND ENTITIES

By Cara Wright

Elements of Intimacy with Entities

Nilofer: So Cara, I wonder what you want to talk to us about entities?

Cara: Good question! I mean what a subject, right? The reason I picked this subject when you asked me to be a part of the "Doorways to Possibility Summit" was because I think that it's such an unexpected doorway into having more of you. For me the doorway opened over 2 years ago when I chose to become an Access Consciousness® and Talk to the Entities® Certified Facilitator within 3 months of one another. After playing with the tools of Access Consciousness for a short while these other interesting classes caught my attention. The 'Talk to the Entities" classes are a specialty class of Access Consciousness developed by Shannon O'Hara with the assistance of Gary Douglas. I started seeing information about these classes EVERYWHERE and my awareness of them increased.

Every time I would see something about these classes my first reaction was "It's not really my thing". One day my sister and I were on a walk and she said, "you should take that class" and I was said right back, "I don't know, I don't think I'm really that aware of entities. I don't really think it's my thing."

Looking back at that conversation now, it is funny because it is the thing I do most that is fun for me and total ease. Anytime I put my attention on entity awareness, anytime I facilitate a class, anytime I'm working with clients and entities it is always an easy flow. Something different opens up to be created and generated.

What I love about this last point is that so many people think they don't have any sort of awareness with entities or if they do have an awareness they've been refusing it because it freaks them out and they don't know what to do with it. There are so many interesting points of view out there about entities. What entity awareness is, what it means and what happens if you choose it?

What I realized early on was that I was functioning from 2 total lies. Number one, I was functioning from the lie that I wasn't aware of entities. Number two, I was functioning from the lie that I was freaked out by it. I remember the first call I did with Shannon O'Hara. It was a Beginner Tele-call and it was everything I could do to stay on the phone. Many times I wanted to throw the phone and run in the other direction. What went through my mind was, "I don't know if I want to be doing this." Choosing to stay on the call, to continue to learn and start to use the tools was a dynamic choice. That choice started to allow me to uncover what it is that I know about entities. It ended up being a huge doorway into not only more possibility but also into being more intimate with me.

The Elements of Intimacy, which is something we talk about a lot in Access are – honor, trust, vulnerability, gratitude and allowance. How does entity awareness and Intimacy even relate? A willingness to acknowledge that I actually have a capacity here, an awareness here and being able to step into that has created so much more of having those elements of intimacy for myself. It's been quite a remarkable exploration and journey, and it's different every day. It builds, expands and grows more every single day. So that is the reason I chose this subject, it can create so much for people and a lot of people tend to shy away from it - Which I totally get because I did the same thing.

It took me like a couple of months to finally go "Ok, fine, I'm going to take this class". I went back and forth a lot! Now I know it was the entities that were encouraging me to choose this work, and I still resisted it at first. I would think "Yes, you are going to take this class" and then "No, no, no, I'm not going to" and they were like "No, no, you are" and I thought "No, I'm not. I think a lot of us actually, familiar with Access and familiar who function from, "Oh, that's really not for me." I get that people do that more often than people choose it, and my question is what if you did choose it? What else is possible? What would it create and generate for your business beyond what you ever thought possible?

N: Yeah, it's so amazing, so there are a couple of things that have come up, so let me ask you a question and then share an experience I had.

C: Awesome

N: Speak about the elements of intimacy – honor, trust, vulnerability, gratitude and allowance. Were you talking about having those elements of intimacy with entities or having them with you? Is it that your work with the entities has facilitated you to have more with you?

C: Well, I think it is both. The interesting thing about entity awareness is that it is very unique to you. We are all born with the ability to be aware of energies and entities. The definition that we use for entity in Talk to the Entities® and Access Consciousness® is an entity is an energy that is defined. This means I'm an entity and you are an entity. Then there are also entities that were in bodies and are no longer in bodies, and entities that are coming into bodies. There are energies that surround you that have never been in bodies, spirits of the Earth and land. Businesses are entities. This Tele-summit is an entity, books, songs, artwork and so much more.

We are all born with our primary language being energy and so everyone is aware of all of these things we define as different entities. The problem is created because it has been made so wrong and so weird. Most people learn to function from, "You shouldn't be aware of entities", "Don't talk about what you are aware of with entities". Most of us can look at our childhood and ask, "At what age did I decide that it was not ok to be aware of entities?" Whatever number just popped into your head, that is usually the time when you basically said to somebody, "I see this" and that person said to you, "No, you can't be seeing that." You may have told your parents that you were aware of some sort of a being in your room and it freaked them out so dynamically and you were aware of that freak out. In the interest of not freaking them out you started to shut it off and shut it down.

The beauty of choosing your awareness again, opening back up to really being aware of entities, is that it does cultivate those elements of intimacy for you. How much of your awareness do you have to cut off to pretend that you are not aware of energy and that you are not aware of entities? For me, as I have claimed, owned and acknowledged what I am aware of and how I am aware of it, a space has been created that allows me to honor myself and trust what it is that I know. Learning to lower your barriers, those energetic blocks we set in place to keep out what we are aware of, is a basic tool of TTTE. In order to be able to interact, facilitate, communicate, and receive from entities you have to have your barriers down. So, the building of the muscle of lowering my barriers has created an uncanny ability for me to step into a different space of vulnerability. The gratitude I have cultivated for me by choosing more of me no matter what others are choosing or what they judge I am choosing is beyond any gratitude I have had for me in my life so far. When you know you are stepping into and playing with entities you must choose to be in allowance of what you know and what others are functioning from that is different.

Being aware of what I'm aware of and acknowledging the spirit world does create a level of intimacy with the spirit world also. At about midnight last night, they all started showing up. It's not odd to me that you have more activity around you Nilofer, because I was going to be on your tele-summit, that's just kind of how it works. What has the spirit world been trying to communicate and even gift to us, that we've just totally been refusing? What have you decided you are not aware of that you actually are? That's my question to you.

N: When you were sharing about how you chose to step into the Talk to the Entities classes it reminded me of something that occurred last year about this time. I was travelling to India and Shannon had her Talk to the Entities® classes in Delhi at the same time. I chose to go for the Beginners class and it was so amazing. What was bizarre was that from the time that I chose the class, got on to the flight arrived the next morning for the class, the exact amount of money that I would require for the 2 classes showed up in my PayPal account.

C: Yay! And you had no idea where that came from?

N: I know where it came from, but I was just aware of all these energies contributing to it and it was like, "You know what, we want you to do this class. You had better get your butt there."

C: Right? I know. That is really what occurred for me too. It was that I literally had this push to do the TTTE classes. It wasn't like this easy "Oh, I'm just going to try that out" choice, it was more like I was resisting it and it was like "No, you are going to do it". I took Beginning class, then right to Intermediate class, Advanced and all the way through TTTE Facilitators'. This created a totally different kind of awareness, energy, possibility, for me that was quite amazing.

Entity work can be confronting in a lot of ways because you do have to really know what you know and trust you! One of the things that I realized very early on was that it wasn't that I had no awareness of entities, I was actually incredibly aware of entities. I just wasn't aware of them in the way that you see in this reality. You know, you have people that are clairvoyant like John Edward! I was obsessed with him by the way. I thought he was amazing and that I just didn't think I had the talent, ability or capacity. There is a tool in Access called everything is the opposite of what it appears to be and nothing is the opposite of what it appears to be. This was a clear case of that!

What is true is how John, or anyone else for that matter, perceives entities is not the way I do and vice versa. One of the things that's really cool is that as you do this entity work, the way in which you perceive entities and are aware of them does change and shift, so you can never really go to conclusion of *"Oh, this is the way that I'm aware of entities"*. It is always the exploration of what are the ways in which I am aware of them?"

I realized that my body actually is a huge contribution to me with entity awareness. I had a lot of stuff going on in my body that I had basically, prior to Access, chalked up to 'I must have a tumor in my head'. I thought I was dying half the time. I had a lot of dizziness. I had a lot of headaches. I had a lot of feeling like I couldn't take full breath. I would feel like I would have to yawn in order to get a full breath. It's just this really interesting thing that happens with the way that I'm breathing, and now I know when those things occur is because I'm aware of something – and it's usually an entity. Sometimes it can be other stuff but it's usually that I'm aware of an entity.

When I started to identify the ways in which I am aware of entities, it began to build a muscle that created a level of allowance for, a level of trust for and total gratitude for myself and my body. Prior to knowing this information I thought my body was ill all the time. I thought my body was incorrect and wrong. I thought my body was doing all sorts of weird things. In my pre-Access life I had done everything that you could possibly do out there to try to fix my body. To find out now that my body was actually just totally willing to be aware of something that I was refusing to acknowledge I was aware of is such a gift.

The level of gratitude that I've gotten for my body and what it's willing to be for me is just – I mean right now, my whole body is just tingling everywhere. Just being able to acknowledge what my body knows and then be able to go "Ok, so am I aware of an entity here?" Or other basic tools of Talk to the Entities® like something as simple as asking *"Ok, is this an entity? Am I aware of an entity?"*

This cultivates a sense of gratitude and trust that I do know what I know. The thing about entities is I could totally be aware of an energy or an entity in a space and no one else in the space is acknowledging that entity at all. You have to start to trust what you know, even if no one else acknowledges what you know. Even if you can't tell anyone else in the room and if you were to tell anyone, they would go, "Oh no, I don't see that" or "I don't hear that". How often has that ever happened to you Nilofer, where you totally perceived an entity or something occurring and nobody else in the room got it? That is where you really start to flex and stretch, build those muscles of trusting that you know even when nobody on the planet knows it the same way that you know it.

N: So for me, I've always been aware of entities and I always have trusted that, so there's never been any doubt in my mind or in my being that my awareness is wrong or anything like that. But you know, what I really got while you were talking was how different my awareness is as compared to this 3D reality. When you were talking about people who talk to entities, the way I'm aware of entities is totally different. It is really interesting that I actually have had this intensity in my head since afternoon today and you are talking about your body contributing to your awareness of entities. There have been times when I have acknowledged that that intensity that shows up is an awareness of entities, and for some reason today I didn't. Duh!

C: Oh that was so cute! Right? I know. Quite funny.

N: So cute, yeah.

C: Yeah, where you can start with a lot of this is just start to acknowledge first and foremost that you are an energetically aware being and that the spirit world does exist. There are things out there. Even going into nature, there's a different energy and that different locations on this planet can have entities unique to them. What if when you travel this planet you could be aware of the different energies and entities that inhabit those areas? I've heard Shannon O'Hara talk about the different places where she travels, for example India, that it is a completely different energy. There's different entities there, there's different ways in which people function with entities. The thing that's interesting about the spirit world and entity awareness is the way in which people have functioned with it really does indicate what you are going to experience in that culture. You may go to places where the culture there has more of an indigenous "perspective" towards the spirit world that it's actually real and exists. It is similar to what you mentioned earlier Nilofer that you never really doubted that entities are real.

For you it is about looking at how you are aware of entities that's been a big shift for you.

For people in North America, entity awareness has been for freaks and it's seen primarily as creepy. People tend to believe if you are aware of a ghost, then that ghost is going to take over your body, or it's going to be like poltergeist. The entity is going to do something awful and come and get you.

There's a lot of spiritual and metaphysical attitudes toward entities where entities are more aware than you are. Just because they are not in a body somehow they know more than you, they are more powerful than you. Or if you are aware of entities, you are only aware of angels. What if entities are just like people? What if there are some that are a contribution? What if there are some that you really don't want to play with? What if it's more practical than we've made it into?

One of the things that I really love about working with the entities is starting to become aware of how people do function with entities, what has been created here with entity awareness and what else is possible for us all. The idea that you can't be aware of entities is now as unbelievable as being aware of them was for me. I had this 'aha' moment about a year ago. I've been working with women who are pregnant for years, for 15 years I have worked with pregnant women as a prenatal yoga teacher and doula. At times felt I had more of a connection with the beings choosing to be born then I did sometimes with the women. As I was going through the Talk to the Entities® class I had a moment,

"Wait a second, am I actually facilitating the beings coming to be born too?" Many times women would choose my classes, without knowing why. I would work with these women and what I started to realize was they chose me because the being that's coming to be their child brought them to me. I was like "WOW, for what reason would I not think that I'm aware of entities when I work with these beings that are coming into bodies all the time?" It was really quite funny because the minute I had that awareness, which actually took me longer than you'd think, my ability to facilitate women during pregnancy and even women who were trying to conceive increased dynamically. Now I can facilitate communication, creation, connection between them and their "babies" even before they conceive. I was doing this and not claiming or owning what I was doing. If you don't acknowledge, claim or own what it is that you're being, it doesn't really grow. It stays the same.

Now it's starting to grow and I'm starting to get a lot more awareness around the whole process of conceiving, being pregnant and birth even. Many times when I'm in a birth space, the being that's coming to be born is the one that I'm actually facilitating the most. So it has been a really interesting shift for me and a really interesting space of asking *"What am I aware of? What are the ways in which I'm aware of what I'm aware of?"*

What if you chose to never come to conclusion but always be curious about what else is possible with the spirit world? What would it look like if we all had much more awareness in the transition places when we are coming in to be born and when we are leaving our bodies too?

It's very exciting to me, you can tell, I talk fast and it is something that I can talk a lot about which is so funny because 2 years ago I would have told you I wasn't aware of entities.

N: Wow, wow. So you know, you are the first person I've actually heard talking about beings coming into bodies in this whole world as entities and as you were talking, I actually started to see how I have actually facilitated people as they are leaving this world. For a long time I used to have a lot of clients who would come to me and who would transition and I was like "I'm a crap healer."

C: Right? Isn't it funny how we do that? Yes, what have you created for these beings that is so far beyond anything you thought was possible?

N: Yeah, absolutely. And I could actually see the beings at the point of transition and I could see the transition process. It was never like a dream, it was more like a vision of what I was seeing at that point of time.

C: So cool.

N: Yeah, thank you.

Question: "Hi Cara, I'm very aware of entities. Where it comes up usually is when I facilitate my clients with entities who want to talk to them. However, when it is for myself, it's often not as clear. Can you help around it being clear for others but not having as much ease with myself?

C: Asking a lot of questions about how you are receiving information is going to assist the fact. What I would ask is this, is it that you are not clear or is it that the information is downloading so fast? It's so fast that you think it's not clear.

So I would invite you to ask when you are dealing with entities that are trying to communicate with you, and you are getting that weird, not clear thing that you are talking about ask, "Is the information down-loading fast?

Entities do not function from time and space like we do. Many times, they will download information so fast, you will be like "Whoa, what is that?" It'll feel very weird. What you can do is ask the entity to slow down and ask yourself to speed up. Over a period of time, if you continue to ask for those things to show up, they will. I have done just that myself because I thought I was very confused with entities and what they were trying to communicate to me and I realized it's because they were coming so fast. So I would say, *"Ok, slow down and what would it take for me to speed up so I can get this communication?"*

Have you ever experienced having more clarity about experiences 6 hours later? 8 hours later? 10 hours later? What I noticed for myself was I would have this interaction and I would feel confused about it and then I would go about my day and later on, I would have this "Oh, that's what that was!"

What if it's not that you are confused, what if it's just that the information is coming to you differently, in a different time, and space. Just be warned as you ask to be that speed you will, and then you will start to talk really fast, and you will then start to get very impatient with people around you, because you will speed up. Everybody else will seem like they are going so slow!

N: So could it even be like what I was experiencing today? We were out and we were actually going to this little spot in nature and we couldn't find it. I mean, we kept going round and round and round in that direction and then after that we moved away from that place and we were going to some other place which we must have gone 1001 times, and we still lost the way. That wouldn't be entities, right?

C: Hmmmm. Was it? I ask all the time, "Is this entities?' My awareness has started to move more to a knowing. There are also certain ways I've identified that I am aware of entities that I am familiar with. Awareness does shift and change, so as it expands, and as you claim, own and acknowledge more of what you be and what your awareness is, you have to use your questions again. So I'm always asking, "Ok, hang on, is this entities?" And sometimes I'm actually surprised by what it actually is. It's totally being in question all the time about what it is that I know and the ways in which I know it.

Question: "So when I look at shit or spit, etc. – things that come out of holes, something wants to go out and eat that. It started a few years back. I've done entity clearings millions of times in the ESB class. Dain has done all those too, but this is still there. One more thing, every time I look at knives, one vision or thought comes to mind – cutting the tongue with it. With needles though, it is how do I stitch the eyes or tongue."

C: Interesting. I would say – how many lifetimes have you practiced black magic?

And what if that's not wrong? Not to go into any sort of significance or seriousness or anything like that. Have you ever employed those methods to create change before in other lifetimes? And is it something you would choose now? If not, just POD POC everywhere you've chosen that in past lifetimes and ask what else is possible? I would also say too, a lot of times stuff like that shows up because you're choosing more awareness. If you were practicing black magic, would that be actually indicative of what you are actually capable of? Was that what was available in whatever culture you lived in at the time? So much of what we as humanoids have available to us, amazing possibilities and capacities, we have these things and then we get born into cultures that have really weird shit they do with them. We basically take our brilliance and we put it into these interesting boxes of 'This is what you do with it.'

My question would be what talents and capacities do you have with energy and entity awareness that you have not acknowledged because you have done weird shit with it in past lifetimes? And all that that is, will you un-create and destroy it all? Good and bad, right and wrong, all nine, POD and POC, shorts, boys and beyonds.

And again, what if it's not wrong, what if you are not bad and what would you like to choose this lifetime? If you start to ask those kinds of questions, then what will show up is what your talents, abilities and capacities are in their natural form, not in the ways in which you've had to deliver them in other cultures or lifetimes.

N: The other thing is – Did you have fun doing all that?

C: Exactly! We've all had really weird, bizarre lifetimes where we've done some interesting shit and what if it's ok? Would we choose that this lifetime and what else is possible? Obviously, you have a talent, ability and capacity. What is it? And start to discover and explore what it actually is and ask questions like "Ok, how can I use it to my advantage this lifetime, in this space that I'm in, in this body I've chosen?" You know, because we are all creating our lives.

I do think it's an interesting question, Nilofer, because I think this is one of the reasons why people refuse their awareness a lot, a lot. They start to get whiffs and insight into what they did with their talent, ability and capacity in other lifetimes and sometimes, it is weird shit. And so you think, "Oh god, I can't. I'm not going to claim, own and acknowledge that I can do that, because I don't want to do what I did that lifetime." But what if you could have the ability and the talent and the possibility and the capacity and you can do something totally different with it?

Something that actually worked for you?

N: Absolutely. It's so wonderful to have that freedom finally.

C: I'm out there doing Talk to the Entities classes and I could perceive everybody going "What the hell is she doing? What is she talking about? This is weird." People do have points of view about being able to talk to the spirit world and being aware of the spirit world. It was like coming out of the closet, a very strange closet. So I chose to practice the elements of intimacy. Honoring myself what it is that I knew. Not divorcing parts of myself based on other people being uncomfortable with what I was claiming, owning and acknowledging. Trusting what I know even if no one else on the planet agrees with me. The willingness to be vulnerable and put my barriers down even when people were projecting thoughts like "What are you doing, you can't talk about that". Having gratitude for what I was willing to be aware of this lifetime and step into. I am still aware many people have questions about what I'm doing and I find myself thinking "Oh, I don't know if I should talk to this person about this!"

I have a funny story about my husband's grandmother, who is kind of a straight-shooter. She shoots from the hip all the time and I'm all over the face book with what I do, so it's not like I'm keeping a secret. I don't directly talk to people about it, that are uncomfortable because there's really nothing that gets created by that. One day she said to me, "So I hear you are talking to ghosts these days." I had this moment of like "oh my god, I don't know what to say to her", you know, because I wasn't sure if she was going to be supportive or not supportive or what. I didn't know. And she goes, "I think I'm interested in that. I think I'd like to have a session with you" and I was floored! I was like "oh my god! Ok, how does it get better than that?"

That muscle continues to be cultivated to claim, own and acknowledge what it is that I know, even with this weird subject that not very many people are open to talking about or they talk to you about it in real hushed tones. People have really interesting and very polarized points of view about the spirit world. Is that ok to be aware of it? In many religions, it's not ok. Why is it not ok to be aware of the spirit world? Well if you were able to talk to your grandma who has passed away. If that created a different perspective on what happens when you die, would the religions have as much control? Being willing to claim this has been a huge stepping into the elements of intimacy for me.

N: Wow. Wow. That's so amazing. Most people judge how other people are going to receive it, but if you lower your barriers, you are just so pleasantly surprised sometimes.

C: Right? Yeah. I recently had an interesting experience where I had to ask a family member to assist me with setting up an email. That email was Cara@talktotheentities.com. He asked about the email and when I went on to explain it to him it felt difficult to find the words. What I have noticed is that when someone can't receive what it is I am doing I never can find the words. So I asked myself, What can he receive? So I said "Oh, you know, it's like business entity, which is true. And it's more than that, but that's what he could receive. I do work with business entities and that made sense to him. He was fine with that. The tool of being aware of what people can receive and not giving them more than that, and never making yourself wrong, creates so much ease. I didn't make myself wrong because I couldn't tell him what I was doing and I didn't disallow what I am doing because he couldn't hear it because I just basically told him what he could receive. It worked.

N: Can I ask you a question?

C: Absolutely.

N: So you wouldn't be by any chance be putting a kind of forgetting spell on him, would you?

C: Ha! More like I said the words required for him to be ease with whatever I said.

N: How does it? Ok, so talk about business. I have a really cool question.

C: Yeah?

N: "So what questions can I ask to the entities to contribute to me with finances? I would like to take all of Shannon's classes. I would like to ask the entities to contribute to pay for them. So what questions can I ask?

C: Ok, so what I would definitely start with are you actually willing to receive it? Start with un-creating and destroying all your projections, expectations, rejections, separations, conclusions, and judgments of what it looks like when entities contribute to you. Would you be willing for it to show up in a totally different way? Also are you asking? If you find yourself facilitating entities and find that entities are coming to you and wanting information, ask to be compensated.

When I am aware of an entity that is requiring assistance with communicating with someone I always ask, "Do I know that person?" No? "Alright, if you want me to facilitate this, bring them to me with money in hand."

– 421 –

It is about getting super-practical about how you ask for it. I think some of us think we have to ask for the receiving of some sort of financial contribution some specific particular way. What if you asked very practically what would it take for the money to show up with total ease? When you have a willingness to receive from entities it can be as easy as "ok, pay me now" or "hey, if you want me to go to that class, I could use a little contribution."

What are your points of view with the spirit world? It is important to be aware of this when asking for their contribution. Do you think entities are more aware, more knowing, more powerful than you? If that is a yes, it is important to un-create and destroy all of that. When you work with, facilitate with, receive from entities its important that you know that they are not more aware or powerful than you just because they are not in a body.

D: So I'm really new to Access and the tools and this is definitely a subject that I feel like both like attracted to and repulsed by.

C: Yes

D: I feel like I don't know what I'm clearing. Am I clearing good stuff? I had heard maybe a month ago Blossom Benedict had run a clearing on entities and I'd only listened to it once, but somehow it must have really stuck with me because I had a dream 2 nights ago and in my dream. I was in a house that was built over a graveyard and the house was filled with spirits and there were all these people living in the house but they were really depressed and unhappy. I said, "of course, you are depressed and unhappy, You are living in a really haunted place." So all of a sudden in my dream, I started doing the entity clearing, like to these beings, except when I tried to say the words, they were caught in my throat and I was like looking for a glass of water, like they couldn't come out. It was like I could feel, even in my dream, there was all this resistance to clear, even though I was like "oh I have this tool. Oh, I can help." And I thought "Well, what if I'm clearing nice beings, like an angel?" Like I feel all sorts of confusion.

C: *All the projections, expectations, rejections, separations, and judgments that you have of what entities are, what they aren't, what you can do and be with entities and what you can't do and be with entities, will you un-create and destroy all of that? Good and bad, right and wrong, all nine, POD and POC, shorts, boys and beyonds.*

Ok, so first how cool is it that you had that dream and my question is were the words required? When you were feeling like it was getting stuck in your throat, was it actually required that you have the words? Or were you being the energy of the clearing?

D: That's an interesting question. I've wanted to ask facilitators or someone can you just think the question? Yes, I guess you can think it and bring up the energy.

C: Right! Because you are dealing with energies and entities, so do you actually need the physical words? And did you actually clear them and you just aren't acknowledging it?

D: Yeah, well, in the end of the dream I was able to get the words out.

C: Cool, the other thing I just want to point out to you is, was that an actual dream or were you actually facilitating that?

D: It felt like I was facilitating that.

C: Ok, so, do you want to claim, own and acknowledge it now?

D: Yes, I didn't know I could, but yes.

C: *Everything that doesn't allow you to claim, own and acknowledge your talents, abilities and capacities with entities, will you un-create and destroy it all? Good and bad, right and wrong, all nine, POD and POC, shorts, boys and beyonds.*

Ok, anything shift?

C: Yes, sometimes it's the refusal of what we are being that actually creates that sense of limitation. You could clear everywhere you are refusing it, and refer to this call a lot. Facilitating can be done without any spoken words. I don't go around speaking out loud to the energies that I'm aware of that nobody else can see.

It is interesting to note that people who have mental illness, people who talk to themselves, like they are not actually talking to themselves. What if they are not actually mentally ill? What if they have a level of awareness with entities that is extraordinary and that's what they are doing.

So it goes back to the ways in which you are aware of entities. What are the ways in which you are aware of them and how are you facilitating entities and energy. We all facilitate – like we all have different ways in which we facilitate entities.

The entity clearing isn't about sending them away. When you do an entity clearing, which is, "Truth, who are you? Truth, who were you before that?" Is that what Blossom did?

D: Yeah

C: Ok. So an entity clearing is basically – and this is great for everybody on this call to know. "Truth, who are you? Truth, who were you before that? And truth, who will you be in the future?" Basically what you are doing is you are putting your attention on the entity and you are giving them the awareness that they have a different choice. You are not actually sending them away from a point of view that they are bad or wrong, or they are good and correct. You are just saying, "hey! You know you have a different choice?" There are a lot of entities roaming around his planet that don't realize they are not in bodies. They don't realize they have a different choice and so you are basically just giving them a choice and they can choose to go wherever they go and it's not up to you. Does that feel better and clearer to do an entity clearing now, knowing that information?

D: Yes

C: So the basic entity clearing is practical and pragmatic and anyone can do it. There is another thing that stops a lot of people from choosing this work is that they feel like if they choose this work, they will forever have to clear entities. You don't have to clear all the entities. You can just be aware of them. You don't have to do anything with them. Just because you know how to clear them doesn't mean it's your job to clear the whole planet of entities.

It can be a total contribution to clear them and sometimes, to not clear them. You can just ask, "Is this generative or non-generative? Is this energy that I'm aware of something that'll contribute and generate more for me or less?" and you can choose based on that whether or not you clear them or not. And also too – it's their choice. You can run an entity clearing and not have the entities clear. So, everyone has choice in that whole regard. As you acknowledge your talents, abilities and capacities here they'll grow, they'll expand and you'll get more confident.

D: So I have a really close connection with Hawaii and I go back and forth. I live on Mainland America and I'm about to go back because the last time I went, I was in Hawaii, which is a really ancient island.

C: Yes, I've been there. I get it.

D: Well, I felt like my awareness of entities there was so huge that I literally felt like I got chased off the island. Like I was supposed to stay for longer and I left early and now I'm supposed to go for a month and I'm scared – like it feels like too much of awareness there. Like overwhelming, and there's a lot of superstition, you know.

C: So you can definitely use the entity clearing to your advantage.

D: Ok

C: The other thing is – are you actually scared or are you excited?

D: Yeah, there's definitely excitement there too. Yeah.

C: Fear is basically something that we use to bastardize and cover up our potency.

D: Yeah

C: *What talent, ability, capacity do you have that you can now claim, own and acknowledge that if you claimed, owned and acknowledged it would make going back to Hawaii more ease for you? Everything that doesn't allow that will you un-create and destroy it all. Good and bad, right and wrong, all nine, POD and POC, shorts, boys and beyonds.*

Hawaiian Islands are very potent and full of entity activity. I totally get what you are talking about. I visited Hawaii some years ago before I had Access and Talk to the Entities tools. I had a panic attack after panic attack and I couldn't breathe. I thought something was totally wrong with me. I basically occurred through my whole vacation. I just went back there in October and the same sensation that occurred in my body then occurred this time, but I just knew to ask, "Is this entities?" And it completely shifted and changed the whole thing. What if what you are aware of isn't scary? For what reason would you let entities chase you away? And let me ask you this, you can start playing with this question – were they actually attempting to assist and contribute to you and you had your barriers up, and you were afraid they were scary?

This is speaking to another element of intimacy – vulnerability. What if you pushed your barriers down no matter what, even if the entities you perceive after you keep your barriers down feel scary to you, what if that's just an interesting point of view, you have that point of view, and you can just be present in the face of a really intense energy? What if there is no such thing as good or bad? Or right or wrong entities? Would you be more comfortable there?

D: Yes

C: What if you could look forward to the trip like "oh my gosh, I'm going to play with what I know about myself now!"

D: Yeah. There's definitely still like physical remnants of that. Physical panic of last time, because when you were describing – I was there in October. That's exactly when I was there, and I was feeling all those feelings and there were moments like – yeah, I love the possibility that you are presenting because that would be a very pleasant experience.

C: What if you acknowledge that it is entity awareness? When you are feeling that, go *"Ok, truth, is this entity awareness? Body, what are you telling me?"* and when you start to acknowledge that it's awareness, that it's not a problem, those symptoms will start to dissipate. Maybe not completely gone but better. It is your body giving you information and when you receive that info instead of the sensations you perceive escalating, they will be able to dissipate and be manageable. Acknowledge that it's awareness and that your body is more willing to be aware in those 10 seconds than you are. How does it get better than that? And what else is possible?

The basic tools of Access Consciousness work wonders in assisting you in intense situations. How does it get better than this? What else is possible? I also would love to add this clearing to these.

What energy, space and consciousness can me and my body be to shift, change and transform all entities and energies with total ease? And everything that doesn't allow that, Good and bad, right and wrong, all nine, POD and POC, shorts, boys and beyonds.

So use that one when you go back, and you'll have to email me and tell me how it goes because I will be dying to know.

D: Cool. Thank you so much.

N: Thank you. That was awesome. You know, I have something to say about that clearing that you just gave. I just feel like I have so many entities show up who wanted me to facilitate them to a different possibility. I had to physically, actually put some time to do it. Then I started running this clearing and now it's really rare that I have to actually do it, as in consciously do it. It just happens.

C: I know!

N: It's brought so much ease.

C: Isn't it awesome? You start to be the energy of the clearing and how does it get better than that?

N: Wow. Wow. Yeah, totally awesome.

N: "So after doing the Talk to the Entities class, I've always perceived entities and never seen them. I therefore, always look for a confirmation of some kind. I'm always being in question and the question is always.. Can I really facilitate the entity or entities? So what would it take for me to be always clear about my capacity and potency? Can you help?"

C: *Everywhere you've decided and concluded that you have to see them to be aware of them, will you un-create and destroy all of that shit right now? And everything that doesn't allow that, Good and bad, right and wrong, all nine, POD and POC, shorts, boys and beyonds.*

That is exactly why I didn't think I was aware of entities. I don't see them with my eyes either. I've seen them out of the corner of my eye, but if I ever put my attention directly on them, I don't see them. There are people that do see them. That is just a way in which they perceive them. Un-create and destroy all your decisions, conclusions and judgments of what entity awareness is and what it isn't, a lot, a lot, a lot. Then start to ask, what are the ways in which I'm aware of them. When you have an awareness of entities, stop thinking you are full of shit, and acknowledge it!

What if you are not full of shit? *What if you went "oh, I'm that kind of aware" and just moved on? What else is possible? What would change, shift, grow, contribute to you if you acknowledged how you are aware of things and didn't just assume it's bull?* That's what so many of us do. We take the ways in which we are aware of the spirit world and we bastardise it and don't acknowledge it, just because it's not how everyone else is aware. I totally get it and you can recover from that, because I did.

N: Also you can clear distractor implants of doubt.

C: Yes! Thank you, Nilofer. How does it get better?

N: How does it get any better?

C: It's interesting too, because Shannon O'Hara always talks about how she thinks it's funny when people say, "well, I can't see them" and that people actually want to see them. I asked her that question in my Beginning class. I asked, "I don't see them. Does that mean I'm not aware?" I'll never forget what she said. "Look, I don't understand why people want to see them," she said, "It's very fucking startling to have one just sitting on your couch and you walk into your living room! It will startle you out of your body half of the time."

All the lifetimes that you did see entities and it freaked you out so dy-namically that you are still unwilling to see them, will you un-create and destroy it all? Good and bad, right and wrong, all nine, POD and POC, shorts, boys and beyonds.

And I mean, I run that a lot and you know, I know at some point I will be able to start to see them and I'm ok if I don't. I'm ok in the ways in which I'm aware of things and what else is possible?

N: Wow, wow. Ok. I have this question, I'm not sure I exactly under-stand what she's saying, but let's go. – "I'm wondering if you've done entity clearings, do you not have access to the contribution of entities anymore? Would you generally wish to clear demons though?"

C: Ok, so first of all, you could clear, clear, clear, clear, clear entities which is basically the entity clearings as we use them in Access. Remember what you are doing is just giving them choice. Clearing them doesn't necessarily mean you won't receive contribution from them.

Sometimes, clearing an entity is a huge contribution to them and when they go, they contribute to you. There are also beings of light, your team mates and more, that are here just waiting to be invited to contribute to you in your life. They are just waiting for you to ask. They don't interfere in your life. They are basically on your team and you've got to call them off the bench.

Doing clearings doesn't mean you will clear them all. You know what I mean?

Now, if you ask the question, "Is this demons?" And you get a yes, it feels light and expansive. Look at the energy is it creating a disruption for you? Then absolutely, do a demon clearing. And the demon clearing is "Return to from whence you came, never to return to me, my body, this reality ever again". Dealing with demons is one of those things that could be a bit tricky. Just run the demon clearing and just keep running it, running it, and it will clear a lot and create a lot of space for you.

All of this is to move all of us into a space where we can have choice. What the Access Consciousness® and the Talk to the Entities® tools are about is creating spaces where people can choose and create their lives from choice. That includes the spirit world.

Demons are entities that have been given jobs. A lot of times they have been given jobs to hide consciousness, to basically project out into the world anti-consciousness and unconsciousness. Clearing demons can be a huge contribution and if that's what it is and if that's what's showing up, go for it!

N: "Can entities ever hurt you? Is that only from your choice and decisions, conclusions, projections and judgments?"

C: Truth, can entities ever hurt you? Is that your point of view or is that something you've picked up from this reality? Is this reality full of projected points of view that dissuade you form ever claiming, owning and acknowledging what you are aware of. How much that is Hollywood or Religion and whatever else being perpetrated out there into the Universe? Remember just because beings don't have bodies does not mean they are more powerful than you, does not mean they are more aware than you and does not mean that they know more than you.

Everything that doesn't allow you to be the dominant entity for all eternity in your life and beyond, un-create and destroy it all. Good and bad, right and wrong, all nine, POD and POC, shorts, boys and beyonds.

You will find people who basically allow entities to mess with them. If you actually look at the specific instances many are actually people that are allowing entities to be destructive in their lives and it is creating something for them. People who choose victim are the people who chose it to have more control of others around them.

So, if you are willing to be the dominant entity and if you are not functioning from "beings out of bodies are stronger than you, are more dynamic than you, are more aware than you" and all of those things, then no, they can't hurt you.

N: Can I say something here?

C: Yeah, absolutely.

N: A few years ago, even before I came to Access, I always was aware of entities. I met this woman and had told her that I was shit scared of entities, and she told me her choice to choose something different. She said on one fine day I chose, "no more, no more. I'm not going to be scared of entities anymore." And from that day onwards, I've never been scared on entities" and I looked at her and I went, you know, "I'm having that."

C: Yes. It's a choice.

N: Absolutely, it's just a choice.

N: So, awesome. Ok, let me take one last question and then we will wind up.

N: "So what if someone asks you to clear the entities and you do and close the portal but they seem to attract them again and again. What would you do in a situation like this?"

C: Well, ask are they really wanting to clear them? Or are they trying to control you with their entity insanity? The thing about portals is that they can be tricky. If somebody is a portal or has portals in their Universe and they don't choose to close them they won't. Basically portals are places where energies come and go from. There are people that are portals, places and things that are portals. The person that you are working with has to choose to change this.

Again, a lot of people use this weird entity insanity and dysfunction with entities to control the people around them. So you want to look at the situation, who you are working and what they are choosing. When you go into the wrongness that you are doing something incorrect and that us why it is not changing it locks you up and them.

Again look at the person that you are working with and ask do they actually want this to change? And if you get a no, that's cool, how does it get better? Choosing to be aware of entities, choosing to do the Talk to the Entities classes or working with people with these entity clearings doesn't mean that it's your job to clear all the entities on the planet. It's not your job to get rid of all the entities in your client's world either. That is their choice. You are just moving them into a choice place. If they don't choose it that has nothing to do with what you are doing, and everything to do with their choice. Sometimes it takes people a long, long time to get ready to change that and how does it get better

What if nothing was a problem? If they keep coming back and they pay you to close the portals and clear the entities and they have to see you more because they keep opening it, how does it get better than that?

N: How does it get better than that?

C: They'll choose something different or they won't. It's not a reflection of you or even relevant to you. So, there you go.

N: Oh that was brilliant. Cara, I'm so grateful. I mean, you have just opened up – I think you've just blasted this whole doorway to a totally different possibility with entities here.

C: Oh, thank you! I'm so excited.

The Place. A Novel by Gary M. Douglas

As Jake Rayne travels through Idahaho in his classic '57 Thunderbird, a devastating accident is the catalyst for a journey he isn't expecting. Alone in the deep forest, with his body battered and broken, Jake calss out for help. And the help he finds changes not only his life but his whole reality. Jake is opened up to awareness' of possibilities. Possibilities that we have always known should be, but have not shown up. Are you willing to have a world where language is not a barrier and people communicate telepathically, where the ability to heal and nurture one another is not limited to the qualified few? Author Gary Douglas is.

http://bit.ly/2dnjbiw

CHAPTER TWENTY ONE

❖

A DIFFERENT CONVERSATION: GOING BEYOND LABELS

By Delany Delaney and Glen Sheppard

Delany Delaney

Change Catalyst, Facilitator, Leader, Song Writer/Composer & Speaker Glen Sheppard Author, Songwriter/Composer, Facilitator, Exploder of Limitations

ilofer: So hi everyone and welcome to another show. We have with us today the really, really, really special guests Delany Delaney and Glen Shepard. Hi Delany! Hi Glen!

Delany: Hi Nilofer.

N: Wow, I'm so excited about this call.

G: Thank you Nilofer. "And I know we are both excited. Firstly let's tell people what's going on. We have a Facilitated Communication board that is styled on how a computer keyboard looks. I tap on the letters and Delany is speaking my words.

I might get Delany to introduce me because she knows me pretty well. "

N: I'm not very good at introductions, so Delany is going to be speaking for Glen and Delany is going to be speaking for Delany. How does it get any better than that? And there's possibility of actually tapping into the energy of Glen and tapping into the energy of Delany. So go for it, Delany, introduce Glen to us.

D: Yes, I will. There's a space that's created with both of us that's really very yummy so everyone's invited to tap into that too. Glen is a pretty unique dude, he has high-level autism. When he was born, his mum was advised that she should lock him up in an institution, that he'd never walk and never really be able to do much of anything, and she did not agree with that. Pam is a pretty amazing woman, she wanted to make sure that Glen could walk and move around, and he does.

When Glen was 16, he was introduced to Facilitated Communication and that was when the world opened up to him and he could communicate with his mother for the very first time. Before that, she would talk with him but he couldn't communicate back with her.

Glen is a published author. As well as a book of poems, he's also written a murder mystery. It's fantastic and gives you a real insight into what it's like for people who do have high level of autism. So Glen uses a board to communicate and then way beyond that. He has a wicked sense of humour.

He is 5 units off completing a university degree. This person who was supposed to be just locked away has completed 19 units of university degree of which 16 were in creative writing. This year, he's actually studying global history and last semester, he actually got a Distinction and High Distinction for his assignments.

Glen also has a Down's syndrome chromosome in there as well, which just cracks me up because he just defies all logic and defies what this reality puts forward as what people with Autism and Down's syndrome are supposed to be able to do.

D: Yeah, he's sitting here grinning with that. (laughs) So it's a very unique thing. Now I'm going to allow him to introduce me. He's already laughing about that – so he's going to say what he thinks should be a good introduction for me. Would that be right?

G: *Delany is pretty unique herself.* D: I do find it a bit of a challenge when he is talking specifically about

me.

G: *She has the ability and the willingness to have her barriers down enough that makes so much unique communication possible. Many of us have the ability to communicate telepathically or even beyond that. How many of us have energy as our first language? What's something unique about Delany is that she has the courage to allow people like me to see or perceive everything that is her. Thank you.*

D: I've had an ability for most of my life to perceive what's beyond what people labeled with a disability are able to contribute. There was a young man who I worked with many years ago, who only had control of the movement of his eyes. He couldn't speak, and he fed through a tube in his stomach. He was so beautiful, and when you were present with him, what he gifted you was a sense of space and peace and joy that was really unique. It really surprised me because when you are willing to be present like that with somebody, you actually get to see way past all their disabilities. You perceive and know that they actually contribute so much, and that they actually know what's going on around them way more than most people give them credit for.

I would see and hear things, mean things or rude things, being said about people with 'high support needs', and it was quite devastating. I knew that they could hear and understand everything that was being said about them, and so, that began my journey in the world of people with unique abilities. That's what I'm always saying, that people labeled disabled have unique abilities and capacities. In fact, some of the things we spend lots of money on trying to find, like joy, allowance, peace - many of them they actually innately be it. If people would be willing to receive it, what contribution would it be?

N: So can you talk more about that Glen?

G: *Talk... Well, to me, Nilofer, it is the reality that so much of this reality passes me by. It's challenged by what I present. It's challenged by the way I move through the world, and by the requirements I have for care. It's funny, isn't it? So many people and so many areas of society actually operate from the deficit, from the glass that is half empty. What we are doing with what we are creating is stepping into a space where this can be challenged in a way that hasn't been challenged before. You see, there've been many people working to create change in the world. Many people that have challenged the mainstream of society about what is disability. Where we are coming from is in some way completely different. We don't want to fight anymore.*

How Do You See This World?

G: *Good question, Nilofer. I see it very differently to you. I fall into spaces and cracks, and colors and sounds and movements so I don't walk through the world in the way that you do. I can be trapped in a crack in the ground and for me that becomes all encompassing. I go into a whole other reality through that crack in the ground. Then when people are trying to get me to interact with them, it takes a huge amount of energy for me to break out of there. Sometimes I'm very grateful for the assistance of people in pulling me out of there. I don't necessarily always want to fall into those spaces. Does that make any sense?*

N: Are those spaces where we are actually not contribut- ing to the Earth but destroying the Earth? Is that what you are aware of in those spaces? Some of them, that is.

G: *That is a very good question, Nilofer. I'm very grateful for that question. And yes, you are correct, you have just assisted me to see something that happens to me.*

N: I'm wondering, Glen, if you could see that, could you also see a different possibility which is available to the Earth? **What capacity do you have to create a sustainable Earth for the next 10,000 years?**

D: That's a really interesting point, Nilofer. I've been aware for a number of years of the possibilities for people with these unique capacities to contribute to healing and generating the Earth. I'm not sure what that looks like, though I do know I've seen things like people being able to contribute to how plants and trees grow, and how food is produced, and the regeneration of denuded soils in areas. So that's a really interesting point. Glen, what have you got to say?

G: *This is so very true. I know that there are so many areas of growth and consciousness that we can contribute to. It's interesting with the planet and the land. I get that there is some kind of catalyst effect and that there is a need for people like myself to connect with other people in doing this. It's not that I can't or don't contribute when I'm on my own but there is something about connecting with somebody or with groups of people that allows me to step into a way of working energetically that doesn't necessarily happen when I'm on my own (or certainly not in the same way.) What I'm aware of since Delany and I have been doing these classes is that it is the interaction with her that allows me - and not just her, everybody in the room - that allows me to expand and be the greatest contribution I can be. Does that make sense?*

Phantasm

N: So Glen and Delany, both of you, are you phantasms?

D: (laughs) Totally! Yes, we are.

N: A phantasm, as defined by Gary Douglas, is a djinn, a genie, a witch, a wizard, this creature of magic which creates life. I actually have had to listen to this so many times before I'm starting to get what is a phantasm. When you be the phantasm, and you interact with other people, are you then showing them the energy of the phantasm they be?

D: That's definitely true. Glen? We had a strong experience of that when we co-facilitated the Certified Facilitator's class for Access Consciousness in December 2014. The people in that room - pretty well most of them - were able to tap into the space that we were being and it expanded their realities. From what people said, they were able to tap into parts of themselves that they previously had not been able to tap into. There were people in that class that said they had acknowledged aspects of themselves that they had never been willing to acknowledge before, and it is continuing on. There are people who say they actually communicate with Glen long-distance quite regularly from all over the world. Someone described it as becoming aware of all their barriers rising up and judgments that they actually didn't realize they had, and then they watched them melt away, it was impossible to hold on to them in that space.

G: *What I see when we are facilitating these classes, is that people can walk in with – as an analogy – 3 meter thick steel walls, and they actually can't keep them there. It is not about forcing anything, it's an energy that we are willing to be that's creating the space that just seems to melt people, which is wonderful and a lot of fun.*

What Can You Gift Us That We Haven't Even Considered Today?

D & G: *I'd like you all to now close your eyes, allow your being to expand out to as big as it can be, and push down all your barriers. And if you would be willing to, pull our energy as we are pulling yours, and let's play with those molecules of judgment. All the places where you have judged what a disability is, judged yourself in relation to that, judged how you judge, and anywhere that you can see a molecule that you can change, would you be willing to change it? And destroy and un-create everywhere that you have made those judgments real. Would you be will- ing to do that? Right and wrong, good and bad, POC and POD, all nine, shorts, boys and beyonds.*

And now keep looking for those molecules of judgment and turn them and turn them again, knowing all the while that it's not real, knowing all the while that you being willing to be you, to be present and not be in judgment, will allow you to receive the space that I be, the space that De-lany be, and what we be together. What will it take for you to allow yourself to know what it is that you came here to contribute? And what will it take for you to allow yourself to know what it is that you know about people with unique abilities and capacities? You are one of them, so why would you separate? There is no need for us to be separate. We are all in this together. It's way easier and it's certainly way more fun. I know that for some people that have been in classes with us, they recall the energy and the space that was created there and that allows them a peace and a space of creation in their day. For me, that's such a gift. And Nilofer, what do you know? What do you know about people with so-call disabilities?

N: I know a lot. I'm so aware of it when I'm with you guys. And what if you were to not make disabilities significant?

D: What would that create? *Let's destroy and un-create everywhere that it has been made so significant and where disability has been made like a cross to bear. It's something that you have to stoically go through. So everything that is, let's destroy and un-create it, times a godzillion. Right and wrong, good and bad, POC and POD, all nine, shorts, boys and beyonds.*

N: *Everywhere that you are so aware of that, will you destroy and un--create it? And everywhere you are buying into it, will you destroy and un-create that? Right and wrong, good and bad, POC and POD, all nine, shorts, boys and beyonds.*

N: When Gary talks about little kids, he talks about them as infinite beings in little bodies. These amazing people, they are infinite beings in bodies, no matter what size the body is.

D: There's something, Nilofer, where people with so-called disabilities themselves actually perpetuate the myths.

N: Glen, do they actually perpetuate the myths or are they so aware of the judgment being directed at them that they buy into those judgments?

Everything that is, will you please destroy and un-create it all? And return it all back to all the senders through all time, space, dimensions, realities. And all the oaths, vows, fealties, comealties, swearings, bindings, bondings, contracts, you have – Oh, have you created that? (laughs)

D: (laughs) You should see the grin on his face!

N: Oh, I got the energy of it. *Everywhere you've created that, and you sold it to everyone, will you now revoke, recant, rescind, reclaim, renounce, denounce, destroy and un-create it all? And return it all back to sender with consciousness attached? Right and wrong, good and bad, POC and POD, all nine, shorts, boys and beyonds.*

G: *Well, the cat's out of the bag now.* (laughs)

Q: The state that Glen functions in, is that similar to the space we can function from as healers and body workers, as well as just be in?

G: *Yes definitely.*

D: We've worked on people together and thanks to a question we became aware that Glen was really amplifying my capabilities and my capacity with bodies. I get that there is that space and if we tap into that more, if we are willing we are not alone in this, that we really are in it together.

G: *You are so aware, and you already know this space. You already operate in this space. So my question is, "What can we be and do to expand this space? What contribution can we be to each other to create healing beyond what we've ever been willing to create as healing before? And so everything that is, would you like to destroy and un-create it all?* Times a godzillion. Right and wrong, good and bad, POC and POD, all nine, shorts, boys and beyonds.

Q: Would you please assist me with my body? It is a disease and no matter how many body processes I have done and I even went to get a SOP session, it has not changed or cured. I have been asking "how does it get any better than this?" and "what else is possible" and a lot more "who does this belong to?" Please help change this. I cannot live my life suffering like this. I was diagnosed with auto-immune PCOD, uterine fibroids, thyroid and a lot more around 8-10 years ago. I was not given any medicine for that, only for thyroid, so I'm not on any medication. I cannot even name the suffering. It started 3 years ago and I have done everything I could."

D: I'm wondering what it is you are unwilling to receive from yourself and the planet. Do you communicate with the planet? Do you contribute and receive from the planet?

What Is It To Be A Healer?

D: If we could look at what it is to be a healer and what does that mean. I've come to know for me that healing is different to what I thought it was, or maybe the word 'healing' and what that means in our reality is not what I get that is required now. I'm really grateful for that lady's question. For me, it really is about what we are willing to receive of ourselves, as well as from others. And there is an innate connection to the planet and the plants and the trees and the air and the sea, that is essential to engage with, particularly at this time.

G: *The planet is in such dire need and it's quite funny, I'm not the kind of person who goes and sits around in nature all the time, but I'm aware of it and I'm connected to it. I wonder what it is that we can be to create the change on this planet that is required for it to continue it's beautiful rolling journey through the cosmos.*

D: It's a living, breathing, entity with which we can commune more than most of us do. Even those of you who are aware of the planet and do connect with it, how many minutes out of every day are you totally present with that? Less than 3? Less than 50? Less than 300 minutes? Less than 4 hours? Less than 12?

I ask, what will it take for us to have the planet in our awareness 24/7? To have that level of communion or that space of communion all the time? What then will we create? What then will we create in relation to bodies and self and this concept of healing? I know that Gary Douglas talks a lot about this energy in his book 'The Place.' What if we are all willing to be the phantasm and create that on Earth? What will that take? And would we be willing to destroy and un-create everything that that is, times a godzillion? Right and wrong, good and bad, POC and POD, all nine, shorts, boys and beyonds.

N: I know we are aware of the planet 24/7. We are just not present to it. So every time you have something show up in your body, is it the planet communicating with you? So what if instead of going "Oh my god, I have this pain in my stomach", you go *"I wonder what my body is aware of? I wonder what the planet is communicating with me?"*

G: *Yes*

N: It is there 24/7 and the intensity of awareness that is showing up 24/7 and instead of asking a question, we go to this conclusion about disease and pain, what have you there.

G: *You know, Nilofer, this is very interesting. I came into this body, I chose this body, I created this body that is not easy to get through this reality in. I am often at war with it, or it can feel like war. Or is that just a projection?*

N: If you were not to define it as war, what would it be? G: *It's a challenge.* N: If you were not to define it as challenge, what would it be? G: *"Just the body that I've chosen."*

N: And even beyond that, is it just an energy? So I wonder, Glen, do you have any barriers for your body? And would you be willing to lower those?

G: *"Yes"* N: And how many barriers are you aware of that people have to their body? And how much awareness is your body giving you about other people's bodies? Wow! (laughs)

G: *Obviously, a lot. (laughs)* N: Oh my goodness.

G: *"I am an awareness unit. (laughs) I operate in even more than one space."*

N: Yes, so I wonder what would it take for you to have ease with that awareness?

G: *"You know, it's very interesting, the more that I am able to facilitate classes, the more that I have been in communication with people – and it has come from many people within Access – the more ease I have, and the happier I am."*

N: And how many other infinite doorways to ease do you have that you are not acknowledging?

G: *"Apparently many. You see, we don't talk about this. We don't have these conversations with people who operate similar to me. It's all about managing behaviour."*

N: Yeah! So what if you could have these conversations, Glen? G: *"Well, we are right now, thanks to you, Nilofer."* N: Do you perceive your body as a jail? G: *"In some aspects, yes."*

N: And how many people have projected that at you? G: *"Most of the planet. Most of anyone who sees me. Even when they see*

a photo."

N: *Would you be willing to destroy and un-create it all please? And re-turn it all back to sender with consciousness attached. All the projec-tions, expectations, separations, rejections and judgments that people have about you, about what autism is like, what Down's syndrome is like, what so-called disability is like, what handicap is like, everything that is, and all the oaths, vows, fealties, comealties, swearings, bindings, bondings, contracts you have to keep any and all of that in place, will you now revoke, recant, rescind, reclaim, renounce, denounce, destroy and un-create it all? Right and wrong, good and bad, POC and POD, all nine, shorts, boys and beyonds.*

I saw this video on Facebook three days ago and it just brings me to tears to even talk about it. There's this amazing being and she was born without two legs, and her birth parents just left her. There was this family who saw that piece of news on TV and they said, "You know what, we don't want this little baby to be alone" and they went and adopted the baby, and the only thing they brought her up on was "There is no 'I can't' in your Universe. You can do everything! And this little girl who had no legs, she went on to do sports like – I don't remember the term – it's like a type of gymnastics, you know, where you jump up and down on a trampoline. She was the state champion of Illinois. She went on to play basketball and now she is in her 30s, and she's a gymnast. She's a performer in Hollywood. That video is amazing. You cannot look at that video and call that woman handicapped or disabled or any of those labels.

D: Exactly.

N: *How many of you have bought into this lie that you are handicapped or disabled? Everything that is, will you now destroy and un-create it all? And return it all back to sender with consciousness attached? Right and wrong, good and bad, POC and POD, all nine, shorts, boys and beyonds.*

And can we all do 1-2-3, 1-2-3-4 on destroying these labels of 'disabled' and 'handicapped' and 'ADD' and 'ADHD' and 'autism' and all of that. Let's do a 1-2-3 on that first. Ok? 1-2-3. 1-2-3. 1-2-3. And now let's create a totally new reality with all the amazing gifts and capacities that we be. 1-2-3-4. 1-2-3-4. 1-2-3-4.

Caller: "Thank you all of you for this breakthrough call. I have always felt restricted by political correctness with people who are different. I know as long as I can be the space, it will be a natural interaction, but I check against political correctness. Thank you for the freedom here. I am so grateful."

D: That's really great to hear, as it's a huge restriction that people put on themselves that they don't know how to communicate with people with so-called disabilities.

You don't have to like everything, nor do you have to feel at ease about everything. It's more about you being you and being present, and that's what the gift is. When you are so busy trying to be politically correct or however you want to term it, can you be authentically you? You can't be. And that's what makes the interactions uncomfortable or not fun because you are not being you. The most paramount thing for me is just be you and it all starts from there.

I don't really like it when there's a lot of dribble, excessive saliva. I don't have to like it. If it's there, I just get a cloth and I wipe it. My friend requires assistance, that's it.

N: Delany, the other thing is how much are you perceiving the things that have been projected on that being?

D: Yes. Absolutely.

N: I mean, when you talk about you not liking saliva, is it you not being comfortable with saliva or are you just aware of the projections on beings that people are not comfortable with saliva?

D: Probably way more that. N: And it's also your awareness of what their body requires.

"What if there is no such thing as disabled? What if it is more like differently-abled people? What if there is greater allowance?"

Possibilities

D: Well, there's so much that we'd like to create and I just would like to thank you, Nilofer, actually, not just for getting us on the show, also for creating a space where Glen actually got to ask some questions to himself and to explore something for him. Recently we were at after a meeting of the 'Brotherhood of the Wordless', all people with Autism who are writers. Believe me the 'wordless' is so untrue. They have so much to say. Anyway, afterwards a few of us had lunch and it dwindled down to just 3 of these young men with autism, and as a rare event they got to talk with each other. One of them has recently moved into his own place for the first time, and he talked about his feelings of abandonment, all the things that he's been going through. Glen was talking about things that made it easier for him and the other gentleman was also talking about his experiences. We realised that these guys have been going to The 'Brotherhood' for years and that was probably the first time they had sat around and actually had a conversation like that.

So when Glen was asking questions and you were asking him questions, that space of being included and having the possibility of asking questions and exploring more about how he can expand his own life, that is a great gift. And as his friend, I'm very grateful to you for that too.

D: We're excited as to where this can go and the space that's been created with this call has really opened up some other possibilities for both Glen and myself, as well as everybody out there and everyone who listens to this in the future.

"Let's keep the questions coming. Let's keep exploring this space where we stop using the word 'disability' in society and actually we start to see that everybody has something to contribute. So what contribution can we all be to changing the disabling judgment that runs rampant on planet Earth? What invitation can we be to ignite, inspire and engage people to join the discussion, to clear the blocks and limitations that we all have around disability, what it means and what people who are labelled disabled are here to contribute?

G: *"These are such exciting times that we live in and I look forward to interacting with you more, hearing more of what you have to say and I'm grateful for the questions that did come in."*

Q: "I have learnt so much from this conversation. Thank you so much. I'm wondering how to develop a way how to communicate without speech, how to communicate simply energetically. What are your insights?"

G: "*The space of expansion with no barriers is really a space that facilitates this and please know that what occurs when running Bars® is a space where you can expand your telepathic communication, your energetic communication. So just know that when you are running Bars®, all these things are there to access, and it's like what you said before, Nilofer, we have the awareness of the planet 24/7, we are just not present with it.*"

N: Can I share something which I have been playing around a lot with these days?

It's to do with the barriers, I will be walking and I'll go "ok, let me lower my barriers and let me receive from everything around me." And I will pass by a car which is parked in the parking lot and I will start to receive this energy from the car and then I will pass by a tree and I will start receiving energy from the tree. I'll start receiving energy from the road. I'll start receiving energy from the clouds. So is that communication?

G &D: (laughs) It sure is!

N: So what if you were to just play that game? "Ok, in these 10 minutes while I'm out for my walk, let me just lower my barriers and let me start receiving energy." You know, my husband is a photographer and they have a photography exhibition going on, so they had their opening night the other day and I was there and as I was passing by each photograph, I was lowering my barriers and I would receive this download of energy from the picture, which was quite amazing. I'm having so much fun with this game. (laughs)

D: Yes, and please be aware of how psychic you are. Recently, I've become aware that when I'm reading a Facebook post, I can actually pick up on judgments even when I'm reading a post and I'm not talking about the words, I'm talking about the energy that is there. I'd have a reaction and I was making myself very wrong, going "Geez! I'm judging that person!" but it wasn't making sense and I started to ask questions and then had this awareness of "oh my goodness, I'm actually able to perceive the judgment they have." So how psychic are we? (laughs)

N: And you are also able to perceive the projections that people are projecting at them as well.

D: Yes.

N: I will often look at a person and when I ask questions around judgments, I get a no for that but then I go "Is someone projecting this at them?" and then I get "wow, yes!" So I mean, you are aware of what people are projecting at someone else as well, and again, how psychic are we? (laughs)

N: So thank you so much, Glen and a huge, huge, huge hug to you and to Delany and a big hug to all our listeners who are listening to us live and in the future. Thank you so much everyone.

G &D: Yes Thank YOU all.

BOOKS BY NILOFER

http://www.nilofersbooks.com

CHAPTER TWENTY TWO

❖

WHAT IF WRITING A BOOK WAS A DOORWAY TO A DIFFERENT POSSIBILITY?

By Nilofer Safdar

Interviewer: Nirmala Raju

Nirmala: You have 4 best-selling books, number 1 on Amazon, isn't it?

Nilofer: Yes.

Nirmala: Wow. Amazing achievement. So tell us more about writing books, please.

Nilofer: So what do you know about writing books, I wonder? You wouldn't know anything about it, right?

How many books have you written? (laughs)

Nirmala: I've written 11 Tamil language books.

Nilofer: So you don't know anything about writing books?

Nirmala: Yes. I have little bit of experience on that but I haven't written anything in English yet. How did you get into writing? When did you start writing?

Nilofer: So, I actually wrote the book by not writing at all. (laughs)

Nirmala: Ok.

Nilofer: People think that you have to actually sit and write. What if you didn't have to write? Can you talk? And can you record while you are talking? So for example, you know, you and I, when we talk, we go to these spaces which are quite amazing. We have these conversations which will go in different directions, which we would not have been able to go to if we were, by ourselves. So you know, writing is that easy.

What if you were to get together with a friend and just start to record that conversation? And then get it transcribed?

Nirmala: Hmm. Really simple. Where did you get this idea? How did all this start?

Nilofer: (laughs) So do you remember you said how many people I have interviewed?

Nirmala: Yeah

Nilofer: I have interviewed more than a hundred people.

Nirmala: Yeah

Nilofer: So, guess what? All those interviews could be chapters in a book? All I have to do is get it transcribed, get it edited, and put it together in a book.

So how many tele-classes have you done?

Nirmala: Oh, I've done loads actually.

Nilofer: So I wonder how many books are hiding?

Nirmala: Wow. (laughs) I never thought about this until now. That's really interesting. How does it get any better than this?

Nilofer: How does it get any better than this?

Nirmala: So do you have all these series as books, Nilofer?

Nilofer: Not yet. But I'm creating. I'm creating some of them. I ask a lot of questions– "Is now the time? Would you like to be in the book?"

And some of them I'm compiling into a book. This book is a also compilation of a telesummit.

Nirmala: Are they all ebooks or did you print them?

Nilofer: Both ebooks and print books.

Now here's the thing, the writing part is really easy. It could be as easy as you having a conversation with a friend on a topic and you just recording it, getting it transcribed and then editing it. It could be as easy as that. So you have your books written down and then is the fun part – to get it published.

And you know what that has created for me? Getting my book published has been nothing short of magical. In Access Consciousness, we talk about judgments. We talk about judgments, we talk about receiving judgment, lowering your barriers and receiving judgments. So for me, writing a book and being a published author is like having a judgment which totally works to my advantage.

I'll just give you an example. When my book became number 1 on Amazon, I had posted it on Facebook. I was in a coffee morning with a few friends and one of them had seen my Facebook update about my book and she told me, "Hey Nilofer, congratulations!" and I said, "yeah, thank you" So everyone started asking her, "So what are you congratulating her for?" And she said, "Well, she wrote a book and she became a number 1 bestseller on Amazon." All of them went "Wow! So what did you write on? And can we have a copy of your book?" and I could see them all change. And these are people who've known me for 2-3 years and they think I'm pretty weird because of all the stuff that I'm doing.

So they started asking questions, "So what is your book about?" and I said, "It's about how you can change your money mind-set so that you can have more money in your life and all of them are "Wow, I'd like to have that. So can I have your book? Do you have copies with you?"

The other example was my husband belongs to a photography club, and the day after my book became number 1 on Amazon, he had a photography club meeting. So in the meeting, he shared with them, "My wife just had her book published on Amazon and she became a number 1 bestseller." Literally they spent their whole meeting talking about my book and being number one on Amazon. And they asked, "Can we have her come and give us a talk on how she did it and stuff like that?" So people have started to look at me differently.

Writing a book is not actually about making money from the sales of the book. You may end up making money from the sales of the book, you may not end up making money from the sales of the book. But writing a book is actually to establish yourself as this figure of authority or to get credence to what you are doing. So when people judge you to be an author or when people judge you to be a number one best-seller author, what happens is, it opens up these doors and these windows of possibility for you which otherwise would not have opened up for you.

Nirmala: That's amazing, Nilofer. You know, publishing a book may be a dream for many people and...

Nilofer: Yes, but most of them go to this space of "No, I can't write."

Nirmala: Absolutely. Yes.

Nilofer: They have already come to a conclusion of "No, I can't write." So my email went out to all these people and there are a lot of people who are on the call, but you know, a lot of people would have gone, "Oh, writing, I'm never going to do it. I'm not even going to be on the call." And the way I look at it is, what if every person were to write a book? I wonder how much their life would change?

I've been talking to a lot of people about writing books and I have a friend who works in a software company and she wants to get admission to the London School of MBA. In my conversation I told her, "Why don't you write a book about any topic which is to do with your business school? And can you imagine that when you apply to London

School of MBA, you send a printed copy of your book with your application. Do you think that would open any doors for you? What kind of credibility will you build?"

I was talking to an old family friend and he is now in his 50s, working in a company in a pretty good position there but what he would like now is to get more money in his position. So I gave him the same idea. I said, "Target some companies that you would like to work for and do a little bit of market research. Find out what is it that they require and take that topic. Once you write a book about it, you can send in your CV enclosing a copy of your printed book to them, and I wonder what that will create?"

Just a few days back, my cousin's son visited me in Abu Dhabi. Now this boy is just completing his engineering degree and he wants to go to the US to do his MS. So I told him, "why don't you write a book on a topic in engineering? And this is how you can apply with that book." So he said, "I don't know what to write."

I told him, "Why don't you go to 10 of your friends and tell them to give you 2 questions to do with that topic. And then what you can do is, you can sit down and either answer those questions yourself or else go to your professors and tell them to answer the questions. And you have your book ready." It was like a light bulb went off in his head and he looked at me and said, "You know what, there is a professor who has written a book and that book is really well known amongst the engineering circle, and that is exactly what he has done. So he created these questions and then he gave it to his students to solve and that has now become an engineering textbook."

Nirmala: Wow. How does it get any better than this? You should probably write a book for dummies.

Nilofer: How does it get any better?

Nirmala: How to write a book for dummies! (laughs) You know, you are definitely inspiring me. I'm sure many of the people who are going to be listening this and probably...

Nilofer: Yeah, it is that easy to write a book. It is that easy to write a book. If you can write down 20 questions about any topic, that is your book.

Nirmala: You know what, you are definitely inspiring. I'm going to share my story, why I stopped writing, and that will probably inspire more people as well because I'm going to start writing now after listening to you. See, I'm a humanoid and if you are in Access, you would know. Humanoids don't like to repeat anything. So what happens is, I get ideas for books, I probably have ideas for 100-150 books by now including fiction, but I don't have patience to write them down because everything is done in my head already. So after writing 11 books, I got bored and I just stopped writing. Publishers asked me, magazines asked me, but I was just bored to sit and write.

Nilofer: Yeah, so would it be fun for you to record it, to talk it out?

Nirmala: Yeah, it'll be really easy for me, really simple for me. And I can even ask my newsletter subscribers to give me questions on a particular topic and then come up with a book.

Nilofer: Exactly! That's exactly what to do!

Nirmala: I'm already doing a book called 'Romance with Money' but hey, that could be really, really easy if I get more questions and I can just talk and get somebody to transcribe it.

Nilofer: Absolutely.

Nirmala: *How does it get any better than that? And how does it get any easier than that?*

Nirmala: And Nilofer, in your experience, how long do you think it would take to get it transcribed and made into a book?

Nilofer: A transcript into a book? Ok, so here's the thing. I don't enjoy editing. Initially, I transcribed some of my interviews, and I tried to edit them myself. I must have edited one before I got really bored of it and I said, "No, this doesn't work for me. I don't enjoy the editing bit." So I was looking for editors and I did not actually know what I was looking for and I had all these points of view in my head about how the book should be and how it has to be edited and blah blah blah and because of that, it was really very heavy for me.

One day, I was having a conversation with another friend and I was just sharing with her this is what is going on and she looked at me and she said, "Do you know that unedited and unabridged books are more valuable than edited and abridged books?"

And I said, "What do you mean?" She said that if you look at a television series, for example, you have the whole edited version. She told me about a video which went viral on the Internet which was the unedited version of a television series. It just went viral and there were millions of views for it. She told me was that the unedited and unabridged versions were more valuable and people appreciated it much more. That was one piece of it.

The other piece of it was that I was in question about editing, that "this is taking too much time", because it took me 4-5 months to get that whole book edited.

I was in question about it and then one day, I picked up a copy of the book <u>Would You Teach a Fish to Climb a Tree?</u> by Anne Maxwell, Gary Douglas and Dr Dain Heer. I was just glancing through it and I saw that there were different styles in which the content was presented in the book. Before that, I had the point of view that there had to be uniformity and I was trying to put a form and structure into the book and then the moment I looked at the Fish book, I got the energy of it. I said, "Oh, I don't have to have uniformity anywhere. I could create it whatever way I would like to create it." Once I got that, within the next 3 days, I found 5 new editors and most of my editing was done in a month's time. It was that easy. You just have to look at the energy you are creating with the book and you have to ask for those people to show up who will edit it, or maybe you enjoy editing. I personally don't.

Caller: "What if you don't do tele-classes or you don't have an email list you can ask questions of?"

Nilofer: That's a great question. Can you invite a group of your friends to come for a coffee morning and tell them that it's going to be on a particular topic (whatever topic you want to write about). Do a little presentation on that topic and invite questions. And record everything. And you might have to do 4 or 5 of these and get it transcribed and then you pick and choose whatever is going to work for you. You can get very, very, creative about this.

Ask your friends, "This is my topic. Do you have any questions for me?"

When I was on a radio show, a lady called in with questions about weight loss and I facilitated her on body issues and weight loss and it was brilliant. It had all the tools of Access, the most basic tools you require for creating your body or having more ease with food, to be more mindful, and there was a different segment in that which was about studying for exams. Guess what I did? I transcribed it and I created it into 2 separate ebooks. (laughs)

Nirmala: (laughs) You are one grand creator!

Nilofer: You can literally go on Facebook or you can just write to a few of your friends and gift them one-on-one sessions with you. And you can actually call it a specific session, like 'Creating more Money' or 'Creating your Business' or 'Creating Your Body', call it whatever session you want and you tell them that the only caveat is that I'm going to record this session to create content from this, and you can also assure them that you are not going to use their actual name and just do that. Give people sessions, record the sessions and it's amazing what comes out of our mouth when we are facilitating people. It is so brilliant! Sometimes I will go and listen to my recordings and I will go, "Oh my God, that was so brilliant. I didn't know I was that brilliant"

I was facilitating someone, and she said that "When I am teaching painting in the class, I'm able to just paint and have so much fun" because it is that group energy. It is that energy, when your energy combines with the energy of another being or a group of beings, you are able to create way more than you are able to on your own. So when that energy shows up, you are able to facilitate people, which is quite brilliant. What if you could record each one of those and listen to the recordings and go, "ok, this one is good" and get it transcribed? You do ten of these sessions and you have a book ready. Ten sessions on that one topic and your book is ready. It's as easy as that.

Content For A Book

Nilofer: There is no minimum content. In my experience from transcribing all the interviews, if there is 60 minutes of audio recording, you get between 20 to 25 pages of transcript.

And depending on how you edit it, it would then reduce to about between 15 to 20 pages of your finished product. So if you want a 100 page book, you would have to do 5 hours. If you want to do 150 pages, you could do between 7 to 8 hours. So with 6 hours on an average, you would have a book between 150 to 180 pages.

Nirmala: That's great. I'm going to write a book every week now. (laughs) Ok, so what are the steps to get into Amazon? Would you be able to share it with us?

Nilofer: Once your book is ready, what I would say to people is first get it published as an ebook.

Nilofer: Ok? Now the best place to get it published is Amazon. So there is something called as KDP, which is Kindle Direct Publishing. Once you go on Amazon, go on KDP and you can create an account there. You require a few things for your ebook. For example, you require a book cover and the book has to be formatted in a certain way. Once you have that done, you can upload the book, and your book is published. KDP has a step by step guide, and you just follow along and very soon your book will be ready and available on Amazon.

Then the second part of it is to get it into physical, print books. So Amazon also has a print division, which is called 'Create Space.' Upload your book to Create Space. They require a different format for the cover page and layout, so you create all that and then publish your book as a print book available for sale online. As an author, you can actually order your copies to come to you at a wholesale price, so can buy a bunch of books and keep them with you.

Imagine this, if you are a healer or you do workshops or even if you have a business, if you give a person your flyer, what happens? If you give a person a visiting card, what happens? They are going to judge you. They are going to say, "prove this to me", but instead of giving them a flyer, if you hand them a copy of your book, what happens is instantly you become a figure of authority in their eyes.

Nirmala: Yeah, I totally get you. I'm with you on this. Absolutely.

Nilofer: So literally if you want to be known as an authority on painting, write a book on painting. (laughs)

Becoming #1 Bestselling Author on Amazon

Nirmala: You make it sound so simple, but not everybody may have the skills to create an ebook from the content and go into Amazon and do all these things. So do you have a publishing house that can help them?

Nilofer: This is one part of my business that I am creating. I offer people this service - you can write your book and give it to me and I will do the whole thing for you. I will put it on Amazon. I will create it as a print book and I will make it number 1 on Amazon.

Nirmala: You are making it so easy. Easy at least. And how does it get even easier than this? (laughs)

Nilofer: So if your book is all written down and you want me to just help you with publishing it and getting it on number 1 on Amazon, that's what I'm promising. If you just have an idea and you would like to take it from idea till number 1 on Amazon, I could coach you and help you with that.

Becoming a Contributing Author in a Bestselling Book

There's another really exciting possibility for people, which I have been playing around with. So for most people, writing a full book can be very overwhelming, so why not start small? I am actually creating these books which are multi-author books, you can be a contributing author in my book.

I'm creating books on different subjects – Money, Business and Marketing, Natural Healing. There's also a book in which Access Consciousness Certified Facilitators can contribute. There is going to be another book for people who are not facilitators and we are going to share the tools of Access in the book. All that is required is that you write one chapter, which is about 20-25 pages, between 4000-5000 words. So literally, it could be something that you could create in 1 week or 2 week's time and give it to me and you could become a part of a bestselling book.

Become a Contributing Author in my next Best Selling Book

Nirmala: You are definitely taking this to a different level, isn't it? So how many authors are you going to create?

Nilofer: I wonder.

Nirmala: What magic can that be for consciousness?

Nilofer: (laughs) Yeah, I wonder. I wonder who wants to play? I wonder how many people want to be published authors with this? (laughs)

Nirmala: Yeah

Tools

Nilofer: The biggest thing for me, in the beginning, was that I had this judgment of me that "Oh my god, I'm really great at interviewing people. I can interview people, but I can't write by myself." That was my judgment about myself so I POCed and PODed all of it. Then last year, I created a series called the Money Circle, which was a series of 9 calls I facilitated. I would just invite people to be on the call and ask me questions and I find that's so easy when people ask questions. It's easy to facilitate them. When people ask you questions, you can just facilitate them and that's what I did. Doing that series changed my point of view. I went from "I can't facilitate" to "I can facilitate" and now I have that whole series. It is also a published book.

Nirmala: Fantastic. How many books have you created so far? Or how many books do you have content for?

Nilofer: I think at least 10. (laughs) So if I were to actually sit down and do it, it would happen. It's all happening in its own time. So at least 2 more books are almost ready. I just have to go through them. If you are doing Access books, then you also have to get the books approved as an Access product, just for you to be aware of that. I have to compile it together and send it off to Access to be approved of as a product. So those two will be ready very soon. And then another 2 are halfway done. How does it get any better than that?

Nirmala: Amazing speed! How does it get any better than this? Nilofer, what targets for the year? How many books are you going to publish and how many books are you going to facilitate?

Nilofer: I wonder... Honestly, if you had asked me before the 7 day event, I would have given you a few numbers, but the 7 day event has changed so many things for me that I right now, I don't actually have an answer for you. The only question that I'm being all the time now is "what's going to be fun for me to do?" And I've been asking for elegance, the elegance of living. So the elegance of living is like doing a tiny effort and creating great results. That's what my target is for this year – the elegance of living. I would like to put in even less effort and get those books out even more, so what would it take, I wonder? (laughs)

Nirmala: Yeah, who else can contribute to you?

Nilofer: Who else can contribute to me?

Books – What Do They Create?

It's not that difficult to be a number 1 bestseller on Amazon, but that label, what it creates for you is just brilliant. I'm just waiting to get my print book, before I start approaching the radio stations, the TV stations in the place that I live in to get media interviews and so on. I've got these screenshots that I got when my book hit number 1, so I actually attach those screenshots and I send it off to people telling them that my book is number 1 and it just opens up these doors for me which otherwise would not have.

You can have a business idea and you can write a book to launch that business idea. If you already have a business going, it's almost the easiest way to promote it. It's just so straightforward and so effective that it opens doors.

Nilofer: I get people all the time, who ask me, "How's your book doing? Is it doing any sales? Is it doing this? Is it doing that?" and I'm just floored by it, because "wow, you have such a tiny little hole that you are looking through. You think that the only purpose of writing a book is to get sales. That is peanuts compared to what more can open up for you once you actually start leveraging your book in a different way."

Caller: Is a book the best calling card you could possibly have?

Nilofer: Yes, absolutely. And the other way I would also put it as a mini-website by itself. If you do the book in a correct way, that means you actually put calls to action within the book, you give away something free so that people go to your website and sign up to be on your mailing list. You will start to build up a subscriber base through that. So all these links you can actually put it within the book. It's just brilliant, how you can create your book like that.

Perfectionism

Nilofer: Most people get caught up in this whole concept of perfectionism. "Oh my god, I'm writing a book. It has to be perfect." It doesn't have to be perfect. Just write it and you can print it and then if someone points out some spelling mistakes or grammatical mistakes or whatever, in the next edition, you can change it. That's my point of view.

Caller: How hard is it to change a Kindle book once you've done this Kindle Direct Publishing?

Nilofer: It's really easy. You can go and upload the changes and it'll be available in the next one. So the people who already purchased the book, unless they have given you their contact details, you will not be able to give them the new version of the book, but for all the people who buy after that, the new version of the book is available. So that's how it is.

Caller: I suppose, you could put an invitation in the book saying "If you find any errors – If you wish to get updates, and we plan on producing a new and improved version fairly soon, just click the following link and give us your email address and we'll use it only for sending you this new and improved version." Because once it's there you can also have the chance to email again, so you could send some other things. Other invitations.

Nilofer: Yes, so that piece is what I was talking about before – the call to action which you put inside the book. It is an invitation for people to get a freebie from you.

Caller: So Amazon doesn't automatically give you the contact details of the people who buy from you?

Nilofer: No.

Caller: Now that you've told me about this call to action, I vaguely remember several years ago seeing something like a call to action. You know, somebody's book said, you can go to my email, here's my website or so forth, but I hadn't even thought about it until you pointed this out. A lot of what you said is just totally new but some of it is a reminder to me. It's so obvious, once it's out on the table it seems like it's simple. This call to action, I don't remember hearing on this last telesummit I attended about writing and publishing a book. 15 different authorities talking about how to publish a book. Nobody said put a call to action offering something free in your ebook.

Nilofer: Here's the deal, you want to learn some of the interesting things that you can do with your book? Go buy my book, Cracking The Client Attraction Code.

You can go on Amazon, you can get my book and then you can see all the interesting things that I've done inside the book and also, there are calls to action inside.

Investment Required

Nirmala: You have inspired so many people, and at least some of them must be wondering about the investments they might require to get it started, other than the content, other than their time?

Nilofer: Ok, so investment you are asking me for how much it would cost to get the thing transcribed and to get it edited and stuff like that. Is that what you are asking me?

Nirmala: Yes. Is it in 100s, in 1000s, 10000s?

Nilofer: Normally, for transcription, it costs about 50 cents per audio minute approximately. It could be a little more than that, it could be a little less than that, so look for transcribers who will give it to you at about 50 cents per audio minute. For editors, I pay them according to the number of pages.

You might actually end up spending more money in the editing. I think I must have spent around $400-$500 when I got my book edited. But you have to remember that it was a transcript from an interview, so the editing is much more difficult.

Nirmala: So how do you select the editor for your work, Nilofer?

Nilofer: I had one piece of transcript and I sent it out to whoever approached me. I told them to edit it and get it back to me, and whichever matched the energy of what I was looking for, I selected those people.

What Questions Can Budding Authors Ask To Create A Book?

Nilofer: Read the chapter by Kalpana Raghuraman in this book. She's an artist and she's got some brilliant questions that she shared in her chapter.

You can ask, so *"what would be fun for me to do?"* And I write down all the different ideas that I have and then I ask *"Is now the time?* Is now the time? Is now the time?" and then once you start creating it, it takes on a life force of it's own and it's going to literally create itself. It's like the 2 books which I said that are almost ready. One of them was just not happening a couple of months back, and then I just let it go as I was busy with another project. Just today, I woke up and it had the energy of "yes, now is the time" so I started working on it again.

One of the tools I use in putting everything together is Google docs. This is a free tool that we use on the internet, so I have created Google Docs for the different books that I am creating. I don't create a book linearly . I don't do Introduction, Chapter 1, Chapter 2, etc, I don't do it like that. So at some point, you know, if I could sit and just write down the introduction or dictate out the introduction and get a transcript of it and at some point, I will write about something which could be chapter 9 or chapter 4 or chapter 7.

What I do is I start creating those different parts within the Google Doc and very soon my book is ready. I actually sat down today and I compiled that whole Google doc for that book. There are a couple of things which are still missing and I'm in question about those 2 chapters, *"Does it want to be in the book? Does it want to be in a different book? Does it not want to be in any of my books?"* So I'm just asking questions around and creating it.

Read the chapter by Kalpana who shared some really amazing, brilliant questions that you can use while creating your book.

Nirmala: Amazing. Thank you.

Nirmala: Can people send their questions about book writing and publishing to you so that you can write a book for dummies?

Nilofer: Yes, yes. You can send me all your writing related questions and I can create a book about writing. How does it get any better than that? Now Nila, I think we both are going to be in competition with each other, to out-create each other with creating books.

Nirmala: Yes, absolutely. Not only between us, we are going to out-create lots and lots of people. You know, I'm quite interested in facilitating and I enjoy facilitating. I have lots of fun facilitating, so you have given me a totally, totally different doorway of possibilities, because sitting and writing is not fun for me anymore.

I had totally closed that door down of writing a book or publishing a book but now you have given me a pathway that is through fun and the fun of facilitating, I can create a book. So watch out girl, I'm going to be publishing one book a week! Beat me!

Nilofer: How does it get any better than that? (laughs) That's an amazing invitation.

Nirmala: Thank you so much Nilofer, for that. It was an enlightening call. I'm all inspired. I'm going to start writing right away. I mean, start talking right away on a subject that inspires me.

ACCESS CONSCIOUSNESS COPYRIGHT NOTICE

Access Trademarks and Trade Names:

1. Access Consciousness®

2. Access Bars®

3. Conversations in Consciousness®

4. Energetic Synthesis of Being®

5. The Bars®

6. Right and Wrong, Good and Bad, POC, POD, all 9, shorts, boys and beyond®

7. All of Life Comes To Me With Ease and Joy and Glory®

8. Ease, Joy and Glory®

9. How does it get any better than this?®

10. How does it get any better than that?®

11. The Body Whisperer®

12. What else is possible?®

13. Who does this belong to?®

14. Energetic Symphony of Being®

15. Energetic Synthesis of Being®

16. Symphony of Being®

17. Leaders for a Conscious World®

18. Consciousness Includes Everything and Judges Nothing®

19. Oneness Includes Everything and Judges Nothing®

THE ACCESS CLEARING STATEMENT

The Clearing Statement is a tool you can use to change the energy of the points of view that have you locked into unchanging situations. You are the only one who can unlock the points of view that have you trapped.

Clearing Statement: Right and wrong, good and bad, POD and POC, all nine, shorts, boys and beyonds.

Right and wrong, good and bad is shorthand for: What's right, good, perfect and correct about this? What's wrong, mean, vicious, terrible, bad, and awful about this? What have you decided is right and wrong, good and bad?

POD is the point of destruction immediately preceding whatever you decided.

POC is the point of creation of thoughts, feelings and emotions immediately preceding whatever you decided.

Sometimes instead of saying, "use the clearing statement," we just say, "POD and POC it."

All nine stands for nine layers of crap that we're taking out. You know that somewhere in those nine layers, there's got to be a pony because you couldn't put that much crap in one place without having a pony in there. It's crap you're generating yourself.

Shorts is the short version of: What's meaningful about this? What's meaningless about this? What's the punishment for this? What's the reward for this?

Boys stands for nucleated spheres. Have you ever seen one of those kid's bubble pipes? Blow here and you create a mass of bubbles? You pop one and it fills in, and you pop another one and it fills in. They're like that. You can never seem to get them all to pop.

Beyonds are feelings or sensations you get that stop your heart, stop your breath, or stop your willingness to look at possibilities. It's like when your business is in the red and you get another final notice and you go argh! You weren't expecting that right now. That's a beyond.

(The majority of information about the clearing statement is from the website www.theclearingstatement.com)

CONTACT OUR CONTRIBUTORS

❖

Rebecca Hulse

Email: Rebecca@rebeccahulse.com

Website:www.rebeccahulse.com

Melanie Clampit

Email: MelanieClampit@gmail.com

Website: www.MelanieClampit.com

Gary Douglas

Email: gary@accessconsciousness.com

Website: http://garymdouglas.com/

Aditi Iyer

Email: info@srishtiholistic.com

Website: www.SrishtiHolistic.com

Stephanie Richardson

Email: Stephanie@stephanierichardson.com

Website: www.Stephanierichardson.com

Nirmala Raju

Email: Light@infinitehealing.co.uk

Website: www.infinitehealing.co.uk

Katherine McIntosh

Email: Katherine@katherinemcintosh.com

Website: www.katherinemcintosh.com

Christine McIver

Email: christine@inspiredchoices.ca

Website: http://www.inspiredchoices.ca/

Rhonda Burns

Email: rhonda@rhonda-burns.com

Website: http://www.rhonda-burns.com/

Heather Nichols

Email: heather@heathernichols.com

Website: http://www.heathernichols.com/

Ritu Motial

Email: ritu.motial@gmail.com

Website: www.boundariesfree.com

Julia Sotas

Email: juliasotas@gmail.com

Website: www.juliasotas.com

Louise Derksen

Email: derksenle@gmail.com

Website: www.louiseestelle.com

Bhagyalakshmi Murali

Email: bhagyalakshmimurali@gmail.com

Website: www.bmpowerednow.com

Rachel Silber

Email: Rachel@Silbers.com

Website: http://ubjoy.com/

Pratima Nagaraj

Email: pratima@pratimanagaraj.com

Website: www.pratimanagaraj.com

Kalpana Raghuraman

Email: Outcreateyoureality@gmail.com

Website: www.kalpanaraghuraman.com

Simone Padur

Email: simonepadur@hotmail.com

Website: https://educationforaconsciousfuture.wordpress.com/about/

Cara Wright

Email: talktocarawright@gmail.com

Delany Delaney

Email: delanydelaney@bigpond.com

Nilofer Safdar

Email: Nilofer@illusiontoilluminationsummit.com

Website: www.nilofersafdar.com

WHO IS NILOFER SAFDAR?

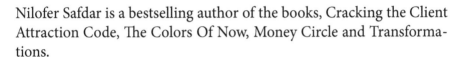

Nilofer Safdar is a bestselling author of the books, Cracking the Client Attraction Code, The Colors Of Now, Money Circle and Transformations.

She is a Certified Access Consciousness Facilitator CFMW. Nilofer helps people change their reality to generate and create a life they desire and require. Her target is to generate a life that is joyful and expansive for everybody she touches.

Nilofer is a Life Coach, Money Mastery Coach, Public Speaking Coach, Relationship Coach and Weight Loss and Anti Aging Expert.

She is a creation junkie and loves to play with infinite possibilities. The latest bee in her bonnet is videos. You will find most of her videos on Facebook and on YouTube.

She is the host of a TV show which aired on JIA News in India called The Nilofer Show.

She is the host of the First online radio show in the Middle East, The Healthy Living Dubai Show, in which she interviews Speakers, Coaches, Natural Healers from the Middle East which empowers the listeners to Create everything they desire in life.

She is also the host of the telesummit, Illusion to Illumination Summit, in which she has interviewed more than 150 Luminaries, Change Agents, Best Selling Authors from around the world including Peggy Phoenix Dubro, the originator of the EMF Balancing Technique, Gary Douglas – the founder of Access Consciousness.

To contact Nilofer for further information about her books, audios, newsletters, workshops & training programs and consultancy or to schedule her for a presentation, please write to:

nilofer@illusiontoilluminationsummit.com

Websites are –

www.illusiontoilluminationsummit.com

www.healthylivingdubai.com

www.nilofersafdar.com

SESSIONS WITH NILOFER

Would you like to have the magic of Nilofer touch you, permeate you and turn your reality on it's head?

Here are some possibilities -

SOP Sessions (Available Online)

Verbal Facilitation on any topic under the sun (Available Online)

Right Voice For You Sessions (Available Online)

Bars (In person)

Bodywork (In person)

MAKE YOUR BOOK AN AMAZON BESTSELLER

Have you written and published a book?

Are you writing a book?

Do you have a book in you that would like to be written and published?

Would you like to write, publish and make your book an Amazon Bestseller?

From coaching on getting started, to helping you with the publishing process to getting your book to be an International Amazon Bestseller, Nilofer offers it all. Contact her to explore the Infinite Possibilities with your book - nilofer@illusiontoilluminationsummit.com

WHAT NEXT

Nilofer loves hosting Telesummits. You can visit www.illusiontoilluminationsummit.com to find her latest offerings.

Past Telesummits:

Creation From Joy

Choice The Liberator

Earth! Love It Or Leave It!

Where Is My Doorway To Possibilities

All the tools and techniques from this book are from the body of work called Access Consciousness.

If you haven't already, I would highly recommend you start with the Access Consciousness Core Classes - Bars, Foundation.

Each of the authors in this book can facilitate these classes and are happy to travel.

You can find more information on these classes at www.accessconsciousness.com

MORE BOOKS BY NILOFER SAFDAR

BOOKS BY NILOFER

http://www.nilofersbooks.com

Cracking The Client Attraction Code

By Carla McNeil & Nilofer Safdar

http://www.crackingtheclientattractioncode.com

Transformations

By Nilofer Safdar

http://www.thetransformationsbook.com

The Colors Of Now

By Nilofer Safdar

http://www.thecolorsofnow.com

Money Circle

By Nilofer Safdar

http://www.moneycirclebook.com

UPCOMING BOOKS

Create Your Life

http://thecreateyourlifebook.com

By Nilofer Safdar

The Magic Of Being

By Nilofer Safdar

http://www.magicofbeing.com

Choice The Liberator

By Nilofer Safdar

Creation From Joy

By Nilofer Safdar

30 Days Business Bootcamp

By Aditi Surti & Nilofer Safdar

Abundance From Kindness

By Nirmala Raju & Nilofer Safdar

No Form No Structure No Significance

By Ritu Motial & Nirmala Raju